MW01096984

WORLDS OF DISSENT

WORLDS OF DISSENT

Charter 77, The Plastic People of the Universe,
and Czech Culture under Communism

Jonathan Bolton

HARVARD UNIVERSITY PRESS

Cambridge, Massachusetts, and London, England • 2012

Library of Congress Cataloging-in-Publication Data
Bolton, Jonathan, 1968–
    Worlds of dissent : Charter 77, the Plastic People of the Universe,
and Czech culture under communism / Jonathan Bolton.
        p. cm.
    Includes bibliographical references and index.
    ISBN 978–0-674–06438–6 (alk. paper)
    1. Charta 77 (Group)—History.   2. Plastic People of the Universe—
History.   3. Dissenters—Czechoslovakia—History.   4. Dissenters—
Europe, Central—History—20th century.   5. Dissenters—Europe, Eastern—
History—20th century. 6. Civil rights movements—Czechoslovakia—
History.   7. Communism—Social aspects—Czechoslovakia—History.
8. Politics and culture—Czechoslovakia—History.   9. Czechoslovakia—
Politics and government—1968–1989.   10. Czechoslovakia—Intellectual life—
1945–1992.   I. Title.
    DB2228.7.B65 2012
    943.704'3—dc23   2011030435

For my parents

Contents

WORLDS OF DISSENT

Introduction

"A specter is haunting Eastern Europe," wrote Václav Havel over thirty years ago: "the specter of what in the West is called 'dissent.'" These opening words of Havel's "The Power of the Powerless," with their echo of the *Communist Manifesto,* are as intriguing and disorienting today as they were in 1978.[1] When Marx and Engels first wrote that "A specter is haunting Europe— the specter of communism," their meaning was twofold. Communism was, indeed, a threat to the European order, a new ideological force to be reckoned with. But the political powers of the old order ("Pope and Tsar, Metternich and Guizot, French radicals and German spies") had turned the word "Communism" into a bogeyman—a specter—and now a manifesto was needed to explain Communism "before the whole world."[2]

Havel's invocation of this manifesto is laced with subversive ironies. In 1978, Europe is no longer haunted as a whole; it has been split into East and West by the very forces Marx and Engels unleashed. What is this new specter, "dissent," which has a name in the West but none in the East? Which half, indeed, is the audience for Havel's text—the Eastern Europe that is being haunted, or the Western Europe that named the ghost? Does "dissent" need a manifesto of its own, to explain its views to the whole world? Or will Havel show us that it is just a phantom?

Havel's essay, the most famous and influential text of European dissent after World War II, is most often remembered for its parable of a greengrocer who places, "among the onions and carrots" in his shop window, a sign that says "Workers of the World, Unite!" (The last line of the *Communist Manifesto* thus makes an appearance, just as the first did.) The greengrocer thereby reinforces the reigning fictions of Communist ideology—the slogans that saturated public space in Czechoslovakia in the 1970s and formed "the panorama of everyday life." He contributes to "life in a lie," a lie that everyone knows is false but pretends to believe. But what if he refuses to put out the sign? He has taken the first step toward reconciling his private convictions and his public behavior—toward "living in truth." He has taken the first step toward becoming a "dissident."[3]

The greengrocer's parable is so bewitching that many readers have lost sight of Havel's extreme skepticism toward the specter of dissent. "The Power of the Powerless," indeed, is nothing if not a sustained polemic with the word and the idea. When Havel's own multipart definition of the word "dissident" appears halfway through the essay, it is ironic, complicated, and intentionally jury-rigged. Dissidents are people who express their nonconformist positions publicly; these positions have won them prestige at home and abroad, which guarantees them harassment but also protects them from excessive persecution; they are "writing people," people "for whom the written word is the primary—and often the only—political medium they command, and that can gain them attention, particularly from abroad"; in fact, they are known abroad because of their writings rather than any other activities.[4] For Havel, the position of dissent is defined largely by the West, and it systematically obscures much of the dissident's life and behavior at home—everything that doesn't illuminate the Western desire for lofty political meditations and courageous nonconformism.

In February 1979, Zdeněk Mlynář—an architect of the Prague Spring reform movement in 1968, who was later expelled from the Party and helped formulate the human-rights proclamation Charter 77—wrote: "The term 'dissident' is one of the least precise in the contemporary political vocabulary."[5] Today, historians have ceased to interrogate the term, but it remains as vague and problematic as it was thirty years ago. Conceptions of dissent are still shaped by the vocabulary of the Cold War. The most common model of the dissident personality is constructed from just a few basic planks—courage, truthfulness, steadfast self-confidence. Dissidents are portrayed with a mixture of romanticism (jailed intellectuals writing prison letters, adventurers smuggling secret publications across barbed-wire borders) and political idealism (a few rare souls with the moral courage to speak out against the state, at great personal risk). Both the romanticism and the idealism contain some truth, but they also speak to Western dreams and desires—a belief in heroes, a yearning for a clear stand against evil, a hope for more fulfilling forms of political participation.

Views of Central European dissent, in fact, have always been shaped by the selective perceptions of the West. Most dissidents considered the term "dissent" to be a coinage of American and West European journalists. During the Cold War, the West—newspaper editors and academic scholars alike—selected a few dissident thinkers and fashioned them into a transnational pantheon that conducted an international conversation about antipolitics, civil society, and living in truth. In this pantheon, there was room for one or two thinkers from each country—next to Havel one usually found the Pole Adam Michnik, the Hungarian György Konrád, and a constellation of other figures, with minor changes from one receiving country to the next, often depending on which dissident writings had been translated into which languages. These political and philosophical debates shaped the way Communism and Central European history were understood in the West, which often thought it was listening in on a conversation that, in fact, it had helped to stage by choosing and translating the thinkers—brilliant and influential thinkers, to be sure—that spoke most closely to its own concerns.

In the years since Havel's landmark essay, his ironic characterization of dissent has been forgotten. Historians speak of "dissent" or "the dissident movement," reducing a diverse phenomenon to a simple, unifying label. They continue to work with terms and definitions inherited from the Cold War, even as the understanding of Communist society and culture has evolved out of a black-and-white Cold War framework. We speak of "the dissidents" as if we knew who they were and, indeed, as if *they* knew who they were. In fact, the very definition of "dissent" was a major concern of opposition intellectuals in Central Europe in the 1970s and 1980s. Was it meaningful, even possible, to bracket off a small group of people and to judge the rest of society using them as the moral measuring stick? And how did society degenerate to the point where so few people seemed to speak for it?

Havel's essay, whose universal formulations are stirring and insightful, was written in a particular world—the world of Czechoslovakia in the 1970s. One aim of this book is to recover that world, better to understand the texture of dissident life, its local practices, its vocabulary, and its obsessions, so as to break through the stereotypes that continue to color images of the dissidents. Dissent was born of a particular world, and that world was born in the fall of 1968.

Pictures from an Occupation

On August 20, 1968, many Czechs and Slovaks were on vacation, spending time at summer cottages, camping and hiking in the countryside, or even traveling abroad—for the last few years, they had been able to leave the country in large numbers, legally, for the first time since 1948. Everyone needed a break. It had been an exciting, eventful, and exhausting summer; indeed, it had been an exciting, eventful, and exhausting year. Back in January, the hard-line leadership of the Communist Party had been maneuvered out of power, and the reform wing of the Party had taken control, under the popular Slovak Communist Alexander Dubček. Dubček and his team had soon begun to implement a set of reforms designed to bring more pluralism, freedom, and openness to Czechoslovakia. Since then, events had accelerated quickly. Economic reforms sought to bring worker governance to factories and loosen up the centralized directives of a command economy. Cultural and political leaders began to speak openly about reform at public meetings; at Prague's Slavic House in March, the screenwriter Jan Procházka, a candidate member of the Party's Central Committee, said: "I think that in a civilized state, freedom of speech is absolutely fundamental, because it is not logical that a person should take so long to learn to talk and then not be allowed to. [. . .] Censorship, friends, is ceasing to exist. Hooray!"[6] Although the Communist leaders were careful to maintain their position as the source of all political power in the state—the Party's "leading role," to use the jargon enshrined in the constitution—they allowed new organizations to be formed, even a group called K 231 representing former political prisoners who, just ten or fifteen years earlier, had been imprisoned for their political beliefs or class background.[7] A commission of historians started work on an account of one of the most sensitive topics in recent history—the show trials of the 1950s—that would begin to acknowledge them as a massive miscarriage of justice.

The reforms came to be known as *Pražské jaro,* the Prague Spring, and for many Czechs and Slovaks they were the most exciting political development in a generation. Heda Margolius Kovály, whose husband had been executed in a 1952 show trial, wrote: "The spring of 1968 had all the intensity, anxiety and unreality of a dream come true. People flooded the narrow streets of Prague's Old Town and the courtyards of Hradčany Castle and stayed out long into the night. If anyone set out for a walk alone, he would soon join a group of others to chat or tell a joke, and we all would listen with relief as the ancient walls echoed with the sound of laughter. Even long after the Castle gates closed, people would remain standing on the ramparts looking down at the flickering lights of a city that could not sleep for happiness."[8] Milan Šimečka, a Communist philosopher who had recently finished a book on the "crisis of utopianism," saw 1968 as a public drama:

> The precipitous course of history in my country could well be described as theatrical in character. Many of the previous changes had occurred in the twilight typical of existing socialism: namely, in secret meeting rooms and in the politicians' well-guarded retreats. The faces of the actors in those political dramas remained hidden or they were covered by the drab masks of officialdom. In contrast, the drama of 1968 was played out on a brightly lit stage. People suddenly began to perceive the politicians and actors in the drama as human beings instead of cardboard cut-outs always spouting the same old platitudes. [. . .] Fatigue, moral dilemma and human weakness were there on their faces for all to see (thanks, of course, to television). Almost in a single moment, public life came into existence and many people, for the first time in their lives, began to view politics as the work of human beings instead of a tedious, infinitely boring, inaccessible and anonymous annoyance coming from somewhere on high.[9]

Not everyone shared Kovály's and Šimečka's enthusiasm. The reforms were led by Communists, many of whom had played a key role in the brutal repression of the 1950s, or had at least sung the praises of the government that carried out that repression. To some, their conversion to the cause of liberalism now felt opportunistic and merely revealed that they could not be trusted—it hardly mattered whether this was because of their cynicism or their naïveté. Nevertheless, after some twenty years of repressive government, many Czechs and Slovaks once again felt that they could take a hand in their own destinies.

The neighbors were nervous. Since 1948, when the Communist Party had taken over Czechoslovakia, the country had been part of the Soviet bloc—behind the so-called Iron Curtain that ran along the Western border of the Communist world, from the Baltic Sea, down the border between East and West Germany, and along the Czechoslovak, Hungarian, and Yugoslavian borders to the Adriatic. Communist governments in neighboring states were increasingly concerned that the Prague Spring would mobilize popular discontent in their own countries—the East German and Polish governments, in particular, feared the pressure for liberalization that was being generated next door. Poland had just repressed student and intellectual protests that rocked the country in March, and was eager to avoid further trouble. The Hungarians had their own experience with Soviet repression; in 1956, Russia had invaded Hungary to put down an anti-Communist rebellion. Of course, the country with the most power over the Eastern Bloc, the Soviet Union, was not happy with the Prague Spring at all. Soviet leader Leonid Brezhnev worried that the reforms were threatening the dominance of the Czechoslovak Communist Party; he feared that Czechoslovakia might try to withdraw from the Warsaw Pact, the military alliance of Communist powers. Brezhnev resented the Prague Spring slogan, "Socialism with a Human Face," with its undertones of a third way between capitalism and Communism. What face, then, was socialism wearing in the Soviet Union?

Czechoslovak leaders found themselves in a difficult position. The more reforms they instituted, the more they mobilized an excited population, which in turn pressed for further liberalization; meanwhile, the Russians were growing more and more concerned that things were getting out of hand. For months, Dubček and his team balanced these competing pressures. They were summoned to meetings of the Warsaw Pact countries and spoke to their own citizens in open assemblies and on radio and television. In June, a forty-one-year-old journalist named Ludvík Vaculík published *Dva tisíce slov* (Two Thousand Words), a manifesto signed by seventy prominent people, including other writers, scientists, and even Olympic athletes. Appearing simultaneously in four newspapers on June 27, it called for Czechoslovak citizens to unite behind the reforms and push them further. It began with a brief history of the Czechoslovak Communist Party, saying it had enjoyed genuine popularity after World War II, but "by degrees bartered this confidence away for office, until it had all the offices and nothing else." Vaculík also warned against the hard-liners still within the Czechoslovak government, who would try to stop reform: "The summer holidays are approaching, a time when we are inclined to let everything slip. But we can safely say that our dear adversaries will not give themselves a summer break; they [. . .] are taking steps, even now, to secure themselves a quiet Christmas! [. . .] The spring is over and will never return. By winter we will know all."[10]

The manifesto enraged the Soviets, and it caught reform Communists by surprise. The Party formally condemned Two Thousand Words in a resolution written in part by Zdeněk Mlynář, one of the sharpest, most skeptical reform leaders. The Soviets were not mollified, and further meetings between Czechoslovak and Soviet leaders took place in Slovakia at the end of July and beginning of August. The well-known playwright Pavel Kohout composed a letter from citizens to the Party leadership, assuring them of popular support as they entered these meetings: "We are thinking of you. Think of us! You are writing a critical page of Czechoslovakia's history on our behalf." Published on July 26 and again in following days in major newspapers, the letter was eventually signed by over a million people.[11] But the high-level meetings failed to resolve Soviet concerns. Things remained tense. By mid-August, the calm of late summer felt like the calm before a storm. Many Czechs and Slovaks were waiting, consciously or unconsciously, for something to happen.

Jan Zábrana, a poet and professional translator who translated both American and Russian poetry, had never been a member of the Communist Party. In fact, he hated the Communists. They had put both his parents in prison in the 1950s, in different cities, and as a young man he had traveled to visit them on alternating weekends. He was not allowed to attend Prague's Faculty of Arts because of his "undesirable political background," and so had spent the 1950s working in various factories. Still, the 1960s had brought some relief. He had been able to publish his own poetry, as well as his translations of the American beat poets. His translation of Allen Ginsberg's poem "Howl"— *Kvílení* in Czech—was a major event in Czech literary life in 1959. Ginsberg's poem, with its vision of a generation stifled and destroyed by the straitlaced and materialistic culture of Cold War America, had spoken to nonconformist Americans when it was published in 1956; Zábrana's translation implicitly transported this vision into Communist society and was equally effective for a generation of young Czech writers in the 1960s. In 1965, Ginsberg had even traveled to Prague, where university students welcomed him, in the words of a secret-police report, "entirely uncritically." They voted him "The King of May" at their annual satirical May Day celebrations, before he was hustled out of the country.[12]

On August 20, 1968, Zábrana was working late, as he tended to do. In the middle of the night, he heard the phone ringing. He didn't answer it. It rang again. He didn't answer. It rang one more time. He didn't answer it. He listened to airplanes circling the nearby airport in Kbely. There seemed to be a lot of airplanes, circling and circling without landing. There were so many planes that they couldn't land on the available runways. His wife was awake, and called to him from the corridor, just two words: "They're here."[13] Those two words were being spoken—in various tones of bitterness, fury, resignation, and disbelief—all over Czechoslovakia.

On that same August 20, Miloš Forman, a young film director, was in Paris with a friend, a French screenwriter named Jean-Claude Carrière. At the age of thirty-six, Forman had already gained celebrity as one of the leading figures of the Czech New Wave, the director of films such as *Loves of a Blonde* and *Firemen's Ball* that thrived on a tension between naïve lyricism and savage irony. Forman and Carrière were writing a screenplay about a New York teenager who runs away from her family. They spent the evening of August 20 in a Paris bar with another friend, Jean-Pierre Rassam. That evening, as Forman later told it to writer Jan Novák, they

> spent a pleasant summer evening getting drunk and talking with a shady, beautiful Israeli named Eva. We were young and did nothing in moderation. Jean-Pierre got smashed and offered Eva a thousand francs to spend the night with him, and they were off in a taxi to her place. Jean-Claude and I finished our drinks and returned to his apartment [. . .]. Jean-Claude had friends on every continent, so there were always exotic guests staying there. He also had a wife, a baby daughter, and a mother-in-law. The whole legion was sound asleep. We tiptoed down the creaking hallway into the kitchen, had a snack, downed a nightcap, and talked some more about our screenplay. It was a while before I got into bed. I had my own room and dozed off instantly. The next thing I knew a telephone was ringing by my head. All the receivers throughout the house were ringing loudly. Finally, someone answered. The clock showed two-thirty in the morning. I started drifting off to sleep again when the door of my room opened quietly. It was Jean-Claude, bleary-eyed, in his shorts. "It's for you, Miloš." I picked up the receiver and heard the slurred voice of Jean-Pierre, a notorious practical joker. "Miloš, the Russians are invading your country!" [. . .] "Listen," I said. "You're drunk and this isn't funny." "I'm not drunk! The Russian tanks are rolling into your country!" [. . .] I hung up and waited to see if I'd been sufficiently cold to discourage him from calling again. He was pretty drunk, but so was I, and I could barely keep my eyes open. The moment I surrendered to the sweetness of sleep, however, all the phones in the house started to ring.[14]

Phones were ringing all over the country. At the Communist Party headquarters in Prague, the phone rang in the Prime Minister's office. The Minister of

Defense was on the line. He was calling to say that there were Soviet soldiers in *his* office. Mlynář has described this night:

> [T]he corridors around the chambers were a hive of activity. Dozens of party functionaries and journalists were running about or standing in little groups waiting for instructions. But there were no instructions. [. . .] Military aircraft bringing tanks and troops to the Prague airport [. . .] were roaring over the Central Committee building at increasingly frequent intervals on the night of the twentieth, and the building itself began to empty as regional and factory functionaries, and journalists as well, returned to their places of work.

One can picture the building, increasingly deserted, while the country's leaders huddled in their offices, writing resolutions and debating what to do.

> Sometime after four A.M. a black Volga from the Soviet embassy pulled up in front of the Central Committee building, followed immediately by armored cars and tanks. Soldiers in Soviet paratrooper uniforms—wine-colored berets and sailors' jerseys under their shirts—jumped out of the armored cars carrying automatic weapons. The tanks and soldiers surrounded the building, and tight cordons of troops blocked off all the entrances. Several officers and a platoon of paratroopers ran inside. I was watching this with all the others from the window of Dubček's office, and I felt the same sensation of unreality that one has watching a film.[15]

Another leading light of the New Wave, Jan Němec, had been making a documentary about the Prague Spring during the month of August. Each day he had gone into the streets of Prague to interview people and portray the new public life that was emerging in the country. On August 21, when he went outside with his crew, the streets were full of tanks, and he quickly converted his documentary about the Prague Spring into one about the invasion, a twenty-six-minute film called *Oratorio for Prague*. Although dozens of people were killed in the invasion—including at Prague's radio station, which came under fire from Soviet tanks and soldiers—overall casualties were relatively light. Instead of fighting, people went out into the streets and protested peacefully. Němec's film captures unforgettable scenes of Czech citizens—angry, pleading, desperate, excited, confused—arguing passionately with the blank-faced Soviet soldiers who are slowly gliding by on tanks and armored cars. A similarly eloquent testimony is provided by the remarkable black-and-white photographs by Josef Koudelka, smuggled out of the country and published anonymously in 1969.[16]

Václav Havel—at the time, not yet a dissident, but a thirty-one-year-old playwright whose absurdist dramas such as *The Garden Party* and *The Memorandum* were enjoying success both at home and abroad—was spending summer vacation at his cottage in the countryside, along with the actor Jan Tříska and their families. Havel and his wife, Olga, had bought the cottage, known as Hrádeček, the previous year. Like many Czechs, Havel was allowed to travel outside the country for the first time in the 1960s, as liberalization progressed, and he had even visited the United States in the spring of 1968. A period photograph shows him striking a pose as a smug bourgeois stockbroker outside the New York Stock Exchange, in an ironic echo of editorial cartoons in the Party press.[17] Back at home for the summer, Havel was following the political events, but he was also spending long, peaceful afternoons and evenings sitting outside his cottage with Tříska, their families, and other visitors. They had a ritual when guests arrived. They kept a 45 record of the Bee Gees' song "Massachusetts" cued on their turntable; when a car pulled up, Tříska would hold the needle while Havel watched from the window. As soon as their guests got out of their car, they would start the song playing as a kind of welcoming anthem.[18]

On the evening of August 20, they had traveled about forty miles to the town of Liberec in northern Bohemia, where they had dinner with some friends who directed a local art gallery. They stayed there all week. Soviet tanks rolled into the town a little after midnight. Havel spent most of his time at the radio station in Liberec, broadcasting protests, commentaries, and directives.

> That week was an experience I'll never forget. I saw Soviet tanks smash down arcades on the main square and bury several people in the rubble. I saw a tank commander start shooting wildly into the crowd. I saw and experienced many things, but what affected me most powerfully was that special phenomenon of solidarity and community which was so typical of that time. [. . .] I remember a typical story: The scourge of Liberec and environs was a gang of about a hundred tough young men called "Tramps" who would go on weekend forays into the countryside. For a long time, the town officials hadn't been able to put a stop to them. The leader was a fellow they called the Pastor. Shortly after the invasion, the Pastor showed up at the chairman's office in the town hall and said, "I'm at your disposal, chief." The chairman was somewhat nonplussed, but he decided to give the gang a trial job: "All right," he said, "tonight I want you to take down all the street signs, so the occupiers can't find their way around. It's not appropriate to have the police do that." The Pastor nodded, and the next morning all the

street signs in Liberec were neatly stacked in front of the town-hall steps. Not a single one had been damaged. And there they stayed until they could be put up again.

For many, the invasion was a moment of national unity and community, of buried differences and improbable alliances:

> [F]or two days, members of the Pastor's gang wore armbands of the auxiliary guard, and three-man patrols walked through the town: a uniformed policeman in the middle with two long-haired Tramps on either side. This gang also did twenty-four-hour sentry duty at the town hall. They guarded the mayor, and checked everyone who entered the building. There were some poignant scenes: for instance, the whole town-hall staircase was packed with these fellows on duty, playing their guitars and singing "Massachusetts," which was a kind of world anthem for hippies then. I saw the whole thing in a special light, because I still had fresh memories of crowds of similar young people in the East Village in New York, singing the same song, but without the tanks in the background.[19]

Streets were full of protesters even as Dubček, Mlynář, and the other Czechoslovak Communist leaders were being rounded up and flown to Moscow. During tense negotiations, when it wasn't always clear whether they were visiting dignitaries or political prisoners, they signed a secret "Moscow Protocol," authorizing the invasion and allowing Soviet troops to remain in the country.

In the countryside of central Slovakia, Ivan Jirous—an art historian who was better known as the artistic director of a Prague rock band, The Primitives Group—was on vacation with his wife, the poet Věra Jirousová. Jirous was one of those skeptics who saw the Prague Spring as an internal affair of the Communist Party, which he considered unreformable. In the summer of 1968, he paid less attention to politics than to the absorbing project of caring for three herons that an ornithologist friend was studying. In August, he and Věra were staying in a cottage on Mount Poľana, with no television, radio, or telephone. One day, as they were lying in the meadow behind their cottage, they saw helicopters overhead. That evening, a neighbor hiked up from a nearby town. She wore a serious expression: "Do you know what's happened?" she asked.

"Well," said Jirous, "I guess the Russians have occupied us, haven't they?"[20]

For many, perhaps most Czechs and Slovaks, the week of the invasion was tragic, but also more exciting, meaningful, and memorable than the Prague Spring itself. The liberalization, significant but clearly limited, had been directed from above, by Communist rulers who struggled constantly to keep reforms in check. In contrast, the peaceful resistance following the invasion was a mass popular movement, one of those moments of national unity that arise in the face of sudden adversity. "It was the most beautiful week I have ever experienced," Milan Kundera told Louis Aragon later that year. In 1988, the actor Pavel Landovský remembered: "As a whole August 68 was a fantastic experience," comparable only to the end of World War II and the first months of Charter 77; "it was a spontaneous, beautiful rebellion."[21] In retrospect, this resistance, rather than the Prague Spring itself, places Czechoslovakia into the pantheon of 1968 protest movements across Europe and the Americas.

The "Czechoslovak autumn," however, turned out to be an end rather than a beginning. The invasion could have been the spark for a broad-based social movement against the Soviet occupation, but opposition, after flaring brightly, slowly burned out over the following months and years. The Soviets, failing in their effort to set up a puppet government of hard-liners who supported the invasion, hit upon an even better solution: they left the Prague Spring reformers in charge, but forced them to preside over the dismantling of their own reforms. A still mobilized population in the fall of 1968 found itself trying to shore up its own shaky leadership. In November, Mlynář saw the writing on the wall and resigned from the Party's Central Committee. Dubček, in a long and ignominious retreat, abandoned one reform position after another until he had little ground to stand on. In April 1969, he was replaced as the Party's first secretary by a fellow Slovak, Gustav Husák.

Husák, himself a former political prisoner, was cagey and chameleonic. For a time it seemed he might hold together a coalition of reform Communists, moderate technocrats, and conservatives who had been sidelined during the Prague Spring but were now riding the Soviet invasion back into power. But Husák either turned into, or turned out to be, a hard-liner himself. He presided over a harsh political crackdown that would set the tone for the two decades following the invasion, years that came to be known as *normalizace*— a term that captures the mixture of ironic resignation, boredom, and often despair that characterized the 1970s for many people, in particular for the writers, artists, and other intellectuals who had taken advantage of the newly creative public life of the 1960s. They were now demobilized into an everyday life that seemed devoid of higher aspirations or a genuine public sphere. Many of them were expelled from the Communist Party because of their allegiance to the reforms and their opposition to the invasion; many were first demoted, then fired from their jobs at universities, research institutes, and cultural journals that had now been shut down or censored out of recognition. Their world was marked by memories of 1968, both the Prague Spring and invasion, and perhaps even more by memories of 1969, when Husák took over, censorship was restored, and they slowly but surely lost their possibilities for publication and free expression. And as the excitement of 1968 receded, so did hopes for meaningful social change—a shift of horizons that was reinforced by the rise of détente, which for many Czech intellectuals signaled an international preference for the gloomy status quo. It felt like the 1970s were going to last a very long time.

Worlds of Dissent

Understanding dissent means understanding the atmosphere of defeat, compromise, and political retreat that had smothered the Prague Spring. But the terms "dissidence" and "dissident" would not come into common usage in Czechoslovakia until the second half of the 1970s. Havel, Mlynář, Kohout and others put these words in quotation marks, until it became too awkward to do so. I will use them without quotation marks, but I hope to reawaken a sense of their complexity and self-contradictory nature, and to do so in two ways. First, I will try to reawaken a sense of dissent, not just as a political stance or political theory, but also as a *world,* a form of experience and behavior. Dissent was a philosophy, but it was also a common set of situations and experiences closely tied to daily life—experiences that had little to do with politics, theory, or Western reception. Writing was an important part of this world, and it is notable that so many dissidents wrote in the first person about their own experiences. The imagination of narrative personae was an important part of dissent, as was the creation of stories, myths, and legends that often blurred the line between real people and their narrative alter egos. Self-writing was not only a record of dissent but also an important part of the whole "dissident experience" for many banned journalists, novelists, poets, and professors.

Second, I hope to give a sense of dissent, not just as *one* world of experience, but as many different *worlds*—a phenomenon that is too diverse to be easily classified, encompassing many characters, styles, and genres, as well as controversies and sharp debates. Just as dissent looked different from country to country, so did it look different from city to city and even from one group of friends to another. In this book, I will focus on the situation in Czechoslovakia (and, to a large degree, on the urban center of Czech dissent in Prague), but even within this framework, I will highlight diversity rather than attempting to offer a unified model of dissent. My hope is that a close-up view will reveal details and insights that are missing in existing accounts of dissent; indeed, I believe that local studies of dissent have generally been shaped to fit universal and comparative models, rather than the other way around.

Nevertheless, before I turn to the particular case, it will be useful to see just where theories of dissent stand today, a task I take up in Chapter 1. My sense is that, twenty years after 1989, these theories have settled into a few standard narratives that capture some important facets of dissent, but also exclude crucial texts, ideas, and experiences. Heroism still takes center stage in many of these narratives, although some of them react against the proliferation of heroes by denying that the dissidents had any real influence. Discussions of dissent consistently return to the same people and texts, as well as the vexed questions of whether the dissidents brought down Communism and whether their political ideas were vindicated (or, on the contrary, exposed as naïve or even authoritarian) by the post-1989 transitions to democracy. These are interesting debates, but when we are attempting to understand the phenomenon and nature of dissent, they are misleading. Rather than weighing in on these questions, I think it will be useful to bring some new voices into the discussion. The dissidents' own first-person writings, from diaries and memoirs to essays and letters, help reveal what dissidents were thinking at the time, and can reawaken a sense of dissent as a form of self-understanding rather than as a political strategy or political theory. This in turn will elucidate the uncertainties, fears, and conflicts that made dissent what it was, and that were the background for the political courage that attracts us to dissent in the first place.

I will then consider Czech dissent by telling three interlocking stories. In Chapters 2 and 3, I tell the story of "normalization," of how writers, artists, and other intellectuals understood the crackdown following Husák's rise to power. Painfully and slowly, over the first half of the 1970s, they came to terms with the new forms of political power that were being wielded against them, and with a new sense of their role as intellectuals or "writing people" in Czech culture. Dissent took shape in what I call the "shadow world" of intellectual life under normalization—the world of journalists, writers, and politicians who had been fired from their jobs and banned from publishing, and were trying to come to terms with a demoralized national political culture shaped by compromise and frustration. I explore the themes of intellectual culture in the early to mid-1970s, just before the rise of dissent proper, and I consider some of the communications networks—especially the unofficial publishing network known as *samizdat*—that were giving shape to an oppositional community.

The second story is the story of the music underground, which coalesced in the late 1960s and early 1970s around a rock band called The Plastic People of the Universe, their spirited artistic director Ivan Martin Jirous (known to friend and enemy alike as "Magor" or "The Madman"), and Egon Bondy, a cranky poet-philosopher whose psychedelic science-fiction novels became cult underground texts of the 1970s. The underground is usually accorded a bit part in the story of Czech dissent: in the fall of 1976, it was a trial of musicians (including members of the Plastic People) that catalyzed Czech intellectuals to draft Charter 77, one of the key documents of Central European dissent—an open call for the Czechoslovak government to observe human rights. The music underground, after its appearance in the courtroom, drops out of most histories of dissent; I will suggest a more nuanced account in Chapter 4, showing how the Charter resulted from a confluence of both "underground" and "intellectual" currents. The underground's penchant for creating legends about itself gave inspiration to the writers, politicians, and philosophers who would coalesce into Charter 77; these intellectuals had a more sophisticated philosophical and theoretical account of dissent, but they also found themselves borrowing the underground's mythmaking techniques. Václav Havel reinterpreted the underground even as he borrowed inspiration from it in helping to found a new kind of oppositional community.

The third story, which I consider in Chapters 5 through 7, is the story of the early years of Charter 77, one of the most philosophically complex of all the Central European dissident movements. I will examine the formation of a Charter community and its response to the different weapons the state wielded against it—a massive media campaign following its proclamation, followed later by attempts to ignore and isolate the Charter, all accompanied by the intensive legal and police persecution that became part of daily life for the Chartists. I will look at the reasons people did or didn't sign the Charter, and I will examine competing conceptions of the Charter's mission that developed among its signatories, as well as the communications networks that held them together and provided a loose identity through clandestine publications such as the newsletter *Information on Charter 77*, or *INFOCH*. Above all,

I will try to recover the polemical background of dissident writings—including Havel's pathbreaking "The Power of the Powerless"—that have been canonized, anthologized, and removed from their immediate context.

Three larger themes are interwoven throughout the entire argument. One is the role played by storytelling in forging group identities. Studies of dissent have become so saturated in conceptions of truth that it is easy to forget that opposition circles thrive on their own myths and legends. Under conditions of police surveillance and censorship, the uneven distribution of information leads naturally to speculation, rumor, and uncertainty. One task of any opposition is to assemble individual experiences into a more structured set of stories that can define the perspectives and values of the larger group; one task in studying Charter 77 is thus to look at how it unified oppositional stories that, until then, had remained scattered and anecdotal. I believe this function of Charter 77 was just as important as its more explicit role of calling attention to human-rights abuses.

A second theme is the question of the dissident public. Who was telling these stories to whom? Who was the audience for dissent, and did the dissidents themselves constitute a public (or proto-public) sphere? As I will discuss in Chapter 1, an important strand of historiography today downplays the dissidents as a tiny, isolated interest group, unknown to the population at large, and irrelevant to larger political currents. Whether or not this is a fair representation (there are arguments on both sides), it doesn't get us any closer to understanding what dissent was, or who the dissidents were. Nor is it really a new insight. From the very beginning, it was a burning question for the dissidents themselves, who feared that they formed a "ghetto" walled off from society at large. Nearly all dissident writing was, at some level, about the question of its own audience—about its own projected, purported, or yearned-for connection to those Czechoslovak citizens who weren't "in dissent." Other strands of historiography today still insist on the questionable hypothesis that Charter writings were aimed at a potentially universal public—anything less would seem unworthy of the dissidents' universal values and their dream of genuine political participation. I will argue that dissident writing uncomfortably straddled two spaces—the space of a universal public, open to all interested parties, and that of a bounded public, theoretically open to all but also defined by particular customs, values, and goals.

The interaction between public, semiprivate, and private writing leads to a third theme, the importance of first-person writing. Indeed, one of my early motivations in undertaking this project was the realization that so many fascinating texts—diaries, memoirs, letters, essays—had not been folded into the study of Czech dissent, precisely because they seemed too local or contingent. The more one reads what dissidents were writing in the 1970s and 1980s—not the proclamations of Charter 77, but the personal writing that was a major form of internal communication inside the opposition—the more one is struck that first-person writing itself was a major *practice* of dissent. The pressures of police surveillance and an often hostile environment turned writers inward, a natural response in a world without a genuine public sphere where one might fashion a more impersonal persona. If "the personal is political" was a feminist slogan of the 1970s in the West, dissidents were forced to take politics personally.

Thus, much of their first-person writing was paradoxically public. Political meditations were framed as personal essays and letters to anonymous friends. Chartists kept diaries, but also published them, albeit in the small world of *samizdat,* where manuscripts would be copied on mechanical typewriters that were known by the strength of their strike—whether they could make an impression through eight, ten, or twelve layers of carbon paper at a time. The audience for these texts was both known and unknown—a core readership of fellow intellectuals (and often fellow dissidents) was known to the author, and perhaps on a first-name basis with him or her; but copies would circulate from hand to hand and could reach dozens of readers by unpredictable pathways. The most important example of such a "public diary" was Ludvík Vaculík's *The Czech Dream Book,* which I will examine in Chapter 7—a diary of the year 1979–1980, and a central text of Czech dissent as well as one of the great works of Czech postwar literature. Vaculík folded descriptions of his dissident activity in with accounts of his everyday activities; on one page he writes about a police interrogation, and on the next he is feeding the canaries or watering the roses. Like Bondy and Jirous, Vaculík thus managed to create a set of stories about the everyday life of dissent, built around the fascinating juxtaposition of public ideals and private life. *The Czech Dream Book* managed to portray the experience of dissent in a way that no writer had yet been able to; the lively debate it provoked among the community of Chartists (many of whom appeared as characters in the book) was a sign that it had touched a nerve.

At one point in this diary, a *New York Times* reporter calls Vaculík to arrange a meeting. The phone, of course, is bugged, and the reporter is unlikely to get to an interview now that he has notified the police about it ahead of time. "I could have met with you," says Vaculík, "if you hadn't called."[22] Accounts of dissent have generally assumed that it had a captive audience—the Western reporters, politicians, political theorists, and Slavic scholars who were, indeed, captivated by the courage and acumen of so many dissident thinkers. It is easy to forget how isolated the dissidents often felt, and how many doubts they entertained about their own purpose and influence. The lenses of "moral courage," "civic engagement," and "living in truth" have obscured the complicated world in which such ideas have meaning—and in which they inevitably blur at the edges, confronted with opposing virtues, incommensurable choices, reasonable objections, and all the messiness of real life. If I bring some of this messiness back into the picture, my goal is not to demystify, unmask, or "expose" the dissidents; rather, it is to reawaken the stories they told about their own lives, and the ways in which their lives were like our own. If we see dissent as a human, and hence imperfect, phenomenon, I hope that we can free the dissidents from our own need for heroes and moral absolutes. In the process, we may better understand what made them exceptional.

1

The Impasse of Dissent

In the 1970s and the 1980s, dissent shaped Western views of Communism and of life in Central Europe. In turn, the image of a repressive Communist state shaped views of dissent. It was hard to talk about one without mentioning the other, since the merciless suppression of all opposition seemed to be a defining feature of Communist rule. Communism systematically violated basic political rights like the freedom of speech, freedom of assembly, and freedom of religion. Communist states may have claimed that other (social or economic) rights were more important, but this claim was belied by the sorry state of their economies, built around privileges for a select few Party members and chronic shortages for everyone else. By the 1970s, it is true, Communist regimes had lost some of their edge; not even the Party's functionaries seemed to take Communist ideology that seriously anymore, and the show trials, prison camps, and white-hot ideological fervor of the 1950s had given way to more colorless forms of repression. "Lawlessness has put on kid gloves," wrote Václav Havel in 1987, "and moved from the torture chambers into the upholstered offices of faceless bureaucrats."[1] In addition to fear, then, these regimes were built on apathy and selfishness. People who spoke out were punished, but the vast majority were willing to keep silent. They would participate in the sham rituals of the regime, vote in rigged elections, and carry a banner at the annual May Day parade, as long as they were ensured a reasonable standard of living and were left alone to live their private lives in peace. In his 1975 open letter to President Husák, Havel complained that the Czechoslovak government had destroyed public political participation and left citizens in "unprecedented drabness and the squalor of life reduced to a hunt for consumer goods."[2] And though violence may have grown more selective, the state still waged war on culture, passed lies off as truth, and brazenly falsified its own history. "Eastern Europe" (the label itself had traditionally suggested a sense that these lands were somehow foreign, backward, and badly run) was painted in shades of gray; it seemed to be a shabby society of memory holes and bureaucratic repression. Whether Communism evoked thoughts of Winston Smith in the torture chamber or the proles in their rundown tenements, the fog of George Orwell's *1984* hung low and heavy over the region.

The fog and night were broken by flashes of light, moments when a courageous few spoke out against the regime. These people were banned from publishing, fired from their jobs, and placed under police surveillance. They endured house searches and harassments by the *Státní bezpečnost* or StB (variously referred to in English as the state, security, or secret police); some were even arrested and imprisoned. Western journalists and academics began referring to these small groups of protesters as "dissidents"—a label that the protesters themselves at first rejected but ended up adopting, albeit often with a certain ironic distance. A few of these dissidents managed to get their ideas out to the West, and they developed an impressively sophisticated understanding of totalitarian power and the moral dilemmas of opposition. The dissidents were, in effect, a sign of everyone else's submission—the evidence that a few people were selfless enough to reject the corrupt bargains on which Communism rested.

This image of Communism often veered close to caricature, at times a hopeless one. Communism *was* a brutal, broken system, but in recent years, historians have started to ask more searching questions about what life under this system was like. During the 1970s and 1980s, the most articulate accounts of Communist rule came from intellectuals—novelists, poets, playwrights, philosophers, journalists, historians—writers all, many of whom had emigrated or been banned in their home countries. Naturally, they were concerned with serious thought and high culture; they took it for granted that preventing a writer from publishing did irreparable damage to both the national culture and the public sphere. They communicated their many experiences with arrest and imprisonment. But historians have begun to wonder if they were too fast to project the devastation of high culture, and the targeted repression of the regime's opponents, onto society at large. How was the miner who only read the sports pages affected by censorship of his newspaper? Just what were the "ripple effects" of surveillance and police harassment on people who did not experience them directly? As researchers learn how to interpret the fragmentary records in the police archives opened since 1989, they are surprised not only by the extent of police power, but also by its limitations.

In an essay calling for new approaches in contemporary history, two Czech historians have suggested paying less attention to "a very influential, but also numerically small group of people, the ruling Communist establishment and the dissident counter-elite." It is more important to understand "the character of consumer socialism," in part as a way of "finally paying attention to the majority of society."[3] The relentlessly political lens of *1984* is being replaced by new understandings of power as well as new accounts of social and economic history that pay more attention to daily life, popular culture, and the growth of a consumer economy. These accounts reveal a more variegated society, shot through indeed with repression and corruption, where the secret police played a significant role, but where many people also built lives around their own projects and values, working both inside the system and outside, both with and against it, depending on their own, often hard-won sense of what was important.[4]

Historians are meanwhile discarding older binaries of "collaboration" and "resistance" in search of a more subtle understanding of how people negotiate with state power. Even broken, immoral, and violent states can generate significant popular support. Since the heady year of 1968, understandings of political power and protest have evolved significantly, under the twin signs of Michel Foucault and Michel de Certeau. Foucault argued forcefully that power is not just repressive but also productive, that it generates cultural forms as well as censoring them, and that selfhood is often tied closely to these forms of censorship. Nevertheless, de Certeau countered, people still have room to maneuver, even in the most controlled situations. They can cross against the light and walk on the grass, reinterpreting restrictions to make them more amenable to their personal projects; they cocreate the contours of their lives, rather than passively accepting dictates from above. The idea that millions of citizens under Communism sold their political souls in exchange for a few consumer goods has come to seem not just condescending, but implausible.

These are painful debates, and still rife with controversy. Even as historians recoup facets of daily life, or try to understand state-run youth groups as something more than just efficient machines for indoctrination, they still take different positions as to the role and extent of violence in Communist (and non-Communist) regimes, the meaningfulness of forms of popular participation, and the effect that censorship has on the population at large. These are, in fact, old questions, and many historiographic debates today recall the political debates of the Cold War. Nevertheless, a more sophisticated "first-person" sense of life under Communism is steadily emerging, and raising new questions. What kinds of life projects did Communism enable, and what kinds did it destroy? To what extent can people blame their failures on the "system" or "regime" in which they live? (Or do they ruin their lives themselves, without any help from above?) In her 2009 novel *To the Sea,* the Czech author Petra Soukupová meticulously reconstructs her characters' life stories without even mentioning Communism. The fall of the regime in 1989 merits just a couple phrases in a section on the availability of fruits and vegetables: "at first of course it was pretty tough, there wasn't much in the stores, but after the revolution it got much better."[5] This is not an oversight, of course, but a gesture. Nor is it confined to a younger generation that came of age after the Velvet Revolution (Soukupová was born in 1982). One of the most popular Czech authors today, Michal Viewegh (born in 1962), has tried to understand the trajectories of his own generation with minimal reference, or none at all, to political repression. In a 2004 novel, three friends, all born around 1960, stagger out onto Prague's Újezd Street after a high-school reunion that has lasted late into the night.

> Not far away, Zoubek's memorial to the victims of Communism is shining in the darkness: the black remains of human bodies. I point at them.
> "That's us," I say stupidly. "Husák's children."
> "Don't fool yourself, you idiot," Hujerová replies sharply. "The tragedy of your life has nothing to do with any regime."
> In fact, she's right. [. . .] "Okay," I say. "Let's find some nice little all-night bar where we can sit down in peace and quiet and analyze the tragedies of our lives."[6]

Viewegh's characters play out this amusing but savage scene in the shadow of Olbram Zoubek's haunting memorial—a series of decaying torsos stretching up a staircase on Petřin Hill. Are the torsos in the process of healing as they proceed down the hill, emerging from a traumatic past into a present when they can be whole again? Or is the monument rather about the decay of memory, with the past slowly disappearing as it recedes up the hill, into the distance? Zoubek's brilliant monument not only portrays lives ruined by Communist violence; it also raises difficult questions about how to remember them.

There has been one anomaly in this historiographical evolution. As the fog of totalitarianism has lifted to reveal the daily lives of people under Communism, the dissidents have remained in the dark, trapped in older models. There has been no corollary evolution that would consider dissent in tandem with a more nuanced understanding of everyday life. Dissent still seems to be anything but nuanced. For many historians, it remains committed to antiquated notions of authenticity; in its dogmatic allegiance to its own truth, it may even end up mirroring the ideology it opposes.[7] For both scholars and laypeople, the "dissident counter-elite" appears less and less relevant, even a bit annoying—a small, privileged micro-society of professional grumblers. They were courageous, of course, but they were also caught up in their own moral superiority, and hopelessly out of touch with ordinary people who were trying to make a living and take care of their families rather than set off political fireworks.[8] It is difficult to work dissent meaningfully into newer and more complex narratives of daily life under Communism. Caught in a methodological time warp, the dissidents are beginning to feel more and more like an anachronism.

Thus, as Cold War history enters a phase of surveys and syntheses, dissidents still appear as "a tiny network of courageous individuals,"[9] "Havel and his friends,"[10] or "islands of civic engagement and solidarity" in a sea of "passivity, conformity, and political irresponsibility."[11] Historians and political theorists have thoroughly worked over a few key texts, such as Havel's "The Power of the Powerless," Adam Michnik's "A New Evolutionism," or György Konrád's *Antipolitics*, while virtually ignoring the letters, diaries, and personal essays of dozens of other dissidents, whose local and personal perspectives might challenge the reigning narratives. Theories of the psychology of dissent remain straightforward, pointing to a few basic virtues (courage, solidarity, devotion to the truth). "The dissidents" appear as a homogeneous group, and there is little recognition of different vectors inside dissent—for example, religious groupings, regional patterns, ideological loyalties on the left or right, professional or class differences. Perhaps most surprisingly, the homogeneous and simplistic view of dissent has taken hold on both sides of the larger debate about the nature of Communism. Whether Communism was the devil or a petty demon, a system of boundless evil or one of shabby corruption and futility, whether the dissidents were a small band of courageous freedom fighters or a self-satisfied elite, they still tend to get flattened out into the same stereotypes. The result is that narratives of dissent circle around the same sets of unanswerable questions and questionable assumptions, until the circle becomes vicious, circumscribing an ever blurrier image of dissent and what it means today.

I believe that much writing about dissent has settled into three larger narratives, each highlighting different dramas and dissident "storylines" within the historiography of Communism and the Cold War. In what follows, I will try to sketch out these three master plots, arguing that they trace a trajectory in Western attitudes toward the dissidents, and that they can help explain why the study of dissent has reached an impasse. For shorthand purposes, I have called them the *Helsinki narrative*, the *parallel-polis narrative*, and the *ordinary-people narrative*. Each of them captures some facets of an intuitive, popular image of dissent; each also suffers from instructive problems of focus and perspective.

The Helsinki Narrative

On August 1, 1975, years of negotiation and planning culminated in the signing of the Final Act of the Conference on Security and Cooperation in Europe, widely known as the Helsinki Accords. Signed by the United States, Canada, and thirty-three states from both Western Europe and the Communist bloc, the Final Act contained agreements to cooperate in a range of areas: European security, commercial exchange, science and technology, cultural contacts, the environment, and other fields, subsumed under the larger headings of four chapters or "baskets." The centerpiece of the negotiations was the ten principles in the first basket, "Questions Relating to Security in Europe," which guaranteed the territorial integrity of signatory states as well as nonintervention in internal affairs. Soviet leader Leonid Brezhnev considered the accords a triumph, "the high point of his career as a statesman."[12] He had pressed for a security conference precisely because he wanted these territorial guarantees, which amounted to a ratification of the post-World War II borders in Europe; the Final Act effectively legitimized Soviet control over its side of the Iron Curtain. Czechoslovakia's rulers were also pleased, as the pact implicitly affirmed the legitimacy of Husák's post-invasion government.[13]

For just this reason, many Czech intellectuals met the Helsinki Accords with anger or despair. In one of the poetic diaries that he kept throughout the 1970s, Egon Bondy wrote that "the iceberg from Helsinki / has crept all the way to the center of Europe" and called this "disgusting pact" a "negotiation of universal subjugation."[14]

In addition to the security agreements, however, the Final Act contained a second set of guarantees. Immediately after principle six, "Non-Intervention in Internal Affairs," came principle seven, "Respect for Human Rights and Fundamental Freedoms, Including the Freedom of Thought, Conscience, Religion or Belief." Further, the third basket of agreements committed signatories to cooperate on a range of humanitarian contacts, calling for more freedom of travel, free flow of information, cross-border contacts between scholars and journalists, and cultural exchanges. The Soviets were not happy about the human-rights principles, many of which were violated daily within their bloc, but they were convinced that the principles of nonintervention would trump any foreign criticism about human-rights violations.

This turned out to be a miscalculation. In signing the accords, Brezhnev had fallen into "a legal and moral trap. [. . .] Without realizing the implications, he thereby handed his critics a standard, based on universal principles of justice, rooted in international law, independent of Marxist-Leninist ideology, against which they could evaluate the behavior of his and other communist regimes."[15] The language of human rights not only exposed the hypocrisy of Communist regimes; it also created "a new political vernacular" that enabled left-wing intellectuals to disentangle themselves from Marxist historical materialism.[16] The traditional Marxist view saw civil rights as a bourgeois mystification, a way of pretending that class interests were universal. In fact, rights were relative to economic structures; freedoms of speech, press, and assembly could only be chimerical distractions in a capitalist market that systematically exploited its workers. The rediscovery of a robust language of rights provided a fixed point from which to get some leverage on the Marxist idea that "History" was an inexorable evolution in which the working class would come to consciousness, seize the means of production, and lead society into a glorious future.

Scholars who highlight the role of the Helsinki Accords have spoken of a "Helsinki Effect," arguing that the Final Act provided a crucial intellectual and organizational impulse for dissident movements, leading to "an unprecedented mobilization of societal actors in Eastern Europe and the Soviet

Union committed to the implementation of Helsinki's human rights norms."[17] There is some plausibility to this argument. New oppositional groupings in the Soviet Union called themselves "Helsinki Watch Groups," organized to monitor abuses of the rights guaranteed in principle seven and the third basket. In the spring of 1976, the older United Nations covenants on political and economic rights (which Czechoslovakia had ratified the year before) came into force; the Czechoslovak government published them in October and even made them available on newsstands. Just two months later, Charter 77 would be drafted; its first sentence appealed to these covenants and their confirmation at Helsinki, and it goes on to index abuses in Czechoslovakia back to specific provisions of the accords.

The Helsinki narrative helps explain why dissent found a ready-made audience abroad. Human rights became something like a lowest common denominator of repression, an Esperanto of resistance—violations could be immediately understood, even by people far away (including foreign journalists) who had little knowledge of local conditions.[18] Nevertheless, the Helsinki narrative poses a number of problems. Precisely because the language of human rights was so general, it does not explain the complex negotiations and decision-making that underlay the mobilization of dissident opposition. In the Czech case, for example, it ignores the significant role in the formation of Charter 77 played by former Communists like Zdeněk Mlynář, who still saw socialism as a viable framework for dissent. Eurocommunism, which has now been relegated to the dustbin of history, was an important inspiration for many in the late 1970s, including figures like Mlynář or Jiří Hájek, the Foreign Minister during the Prague Spring, who placed as much hope in the upcoming congress of European Communist parties in 1976 as they did in the Helsinki process.[19] Other dissidents tended to reject the idea that Charter 77 arose out of Helsinki; as the Slovak political scientist Miroslav Kusý wrote in the late 1970s, the Charter "cannot be understood or explained either by external factors and influences such as the familiar International Covenants or Carter's human rights campaign, nor by general and abstract political and moral principles such as Freedom, Truth, Equality."[20]

The Helsinki narrative also ignores the fact that the philosophical roots of Czech dissent were located elsewhere—not in "rights talk," but in phenomenology and existentialism. Rather than speaking of human rights (or even, in the language of the Final Act, the "human dignity" from which those rights derived), Czech dissidents were generally more at home with a vocabulary of alienation, crisis, subjectivity, and authenticity, often embedded in larger theories of History (albeit not the Hegelian variety). Jan Patočka's 1975 work *Heretical Essays on the Philosophy of History*, for example, worked with the notion of a "community of the shaken," an idea that dissidents adapted to their own situation. Rights were not the only political vernacular available to opponents of the regime.[21]

Further, the Helsinki narrative tends to emphasize ideology over motivation—the mere existence of an internationally recognized standard of human rights is seen as generating Helsinki Watch groups to claim and defend them. This leads to a simple cause–effect explanation, as if a strategic opening and a bit of daring were all that intellectuals needed in order to criticize their government: "What this meant was that the people who lived under these systems—at least the more courageous—could claim official permission to say what they thought."[22] Precisely because of this "if you build it, they will come" model, the Helsinki narrative tends to work with an impoverished psychology of dissent. It needs a "mobilized local constituency"[23] to help explain why a state might be forced to respond to international norms, but it doesn't tell us much about the mobilization process.

In fact, Helsinki does little to explain how and why people took the painful first steps into open opposition, putting themselves and their families at risk. And while it is true that "rights talk" gave dissent a common language, one particularly useful for the proclamations and reports that were generally written with half an eye to their Western reception, the rhetoric of rights did not play a major role in the self-understanding of many dissidents. Consider, for example, this statement by the poet Zbyněk Hejda, one of the original 241 signatories of Charter 77:

> I perceived the 1970s as an enormous despondency, which was caused by—let's call them external circumstances, but also by the fact that people weren't actually doing anything *in opposition*. That's why I very much welcomed Charter 77. [. . .] For me it was a liberating experience, that a person can actively oppose something he perceives as an enormous villainy.[24]

This passage comes from a 2001 interview with Hejda, but it captures a feeling that is well documented in texts from the 1970s and 1980s: Charter 77 had more to do with a sense of activity, an assertion of autonomy, a taking control of one's fate, than with any articulated allegiance to human rights. To use Václav Havel's more existentialist vocabulary, "it was time to stop being merely a passive object of those 'victories written by history' [. . .] and to try to become their subject." Looking back in 1986, Havel considered the year 1975 to be "the first noticeable break in the long and boring sentence of the 1970s," but he did not even mention the Helsinki Accords signed that year.[25]

Another facet of the rights-based narrative is even more problematic in understanding the intellectual and psychological complexity of dissent. The Helsinki claims, by their very nature, are maximalist and decontextualized, speaking of "the universal significance of human rights and fundamental freedoms."[26] They are meant to apply in all cases, without exception. This universality is precisely what gave them their force across different countries and on both sides of the Iron Curtain, and made them so dangerous for the Communist governments. But this maximalism also made them a blunt instrument. The Helsinki Accords, once they had been translated into human-rights platforms in individual countries, implicitly condemned all the gray zones, compromises, and rough moral edges that characterized the lives of most people, dissidents included, living under Communism (or anywhere else, for that matter). They did not speak directly to the millions of citizens who had made their peace with the Communist system and had no interest in an uncompromising attack that would shake the foundations of the society they had learned to live in. Thus, the greatest strength of human rights, their universality, was also their greatest weakness. The Helsinki narrative explains why dissidents could speak to the international arena, but not how they sounded to their neighbors at home, or even to themselves. In fact, by committing themselves to this maximalist program, the Chartists risked *weakening* their appeal to all those people who had made different calculations (both moral and strategic) about the value of dissent. As I will argue in Chapter 6, the Charter would spend the first few years of its existence trying to define its audience, which often seemed much better delineated abroad than it was at home.

Civil Society and the Parallel Polis

Instead of asking what common ideas or ideologies held the dissidents together, some historians and political theorists have asked what kind of political communities they formed. Theorists who approach dissent along these lines, while acknowledging the role of human-rights discourse, place more importance on the forms of political debate and civic deliberation that the dissidents took part in. Such accounts tend to de-emphasize human rights as a motivating strategy for dissident behavior, and instead consider dissent as an end in itself, often with recourse to two key concepts, civil society and the parallel polis.

"Civil society" is a loose term that has meant many things to many different theorists; as part of the vocabulary of dissent, it has generally referred to the independent organizational life of society, to forms of social and political life that are neither state-sponsored nor wholly private, but fall somewhere in between. In "The Power of the Powerless," Havel speaks of "pre-political" activities and "the independent life of society." For Czech dissidents, the prototype of such an independent life was cultural—the informal concerts of the music underground in the early 1970s; samizdat publishing; art exhibits, plays, or philosophy seminars held in private apartments.[27] These independent structures could be envisioned in different forms—as the isolated outpost of a better society, one that might inspire the rest of the population (or even the state) by example; as a limit on state power, preserving "islands of freedom" against official interference; or as a genuine alternative that would ultimately take the place of the corrupt state.[28] In all these forms, civil society is a schooling in public life for citizens, who can learn to deliberate together and realize their aspirations at a local level. Dissent can be seen as providing just this sort of pre-political schooling. On this reading, the human-rights claims of dissent actually had less to do with the claims themselves than with the communities that formed around them. Dissent offered a vision of collective life in which people realize themselves through political deliberation in small communities.

What's more, Central Europe did not have a monopoly on political anomie and consumerism. Dissent did not just condemn Communism; it pointed to a crisis of mass consumer society both East and West, and suggested that liberal institutions, too, "are chronically liable to corruption" and must be preserved and "reinvigorated" through "conscientious engagement in public affairs." Dissent was not just concerned with human-rights violations; it was sensitive to larger currents of "political disempowerment and alienation characteristic of modern industrial society."[29] It therefore sought to work out a "notion of politics imbued with morality, authenticity, and active subjectivity" as well as "the ethos of social solidarity." The result is a "broad re-definition of politics itself" that emphasizes citizens' self-empowerment and the recovery of their own subjectivity within a community.[30]

Like Helsinki, civil society explains some things while obscuring others. It does a better job of accounting for the philosophical language of Czech dissent, in particular the rhetoric of alienation, authenticity, and subjectivity that is so central to Havel's and Patočka's writings. It raises the crucial question of what dissent looked like "on the ground," and thus provides a theoretical backdrop to explain why dissent could be *fulfilling*, a form of political life vastly superior to the empty public rituals of Communism in the 1970s. Nevertheless, its account of dissident practices remains thin and idealized; indeed, the civil-society account totters precariously between a realistic description of dissident activities and an idealized theory about how civil society should function.

This tension can be seen clearly in Western accounts of an essay by Charter signatory Václav Benda called "The Parallel 'Polis.'" In May 1978, Benda took stock of the Charter's impact and influence after a year or so of activity and concluded that it was in a "blind alley." He saw the Charter as "schizophrenic": was it taking "an abstract moral stance" (which would lead to "disillusionment and deep skepticism"), or did it hope to make real reforms in the life of society (a cause that seemed quixotic given the government's implacable opposition)? While it was important "to compile basic documents which draw attention to the denial of human rights," Benda feared that the Charter was in danger of "becoming a mere producer of dry, rustling papers."[31] His solution was to harness the Charter's moral energy in the creation of parallel structures that would supplement the broken institutions of the regime. In addition to the parallel culture of samizdat publishing and underground concerts, Benda called for the development of educational systems, information systems, economic structures, and at least the beginnings of a parallel political life and even foreign policy.

Benda's "plan" resonated in both East and West. It proved to be "both a powerful metaphor and rhetorical rallying point across the region" of Central Europe,[32] but it also spoke to Western theorists, who saw it as an appealing vision of more genuine forms of political life. One of the best discussions surrounding the parallel polis was generated by a Canadian scholar, H. Gordon Skilling, who circulated a questionnaire to a number of Czechoslovak intellectuals in 1986 and 1987. He asked them whether the idea of an "independent society" was meaningful, and if so, what its purposes and prospects might be.[33] The resulting volume, containing Benda's original essay and the responses to the survey, provides an excellent survey of the intellectual world of Czech dissent in the mid-1980s, although it also produces a certain "echo chamber" effect—the discussion of Benda's essay is a result of foreign interest as much as conditions within Czechoslovakia. Although Skilling was aware that the whole idea of a parallel polis might function more as moral support than as a real plan of action, his questions pointed to a pronounced faith in the possibilities and existence of independent society.

Nevertheless, Benda's essay is more interesting as a self-diagnosis (and therefore a symptom) of the malaise in the Charter community; one cannot help thinking that its intellectual force has been overestimated. The idea of parallel structures had been floating around oppositional circles for years, for example, in Ivan Jirous's idea of a "second culture," which I will examine more closely in Chapter 4, or in Ladislav Hejdánek's account of parallel structures in his cycle *Letters to a Friend*.[34] Benda did not provide any real account of how different parallel structures might come together, or indeed why they should be related at all—why an underground rock concert, for example, should have anything to do with a secret university lecture, let alone with a parallel foreign policy. Hoping to appeal to both radicals and reformists, Benda also remained agnostic on the crucial theoretical question of how parallel structures would lead to meaningful social change—would they cause existing structures to collapse, or merely inspire them "to regenerate themselves in a useful way"?[35] Rather than a work of theory or argument, Benda's essay was an attempt to brainstorm and raise morale.

Despite its sketchiness, however, the notion of the parallel polis has served as a rhetorical hinge in civil-society accounts, allowing historians to move from the idea that dissent *promoted* civic engagement, to the idea that dissent was a *form* of civic engagement—and not just a form, but a whole worked-out proto-society of cultural, educational, social, and even political structures. How widespread were these structures? The situation varied enormously from year to year and from country to country. In general, an independent civil society was most developed in Poland; for the other countries of Central and Eastern Europe, however, seeing dissent as a form of civic engagement means asking difficult questions about how extensive the "islands" of dissident activity really were.[36] And were there other islands of freedom that had nothing to do with dissent at all? Invoking an imaginary polis, Benda's essay allows a sleight of hand, concealing the fact that dissident activities were often woefully limited and invisible to society at large.

How extensive does, say, a network of underground university lectures have to be before it becomes a genuine "parallel structure" that fulfills the functions of civil society? In fact, there is relatively little work analyzing the actual forms of dissident life, including the purportedly parallel structures. Paradoxically, the civil-society narrative has tended to flatten out our accounts of what dissident organizational life really looked like.[37] Further, there was much more to the dissident experience than political debate, self-organization, and the construction of alternative spaces. For one thing, there was police harassment. Like the Helsinki narrative, the civil-society narrative sees imprisonment, beating, and other forms of persecution as an exceptional and unfortunate postponement of dissident activity, an epiphenomenon or temporary abeyance rather than an essential part of the dissident worldview. But surely any account of dissent has to ask how it was shaped by persecution. "Over the years," wrote Ludvík Vaculík in 1980, "we have worked out ways to behave during interrogations, how to escape with documents, smuggle information. We've worked out our position and tactics against the StB, but have we done so with respect to the masters above? After all, the StB is only a stick in the master's hands. We gnaw gloriously at the stick, like free dogs, and the master hardly knows we're there."[38] Dissent, in other words, was not just secret university lectures, but also the police raids on those lectures. In one particularly egregious case, police planted a bag of brown powder in Jacques Derrida's suitcase when he came to Prague to deliver an underground lecture; they arrested him at Prague airport, accused him of drug trafficking, and threw him in jail for a night before expelling him from the country.[39] Was Derrida arrested in the parallel polis? Considerations such as these are a reminder that dissent was about distrust and even paranoia as well as courage and fortitude—about fear as well as fearlessness. "Independent activities" could be distorted by regime pressure, even becoming a different sort of political training and political deliberation. How thin is the line between civic engagement and conspiracy? Some of the most heated debates within dissent had little to do with the parallel polis at all—for example, debates about whether to call out and excommunicate suspected police informers.[40]

The parallel-polis narrative has another blind spot. Many common experiences—hiking trips, visits to the dentist, dinner parties, conversations in the pub, going to the movies, looking for babysitters, lovers' quarrels, and so on—tend to fall under its radar. Thus, even as it gestures toward an exaggerated view of the "civil society" constituted by the dissidents, the parallel polis fails to ask about much of the daily life of dissent, proposing instead an idealized, ultimately unhelpful view of its political and social life.

Ordinary People and Everyday Life

Jiří Gruša, a poet and novelist who signed Charter 77 and later emigrated (and eventually served as the Czech ambassador to Germany and Austria after 1989), objected to the term "parallel polis" in a 2004 interview. "In Benda's alliteration, I couldn't quite figure out one thing: what our polis was supposed to be parallel to." Gruša preferred to see the Charter as a *res publica*, a public affair founded "loudly" in the space of a silent society.[41] Gruša foregrounds the question of how dissent might speak to a broader public, rather than just setting up an alternate universe of right-thinking intellectuals. Many Czech dissidents posed the complicated, even painful question of just how the Charter's islands of civic engagement were supposed to address society at large. Poland was the only Communist country in which dissident protest joined with a mass movement, in the form of the ten-million-member labor union Solidarity; in other countries, open dissent encompassed only a fraction of the population. No matter how universal the dissidents' claims may have been, many people had never heard of this small group of people. Only 241 people signed Charter 77 when it was published, and the final tally of signatories comes in below two thousand—about a hundredth of a percent of Czechoslovakia's population of fifteen million. In December 1989, during the Velvet Revolution, it was Communists in the Czechoslovak parliament who pushed for the direct popular election of a new president; they calculated that Václav Havel was largely unknown and would have little chance of beating their candidate, Ladislav Adamec, who could present himself as a populist reformer and advocate of perestroika. The dissidents at the head of Civic Forum performed the same calculation, and so they opposed the idea of a popular election, arranging instead a parliamentary vote for president, where they had a better chance of negotiating their candidate's success.[42]

Not only were the dissidents few in number; their own experience of Communism was, by any measure, unusual. They came under far more fire from the state than the average citizen; they were closely watched, subjected to psychological harassment, even beaten and jailed. When Havel walked his dog, a secret policeman followed a few steps behind. The dissidents were quite aware of such absurdities; it only takes a slight shift of perspective to see dissent as highly unusual, even esoteric or bizarre. From there, one might reason that historians have been devoting entirely too much time to this strange group of eccentrics—what can dissidents really tell us about daily life under Communism or the functioning of the Communist regime?

In light of such considerations, some historians, sociologists, and anthropologists have proposed a new focus on the majority of ordinary citizens who were neither dissidents nor Communists, neither in opposition nor actively involved in the Party or the police. This shift is part of the larger sea change in the understanding of Communist and other dictatorships that I discussed at the beginning of this chapter. Recent scholarship on Stalinist Russia, for example, has sought to understand society as an actor in its own right, asking how Stalinist culture could be productive as well as repressive, and examining how ordinary people accommodated and negotiated state power in their everyday lives.[43] Ordinary Soviet citizens in the 1970s and 1980s may not have been waiting for the regime to fall; many of them sincerely supported their government, and many others took an ironic stance toward ideological directives even as they paid lip service to them.[44] In the historiography of East Germany, discussions of resistance, opposition, and everyday life have been in full swing for years, and many of the basic theories and categories had already been worked out in discussions of popular resistance (or its absence) under the Nazi regime.[45]

Many of these accounts have turned away from exceptional cases of terror and violence, looking instead at everyday life or the lived experience of ordinary people. A notable recent contribution to the East German debate argues that an exclusive focus on state repression cannot really do justice to the experience of Communism:

> Faced with accounts of repression, complicity and collusion, former citizens of the GDR claimed that their own memories and experiences told them otherwise. Their own biographies did not seem to fit easily within the bleak picture of oppression and fear. [. . .] The experience of East German citizens was far more complex: the distinctions between a brutal repressive state and a subordinate, repressed, or complicit society could not be drawn so neatly.[46]

Newer approaches to Communism show an appreciation of "consumer socialism" that looks for common ground with West European countries, which were also making the postwar transition to modern industrial society. These approaches are often marked by an appeal to notions of everyday life, lived experience, and ordinary people.

Nevertheless, the invocation of experience—and the closely related invocation of people's memories of their experience—is a complicated one. To some extent, the question is one of emphasis: at what point does a historian's shift of

attention from police repression to "everyday" behavior become "a trivializa-
tion of coercive mechanisms"?[47] And what do these accounts say about (and to)
people whose lives *were* shaped by those coercive mechanisms? The invocation
of "ordinary people," "everyday life," and "lived experience"—all these terms
deserve scare quotes—is never an innocent appeal to some unmarked sphere;
it explicitly suggests that some group of people, or some type of experience, is
more typical than others, and asks the historian to orient his or her research
program appropriately.

Inevitably, the everyday-life narrative remains in an uneasy relationship
with dissent. In his introduction to *Obyčejní lidé. . . ?!* (*Ordinary People. . . ?!*),
a collection of oral histories of non-dissident workers and professionals about
their lives under normalization, the Czech historian Miroslav Vaněk offers
a brief but insightful examination of the tensions between "dissent" and the
rest of the population. Vaněk reasonably complains that older histories have
given pride of place to the dissidents, and have contented themselves with a
"shallow, black-and-white and above all superficial characterization, depict-
ing Czechoslovakia's population as apathetic, frightened, escaping from a
disconsolate reality into temporary refuges" such as their weekend cottages.
"An obtuse and silent nation, interested only in its physical possessions and
material prosperity, is placed over and against noble ideals and 'idealistic'
dissidents."[48] Much of the history of normalized Czechoslovakia, Vaněk
points out, was not only shaped by images of dissent, but was actually written by dissident historians and popularized by dissident journalists. Vaněk
does not idealize the past and rejects nostalgia for the good old days under
Communism, but does ask us to remove the dissident lens and consider normalized society on its own terms, without defining it in terms of fear and
cowardice. Indeed, the fascinating oral histories contained in *Ordinary People. . . ?!* make an important contribution to this sort of "first-person" account
of normalization.

Vaněk's title *Ordinary People. . . ?!* derives from (and ironizes) a comment
made by Czech president Václav Klaus in a 2003 article written for the fourteenth anniversary of the fall of Communism:

> I don't agree with those who reproach ordinary people for collaborating
> with the totalitarian regime, for not revolting, for not demonstrating, for
> not founding various opposition groups, as was done by a group of intel-
> lectuals—for the most part former party-members—in several group-
> ings in the 1970s and 1980s. That mass of "ordinary citizens" did have a

reaction to unfree conditions: resistance, inefficiency, alternate individual
activities, the atomization of society, mere passive living against the backdrop of propaganda that no one believed any longer. But it was just these
people who, through their behavior, created the preconditions for November 17, 1989.[49]

Klaus's short article provoked a great deal of controversy.[50] His account of
the dissidents as "a group of intellectuals" and "former party-members" is
unmistakably disparaging, as is his failure even to mention Charter 77. In
contrast, Vaněk's oral histories maintain some distance on the idea of "ordinary people"—thus the ellipsis, question mark, and exclamation mark added
to the title of his team's interviews—and he does go to great pains not to
denigrate the dissidents: "Nevertheless, we would like to emphasize that
dissent, whether it stood on the ideological right or left, deserves historical
appreciation and respect."[51] These sorts of caveats are almost obligatory in the
ordinary-people narrative. They register not just genuine respect, however,
but also a certain helplessness—as if the dissidents were a museum exhibit
belonging to an older classification system.

Vaněk's ironization of the term "ordinary people" is a salutary reminder.
One of the difficulties here is the very idea that an appeal to experience or
ordinariness can direct researchers toward a particular group of people. Surely,
everyone living under Communism had a lived experience of Communism,
and everyone had an everyday life, although different everyday lives may have
looked quite different—some people had encounters with the police almost
every day, others hardly ever. Invocations of "lived experience" or "everyday
life" simply postpone the question of how historians have chosen their sub-
jects, and often hide the absence of a clear criterion for bracketing one sector
of the population off from others. In fact, these invocations generally hide an
assumption that some people's experience is more "lived" than others'—that
some people's lives were simply more typical, emblematic, or important.

The value of the ordinary-people narrative is that it refuses to write off
whole populations as apathetic and immoral. It can even help illuminate dissent by keeping alive the painful questions that dissidents themselves faced,
about whether and how to judge the majority of society that did not join
them in opposition. It may be no surprise that Paulina Bren's recent treatment of popular culture and everyday life under Communism is also one of
the first works by an American historian to explore some of the many divisions and different approaches *within* the Czech dissident movement.[52] The

ordinary-people narrative helpfully identifies a spectrum of responses to the regime, ranging from total support to total rejection (with nearly everyone located somewhere toward the middle). Nevertheless, it is difficult to draw the line anywhere along this spectrum and coherently argue that some set of experiences is more important (typical, enlightening . . .) than others. Because there is no way of drawing that line, the ordinary-people narrative just inherits and recycles the same anachronistic vision of dissidents as a small band of courageous heroes. Even worse, it creates the impression that dissidents had no everyday life of their own. What was the lived experience of dissent, anyway? And how much claim should it have on the historian's attention? We seem to be back where we started.

The three narratives trace a certain trajectory in how the West has understood dissent. The Helsinki narrative sees the dissidents as the moral conscience of society, courageous spokespersons for universal truths that most people are afraid to support. This is a comfortable position for the historian (not to mention politician or op-ed writer) to occupy, and it is characteristic of the more triumphalist narratives built around a United States victory in the Cold War. But its account of dissident thinking remains thin, nor does it give a clear sense of what activities the dissidents actually engaged in. It threatens to leave us with a collection of Benda's "dry, rustling papers"—proclamations and accounts of human-rights violations—without explaining the texture and psychology of dissident life. The civil-society narrative answers this challenge, turning its attention to local organizations and political deliberation. It sees dissent as an end in itself—a meaningful form of civic deliberation and political activity—sometimes with a suggestion that Western forms of democracy in the Cold War were themselves flawed. On one model, the dissidents used the weapons the West had given them; on the other, they yearned for a higher form of political life than Western democracy could provide. Both accounts remain idealized, built around an abstract notion of civic engagement. What's more, both accounts are committed to the idea that society at large was apathetic or cowardly. The dissidents begin to look more and more like a self-important sect. The result is a narrative of "ordinary people" or "everyday life" that seeks a deeper understanding of people's lives under Communism, but only *some* people's—it still inherits an older view of the dissidents, keeping them at a respectful but uncomprehending distance.

This trajectory leads into what I would call *the impasse of dissent*: lacking a persuasive account of dissidents' lives, of their varied motivations, fears,

and failings, we throw up our hands and simply bracket the dissidents off
from our accounts of Communism altogether. In the absence of a richer
sense of their personalities, their undeniable courage comes to seem one-
dimensional, puzzling, and above all unnecessary. They seem to have taken
a wrong turn and ended up somewhere out of power, out of touch with their
compatriots, and ultimately out of the history books, which are now moving
on to the intriguing and complicated project of understanding the daily life
of consumer socialism. Starting from the noble rhetoric of human rights,
we have ended up abandoning the dissidents without even answering the
most basic questions of all: Who *were* they? And why was it, again, that we
thought they mattered?

Dissent in the First Person

Imagine that, instead of asking about the features of the parallel polis, a
Western scholar had distributed a different sort of questionnaire, with questions like "What have you been reading lately? Which newspapers do you
follow? How have your closest friendships evolved since you lost your job at
the university? Could you describe a recent house search by the secret police?
What compromises would you be willing to make in order to publish with an
official publishing house? Do you talk about politics with your children? How
have you been sleeping?" We might know less about the theory of the parallel
polis, but I think we would know a lot more about the dissidents themselves.
We might have a better sense of their "lived experiences," of how they saw
themselves and their friends, and a better way of using these experiences to
help us understand dissent in other countries and at other times. Such questions might offer a way to approach both the failures and successes of dissent,
rather than forcing the dissidents into the airless categories of courageous
heroes or irrelevant intellectuals.

In fact, there *is* such a questionnaire—a book of interviews, actually,
called *České rozhovory* (Czech Conversations), conducted by the journalist Jiří
Lederer in 1975 and 1976. It paints an intellectual portrait of banned Czech
writers and journalists in the years before Charter 77, and it is just one example of a whole world of first-person writing from the 1970s and 1980s, most of
which has not been tapped in histories of dissent or philosophical investiga-
tions of civil society and human rights. A brief survey of some of these texts
may give a sense of just how much information, and how many perspectives,

have been left out of accounts thus far. In addition to *Czech Conversations*, there is Eva Kantůrková's *Sešly jsme se v této knize* (We Have Gathered Together in This Book), a collection of interviews with women from 1980, as well as many other interviews scattered throughout the samizdat press. There are anthologies of feuilletons, the genre of personal essay that was a favored form of self-expression for many banned writers, such as the annual volumes *Československý fejeton/fejtón* (Czechoslovak Feuilletons) edited by Ludvík Vaculík from 1975 through 1979. There are books of letters, such as the philosopher Ladislav Hejdánek's *Dopisy příteli* (Letters to a Friend), addressed to an anonymous young student who wants to sign the Charter. There are diaries—some by writers who opposed the regime but kept their distance from dissent, such as Jaroslav Putík's *Odchod od zámku* (Departure from the Castle) or Jan Zábrana's *Celý život* (All My Life), and some by dissidents themselves, such as Jan Vladislav's *Otevřený deník* (Open Diary), František Vaněček's *Všivá doba: Z deníku chartisty* (Lousy Age: From a Chartist's Diary), or Ludvík Vaculík's *Český snář* (The Czech Dream Book). There are memoirs, such as Jiří Lederer's *Touhy a iluze* (Desires and Illusions); František Janouch's *Ne, nestěžuji si* (No, I'm Not Complaining); Ivan Jirous's *Pravdivý příběh Plastic People* (The True Story of the Plastic People); or Eva Kantůrková's prison portraits *Přítelkyně z domu smutku* (My Companions in the Bleak House). There are autobiographical novels, such as Pavel Kohout's "memoiroman" *Kde je zakopán pes* (Where the Dog Is Buried), and the unclassifiable, melancholic soliloquies of Egon Bondy such as *Leden na vsi* (January in the Village). There is also autobiographical poetry, such as Bondy's poetic notebooks or Ivan Jirous's prison poems, *Magorovy labutí písně* (Magor's Swan Songs). There are first-person political accounts, combining dispassionate analysis with autobiography and highly personal self-examination, such as Milan Šimečka's texts from the 1970s and 1980s—his well-known *Obnovení pořádku* (*The Restoration of Order*) is still unsurpassed as an analysis of late socialism, but is also an autobiographical essay about his own path from reform Communism into dissent. To these accounts could be added interviews and memoirs written after 1989, as well as the more recent work conducted by the Center for Oral History at the Institute for Contemporary History in Prague, which published, in 2005, dozens of interviews with former dissidents and Communist Party functionaries. These are an invaluable source of information on the texture and daily life of dissent (and they, too, have hardly been tapped in Western scholarship).[53] Collectively, these books and interviews sketch out a different picture of dissent—one that embeds the theoretical concerns of political opposition in the immediate concerns of family, friendship, work, and leisure, all shaped by the effort to understand oneself through first-person writing.

These accounts must be handled with care, and it may be useful to say a few words here about how I have approached first-person documents while writing this book. Memory is often, perhaps always, deceptive, and every experience gets changed in the telling, not to mention the hearing or reading—or the retelling! Oral histories often reflect the concerns of the questioner as well as those of the subject, and need to be read as a dialogue between two forms of memory rather than as a straight confession or autobiography. And self-deception and self-stylization can distort one's memories even when one tries to be open and honest. Short-term memory can play as many tricks as long-term memory, and when people record their experiences, they are subject to pressures imposed by various anticipated audiences, whether they be friends, family, strangers, a future self, or even the state police. In short, memoirs, diaries, interviews, and other first-person texts present many puzzles for the researcher, who must approach each of these texts with healthy skepticism.

I have tried to mitigate the uncertainties in three ways. First, I have tried to provide as much context as possible for the works I cite, indicating when they were written and keeping alive a sense of the author's blind spots and interests. To an alarming extent, foreign historians have tended to take dissent at its word; because of the dissidents' open commitment to telling the truth, as well as their undeniable charisma, the historian is reluctant to see their accounts as self-serving, self-reinforcing, or simply wrong. Wherever possible, I have tried to cross-check and juxtapose the memories and stories of various actors. I hope readers will perceive the resulting picture as a loose mosaic in which each tile has some freedom of movement, while still limiting the movement of the tiles around it and contributing to a larger image that is relatively clear. Or, to switch metaphors, readers may listen to these stories as a much richer polyphony of voices than has been heard until now; some voices will get the occasional solo, but I hope that none will drown out the rest. In the end, if this book is successful in bringing many new voices into discussions of dissent, it should also indicate just how much of the variety of dissident experience remains to be narrated. Indeed, my own reading on dissent in Central Europe has convinced me that a significant influx of new texts and translations may be necessary if historians are to develop new comparative and theoretical narratives.

My second methodological principle has been to return as often as possible to texts written at the time. I do not presume that letters, diaries, and personal essays are closer to the truth—indeed, the errors of memory often result, not from distance, but from all the minor self-deceptions and rationalizations that people accumulate in the daily business of living. But I have looked on contemporary texts from the 1970s and 1980s as relatively reliable guides, at least, to what people were thinking and saying (true or false) at the time. I have paid particular attention to the changing names of phenomena that, at first, enjoyed no established definition—asking questions such as when a trial of four members of the music underground became known as "the trial of the Plastic People," or when the signatories of Charter 77 came to be called "dissidents." Misnomers are often more telling than names, and stories can reveal the most about a storyteller at the moments when he or she is bending the truth. A return to older texts can also help reawaken the uncertainty that is such an important part of human experience, and can turn our attention to the crucial question of who knew what when. This turns out to be one of the most interesting questions that dissent poses for the historian today, and it is elided in the three narratives I sketched out earlier, which see dissent as a unified phenomenon, a set of ideas held or strategies practiced in common. In fact, dissent always grappled with an unequal distribution of information.

Finally, I have tried to pay special attention to the linguistic form and genre of sources. For example, rather than accepting reports on human-rights abuses as simple information-delivery systems, I have asked how they draw on established literary conventions, such as the primitivism that was so assiduously cultivated in the writings of the music underground, or the conventions of the open letter as it evolved during the 1970s. Many of the dissidents were themselves masters of rhetoric and literary form; many of them had years of journalistic training, which meant they knew how to write quickly according to basic conventions of style, length, genre, and tone. Dissidents worked hard on perfecting the objective, dispassionate voice of Charter documents, but the very same writers felt the need to express themselves more eloquently, with less restraint, in personal essays, interviews, and other genres. Style mattered, and attention to the written traces of dissent needs to keep questions of form, genre, and language at the forefront.

It may also be useful to say a few words about why these texts have not made it into English-language discussions of dissent. The language barrier has played a role, of course, but they have also fallen into a blind spot of the narratives I described earlier. First-person writing highlights the local, the contingent, and the personal, whereas the study of dissent has generally been filtered through the theories of its protagonists rather than through their behaviors or practices.[54] Where history *is* interested in the actual lives of dissidents, the focus tends to be on arrest, interrogation, and imprisonment, but even these experiences, in turn, are interesting either because they shape dissident thought, or because they don't—because dissidents reflect on imprisonment, or fail to be broken by it. For Western observers, a central dissident genre has always been "letters from prison," imbued with both courageous idealism and hard-minded realism. And many of them are—such as Adam Michnik's *Letters from Prison* or Havel's *Letters to Olga*, whose very philosophical abstruseness was honed on his struggle with the prison censor. But the genre may look like this because works that don't fit the mold have been pushed to one side. For example, Eva Kantůrková's ironic portraits of fellow prisoners in her book *My Companions in the Bleak House* have hardly been noticed in discussions of dissent, even though they were translated into English in 1987. Kantůrková pays close attention to the illusions and self-deceptions of her fellow prisoners; she offers a panorama of life under normalization, inside and outside prison, that looks closely at how people incorporate both personal truths and self-delusions into their life-stories. This is a far more complex rendering of truth and lie than the standard accounts of dissident philosophy.[55]

The heroic view of dissent has tended to paint it as an individual, often lonely activity—in fact, just like writing. This view ignores the communal structures that make such writing, and protest more generally, possible—not the abstract "civil society" of political theory, but simple things like pubs and cafés, family and friends, and above all a wife or husband. Indeed, many dissidents might best be thought of as "spousal units." Dissident couples often worked out a clear division of labor, in which one member remained politically engaged while the other held down a job (and thus avoided public protests that might have led to being fired) in order to support the family financially, and often took care of the children as well.[56] (Usually it was the husband who took on the "public" role, but that was not always the case.) Many "writing" dissidents had a partner who wrote little but played a vital role in community-building—for example, Dana Němcová, the "spiritual mother" of the music underground who offered her home to musicians when they had no place to stay, or Olga Havlová, who played a vital role in organizing the many parties, concerts, seminars, and meetings that helped intellectual dissent crystallize around her husband in the mid-1970s.[57] Even those collections of prison letters were generally addressed to a spouse or lover who then played a key role in collating and distributing them.[58]

There is an unmistakable gender dynamic here. The dissident theorists and thinkers who make it into Western accounts are almost all male; the closer we come to seeing dissent as a transnational dialogue about human rights or civil society, the more women seem to be erased from the picture. The idea that a whole world of dissent is missing from historical narratives was broached most forcefully in recent years by Shana Penn's book *Solidarity's Secret: The Women Who Defeated Communism in Poland*. Penn opened up discussion of the role of women in Solidarity; her work was also skillful in describing the mechanics of opposition work in general, from techniques of underground publishing to the hiding of forbidden texts in the "feminized spaces" of domesticity (such as laundry chutes, a child's bedroom, or pickling jars).[59] Penn made a convincing case that a crucial chapter of Solidarity's history had been neglected, but her argument was weaker in framing the everyday life of dissent as an inherently female or gendered realm; many underground activities Penn describes were carried out by both men and women, and I believe much more examination of contemporary texts is needed before we can see whether and how different genres of underground activity were marked as masculine or feminine. Penn's book may have reflected less an occlusion of women's roles—although that is certainly part of the equation—than a larger exclusion of private life and daily practices from discussions of Solidarity. This remains true of Czech dissent, as well, and reflects the blind spots of narratives that focus on theory and politics rather than the stories dissidents were writing about their own lives.

Did the Dissidents Bring Down Communism?

Research on dissent has been distorted, not just by the preference for theory over practices, but also by a somewhat contradictory conviction that dissent should get results. The recent anniversary of the 1989 revolutions occasioned a new round of questioning as to whether the dissidents "brought down" the Communist regimes. Although the question in this form is little more than a journalistic hook, serious histories have nevertheless tried to grapple with it in more nuanced form. Answers have varied widely, from detailed micro-histories of the roles played by specific dissidents in the day-to-day course of the revolutions[60] to the strong thesis that dysfunctional regimes imploded on their own, with minimal or no input from domestic opposition.[61] Similarly, studies have looked back from the postrevolutionary era to ask whether the dissidents' experience under Communism was a benefit, a liability, or simply irrelevant when it came to negotiating regime change and founding new political and economic structures—a common thesis, for example, is that the fascination with "antipolitics" and civic initiatives led the dissidents to scorn political parties, fatally weakening themselves in the rough-and-tumble of democratic politics.[62] Others have challenged the myth of "dissident failure," pointing out that former dissidents are still prominent in Central European politics and culture, even if the parties they formed in the days of revolution have disintegrated or been voted out of power.[63]

Seeing dissent through the lens of 1989 is important for understanding 1989, but it is not important for understanding dissent. Indeed, one of the most important tasks in approaching dissent is to discard this line of inquiry.

Why is the 1989 question so problematic? There are at least three reasons. First, it assumes agreement about what actually happened in 1989. This frequently involves the "triumphalist" thesis that the West won the Cold War: Communism was overthrown in the name of democracy and market capitalism. As with so much writing on dissent, this perspective homogenizes the diverse perspectives of oppositional groupings in the 1970s and 1980s. Indeed, if you had asked different Czech thinkers in 1988 what it would mean to "bring down" the regime, you would have gotten many different answers—from negotiated transition to a revolutionary clean sweep of all offices. The same goes for the question of what would come next. Social democracy, market socialism, Thatcherite free enterprise? Proportional voting or majority rule? A strong or weak president? A traditional party system or structured competition among civic initiatives?[64] The list of uncertainties goes on and on; most people had hardly thought seriously about these questions before the heady days of November and December 1989, when they suddenly had to be answered quickly, often on the fly. Czechs today do not even agree on whether the Velvet Revolution was a genuine revolution, or merely a transfer of power carried out within the institutional structures of the old regime; many Czech intellectuals are more skeptical about the "triumphalist" narrative than former cold warriors in the West.[65]

A second problem with the 1989 question is that it judges dissent based on its efficacy, on its success at performing this vague task of "bringing down" Communism. Rating different dissident practices according to which were most "effective" or most useful in the post-1989 transitions, it treats dissent as a proto-political party with particular goals and strategies, rather than as a form of culture, a set of common stories, a style of political behavior, or a collection of practices that had meaning in and of themselves. It would make just as much sense to ask whether the French *philosophes* brought down the *ancien régime*, or the Romantics caused the revolutions of 1848—the question is worth asking, but any plausible narrative answering it would have to simplify its subject, ignoring many of the writings and practices that made the Enlightenment the Enlightenment and Romanticism Romanticism. In other words, dissent should be seen as a cultural-political movement whose fortunes are not necessarily tied to some particular (and inevitably oversimplified) narrative about historical change.

Finally, the 1989 question removes all the uncertainty from dissent. Why *not* oppose the regime if it's going to collapse? There were a mere thirteen years between the proclamation of Charter 77 on January 6, 1977, and the first major demonstrations of the Velvet Revolution in November 1989. It is easy to forget how long those thirteen years seemed. Those who emigrated (many would soon be returning unexpectedly) thought they would never see their friends and family again. It is difficult to recover the force of this "never" today. Those who went to jail thought their imprisonment might be swallowed up in the depths of history, rather than becoming a discernible stepping-stone on the way to a free society. The structures of the Cold War seemed implacable, and the division of Germany seemed as inevitable, even logical, as the division of Korea may still seem to many people today.

In taking the fall of the regime as a starting point, we thus lose touch with all the complications, fears, and uncertainties that made dissent *difficult*—and continue to make it difficult under regimes and ideologies that today seem as stable and everlasting as Communism did in 1975 or 1984. This sort of "backshadowing"—narrating past behavior in the light of later events—not only leads to Whiggish histories, but also loses touch with the unshaped quality of experience, the very thing that makes choice meaningful (and often fails to dispel doubts even after a choice is made).[66] It is easy to forget that dissent was an ongoing decision, endlessly revisited, and a constant puzzling-through of questions with real consequences: Am I doing the right thing? Are the sacrifices I am making (and inflicting on my family and friends) really worth it? What kinds of beliefs will sustain me over time? How long can I hold out? As we return to the dark days of 1969—following the Soviet invasion, the ignominious collapse of reform leaders, and the rise to power of the enigmatic Gustav Husák—it may be useful to keep that uncertainty in mind.

2

The Stages of Demobilization

In the years following the invasion, the physicist František Janouch descended down the same spiral as many other Communist intellectuals. Janouch, born in 1931, had grown up in a Communist family and was fascinated by the Soviet Union from an early age—he even learned Russian as a boy, during World War II, and helped interpret for Red Army soldiers when they arrived in Prague at the end of the war. He studied physics in Leningrad and Moscow, where he completed his university and doctoral studies. He became head of the Theoretical Nuclear Physics division at the Institute for Nuclear Research near Prague. A spokesman for reform during the Prague Spring, he continued to support the reform course after the invasion.

In November 1969, while painting his apartment, he discovered a hole in the wall containing a listening device. Three months later, he was expelled from the Communist Party for "opportunism" and "anti-Sovietism." In September 1970, the director of the Institute for Nuclear Research called Janouch in to his office and gave him notice that he was being released, at the same time offering him an alternative: if he resigned his position voluntarily, he still might be able to find a decent job elsewhere. Otherwise, the black mark on his record would surely keep him from finding work commensurate with his abilities. Janouch rejected the offer as "indecent and cowardly" and "more advantageous" for the director than for him. The director then handed him a short letter on the institute's letterhead: "Dear Comrade," it read, "because in the recent past you have disrupted the socialist social order with your political and public activity [. . .] I am dissolving the working relationship between you and the Institute of Nuclear Research [. . .] by means of this notice, in accordance with statute 46, paragraph 1e) of the legal code." Janouch sued the Institute for firing him illegally; when a first judge ruled that, indeed, no valid reasons had been given, she was replaced with a second, who affirmed the dismissal. Janouch appealed the decision and lost; the appeals court noted, among other things, that Janouch had disrupted the state's Marxist-Leninist educational system by calling for an end to censorship.

Janouch and his wife began to support themselves by translating technical documents. He continued to send protest letters to state representatives, as well as to his colleagues abroad. Shortly before elections in November 1971, three cars appeared outside his apartment building, and for several days he was followed everywhere he went. One morning, Janouch later wrote, he happened to drive past President Husák's car and noticed that his own police escort was larger than the president's. Janouch began to carry a "prison kit" around with him at all times—a briefcase with a small towel, a toothbrush, an empty notebook, and reading materials (one book on mathematics, one on theoretical physics, an Italian textbook, and the Czechoslovak legal code). He began to be called in for interrogations, whether as witness or as the accused. He continued to write protest letters, as well as letters to friends in prison, such as the journalist Karel Kyncl, who had been arrested in January 1972 and was serving an eighteen-month sentence.

In September 1973, Janouch sent a letter to *The Times* of London advocating a Nobel Peace Prize for his fellow physicist in the Soviet Union, Andrei Sakharov, who was the object of constant attacks in the Soviet press. A few days later, Janouch received an anonymous letter accusing him of being a tool of the international Zionist conspiracy and of "veiling his intentions, as Jews usually do, with lofty words about freedom and democracy." In September 1973, he was threatened with prosecution for having given an interview to visiting British reporters and spreading disinformation about Czechoslovakia—a crime punishable by up to three years in prison. At the same time, it was suggested that he accept the offer of a guest professorship at the Royal Academy of Sciences in Sweden. (This position had been offered to him in 1970, but at the time Czechoslovak authorities had responded by simply canceling his passport.) On December 26, 1973, Janouch, his wife, and their two children, in a car packed full of their belongings, drove to Železná Ruda, a sleepy town on the Czechoslovak–German border. The border guards were surprised—Janouch had told his friends, over his (bugged) telephone, that he would be leaving on the 28th from another crossing some hundred kilometers to the north. After five hours of questioning, Janouch crossed the border and emigrated to Sweden. The Czechoslovak government, which had once taken away his passport, was now glad to get rid of him.[1]

In a letter composed at the end of 1973, Janouch wrote up his own diagnosis of Czechoslovakia after the invasion. Among other things, he noted that the Communist Party:

> had gotten rid of its brain [*mozkové centrum*]—those hundreds of thousands of socialist intellectuals who were capable of independent and critical thought, of analysis, of evaluating the past and present and of thinking through perspectives and variants of the future socialist development of our country. Today there exists, outside the Communist Party, a strong (both in numbers and intellectual capacity) group of former Party members as well as non-members who would be capable of determining and leading future political changes in our country. These people, however, are on the periphery of society; they form a ghetto of outcasts with no rights; the mechanism that could return them to active participation in the activity of society is not at all clear and probably is not a simple one.[2]

Janouch was not the first or last to voice such a lament. By punishing so many writers, artists, and scholars who refused obeisance to the post-invasion government, the Communist Party was destroying the country's intellectual base. But the most striking thing about this analysis is a word that is missing: *dissident*. Just a few years later, it would have been difficult to write these sentences *without* mentioning dissent, if only to put it in quotation marks and lament the lack of a better term. In 1973, it was still difficult to conceptualize this nascent intellectual opposition—consider how many words it took Janouch to describe it. It is also striking to see how difficult it was for an ex-Communist to separate the idea of intellectual opposition from the Party itself—Janouch, who himself had been a longtime Party member with a prestigious academic position, is clearly thinking here of "socialist intellectuals" expelled from the Party, although he remembers to mention "non-members" as well.

Janouch's analysis raises the larger questions of what the world of dissent looked like before it had a name—who were the dissidents, and what were they doing, before their activity had been reconceived as an organized opposition, endowed with a philosophy and even a manifesto, Charter 77? What did dissent look like before the term existed? To understand these questions, we must place them firmly in the context of the Czech lands in the early 1970s. Czech dissent was a reaction to a specific set of conditions: the decimation of public cultural and political life after 1968, the particular forms of persecution (severe, but generally not crippling) that people were subjected to, and the forms of community that intellectuals imagined for themselves during the first half of the 1970s.

The Rise of Gustav Husák

Warsaw Pact troops were met by a remarkable outpouring of peaceful resistance. Historians of the invasion have tended to agree with what United States Secretary of Defense Clark Clifford told his staff meeting on August 26: "From a military standpoint it was a sophisticated operation but politically it was a bust."[3] A puppet government of pro-Soviet Communists never coalesced, while tens of thousands of people protested in the streets. But the resistance was destined to dissipate over the coming months, in the absence of any effective leadership from Dubček and his team. Indeed, the reform politicians returned from Russia "in one piece," as Milan Šimečka put it, but "with [their] spirit and morale shattered." During their Muscovite captivity, they had signed the so-called Moscow Protocol, a set of fifteen demands that immediately put the reformers on the defensive. The protocol nullified the emergency Fourteenth Congress of the Communist Party that had been called in the Prague district of Vysočany immediately after the invasion; it promised regulation of the media as well as a ban on activities by the fledgling non-Communist organizations that had begun to organize themselves during the spring and summer; and it said that "allied troops" would only be withdrawn when "the threat to the gains of socialism in Czechoslovakia and the threat to the security of the countries of the socialist commonwealth" had subsided. There were only a few concessions to the Czechoslovak side—references to the Prague Spring as a "counterrevolution" were removed, although of course the idea that there had been a "threat to the gains of socialism" already signaled a new interpretation of the events of the spring and summer. There was also an unconvincing promise that the occupying troops would not intervene in internal affairs.[4]

For the Czech and Slovak populations, the hazy arrangements emerging from Moscow could be seen, at best, as a necessary evil that might block a major crackdown until the reform leadership could reorient itself and build on its massive popular support. For the Soviets, the Moscow Protocol was a blueprint for the gradual demobilization of the population. Brezhnev understood that the invasion had provoked too much opposition for an immediate change of leadership to take place, but also shrewdly calculated that there was no reason to rush; reforms could be rolled back more decisively by the indecisive reformers themselves, rather than by the puppet government he had originally hoped to install. In Soviet eyes, the Moscow Protocol was a minimal program for the consolidation of Communist rule, a process during which the reform leadership would be gradually undermined and replaced with more palatable rulers. The astute Šimečka, analyzing the situation in early September, wrote: "This is the treachery of the Moscow agreements: in reality, they mean that Moscow's policy will be carried out by the people who gained popularity precisely because they took a stand against it." (Šimečka refers only to the "Moscow agreements"—one of the fifteen demands was that the actual protocol would be kept secret, in order to avoid a popular outcry.)[5]

The reformers' first concessions and retreats can be seen in this light, and they focused on clearing the stage of alternate power centers.[6] The Moscow Protocol spoke of "personnel changes," understood to be aimed at the most radical and stubborn reformers, who now were removed from positions of power. These included František Kriegel—the only leader brought to Moscow who had refused to sign the Protocol at all; Minister of the Interior Josef Pavel; Minister of Foreign Affairs Jiří Hájek; vice-premier Ota Šik, who had masterminded the economic reforms of the Prague Spring; and the directors of state television and radio, Jiří Pelikán and Zdeněk Hejzlar. Two of the major civic organizations that had evolved outside of Party structures during the Prague Spring—KAN, the "club of engaged non-party-members," and K 231, the group of former political prisoners—had their requests for official registration refused; preparations for a new Social Democratic Party were also halted. In the week after the invasion, the Vysočany Congress—not knowing what had happened to Dubček, Smrkovský, and the other kidnapped leaders—had elected an alternate Central Committee. This second leadership had to be persuaded to step aside; in return, some of its members were "co-opted" into the existing Party leadership. A new censorship office was instituted, although its restrictions were fairly mild—open criticism of the Soviets was forbidden, as was reference to an "occupation" or "occupiers." Otherwise, there were few limits on what could be published.[7] Indeed, many journalists and writers remembered the fall of 1968 and the spring of 1969 as a time of significant press freedom, perhaps the freest under Communist rule.

Nevertheless, the true balance of power quickly began to make itself felt. The levers of power in the Communist state traditionally rested in the Central Committee of the Party, which itself was controlled by its presidium. When the Central Committee co-opted eighty members of the Vysočany Congress (ending up with 191 members in all), it seemed to contain a strong coalition of reformers. The presidium, too, was increased in size to twenty-one members, with reformers well represented. But in the chaotic atmosphere of the fall, when contacts with Soviet leaders were all important, real power was focused in the hands of a so-called "Group of Five." The strongest reformers in this group were Dubček himself, still holding his post as the Party's First Secretary, and Josef Smrkovský, who was president of the National Assembly; the other three, Prime Minister Oldřich Černík, President Ludvík Svoboda, and head of the Slovak Communist Party Gustav Husák, had all shown themselves to be far more pragmatic and willing to make concessions. Dubček, Černík, and Husák went to Moscow in the beginning of October for direct negotiations with Brezhnev; but rather than making headway against his demands, they brought back a treaty on foreign troops that effectively ratified the Soviet military presence. While arranging for the departure of some soldiers, it accepted the presence of about seventy-five thousand Soviet soldiers in Czechoslovakia, with no clear date given for their departure. This treaty was approved by a vote of 228 to 4, with ten abstentions, in the National Assembly on October 18.[8]

If the Moscow Protocol had been accepted as a concession to brute force and unpleasant reality, the troop treaty was a clear defeat, a signal that reformers were now steadily losing ground. The continued presence of Soviet soldiers—effectively a legalized occupation—would give hard-liners the upper hand in all the internal Party power struggles from now on. The signing of the treaty provoked demonstrations, particularly among students, but at a November meeting of the Party's Central Committee, reformers continued to lose ground to two other factions now clearly taking shape: a group of hardline reactionaries, many of whom had opposed the Prague Spring to begin with, and an emerging group of "realist" figures like Husák and Černík, who were increasingly willing to negotiate away reforms in order to consolidate their own position. In the middle of this meeting of the Central Committee, Dubček, Černík, and Husák fended off an attack from the Party's conservative wing by flying off to Warsaw for a secret night meeting with Brezhnev; the Soviet leader strengthened their hand by approving their draft of the Central Committee resolution, but also forced them to insert even sharper language against "the right-wing danger" of reform. Reform Communists were sliding down "a slippery slope of constant compromises," lacking both the strength and the will to take advantage of their still considerable support among the population at large. Zdeněk Mlynář, who for all his cautious maneuvering was still one of the most committed reformers, saw the writing on the wall and simply resigned from the Central Committee.[9]

By contrast, the November Party plenum, as well as the recent decision to temporarily cease publishing two reform journals, *Politika* and *Reportér*, the weekly of the Journalists' Union, provoked a major protest from the artists and writers who were united in the Coordinating Committee of Creative Unions—an umbrella organization that brought together the various official unions of writers, journalists, architects, musicians, workers in television and film, and others. On November 22, they called a major meeting of Czech and Slovak cultural figures at the Slavic House in downtown Prague. The high point of the meeting was a speech given by reform journalist Jiří Lederer, an editor at *Reportér* who had reported extensively on the events of 1968 in Poland as well. "Culture will set the terms," said Lederer. "Not for the first time in our history has it become the most important factor shaping politics—if I understand politics in the broadest sense of the word, not simply as an immediate effect on the mechanism of power."[10]

The mechanisms of power, however, kept operating. The November Party plenum saw one leader in particular, Gustav Husák, begin to consolidate his position. Husák had stationed himself among the "realists," as someone who supported the reforms but was willing to make concessions in order to save them; at the same time, he was sending clear signals to the Soviets that he was a man they could deal with. In November, in an effective speech—long banned from public life, Husák was turning out to be one of the more proficient orators in the Party leadership—he characterized the Prague Spring as a deformation of the initial reforms of January 1968 and called for a more realistic approach.[11] Husák further strengthened his own position in December, when he maneuvered one of the most popular reformers, Josef Smrkovský, out of power. Smrkovský was chair of the national parliament and had held on to his position as a member of the ruling five, but the ground began to give way beneath his feet as the Soviets looked for new concessions and excluded him from their meeting with Czechoslovak leaders in Kiev in the beginning of December. Now clearly serving Soviet interests, Husák argued that since Czechs occupied two of the highest state functions (Ludvík Svoboda was president, Oldřich Černík was prime minister), the president of the Federal Assembly should be a Slovak and Smrkovský should therefore step down. Smrkovský was popular, and workers from the large metalworkers' union prepared to strike in his behalf. In early January, however, he gave way for fear of promoting open clashes—first asking workers not to strike, and then conceding chairmanship of the assembly on January 7.[12]

Although Smrkovský remained in the Party presidium, his demotion was a clear signal that neither he nor Dubček was willing to persist in open confrontation with Soviet wishes. His concession replayed in miniature the entire dilemma of the months following invasion, in which reform leaders enjoyed immense popular support, but were unwilling to mobilize it for fear of open clashes. The dominant political reality, after all, was still the ongoing presence of Soviet troops and the active interference of Soviet advisors. Reformers thus cautioned their own supporters, calling for patience—and further weakening their own position in the process. That fit precisely into the Soviet playbook, according to which the reformers were useful for one thing only—demobilizing their own followers—and only had to be kept around until the threat of popular action had been defused.

The remaining months of Dubček's rule would be marked by two outbursts of popular discontent and frustration. The first began on January 16, 1969, when Jan Palach, a student of history and political economy at Prague's Charles University, set himself on fire in Prague's main Wenceslas Square; he would die three days later from his burns. Palach's farewell letter made two demands—an immediate end to censorship and a ban on the distribution of *Zprávy*, an aggressively pro-Soviet newspaper set up by the invading forces. Palach's rather specific and limited demands, so out of proportion with the gravity of his deed, remain puzzling—as the writer Jaroslav Putík noted in his diary, "Parts of the letter don't make sense and so it is probably genuine. [. . .] Why did he take aim at *Zprávy*—why, nobody reads it anyway."[13] But Palach's deed may be best understood not as an attempt to achieve particular political goals, but rather as an expression of disillusionment with the reform leadership, and of desperate frustration with the steady rollback of reforms.

It was also an attempt to provide a now-leaderless movement with some kind of focal point or catalyst; in addition to its undeniable courage and moral pathos, Palach's self-immolation reflected a clear recognition that the public sphere opened up by the Prague Spring and the invasion week was now shutting down. Democratic and civic activity had been buried by the backroom dealings of the Party's inner circles, and drastic action would be needed to revive it. But Palach's sacrifice, while it mobilized a massive show of sympathy, could not provide the practical, political leadership of whose very absence it was an emblem. Thus, although there was a major march in his memory the day after he died, and his funeral on January 25 became a *de facto* demonstration against the occupation and the retreat of reforms, no more significant or structured protest resulted. The fate of three others who burned themselves in subsequent months—Jan Zajíc on February 25, Evžen Plocek on April 4, and Michal Leučík on April 11—is even more depressing. Media coverage of their deaths was suppressed, and they never really entered into the national pantheon alongside Palach—a tragic reminder that even the starkest and most courageous deeds of moral pathos rely to some degree on successful staging as well as "management" of their legacies.[14]

A second groundswell of popular frustration came two months later. On March 21, in the first round of the world ice hockey championships in Stockholm, the Czechoslovak team beat the Soviet Union. In a clear protest against the occupation, they refused to shake hands with the Soviet team after their victory. A couple thousand people gathered in Wenceslas Square, some chanting anti-Russian slogans, and cars honked their horns. These mild protests were an augur of things to come. Already rattled by the Palach demonstrations, the Soviets were preparing to take advantage of any popular outbursts. A week later, on March 28, the Czechoslovaks beat the Soviets again in a dramatic 4–3 victory. Around 10:00 P.M., Czechs and Slovaks poured into the streets—150,000 people gathered in Prague, and some eight to ten thousand demonstrated in front of the Soviet embassy in Bratislava. Jubilant crowds celebrated the victory, hoisted anti-Soviet banners, and called out slogans. In Prague, the offices of Aeroflot and Inturist, the Soviet airline and tourist agency, were ransacked, almost certainly a provocation by Czechoslovak secret police. In smaller cities, as well, demonstrations sometimes turned violent, often because of secret-police provocation. Windows were broken at the Soviet barracks in Mladá Boleslav, and armored vehicles were torched in Ústí nad Labem.[15]

The Soviets reacted with precalculated fury and portrayed the "hockey riots" as an organized anti-Soviet demonstration, evidence that "counter-revolutionary" forces were still strong and that Dubček had failed to properly implement the Moscow Protocol.[16] On March 31, Soviet Minister of Defense Marshal Andrei Grechko and Deputy Foreign Minister Vladimir Semenov arrived in Czechoslovakia, effectively to begin interviewing replacements for Dubček. At the beginning of April, the Party presidium announced a range of measures designed to reestablish order. A key step was to institute more rigorous, long-term, and broad-based censorship, which would now regulate far more than just references to the Soviet Union. The government paid special attention to bastions of reform like *Reportér* and *Listy*, the weekly of the Czechoslovak Writers' Union and one of the main tribunes for reform intellectuals. (Neither journal would last for long under the new restrictions.[17]) In effect, the Czechoslovak leadership had accepted the Soviet interpretation of "hockey week" as an organized anti-socialist uprising. This further retreat was "devastating. [. . .] The Dubček leadership had, for the first time, fully identified with its Soviet critics; in doing so it parted ways with the public it had courted for over a year."[18] It was in this atmosphere that two more people burned themselves to death in protest: Evžen Plocek, one of the delegates to the Vysočany Congress, on April 4 in Jihlava; and Michal Leučík, a Slovak soldier, in Košice on April 11. The press, now increasingly censored, was not allowed to publicize these events—many found out about Plocek, for example, only from fliers printed up by students.[19]

The stage was now set to get rid of Dubček completely. Grechko and Semenov were auditioning a number of friendly leaders, such as Svoboda, Husák, and Černík, for the role of his replacement. Husák, long a Soviet favorite, rose to the top in this process, and on April 13 made a secret trip to Uzhgorod, in the Soviet Union, to meet with Brezhnev and win his blessing.[20] On April 17, the Party presidium voted to accept Dubček's resignation and replace him as first secretary of the Party with Husák; this decision was accepted by the full Central Committee later that day.

Dubček's public image was avuncular, complaisant, and smiling. Many of his opponents had underestimated him at their own peril, but despite his long experience with Party power struggles, he often seemed beleaguered and vague. Husák, by contrast, was a tough, effective orator who knew how to trade on his own roughness and even vulgarity. In the confusing power struggles of late 1968 and 1969, his brusque combativeness was appealing to many

for its quality of forthright honesty, especially compared to Dubček's vacil-
lations. In the 1950s, Husák had served prison time on trumped-up charges
of treason; his refusal to confess had helped save him and his codefendants
from a death sentence. For many, his past seemed a sign of his character and a
guarantee that he would not resort to the same abuses of justice. He was also
thought to be someone who could hold off the vindictive conservative wing
of the Party, which was now clamoring to return to power and redress the
insults it had suffered during the Prague Spring. Husák thus came to power
with a great deal of support, even among intellectuals, who were not always
sure what to make of him but often gave him the benefit of the doubt. Some,
indeed, were more skeptical—on January 10, 1969, Putík wrote in his diary,
"come on—he's a demagogue and a liar," and in a May 1969 letter to Vilém
Prečan, Šimečka commented on one of Husák's television speeches: "It's absolutely clear that he's an insane psychopath. He managed to say things that
strongly recalled the screeches of a troglodyte from the 1950s." Nevertheless,
there were plenty of writers and journalists who thought Husák would avoid
excesses while bringing consistency and a firm hand to high politics after
the chaos of Dubček's rule. Husák successfully presented himself as someone
who wanted to restore peace and quiet in order to get on with the business of
governing and repairing the economy.[21]

The first years of Husák's rule saw the gradual disappearance of both popular demonstrations and organized opposition. The last major public demonstrations against the occupation regime took place across the country on
August 21, 1969, the anniversary of the invasion. They were suppressed by
army and police units. Petr Pithart, a twenty-eight-year-old journalist and
instructor at the law faculty, and his wife went to the demonstration on Wenceslas Square; Pithart later remembered his shock at seeing armored cars with
Czechoslovak rather than Soviet markings come roaring out in front of the
National Museum.[22] On the same day, a number of writers, academics, and
politicians issued a petition called Ten Points. It was written by Ludvík Vaculík, author of the famous Two Thousand Words manifesto from the spring of
1968, and it showed his usual flair. It began by rejecting the Moscow Protocol
as the humiliation of two nations (Czechs and Slovaks) that suffered "the bad
luck of having got caught between two superpowers fighting for the world." It
criticized the steady series of concessions brought on by "foreign interference"
after April 1969; it attacked censorship, the sorry state of the economy, and
the purges carried out "to the benefit of less capable, but obedient people, or

those who have lost the confidence of citizens." It refused to place the category
of Party membership above that of citizenship: "Noncommunists, who are in
the majority, are not obliged to live under conditions they cannot influence."
Although the manifesto was formulated as a petition to the government and
was therefore protected by the constitutional right to petition, police began
investigating the signatories; sociologist Rudolf Battěk, historian Jan Tesař,
and chess grandmaster Luděk Pachman were arrested and detained for a
year. The case never came to trial (although the charges were never formally
dropped), perhaps because in late 1969 Husák's government did not yet feel
strong enough to initiate a high-profile political trial with inevitable international repercussions.[23] But Husák continued to crack down on opposition.
A number of writers and prominent opponents were arrested, including Jiří
Lederer (once in 1970, and again in 1972), Kyncl, and the journalist and television personality Vladimír Škutina.

In late 1969, the government also moved against a student group called the
Movement of Revolutionary Youth. One of the movement's founders and old-
est members was twenty-eight-year-old Petr Uhl. In 1965 Uhl had hitchhiked
to Paris, where he came into contact with radical students who thought the
French Communist Party was too conservative. Ultimately he would work out
his own brand of political radicalism that would long outlast his student days.
By the standards of the Western New Left, Uhl was not an extremist, but his
combination of Marxist and anarchist ideas with energetic student activism
put him well to the left on Prague's political spectrum. In November 1968,
when students went on strike to protest the Central Committee's resolution,
Uhl tried to sustain their momentum and became, in December, one of the
founders of the Movement of Revolutionary Youth. This was an idea whose
time had already come and gone, but it was also a sign of how fluid the situation after the invasion was, and how some social groups were more radicalized
in the fall than they had been in the spring. For the one-year anniversary of
the invasion in August 1969, the Movement printed thousands of copies of a
pamphlet called "The Proclamation of the Ideological Section of the Revolutionary Socialist Party"—a mixture of antibureaucratic, antiestablishment,
socialist, and anarchist ideas that called for an alternative to "Nixon, Brezhnev, and Franco." This kind of rhetoric was increasingly out of place, and
increasingly dangerous, in normalizing Czechoslovakia. In November and
December 1969, nineteen members of the group were arrested, and they were
eventually put on trial in March 1971. Uhl got four years, and a number of

others of those convicted—such as Jaroslav Bašta, Pavel Šremer, Ivan Dejmal, Jaroslav Suk, and Petruška Šustrová—would go on to number among the first signatories of the Charter.[24]

A further wave of arrests began in 1971, when the Socialist Movement of Czechoslovak Citizens—an attempt to formulate an oppositional platform around a revitalized socialist movement—put up posters and distributed leaflets encouraging Czechoslovak citizens not to vote in the upcoming November elections. (In the end, over 99 percent of eligible voters voted, and over 99 percent of them endorsed government candidates.) In December 1971 and January 1972, some two hundred people were arrested, and a series of trials was held in Prague, Brno, and Bratislava in the summer of 1972. Sentencing was harsh: Jan Tesař and Rudolf Battěk (both still charged with participation in the Ten Points manifesto) received six and three and a half years respectively; student leader Jiří Müller, five and a half; and Jaroslav Šabata, a psychologist who had been a leader in the Brno Party and one of those elected to the Central Committee at the Vysočany Congress after the invasion, six and a half. Along with Šabata were arrested his two sons, Václav and Jan, and his daughter, Anna, who received shorter sentences of six months to two years.[25]

These political trials sent a clear signal to anyone contemplating organized political opposition. They also created a recruiting ground for future dissidents; many of the prisoners from the early 1970s would become founding signatories and active members of Charter 77, and would supply a certain streetwise toughness to dissident initiatives. Ultimately, however, dissent would emerge, not merely from the ranks of seasoned political prisoners, but even more noticeably from the many intellectuals and artists driven out of the Party and public life after 1969.

Screening the Party

Husák's rise to power in April 1969 marked the end of the first phase of normalization. After Mlynář's resignation in the fall of 1968, all the major reform Communists had been maneuvered out of power (like Dubček and Smrkovský), had renounced their earlier support for reforms (like Husák), or both (like Černík, who would resign from the presidium in January 1970 after the usual abject self-criticism).[26] With the reformers definitively sidelined, the higher Party echelons—closely watched by Soviet leaders—were now firmly on the side of the occupation. But support for the reforms, and opposition to the invasion, were still strong at lower levels of the Party, as well as in society at large. Even after Husák had taken control, there were still capable leaders at regional and district levels, or in local Party organizations from factories to agricultural cooperatives to academic research institutes, who had not been cowed into submission. Husák's next order of business, therefore, was to reestablish control over the Party's base as well as its unruly intellectuals. He chose to do so through a screening process, framed as a reissuing of Party membership cards, during which each and every member would have to affirm his or her support for the new Party line.[27]

The reissuing of cards had taken place before, in 1950, 1955, and 1960, and was a standard way for the Party to update its records as well as expel members who were disobedient, inactive, or otherwise undesirable. In 1950, when the re-registration was tied to a purge of "alien class elements" (for example, those who had only joined the Party after its takeover in 1948), 8.4 percent of members lost their cards.[28] A new exchange of cards was overdue, and had been in the works for some time. After Husák's rise to power, however, this process was reconceived as a massive screening process that could accelerate the "consolidation" of the Party.

The purges pursued a number of goals at once. Historian Kieran Williams has emphasized the need to redress a long-term, ideologically embarrassing decline in the number of working-class members of the Party; in general, since workers were pampered by the state already, they had less incentive to join the Party, whereas white-collar employees often saw Party membership as a necessary step for promotion and advancement in their careers. By 1966, the percentage of Party members who were workers had dropped to 30 percent (compared with 57.7 percent in 1946), and this trend only accelerated after the invasion.[29] But the purges were also an inevitable result of the rapid changes at the top of the Party—after the decisive shift in leadership that had taken place between November 1968 and April 1969, consolidation in the lower cadres had to catch up with the Party's Central Committee. Husák and his allies needed a more reliable and malleable rank-and-file apparatus that would stop using words like "invasion" and "occupation." In the spring of 1969, Husák had declared that there would be no screening of the Party and that members would "screen themselves" through their own hard work, but by the summer of 1969 he became aware of the need for a firmer power base.[30]

Nevertheless, the purges were not a Stalinist terror reaching into every corner of political and social life. They were less about ferreting out all traces of opposition and more about getting rid of high-profile reformers, while giving everyone else the chance to switch rather than fight. They involved formal boards of inquiry, not police interrogations. In a top-down process, reliable cadres at the top would screen for a "healthy core" of regional and district leaders, who would then screen the next level down, and so on. Individual members were invited to have a talk with a screening commission of perhaps four or five people. In the first stages of the purge, there seems to have been some genuine discussion involved; not only did screening commissions entertain arguments that Party members made in their own defense, they were often unable to refute them. Chess player Luděk Pachman, whom the Soviet press had already labeled "a grandmaster of demagogy and ambiguity," wrote that his own commission argued with him for six and a half hours at the beginning of July and could not come to a decision about his expulsion; it was adjourned so it could be "reinforced by ideologically strong members," but a second six-hour meeting yielded the same result. Eventually he was simply arrested, and the district Party committee expelled him in September, while he was in detention.[31]

With time, however, the process took on a momentum of its own; once the regional and district Party committees had been screened, they pushed the Central Committee for an even faster, harsher purge. Most commissions prepared their decisions beforehand, but still required members to speak on their own behalf. In practice, the actual meeting of the commission became a mere ritual of expulsion or submission. As Šimečka remembered: "There were thousands of 'trials' and the verdicts were decided at the outset. The board members then diligently obtained information, asked questions, cleaned their nails, made doodles on their note pads and thought about what was for dinner, while those who were condemned in advance spent sleepless nights trying to think of what to say in their defense."[32]

In fact, the point was not to defend yourself in fair debate, but simply to acquiesce in the official interpretation of 1968. Party members were asked about their own political history (in particular their activities during the Prague Spring, now rechristened as a right-wing counterrevolution) and their current political attitudes (especially their gratitude for the "fraternal assistance" supplied by Warsaw Pact armies in August). The atmosphere was often polite and formal, even cordial, although few people on either side of the interview table had any illusions about the final result. For those who did not receive new cards, there were two possibilities. Irredeemable and high-profile reformers—in many respects, the most imaginative and capable Party members—were expelled from the Party; for white-collar workers, and above all for intellectuals, this generally meant being fired as well. Journalists, academics, doctors, and many others found themselves frozen out of their familiar professions and had to find other jobs, generally working-class ones. Those who were less prominent supporters of reform, or who were willing to make certain compromises with the new regime, faced a lesser sanction: "cancellation of membership." They could expect to be demoted at work, but not necessarily fired. As Paulina Bren writes: "With party membership renewal one could reasonably expect career advancement; party membership cancellation signaled the possibility of demotion; and party expulsion meant the difference between having an office and cleaning one."[33] The purges were effectively complete by 1970 or 1971. At the beginning of the process, the Party had 1,535,937 members; as of October 9, 1970, fully 1,508,326 had met with screening commissions. About 78 percent received new cards, while 17.2 percent—260,000 people—had their membership cancelled. Another 67,000, or 4.5 percent of the Party, were expelled outright.[34]

If we are to understand the soil from which dissent would grow, we must take some time to consider the overall effects of the purges. In absolute terms, their impact might not seem so imposing. Indeed, Kieran Williams has pointed out that "the brunt of 'normalisation' in the party [. . .] was borne by a group that represented only 4 per cent of its January 1968 total, or 0.5 per cent of the country's population (slightly more once we factor in their families)."[35] But this line of approach is misleading for a number of reasons. First, if we include family members, we would probably want to double or triple the number of those affected, a significant increase. Children, for example, often had trouble getting into university if their parents had been expelled; spouses could be demoted; and sometimes the effects of expulsion could spill over onto parents or siblings as well.

More broadly, though, we must be careful about seeing the purge as directed only at its victims. Historians have tended to approach the purges from the point of view of those being screened, but it is important to remember the whole process was aimed at the *screeners* as well. Ultimately, 235,000 Party members served on over seventy thousand screening commissions—many saw the process from both sides. Further, we must also remember that the screening was aimed as much at those who *passed* as at those who failed—and, as I mentioned, a million and a half people went through the entire process. The screenings did not merely identify a class of people designated for further persecution; they also instituted and institutionalized, nationwide, a particular kind of political theater, founded on ritual humiliation and the performance of insincere obedience, all couched in the absurdly wooden language of bureaucratic Communism. For most of the screened, the commission did not involve getting raked over the coals for one's beliefs, but rather making a formal commitment to a set of absurd theses that no one believed: Czechoslovakia had been threatened by a right-wing counterrevolution and had been rescued in the nick of time by selfless allies.

The screening commissions can be well understood as "disciplinary mechanisms" in the sense described by Michel Foucault, who would publish his classic work, *Discipline and Punish*, in France just a few years later. They did not merely repress certain types of behavior, but created a model of how people should act and defined certain beliefs as more politically salient than others. They did not merely silence people; they helped shape each individual's identity in terms of a "cadre profile," and highlighted what sorts of statements and activities would be registered by the regime and what would be ignored. They also reinforced a public–private split that rewarded dissimulation, opportunism, and self-preservation over the open proclamation of one's beliefs. Thus, the purges did not merely punish one group of people; they also trained a far larger group in the rules of the new game. This was an ongoing process; in a 1973 article published under a pseudonym in the exile magazine *Listy*, Vilém Prečan wrote: "[. . .] this wasn't a one-time act: only during the course of 'the purge' did its organizers and executors give it a final shape, form and content."[36] The purges were an ongoing rehearsal of new power relations, and, of course, they gave momentum and confidence to the "healthy core," the groups of Communists who were now rising to the top by signing on to the Soviet interpretation of events.

But there was yet a third reason the purge cast a shadow far out of proportion to the number of people directly affected. The purge devastated a particular section of the country's elite—the large group of reform-minded, modernizing Communists who were university-educated and committed to open, public debate as the best way to understand and solve social and political problems. These people did not compose the *entire* intellectual elite—some people scraped through the screening commissions without fully compromising themselves; a far greater number had never been Party members in the first place, and had remained disadvantaged members of society even during the Prague Spring. But the purges did push thousands of capable thinkers and leaders, on both the national and local scale, out of their professional roles, and cleared the way for a new class of people—those who valued advancement above consistency or principle. Again, not everyone who survived the screenings was this sort of careerist, but it is undeniable that thousands of people who had trouble getting promoted when competition was tougher now found an abundance of job vacancies beckoning to them from above. The early 1970s saw a widespread replacement of talent by mediocrity.

In other words, the real brunt of the expulsions rested on a specific subset of Communist Party members, the university-educated professionals, intellectuals, and artists who, as Paulina Bren writes, "had been the most instrumental in firing up the engine for the Prague Spring and then fueling its passage into the consciousness of the larger population."[37] In Czech this grouping is usually called the *inteligence*, and they might be called "intellectuals" as a reasonable English shorthand. They included journalists (in radio, print, and television); writers (novelists, poets, playwrights, and screenwriters, as well as translators, editors, and publishers); people involved in theater and film (actors, directors, producers, set designers, cameramen, and others); academics (students, university teachers, and researchers employed at research institutes); economists; architects; lawyers; doctors; government administrators at the national, regional, district, and city levels; and the large class of so-called "production and technical *inteligence*"—engineers, mathematicians, chemists, physicists, and other scientists, whether employed in education or—a significant sector—in research, development, design, and management roles in state-owned firms and factories.

Intellectuals and professionals "accounted for more than half of the members who were being expelled" and "about 41 per cent of all members who were losing their cards."[38] The most detailed breakdown of the effects of the purge by occupation, region, and other variables is the Party's own internal report from December 1970. On this basis, historian Jiří Maňák has drawn up "persecution coefficients," comparing the percentage of various occupations in the Party to their share of the people purged. These reveal that intellectuals in the arts and humanities—"artistic and cultural workers," in Party jargon—were hit out of proportion to their numbers; their percentage among the purged was over two and a half times their percentage of the pre-purge Party base. An amazing 56 percent of the Party's "artistic and cultural workers" lost their membership during the purge. They were closely followed by academics and scholars in research institutes; here, the social sciences were particularly hard hit.[39] The purge seemed to hit engineers and scientists somewhat less severely. Party documents suggested that the "production and technical *inteligence*" was falling into line faster because of "its rational approach in the evaluation of social phenomena, its sense for organization and discipline, and its inner need to participate in solving the problems of the national economy."[40] In fact, the somewhat lighter effects of the purge on scientists and engineers, many of whom were employed directly in factories, may have resulted from the Party's desire not to disrupt productivity by getting rid of highly qualified workers.[41] Such reservations were not as strong in the case of "cultural workers" such as painters, writers, or even journalists, long seen as more of a nuisance than anything else, and as being easily replaceable. The arts were the one sector of the *inteligence* where you could get ahead without a university education.

Even these numbers, however, don't tell the whole story. In April 1970, when the Party's Central Committee decided to intensify the purge, it paid special attention to organizations "strongly impacted by right-wing opportunism"—groupings, for example, like the Journalists' Union, the Union of Czechoslovak Writers, or the Historical Institute of the Czechoslovak Academy of Sciences, where reformers were strongly represented and had managed to close ranks and hold off the worst effects of the first round of screenings. The Central Committee decided to dissolve these organizations by identifying a few loyal members in their leadership, a "healthy core" that would temporarily suspend everyone else's membership and then, effectively, reconstitute an entirely new organization. They would allow some members back via self-compromising screening interviews, but would expel many on the spot—or, in Party jargon, "immediately resolve the question of membership" for all "carriers of revisionism, right-wing opportunism and anti-Sovietism." This tactic would destroy the organizational base of many reformers, and would multiply the effect of the purges beyond the mere numbers of people expelled.[42]

One example of the liquidation of an entire Party organization was the Czech Writers' Union, founded in 1969. An earlier Czechoslovak Writers' Union had fired off some of the first salvoes of the Prague Spring at its fourth congress in June 1967, when controversial speeches by Vaculík, Havel, and others had opposed censorship and pushed for broader reforms. After the invasion, the union was split into Czech and Slovak sections; the reassembled Czech Writers' Union voted the distinguished poet (and future winner of the

Nobel Prize) Jaroslav Seifert as its chair. "Seifert's Union" was able to hold off the massive personnel changes affecting other organizations, and strove to protect its members while engaging in dialogue with the regime. Ultimately, though, it had to give in to the increasing pressure and effectively ceased activity in December 1970.[43] Subsequently, the regime just replaced it with a different organization; as Vaculík wrote in his diary on January 5, 1971: "They had an easy time liquidating our union. They simply stopped negotiating with us and began negotiating with another group of people."[44] Overall, the tactic of reorganizing whole institutes and professional organizations had a built-in "multiplier effect," not only expelling individual members, but also shutting down research teams and professional organizations, breaking up workplaces where scholars and artists had once been able to meet and exchange ideas, and stopping work on long-standing research projects. Many academic institutes and university departments were decimated; whole disciplines, particularly in the humanities and social sciences, were devastated and would take years to recover.

For all these reasons, mere numbers do not capture the force of the screenings, underestimating in particular the tremendous, and largely unquantifiable, damage they did to cultural and intellectual life. But we must also remember that the purge itself was only one element of a much larger muffling of cultural activity. There were countless writers, artists, and other intellectuals who had never joined the Party and had been disadvantaged, persecuted, or imprisoned in the 1950s. Many of them—even those who maintained some skepticism about reform Communism and "socialism with a human face"— had benefited from the freer conditions of the 1960s, enjoying new publishing possibilities and even cooperating with Communist colleagues in research institutes, the Writers' Union (in which a club of non-Communist writers had been formed), and magazines like *Literární noviny* (Literary News). After 1969, they, too, were demoted, fired, and banned from publishing. The sanctions against Party members have been well covered by historians, in part because they were part of a relatively coherent campaign and we have the Party's own records to draw on; there was no centralized record-keeping for tracking sanctions against non–Party members, so it is more difficult to come up with an estimate of the numbers affected. It may be instructive to consider the cases of two of the towering figures of Czech intellectual life in the twentieth century, Václav Černý and Jan Patočka, who would each play an important role in the story of dissent.

Černý, born in 1905, was the son of a literary historian, and became one himself. He did his baccalaureate degree in Dijon, returned to Prague for his PhD, and in the first half of the 1930s worked at the Institute for Slavic Studies in Geneva. In the mid-1930s he returned again to Prague, where he became a fixture in the culture life of the interwar republic; he founded the legendary journal *Kritický měsíčník* (*Critical Monthly*), which was eventually shut down during the German occupation. Černý joined the anti-Nazi resistance and was arrested at the end of 1944. After the war ended, he restarted *Critical Monthly*, in whose pages he both supported socialism and launched polemics against the Communist Party. In 1945 he was named professor of comparative literature at Charles University, where he taught for five years; his lecture series on existentialism in both Czech and European literature would become legendary. In 1950, however—two years after the Communist takeover—he was told to take a research leave that he hadn't asked for; he was then fired, in May 1951, for not carrying out his duties. (In his memoirs, Černý described a Ministry of Education memo from 1950, with a list of professors who were to be fired; his characterization there read: "Advocate and admirer of Nazi philosophers, an extreme individualist, an anti-Marxist. Negative stance toward people's democracy.") The department of Comparative Literature was shut down, and Černý was shuttled off into less significant positions; in September 1952 he was arrested and sent to trial, but he was ultimately released.

Not allowed to teach, he worked in various research positions and spent time archiving the libraries of monasteries and aristocrats' estates that had been confiscated by the Communist regime. If this work was intended to marginalize him, it failed; in 1960, he discovered a previously unknown manuscript by the seventeenth-century Spanish writer Pedro Calderón de la Barca—proof that you can't keep a good philologist down. In 1968, he was allowed to return to Charles University, but he became an early target of the normalizers and in 1970 was forced into retirement as soon as he turned sixty-five. (The Ministry of Education had directed that only "full professors who were unequivocally committed to the benefit of socialism" could teach past retirement age.) Further, in April 1970, Černý became a target of one of the nastiest attacks of the early normalization regime, when Czech television broadcast a two-part "documentary" consisting of private conversations (including unflattering opinions of reform leaders, the working class, and so on) that police had taped through the bugging of Černý's apartment. These

were edited and taken out of context in an attempt to blacken the names
of Černý and a range of other intellectuals, most particularly the prominent
reform Communist Jan Procházka, making them appear nasty, backstabbing,
elitist, and counterrevolutionary—all in what the Party press had the gall to
call "a political and moral 'striptease.'" The unprecedented episode made an
enormous impression, for its pettiness, its brazen manipulation of the truth,
and its destruction of the private sphere. Procházka fell seriously ill that summer; Černý withstood the pressure, thriving as so often on his own fury, and
remained an active scholar during the 1970s, although he couldn't publish
officially. Among other things, he devoted himself to finishing his memoirs,
some fifteen hundred pages of brilliantly complex prose and savage polemics,
sometimes wildly entertaining and sometimes disturbingly harsh, directed
against his literary and political enemies, who were legion.[45]

Černý was a famously prickly figure who loved a good fight; given his long
history of polemics against Communist politicians and cultural figures, it
was hard to imagine that the normalization government would accommo-
date him. Jan Patočka was milder, but just as firm in his convictions. Born
in 1907, he had, like Černý, come of age in the democratic interwar republic;
after finishing his PhD in Prague, he too had studied abroad, in Paris at the
Sorbonne and in Berlin and Freiburg, where he was a student of the great phe-
nomenologist Edmund Husserl and attended lectures by Martin Heidegger.
His philosophical interests were broad, influenced by Husserl and Heidegger,
but he also dealt extensively with questions of Czech national identity and the
seventeenth-century Czech philosopher Jan Amos Komenský. After returning to Prague in 1934, he taught in high schools as well as at Charles University, and cofounded the *Cercle Philosophique*, a German-Czech organization
that became a center for German philosophers who had escaped from Hitler's
Germany. When the Nazis occupied Bohemia and Moravia, he had to leave
the university, and in 1944 he was, like many other Czechs, assigned to hard
labor. But after the war he began teaching again, in Prague and Brno, until
1948, when the new Communist government once again pushed him aside
and he began work as a librarian.

During the 1960s, he was gradually allowed to return to public life, even
to lecture abroad, and he returned to Charles University in Prague in 1967.
According to legend, he stepped up to the podium for his first university lecture in twenty years and said to the hushed crowd: "Ladies and gentlemen,
last time we were talking about Aristotle's *Poetics*. . . ." A complex and often

abstruse thinker, he was also known for his warmth, optimism, and openness. In 1972, he was forced into retirement—the third time he had been
forced to leave the university. But he continued to teach a new generation of
students in philosophy seminars held in private apartments.[46] Like Černý,
Patočka was one of the dominating figures of Czech intellectual life, someone
of vast learning and broad perspectives, a scholar and a teacher who persisted
in academic life even as he was repeatedly slandered and banned, a thinker
who developed his own beliefs in a lifelong project that frequently brought
him into conflict with the authorities. Černý and Patočka are just two representatives of the enormous group of non-Communist intellectuals who had
suffered from Party rule long before 1969; they are reminders that the Party
screenings were only one piece of a much larger effort to marginalize independent thinkers in many different fields. The screenings had a massive spillover
effect on all areas of intellectual and cultural life, affecting non-Communists
as well as the newly minted class of ex-Communists.

How, then, do we measure the effects of the Party screening? In a 2003
interview, Jan Urban called it "a sociological experiment of unusual force."[47] It
was a self-inflicted lobotomy, a brain drain of unheard-of scope. To a considerable extent, it was also an experiment in the necessity of the arts, humanities, and history, posing the question of what happens when a polity silences
a major proportion of its best philosophers, writers, critics, historians, and
artists. The purges created a pool of discontented, demoted, educated, and
creative people who would "staff" dissent in the years to come, providing
one of its most important recruiting grounds. The targeting of the purge also
helps explain why artists, writers, journalists, and ex-academics would make
up such a large proportion of the initial signatories of Charter 77, particularly among its leading figures. As Prečan wrote in 1973, the new group of
expelled intellectuals was "a lasting, unsolvable problem" for the Party leadership: "It has become a ghost similar to the one that persecuted Lady Macbeth
in Shakespeare's tragedy."[48]

In the summer after the broadcast of his private conversations with Černý,
Jan Procházka fell ill. For many, he was a symbol of the Prague Spring. A
cultural figure who had been a candidate member of the Party's Central
Committee and had the ear of highly placed politicians including first secretary Antonín Novotný, Procházka was a critical voice with a genuine faith
in democracy and in the free exchange of ideas, which, he had said, would
show Czechoslovakia the path "back into Europe." Procházka had become

a well-known and popular speaker at the public gatherings of the Prague Spring; he was intent, impassioned, energetic, influential. He was also an accomplished writer, capable of both biting irony and undeniable pathos. His novels and screenplays had become touchstones of liberalization, often trying to come to terms with painful episodes of the past. In the 1967 film *Night of the Bride*, a former nun whose convent has been shut down returns to her village at the height of the collectivization campaign in 1950. *The Ear* was a satiric film about the regime's surveillance of its own functionaries, with clear allusions to the Slánský trials; finished in 1970, it was locked away as politically undesirable for almost twenty years.

The media campaign against Procházka, allied with police surveillance and harassment, was meant to destroy this charismatic figure. When Vaculík visited him in the hospital in February 1971, he wrote in his diary: "Jan Procházka must be dying. [. . .] If we didn't know it was Procházka, we wouldn't have recognized him. He has neither his form, nor his voice. His elegant, wavy grey hair has changed into forlorn strands, his bones stand out, his pale hand moves in wan gestures above the white blanket [. . .]." For his friends, his diminishing body, subjected to repeated operations since the fall of 1970, was an emblem. Pavel Kohout saw him on his deathbed and found, "instead of a giant, a white knot of cut-up flesh." Procházka died on February 20, and a few hundred people—including many reform Communists and other recently prominent figures—would gather at Košíře Cemetery in Prague for his funeral.

Accounts of the funeral are a reminder of how many different perspectives were present in the nascent intellectual opposition to normalization. Jaroslav Putík attended, and noticed two of the most prominent reform Communist politicians who had now been sidelined: "I saw František Kriegel. His black eyes have an unextinguished, combative gleam: why are you surprised; what happens, happens; there are worse things in the world. Smrkovský shuffles along on crutches; he is tall, haggard, grey." If Putík saw the funeral as an ambivalent requiem for the Prague Spring, Ludvík Vaculík saw it as a meeting of the new class: "There were maybe 300 people there, some say more. But it was a gathering that defined itself very precisely, made up entirely of people who did not need to get an excuse from work, because they have no jobs [. . .]." The whole group, he wrote sardonically, "comprised an ideal, well-chosen allotment for a mass grave." Pavel Kohout, who spoke above Procházka's grave, remembered the event a few years later more melodramatically: "That small cemetery was the first giant crossroads where fates diverged." Many people had been warned away from the funeral by their superiors and decided not to attend; others came despite the risks. "In the following days, many received serious warnings. For some the time of resistance ended, while for others it began."[49]

3

The Shadow World

For the long demobilization and political crackdown following Husák's rise to power, two terms caught on. On October 27, 1969, Jaroslav Putík wrote in his diary: "Those hideous words 'consolidation' and 'normalization' are not, from the point-of-view of the regime, bad inventions. They capture some kind of thermodynamic law about the tendency toward calm and stasis. In other words: people want to be left alone."[1] "Consolidation" was a frequent term in the early 1970s, but among historians, "normalization" has won out as the blanket label for a number of different phenomena: the retreat of reform leadership between August 1968 and April 1969 (what historian Kieran Williams calls "Dubček's normalization"); the early years of Husák's rule in which he firmly established his own power; and the whole twenty-year period between 1969 and 1989.

As useful as it is, however, the term "normalization" began life as a dishonest euphemism, a word used in bad faith on both sides of the newly drawn battle lines. For Czechs and Slovaks, armed intervention had created an abnormal situation; for the Soviets, an abnormal situation had required armed intervention. For Czechs and Slovaks, nothing could return to normal until Soviet troops were withdrawn; for the Soviets, troops could not be withdrawn until things had gotten back to normal.[2] *Normalization* was thus an appropriately vague word, providing a common ground for Soviet duplicity and Czechoslovak self-deception. The Soviet communiqué about the Moscow talks, published on August 28 in the Party organ *Pravda*, called for "the swiftest possible normalization of the situation" and suggested that troops could be withdrawn from Czechoslovak territory "as the situation there is normalized."[3] Dubček and other reformers, however, picked up the term as a way of talking about the occupation without going into detail about just what was "normal." In a September 14 speech to the country, Dubček said: "The fundamental question for us today is the normalization and consolidation of conditions and the departure of the troops of the five countries from our republic." Typically, this formulation carefully fails to clarify which would come first, the troops' departure or normalization. Dubček went on to confess that the word itself was unclear:

> How are we to understand the term "normalization"? A variety of comments and all sorts of speculations are today being spread by various quarters about this question. Normalization certainly includes fully restoring the economic, political, and cultural life of the country. It includes developing the activities of the legally and democratically elected organs of our working people, the further unequivocal socialist development in the country, and enhancing the leading role of the party and working class.[4]

The uncertainty about the word's meaning was more important than the vague definitions Dubček provided.

"Normalization," in other words, was a blank screen onto which different political actors could project what they liked. Husák's conception of normalization—which, of course, would eventually win out—offered a vision of society in which citizens traded any meaningful public or political life in exchange for relative economic well-being. In his book on normalization, aptly titled *The Restoration of Order*, Milan Šimečka called this process "adaptation"; he also picked up on a concept coined in the early 1970s by Antonín Liehm, who spoke of a "new social contract" according to which people would pretend to support the regime as long as they were left alone in their private lives.[5] In a January 1970 article published in *Rudé právo* (Red Right), the main Party newspaper, Husák spoke of:

> a quiet life for people, upholding legality, the free development of society, favourable conditions for the development of economic activity, stability, social and existential certainty, a perspective for people, so that they do not live from week to week, so that there be no scares with supplies or the currency. It all creates conditions to live well and quietly, so that it is worth living.[6]

This ideal of a quiet life would acquire great resonance in the 1970s. A typical phenomenon of normalization was the boom in weekend cottages, for example, some one hundred thousand of which were built between 1969 and 1981. Many people devoted immense time, energy, and resources to building and maintaining these refuges—finding materials and expert labor on the black market was often an immensely complicated task. For many, country cottages were an asylum for the preservation of private and family life; for others, they became an emblem of widespread political apathy. In larger cities, nearly half the population—including Communist functionaries, dissidents, and everyone in between—might disappear to their cottages for the weekend.[7]

Accounts of the onset of normalization, both in English and in Czech, tend to work with generalizations about the widespread mood of apathy and despair—"feelings of disappointment, skepticism, and despair were gaining ground."[8] Apathy and disillusionment were indeed widespread, perhaps inevitably so; no society could have sustained the excitement and unity of purpose of the week following the invasion. But there were also countervailing feelings of protest and anger that did not disappear so quickly; the arrests of the early 1970s are evidence of this. What's more, the apathy itself was nuanced, built around a number of key ideas that help elucidate the responses of the cultural elite to the new kinds of power and sanctions exercised under Husák. A few themes recurred frequently in contemporary discourse and would become central to the self-conceptions of many intellectuals in the first half of the 1970s.

"Nobody wants to go back to the 1950s"

On Tuesday, May 24, 1949, a twenty-year-old boy wearing a jacket and tie got off the train at Tachov, a town some ten miles from the German border. Karel Pecka had decided to leave Czechoslovakia. The previous fall he had been denied entrance to university—he had failed the entrance exams, which contained questions about his political views rather than journalism, the field he wanted to study. Without a student's exemption from military service, he would soon have to report for duty. He decided to emigrate instead. While searching for a way to get across the border, he worked as a clerk in a radio company in Prague, and met some other boys his age who worked at Prague's film studios. They started a small magazine, *Za pravdu* (For the Truth), where they wrote, under pseudonyms, film reviews as well as articles criticizing the new Communist government. They produced two issues, which they mimeographed in seventy or eighty copies and then distributed in people's mailboxes. Finally, an acquaintance of Pecka said he could arrange the trip across the border—one of his relatives was a guide who smuggled people across in exchange for payment, but he would add Pecka for free to an existing group.

In Tachov, two men were standing at the train station entrance and observing the hikers and backpackers who got off the train. They stopped Pecka and asked him where he was going. In accordance with his instructions, he said he had come to Tachov to apply for a job with a certain Mrs. Revel. They asked him politely to come with them to the police station. Once there, they took him upstairs and told him that there was no Mrs. Revel at the address he had given. The policemen found copies of both issues of *For the Truth* in Pecka's suitcase. They stripped him naked, blindfolded him, tied his hands, and began hitting him with clubs. Then they released an attack dog on him. Pecka confessed that he had been intending to cross the border. (In fact, the police already knew he was trying to emigrate—apparently the guide had given him up ahead of time.) Pecka was sent to Prague, where he slept in a cell with thirty other prisoners, and was taken out for interrogations at which his fingers were burned, needles were stuck under his fingernails, and the soles of his feet were whipped with cords. "In Tachov," he remembered some fifty years later, "they were good old boys who hit you wherever the blows happened to fall. In Prague they were sadists." Pecka managed to send word to his friends that he wouldn't hold out forever and that they should leave the country, but they didn't. They were also arrested, and on November 2, 1949, all four were convicted of forming "an antistate conspiracy" and were sentenced to prison terms of eleven or twelve years. They felt fortunate not to have been given a death sentence, and hopeful that Communist rule could not last for more than another year or two.

Pecka spent a year in forced labor at the coal mines in Kladno; in December 1950, he was sent to the uranium mines in Camp Svornost (Harmony) near Jáchymov. Later, he was sent to Camp Nikolai, where the prisoners were awakened at 4:00 A.M. and marched to the mines a mile away, grotesquely bundled with barbed wire into groups of five. With no protective gear, miners choked on uranium dust, boiled radioactive water for tea, and walked through the underground passageways with Geiger counters in order to find pockets of ore that hadn't been collected. All together, Pecka would spend ten years in various camps, mining uranium and hearing faint echoes of the world outside. When the entire world-championship Czechoslovak hockey team was arrested in March 1950, Pecka worked in the mines beside one of their star players, Stanislav Konopásek. Stalin's death in 1953 led to an increase in rations. This was about the time that Pecka began writing poetry—laconic poetry, given the shortage of paper to write on. (Eventually, he would publish a novel, *Motáky nezvěstnému* [*Messages to a Missing Person*], based on his prison experiences.) Pecka spent the last five years of his sentence in the Bytíz camp; from the roof of one of the buildings, he could see the Dobříš Chateau off in the distance—an estate that had been turned over to the Czechoslovak Writers' Union as a retreat for its members.

Like many other prisoners, Pecka refused to ask for a pardon because that would have meant acknowledging the validity of his sentence. Eventually he was released six months early, in December 1959, after ten years of hard labor. His official release form expressed "justifiable hope that after his release he will conduct the proper life of a worker, and that the part of his punishment already served has fulfilled its educative purpose." Ten and a half years of hard labor were apparently just as educative as eleven. When he arrived that night in Prague, he had no idea which trams went where or how much a ticket would cost. He couldn't get hold of either of his friends in the city, and so he spent his first night of freedom at the main train station.[9]

Tens of thousands of people shared fates similar to Pecka's in the brutal years following the Communist takeover in February 1948. Many of them were just as surprised, arrested out of the blue for trivial-seeming expressions of discontent, or simply for their class background or political past. Pecka's mimeographed magazine and attempt to cross the border qualified as treason. In 1975 Milan Šimečka described the terror of the 1950s, in which the secret police came to seem like "an instrument of fate" rather than a rational actor:

> Most of the acts for which people were punished were either invented or provoked, and they were indictable offenses only in a situation of political lawlessness. People would get ten years in prison for having offered a bed to a friend who tried to escape across the border the next day. One still comes across people all over the country whose fate was decided by just such an absurdity at some time or other.[10]

In a speech from September 1968, shortly after his return from Moscow, Dubček said: "I consider it a very important factor for consolidation to assure the Czechoslovak citizen that he is really at home in his homeland, that he enjoys the protection of the law and all the guarantees based on the laws and constitution of this country. This is a basic question of sovereignty upon which we shall firmly insist. There can be no alternative nor must there under any circumstances be a repetition of the fifties."[11] Six months later, Dubček's most dangerous enemy, Gustav Husák, would voice the same sentiment at the April meeting of the Party presidium that voted him into power: "We don't want to return to the 1950s." At the Party plenum a few hours later, Oldřich Černík proclaimed: "Comrade Husák [. . .] is a guarantee that, under his leadership, the party will avoid possible relapses of the fifties."[12] On January 26, 1970, the film director Pavel Juráček wrote in his diary: "Everything is starting all over again; we've found ourselves in the fifties again, and there's no hope for a miracle."[13]

The 1950s were one of the key themes of the 1970s. They became a short-hand for show trials, mass arrests, and labor camps—the lethal combination of sincere ideological fervor and police-state violence that had marked Communist rule from its very beginnings in February 1948. "The Fifties" meant police terror, political prisoners, and—above all—show trials, perhaps the most expressive symbol of regime injustice and violence. The early 1950s had witnessed political trials both of the government's alleged opponents (such as Milada Horáková, who was executed on trumped-up charges of conspiracy and treason in 1950) and of its own leaders (the notorious trial of Rudolf Slánský, the number-two man in the Party apparatus, executed along with ten others as "Trotskyite-Titoist Zionists, bourgeois nationalist traitors and enemies of the Czechoslovak people"). For those who believed the charges, the show trials were a terrifying sign of the intense hatred harbored toward Communism by its imperialist enemies. Treasonous conspiracies reached into the highest level of government, demanding ever-greater vigilance. For those who saw through the wooden, scripted testimony in which broken defendants confessed to fantastic crimes, the trials were a terrifying sign of the new regime's strength, its ability to portray outrageous lies as the truth, and its readiness to turn on anyone at all, even its most loyal supporters.[14]

Soviet advisors played a major role in scripting and staging the trials, but much of the Czechoslovak Party leadership in the 1960s, including first secretary and president Antonín Novotný, had played a direct part as well. Novotný fought a long delaying action throughout his rule to prevent this information from being widely publicized. The threat of coming to terms with the show trials was thus a political weapon in the hands of his opponents, but it also expressed a sincere impulse on the part of many reformers and ordinary citizens to confront at least one form of the political violence of the past, to "rehabilitate" people who had been falsely accused and convicted, and to arrive at a more accurate rendering of the country's recent history. Novotný's strategy was to create government commissions with the task of reviewing the trials, and then to keep tight control over their access to archives, as well as the potential range of their findings—it might be possible to rehabilitate some of the victims, but not to stray too far toward the question of how closely the Czechoslovak Communist leadership was involved, or to what extent they had been directed by Soviet advisors and ultimately by Stalin himself.

A first commission was headed by Minister of the Interior Rudolf Barák, whose fate indicated how explosive the issue of the show trials was: when Barák threatened to become too powerful a rival, Novotný had him arrested for embezzlement. But he allowed the less explosive report of a commission headed by Drahomír Kolder in 1962 and 1963. A third commission was known as the Barnabite Commission, after a former convent for Barnabite nuns, now a government-owned building near the castle, in which members were allowed to examine the closely guarded archival materials. This report helped lead to Husák's rehabilitation in 1963. But it was only the Prague Spring, and the partial emergence of the show trials into public discourse, that fully opened up the possibility of a genuine reckoning with the past. The formation of K 231, the group of former political prisoners, as well as the relaxation of censorship, helped promote a widespread demand for some kind of accounting with the show trials and the people who had staged them. A new commission, headed by Jan Piller, was given a much broader brief as well as fuller access to sensitive materials, and its final report, which spoke clearly of torture and Soviet participation in the trials, would become one of the time bombs of the liberalization movement. After several postponements, it was scheduled for discussion at the April 1969 Central Committee meeting, but reformers did not muster the strength to force through their agenda—instead, this became the meeting at which Dubček resigned and Husák took his place.[15]

Husák helped suppress this report, but nevertheless the fifties were an extremely useful reference for him. He himself had been a political prisoner.[16] Despite being a loyal Communist, he had been arrested in February 1951 in a campaign against Slovak "bourgeois nationalists" who were said to place Slovak national interests ahead of the Party. Husák behaved courageously in prison, refusing to confess to crimes he hadn't committed; his stubbornness undermined the show trial's script, helped delay it until 1954, and likely won him and his fellow defendants a life sentence rather than execution. Husák was eventually released in 1960, whereupon he quickly began his rapid rise to the top of the Slovak and then Czechoslovak Party structure.

Husák's past as a political prisoner was crucial to his chameleonic ability to appeal to a wide spectrum of the Party leadership and Czechoslovak population in the crucial months between the invasion and April 1969. Since he had been imprisoned for supporting Slovak national interests, his jail time helped reinforce his support among Slovak Communists. Among Czech reformers, his own persecution seemed a guarantee that he would not return to the savage repressions of the past, as well as a sign of self-discipline and strength. At the same time, Husák could and did repeatedly play the "1950s card" in fighting off the Party's extreme conservative wing, in the main an older generation of hard-liners who were pushing for an even harsher settling of accounts with the reformers and an even tighter bear hug with their Soviet overlords. Many of these figures had also been implicated in the show trials, and they could not afford an open discussion of them. Husák's invocation of the previous decade was thus both a reassurance to moderates and liberals, and a veiled threat to hard-liners. Nobody wanted to return to the 1950s.

At an interrogation in December 1969, during the investigation into the Ten Points manifesto, Ludvík Vaculík told his interrogator that Luděk Pachman had been writing him from his prison cell: "I mentioned what beautiful letters Luděk was writing me, how I read them everywhere and that this made a good impression on people: maybe something really had changed in comparison to the fifties."[17] Vaculík was already registering a certain ironic distance from this topos, which eventually turned into a cliché and even an in-joke. In 1973, during one of his interrogations, František Janouch refused his interrogator's offer of a cup of coffee or mineral water. "Surely, doctor, you don't believe those tall tales about the horrors of the 1950s," his interrogator replied, shaking his head.[18] The implication was both that the coffee was not drugged, and that interrogator–interrogatee relations could be altogether more genteel and civilized in this new era.

Eventually, it would become clear that invocations of the 1950s were a red herring. Violent repressions were not in fact repeated, with a few exceptions. The concept of "the 1950s"—a bit like the word "normalization" itself—provided a way of talking about the new situation without fully understanding it; meanwhile, it became more and more urgent to define and describe the forms of repression that *were* being implemented. Meditations on the difference between the 1950s and 1970s would become a staple of dissident thought. Vaculík had already recognized some of the main questions in December 1970:

> Personally I am not experiencing any oppression; actually nothing is happening to me; I'm just experiencing mild amazement at how things are going, how everything is going. They have found a genuinely new method of terror directed at the whole nation. The propaganda is stupid; nobody believes it and I think they're doing it more for themselves, for a feeling of the completeness of their policies. After all, absolutely none of these interventions against the people, culture, the nation, morale, and law can stand up ideologically. They know this perfectly well, which is why they don't enter into any ideological arguments at all; Marxism has shriveled up into the most primitive dogma. It's extremely interesting to observe; it will be rich material for the study of modern dictatorships. It's so new that it's worth the unpleasant experience.[19]

Šimečka's *The Restoration of Order*, written in the mid-1970s, would provide one of the deepest analyses of this theme. Operating with the 1950s–1970s comparison, Šimečka wrote that "the old explicit forms of violence" had been discarded in favor of what he called "civilized violence":

> Heads of staff took leave of the victims with a handshake. When giving people notice of their proscriptions, those in charge would smile guiltily and urge the victims to save themselves by means of self-criticism. People were silenced in a dignified manner and not with a punch in the mouth. No representative of the Czechoslovak intelligentsia really underwent third degree treatment. No one was forced to die of hunger or beg for a living. In prison, convicted academics would be treated according to regulations. In certain cases, people were free to choose exile. Despite being banned, people could continue to occupy their flats and drive around in their cars. Banned authors could take the risk of publishing abroad. StB interrogations would take place during normal office hours. People would not be woken up at four in the morning. Interrogators would not taunt accused persons, nor rough them up. When bugging devices were installed in people's flats, it would be done without damage to the furniture. If you had no objection to being questioned about it afterwards, you could meet foreign journalists and mix with those of your fellows in the same boat as yourself. Everyone had the chance to write a denunciation of themselves or their friends, which could win them a review of their case, albeit skeptical, and the chance of being accepted as a reformed sinner.[20]

These forms of "civilized violence" were corrosive in their own way. The goal was to neutralize opposition and silence discontent by "converting" those with less resolve, those who had the most to lose, and those who did not want to sacrifice the life chances of their families; only those who persisted in their disagreement would be made an example of. Civilized violence was one of the most important preconditions for dissent. Put simply, dissent arose from a system that persecuted its opponents, occasionally brutally, but rarely destroyed them.

Superimposition and the Absurd

Civilized violence carries another connotation that Šimečka does not explore. Starting in the early 1970s, the new round of arrests, interrogations, and surveillance was being "superimposed" onto the still-surviving accoutrements of a more civil and free society, and this strange juxtaposition created a lasting sense of cognitive dissonance. Although in retrospect we tend to see the beginnings of normalization as a series of defeats leading inexorably to full-scale repression, the process was uneven and inconsistent. The timelines of repression were different for each person; when all these individual tales were superimposed on one another in a society-wide mosaic, it could be difficult to see exactly how well, or badly, one stood in relation to everyone else. In part, this explains why so many people held out hope for partial victories or the salvaging of reform, even into the early 1970s. It also explains another characteristic topos of early normalization, the sense of absurdity, irony, and incongruity that attended much of the early repression and continued to exist as a hallmark of "civilized violence" throughout the 1970s and 1980s.

Indeed, one of the things that made the 1970s different from the 1950s was—the 1960s. A week after mailing in his Party resignation on June 25, 1969, Putík wrote: "What's going on around us these days is total Hitchcock."[21] But for many intellectuals, an even clearer reference point for the first months and years after the invasion was the Theater of the Absurd that had come to Czechoslovakia in the 1960s—particularly in the plays of Václav Havel—and the films of the Czech New Wave. If the postwar 1950s were marked by existentialist themes of guilt, isolation, objectification, and the confrontation with death, the 1960s took its alienation in a somewhat lighter form, with a sense of humor, tragicomedy, and even occasional lightness; absurdity could be horrifying, but it was also diverting. Milan Kundera's classic works of the 1960s, the novel *The Joke* and the story collection *Laugh-able Loves,* captured the super-seriousness of the dedicated young Commu-nists of the 1950s at just the point when it was beginning to seem overblown and tragically silly. Over and over again, the films of the Czech New Wave portrayed the encounter between individuals and a highly ornate, scripted culture that they only vaguely understand; this conflict between an unwitting character and an unknown script was implicitly recreated when directors like Miloš Forman used nonactors in their movies, often asking them to improvise their dialogue around certain words and themes. The results, in films such as Forman's *Loves of a Blonde* and *The Firemen's Ball,* Jan Němec's *Report on the Party and the Guests,* or Jiří Menzel's *Closely Watched Trains,* were often brilliant set pieces in which characters seemed to uneasily inhabit the larger scripts of Communist culture, highlighting both their own lack of autonomy and the artificiality of the official world.

These are the cultural touchstones that helped many intellectuals under-stand the early 1970s; their descriptions are marked by a theatricality and self-referentiality that are missing from the more serious 1950s, when the stakes were higher and one's accusers tended to be convinced of their own gravity and significance. We find a fine sense for the absurd, for example, at the end of *Nightfrost in Prague,* Zdeněk Mlynář's 1978 memoir about the Prague Spring, particularly in his discussion of the signing of the Moscow Protocols. When Brezhnev and the whole Soviet leadership demonstratively left the negotiating table after Dubček began to argue with them, Mlynář wrote, "it impressed me as a theatrical trick." The finale is described in terms worthy of absurdist theater:

> Sometime around midnight, it was all completed and the moment of sign-ing came. Suddenly a huge door flew open and about ten photographers and cameramen stampeded into the room. As if on command, the entire Soviet politburo simultaneously rose to its feet, and each of them leaned across the table to the Czechoslovak opposite with arms wide, ready to embrace him. It was an absurd scene that the photographers' flashguns illuminated: dozens of arms belonging to the Soviet politburo stretched out and waved across the table in a row, and I suddenly imagined that a fantastic carnivo-rous plant was trying to entrap us in its sticky tendrils. Instead of standing up and making a reciprocal gesture, I pushed my legs against the trestle of the conference table, and my chair went skidding backwards over the polished parquet flooring towards the wall about three meters behind me. I

came to rest besides Ambassador Koucký, who was sitting by the wall along
with those for whom there was no room at the table.[22]

This wonderfully described scene, a mixture of horror and Keatonesque slap-
stick that any novelist might envy, is in fact the climax of Mlynář's entire
memoir, which itself is framed as farce more than tragedy. It is difficult to
imagine these words written in 1968 rather than 1978; the scene does not
reflect the genuine, intensely felt tragedy and trauma of the invasion, but rather
transmutes it ten years later into a classic Theater-of-the-Absurd moment, in
which the spontaneity of the little man is entangled by the "sticky tendrils"
of power, politics, and the gaze of others. Mlynář's use of the device is a bit
self-serving, of course—he was a responsible politician, not a puppet, and he
did eventually sign the protocol, even as he refused the smothering embrace
of his captors—but however the scene actually played out, his evocation of it
captures the sense of Czechoslovakia as drawn into the absurdities of a power
play for which it didn't write the script.

Jaroslav Putík recorded a moment from the invasion week that stuck in the
memory of many Prague residents:

> A scene from Wenceslas Square. A taxi rides in and out among the tanks
> that have overwhelmed the whole square. A young man is leaning out of
> the window from the waist—and playing the violin. He is playing for the
> tanks; he is playing to enrage those horrible anti-muses: it's a challenge, it's
> beautiful, I rub my eyes, pinch myself, I can't believe what I see, but the taxi
> surfaces again and again and the man plays some kind of devilish czardas.
> Tears come to my eyes when I think of how nonsensical and beautiful it is.
> I will never, never forget.

Jiří Lederer described a similar (perhaps the same) scene:

> And here, from the Powder Tower [a few blocks from the base of Wences-
> las Square], another car approached. An older man with tousled hair was
> leaning out of the window and playing a melancholic melody on the violin.
> The violinist's face was fascinating—expressionless, there was neither joy
> nor sadness in it, just his large, staring eyes. The first day of normalization
> was arriving.[23]

What these two scenes have in common—despite the divergent memories
of the violinist's age and the song he was playing—is a fascination with an
absurd moment in the midst of great historical events, a fascination that helps

set the tone of both Lederer's and Putík's literary accounts of the early days of normalization.

A further touchstone for the absurdity of the 1970s was Franz Kafka. In the 1950s, Kafka was ideologically undesirable, out of step with the forced optimism of official propaganda; he resurfaced after a major conference on his work in 1963, one of the early harbingers of liberalization, which (according to the book jacket of the conference proceedings) "rehabilitated" him for a social-ist audience. The rediscovery of Kafka in the 1960s now made his novel *The Trial* an inescapable reference for intellectuals, especially since the secret police often traveled in pairs when they went to detain suspects or witnesses, just like the two guards who turn up at the beginning of *The Trial* to arrest Josef K. Indeed, it was only in the 1970s that the Kafkaesque nature of Communist power came into its own. *The Trial* was not actually a very useful reference for the repressions of the 1950s, when a squad of policemen might pluck you off the street, or barge into your apartment in the middle of the night, and drag you off to a concrete cell in the depths of a prison, where you would be inter-rogated and beaten. But when two officers, perhaps quite polite ones, knock on your door and then escort you to an office where they spend hours ham-mering out a protocol with you in the presence of a chatty stenographer, Kafka begins to seem more prescient. Kafka's tendency to merge public and domestic spaces, his endless interpretation of inscrutable texts, and the bewilderment of his characters, who are never quite sure what position they occupy in a vague hierarchy that threatens to crush them and yet responds to their every word and gesture—these were recognizable, even literal-seeming descriptions of life for many who got on the wrong side of the normalization regime.

In the spring of 1970, after he was released from detainment, Jiří Lederer had to visit the Ruzyně prison three or four times a week for interrogations, at which he was asked to subject his own newspaper articles to a kind of absurd midrash: the investigating major would read aloud passages from Lederer's journalism about the events of 1968 in Poland, asking him questions such as: "What were you getting at with the comment in parentheses?" or "What did you want to suggest to the reader with those three periods?" After Luděk Pachman gave an interview to Dutch radio, his interrogator wanted to know how far they held the microphone from his mouth.[24] The absurdities of this sort of interrogation were a common topic for essays and short stories in the early 1970s; Vaculík became a master at this genre, in part because his own exquisite sense of Czech made him hypersensitive to the twists and turns of the interrogation protocols, in part because his ability to think his way into other people's minds often lent his accounts a surprising degree of empathy for his interrogators and the strategic goals they were pursuing. One of his short essays, "A Cup of Coffee with My Interrogator," became a classic. Václav Havel, too, not only continued writing plays, transplanting his own strain of absurd theater from the more liberal 1960s to the normalized 1970s, but also skillfully mined the Kafkaesque vein in essays such as "Report on My Participation in the Railway Workers' Ball," where he accompanies a friend to the police station to testify as to his innocence—only to end up in an interrogation room and discover that, somewhere along the way, he has been arrested as well.[25]

This does not mean that arrests and interrogations were funny, but simply that people's understanding of normalization was shaped by their sense of irony and sensitivity to the absurd. Nevertheless, incongruity was not just a literary device. One of the side effects of "civilized violence," with its bureaucratization of repression, was that persecution was remarkably inconsistent, especially in the early years of normalization. In countless instances, even the regime's targets found themselves faced with surprising gaps in the wall of repression. When František Janouch and his wife were supporting themselves doing technical translations from Russian, they were hired several times (and paid well) by workers at the Ministry of the Interior to translate secret instructions for dealing with the opposition—on how to identify typewriters according to their typefaces, for example. After Jiří Lederer's first stay in prison, his wife Elžbieta, who was from Poland, managed to get a job as an interpreter and found herself invited to the resort town of Karlovy Vary to interpret for visiting officers from the Polish secret police. She was so well liked that they offered her a steady position at their private resort, and it was only when the Polish Minister of the Interior himself visited that they did a background check on her and realized that her husband had been charged with hostile activity toward the People's Republic of Poland. She was immediately sent home to Prague. No car was free, and so she was taken home, as the only passenger, in a Ministry bus that happened to be present on the grounds.[26]

These were administrative glitches, but the incongruities of oppositional life stretched even further. In September 1973, when Janouch wanted to send an open letter to *The Times* of London in support of Andrei Sakharov, he simply went to the post office, paid 140 crowns, and sent a telex to London.[27] When journals were shut down for political reasons, subscriptions were refunded.[28] In the first years of normalization, it was quite common for writers to be banned from publishing, have their contracts cancelled, and yet still be paid in full. Elžbieta Ledererová, for that matter, received full payment even after she was fired from her interpreting job for the Polish secret police. Many well-known critics of the regime were allowed to keep advantageous apartments and country homes. Pavel Kohout, one of normalization's most vocal opponents, lived in a huge apartment adjacent to Prague Castle—one of the nicest pieces of real estate in the city, in the same building as the Swiss Embassy. He also had a country house in Sázava, where secret police painted swastikas on his garage door, staged a break-in, and started a fire inside the house; but they let him keep both homes, and only forced him to move out of his apartment on Castle Square after he signed Charter 77. Václav and Olga Havel also kept their country cottage as well as their apartment in Prague.

Havel and Kohout were already well-known writers with many contacts abroad, which may have protected them, and if their homes became gathering places for opposition-minded intellectuals, this was not necessarily against the wishes of the police, since it could easily keep tabs on who was meeting with them. The sociologist Ivo Možný has pointed out that the prestige and foreign income of some dissidents was itself a useful propaganda tool for the regime, which portrayed dissent as elitist and out of touch with ordinary people. But Karel Pecka, not nearly as well known, was able to exchange his small, one-room apartment far from the city center for a new one with vaulted ceilings on Nerudova Street, just down the hill from Prague Castle, and to renovate it using money from his contract with a Swiss publishing house; it would also become a gathering place for his dissident friends.[29] Many other people who had been fired or banned from publishing were nevertheless able to buy country cottages with relatively few problems. Many were also able to secure a disability pension. Luděk Pachman, one of the regime's main targets in the early 1970s, could not find a job because of his political sins, but he did get a disability pension of 610 crowns a month. (The day before he was awarded this pension, he had been stopped by police and arrested on a false drunk driving charge; the day after, an article smearing him appeared in *Rudé právo*.) In 1975, Ivan Klíma arranged a 630-crown-a-month pension for his pollen allergies, thanks to well-wishing doctors who signed off on his paperwork—not much money, but enough to qualify him as having a regular income and thus keep from having to find other work.

Pecka described his own successful efforts to obtain a small invalid's pension in 1979; a psychiatrist told him what symptoms to describe, and a clinic then helped shield him from the StB's attempt to verify his diagnosis.[30] These were small victories in the midst of an otherwise difficult life; but it is interesting to note that the regime missed many, many opportunities to make life even more difficult for its opponents.

There were several reasons for such incongruities. Zdeněk Mlynář suggested that selective repression was more efficient than mass terror; the tactic of scaring everyone into submission by persecuting a few people represented a more rational use of the state's resources and was, in effect, a "symptom of modernization."[31] But as I mentioned earlier, the regime generally did not want to destroy its opponents in the early and mid-1970s. After Charter 77, it got tougher, at least in some cases, but before then it was content with making people's lives difficult, rather than impossible. Arranging for an expelled Party member to be fired and take up an unskilled job was often seen as punishment enough; there just does not seem to have been a conviction that further abuse was necessary. And the idea of a philosophy professor working as a taxi driver or night watchman did not have the glamour or frisson of resistance it may seem to have today; it was simply an effective way of silencing a potential opponent.

At the same time, the incongruities of repression were themselves a form of harassment. They gave the state hostages to fortune and room for maneuver; if a disability pension had been granted, it could be taken away. Inconsistency created uncertainty, which could cause significant stress (and, not incidentally, aggravated many long-term illnesses). It was a cheap, reliable, and low-maintenance way to scare people. We should also remember that the state had acquired many new functions since the 1950s, and it just didn't know how to make use of all of them for the purposes of harassment; many forms of repression were as new to the regime as they were to the victims. Thus, when Pachman was arrested on the false drunk driving charge, he asked doctors to take a second blood sample to prove his innocence; they willingly obliged, and so police had to intercept the second sample before it reached the forensics laboratory. Eventually, they would figure out how to run such operations more smoothly.

There was thus a complex dialectic, evolving over time, between the increasing abilities of the state to harass opponents (as well as its increasing awareness of those abilities) and its fluctuating desire to do so. Some forms of harassment required complex coordination, for example among Party, police, and state officials, or among the many institutions of a modernizing society. The structures of a modern bureaucracy and economy left plenty of room for maneuver at the lower levels. Thus, a doctor might find it relatively easy to help a friend in need by vouching for a disability pension. But by the same token, many of the abuses of normalization had as much to do with the vindictiveness of individual policemen or bureaucrats as they did with directives from above. Husák's rise to power and the Party screening saw a long process of individual score-settling, often motivated by jealousy, envy, slighted pride, or revenge. There was room for this in the system, too. The sense of incongruity, then, was part of a mosaic of opposition and repression, in which general trends were visible, but their enforcement at the individual level was often a result of random or personal factors. Here again it is useful to think in terms of superimposition: the political crackdown of the 1970s should not be seen as a portcullis slamming shut, but rather as a blanket of snow settling slowly over a landscape, with familiar landmarks still occasionally peeking through.

The Shadow World

Given the state of the Party, getting kicked out of it was not such a tragedy. Many ex-members walked out of their screening commission with a sense of elation. Far more serious were the two associated punishments: being banned from publishing (or public performance, in the case of stage and screen actors) and—above all—losing one's job. Intellectuals expelled from the Party were not only fired, but were generally prohibited from working in their field at all—often they moved into manual labor. (The same fate was meted out to many others who had never been Party members; for them, this was, indeed, a replay of the 1950s.) Normalization thus witnessed the disorienting displacement of tens of thousands of artists, academics, and university-trained professionals.

Losing one's job was not only demoralizing and a financial problem; it was a legal hassle as well. Section 203 of the legal code forbade "parasitism" and required all Czechoslovak citizens to be able to demonstrate a source of income, generally with an employer's stamp in their *občanský průkaz* or identification card (a booklet, actually). For most intellectuals, as we will see, the solution was to find some kind of working-class job. The parasitism clause may have had more to do with persecution than prosecution; although it was relatively rare for these cases to actually go to trial, the threat was an effective weapon and a convenient pretext for an interrogation. People would often have to look in many places in order to secure a job; often they might be accepted and then turn up for work only to find that their employer had, in the meantime, found out about their political profile and no longer needed their service. Workers thus had to be careful about losing even menial, low-paying jobs. Securing a steady income, as much for legal as economic reasons, became one of the central concerns of the early 1970s.[32]

A related concern for journalists and writers was being banned from publishing—often the equivalent of losing one's job. Publication bans were sometimes sudden and unequivocal, but often constituted a subtle process with different stages, another instance of "superimposition." Many literary magazines and political journals were shut down over the course of 1969 and 1970, depriving editors and writers of their "home base" and a salary or a steady source of honoraria. Writers who then refused to join the new Writers' Union in 1971 had their official status revoked and had to find other work. At the same time, they found it more and more difficult to publish anywhere, so that even freelance work would be difficult. Manuscripts that had already been accepted were returned, often without any clear reason being given. Vaculík relates a characteristic story in his diary. He had written a preface for the reprint of a novel; in 1971, two editors, "embarrassed by their mission," visited him personally to explain that the book would still be released, but without the preface, and to reassure him that he would still get paid but "in a roundabout fashion"—as if he were being paid for writing a reader's report. A week later another editor came to give him the money in person, so that, Vaculík presumed, "this honorarium and my address would not be moving publicly through the postal service." Vaculík was paid eight hundred crowns—more than he would have received for the preface itself.[33] This little story from February 1971 speaks volumes about early normalization: the publishing house's embarrassment, its desire to make things right—and its fear of doing so too openly. There were still many cracks in the wall of repression, but it was ever clearer who was on which side.

Vaculík, a notorious "counterrevolutionary" as the author of Two Thousand Words and Ten Points, was not surprised to find himself silenced. For other writers, bans took effect slowly and unofficially, communicated only through repeated rejection. Once the editors at various publishing houses were replaced, it became obvious to many writers that they had no hope of getting published, and so they ceased trying. Some writers were lucky enough to have an independent source of income from foreign royalties. Havel and Kohout could rely on foreign performances of their plays; Kohout, quickly proving himself to be one of the new regime's tougher opponents, negotiated a contract in November 1969 whereby Dilia, the Czechoslovak agency that handled foreign rights, gave a West German publisher the right to arrange all foreign performances of Kohout's plays for a period of five years. Kohout also helped arrange for foreign publication of a number of other writers such as Vaculík, Alexandr Kliment, Ivan Klíma, and others. Such an arrangement could be advantageous to both writer and state; not only did the state take a percentage of all royalties, but it controlled the transactions and currency conversions at both ends. After receiving the foreign currency, it would issue the recipient a special currency called the *bon*, which could only be used in the network of special "Tuzex" stores. The state thus received foreign currency while maintaining control over how much it was worth and where it was spent. Eventually, though, the state raised its commission on foreign royalties from two to 40 percent, meanwhile exempting all authors from this rule unless they were banned at home or had written "antistate" or "antisocialist" works. Banned writers thus had to find other avenues to receive their foreign payments—royalties would often be sent in cash via friends, visitors, or diplomats.[34]

A second option was to support oneself through translations, whether literary or technical. Banned writers could often find a *pokrývač*, literally a "roofer" or "tile layer"—someone who would publish their translations under his or her own name and then give them all or part of the payment.[35] František Janouch wrote: "I supported myself any way I could. Mainly through translations." He and his wife did a last-minute translation of a six-hundred-page technical proposal for a Prague subway line—it had been written up at the last minute, and needed to be submitted to Soviet experts. "We worked sixteen hours a day. Our fingers were swollen from the typing—every strike caused sharp pain."[36] Other writers switched over to literary translation more or less full-time: "I translate to support myself; there's not much time left for my own writing," said Putík, a sentiment echoed by Jan Zábrana, who had published three poetry collections in the 1960s but would not publish a line of his own poetry for the rest of his life.[37]

Others found jobs in out-of-the-way places, often with the help of a manager, director, or editor who had survived the purges, stayed in the Party, and was able to protect people who were not entirely anathema to the regime. Many academics found work in out-of-the-way archives or libraries where they could work on long-term projects, like foreign-language dictionaries, without attracting much attention. Zdeněk Mlynář retreated to the entomological department of Prague's National Museum, where he carried out research on beetles.[38] An emblematic story is that of literary theorists Milan Jankovič and Miroslav Červenka, who found temporary asylum in the National Literary Archive; sharing a tiny office, they organized the papers of two nineteenth-century poets until they were forced to move on—Jankovič working as a night watchman, Červenka translating poetry under other people's names until he found a new job as technical librarian at Pragoprojekt, a Prague firm that designed roads and bridges. In the 1980s, thanks to the good offices of a highly placed Party member at the firm, Pragoprojekt turned into a curious asylum for a number of literary theorists; Jankovič, a photographer as well as a literary scholar, got a job there taking documentary photos of bridges, roads, and public transportation around the country.[39] Such peripeteias marked the careers of many a Czech intellectual in the 1970s and 1980s.

All the same, many intellectuals considered themselves lucky if they could continue to make a living by writing and research. A great many took jobs at manual labor. Many women who needed work ended up as cleaning women. Milan Šimečka got a job as a bulldozer driver. Havel did unskilled labor at a brewery for a time, when he didn't have enough money to support himself and Olga.[40] A number of jobs became common for fired intellectuals. Milan Jungmann, who had been the editor of *Literární noviny* in its glory days in the 1960s, worked as a window washer, as did Luboš Dobrovský, a translator and journalist who had been the Moscow correspondent for Czechoslovak radio in 1967 and 1968.[41] During the revolution in 1989, when the democratic Civic Forum was negotiating with the Communist Party to form a transitional government, Pavel Rychetský would lament: "They are professionals who have been moving inside these structures for twenty years. We've been washing shop windows [. . .]."[42]

Work as a stoker—monitoring the heaters and boilers of large buildings—was particularly common. Stokers at coke fuel boilers had to fill them with fuel, monitor the temperature, and eventually remove the burnt fuel and load a new batch; while each load burned, stokers had plenty of time for reading and writing. Gas boilers were easier; they simply had to be monitored and adjusted when necessary, leaving even more time for work.[43] Boiler rooms often saw one PhD replacing another from shift to shift. Karel Kaplan, a historian and formerly a high-level Party member who had served on several of the commissions that revisited the show trials of the 1950s, found work in the boiler room of Mitas, a Prague tire factory, along with a number of other banned historians. Kaplan remembered the work as undemanding: "I wrote a whole book there, on Czechoslovakia from 1945 to 1948 [. . .]."[44] Another common job was with the state water company, measuring water depth and pressure at various places around the country; groups of two or three workers would live in trailers in the countryside, installing pumps and taking measurements, often alternating in long shifts that left them several days at a time to return to Prague. If a writer said he was working *v maringotce*, "in a trailer," this is what he was doing. Karel Pecka found such a job, and used the long stretches of free time to work on his novel about the labor camps of the 1950s.[45]

This transposition of intellectuals into working-class jobs was one of the defining features of Czech intellectual life in the 1970s and 1980s, and created a "shadow world," an alternate universe existing just behind and beyond the official sphere. Publishing houses, academic research institutes, universities, theaters, and radio programs continued to exist, but for the most part they had new personnel at the top; genuine institutions like the Writers' Union were gradually replaced by "ersatz" ones, staffed for the most part by careerists and mediocrities, but appointed with all the trappings and perquisites of an official institution. For many, this created a strange sense of juxtaposition. The disorientation was intensified by seeing friends or respected colleagues suddenly turn and begin to support the new order, or by seeing nonentities pop up in leadership positions—Putík spoke of those "who vaulted out of nowhere to the front of the parade of the faithful." The surface world seemed a corrupted copy of its former self. In a 1978 essay, Vaculík would sum up the overall sensation: "A kind of neutron bomb: undamaged empty figures carry on walking to and from work."[46]

Meanwhile, a huge swath of the former intellectual elite recognized itself reappearing in the shadows, as the shadow world itself became more and more real. "I began to encounter many friends and close acquaintances," wrote Lederer, "as taxi drivers, parking lot attendants, night watchmen in factories, window washers, salespeople at news stands." In the 1950s, people had simply disappeared; in the 1970s, they kept turning up in unusual places. Jaroslav Putík nicely captured the sensation in a brief portrait of a former colleague: "Mirka Rektorisová, driven off the editorial board of *Literární noviny*, is selling flowers at a well-known flower shop. She grimaces ironically, as always, squints her left eye and politely distributes information about how to take care of freesia, or what she would recommend for a wedding bouquet. White roses? Aaron's rod? A smiling sigh in her eyes: If only I had your problems."[47] Putík captures the strange experience of seeing one's friends and colleagues, or former public figures, appearing in completely new roles—as if the cultural world had been phase-shifted or translated into a new reality in which people were mere images of their former public selves.

This common experience was an important defining moment, almost an initiation, for thousands of intellectuals in the 1970s. It was not entirely bad. Manual labor provided new experiences, often useful for a writer, and many of the new jobs had their positive sides—intellectually undemanding, they left plenty of time for thinking, writing, and discussing politics, literature, and philosophy with one's colleagues, many of them in the same situation. But the phase shift was also, undeniably, stressful and disorienting. Many emerged from the early 1970s with permanent health problems, or an irrevocably darkened view of the world. Not everyone in the shadow world would sign Charter 77, of course—many emigrated, or held back from open dissent in order to protect what little independence they had—but it was still the major pool of potential "recruits" for dissent. More than anything else—and more than the actual prosecution and imprisonment of a much smaller number of people at the beginning of the decade—the shadow world created a sense of solidarity and common misfortune while encouraging its inhabitants to begin talking about their situation and how to change it.

From Salons to Samizdat

The apartment of Klement Lukeš on Celetná Street in Prague, just off Old Town Square, had been a meeting point even before normalization. Lukeš was a charismatic figure, with a wide range of friends in politics, theater, journalism, literature, and the arts. Born in Moravia in 1926, he attended a school for the blind before moving to Prague in 1946. He soon joined the Communist Party and became a well-known figure in the Prague Party leadership—tall and handsome, with dark hair and dark glasses, he was an excellent speaker and conversationalist with a legendary memory. Lederer remembers seeing him at a Party meeting in 1953: "He is blind, but he moves with sovereign certainty, and in fact he even reacts to changes in the faces of his listeners." Lukeš was arrested in 1961 as part of a group accused of criticizing the show trials and of being in the service of Yugoslavia. He was expelled from the Party, and was then "exiled" from Prague; after four years in Moravia, he was able to return to Prague in the more liberal conditions of the mid-1960s. In 1973, he was fired from his position as a researcher at the Public Opinion Institute. He was among the first signatories of Charter 77 and participated actively in dissent—among many other things, in making recordings of samizdat literature for the blind.[48]

Lukeš did not run a formal salon, but his apartment served, *de facto*, as a meeting-place for his large group of friends—many of them reform Communists expelled from the Party, but others too—as well as a clearinghouse for information. Lederer's memoir, written some ten years later, paints a vivid picture of these meetings. "There was not a week," he says,

> that I didn't stop by Klema's at least twice—for several hours each time. [. . .] It was always a quite diverse community—politicians, journalists, artists, writers, academics and people with completely normal jobs. [. . .] Each of us would occasionally bring something—coffee, a bottle of wine or the rum that Klema took a liking to, bread rolls and salami. People felt like they belonged there, like they had a place there. The friendly atmosphere—in which we forgot about our personal difficulties, as well as society's—drew us there, even though we talked about those difficulties too, actually. Sometimes in a whisper, to make things more difficult for the listening devices. It was a kind of lay chapel for us, necessary for our survival. Klema was always the center. Not so much for his erudition, limitless tolerance, and Moravian hospitality, but above all for the internal tranquility that shone from him [. . .].[49]

Vaculík was another of Lukeš's visitors, and paints a slightly ironic but still appreciative picture:

> There's always someone at Klement Lukeš's apartment, and today there was someone there, too, and before I left, two more people came, one of them a Polish woman. A man was there reading a biography of Catherine the Great to Kléma. [. . .] When he speaks about something serious, Kléma always feels about for the radio to turn it on. He smokes and gropes about for a cigarette, offers us wine from Rakvice. He is absolutely sure there's a listening device in his apartment, and if they had anything to latch on to, they could have an enormous trial around Kléma, with many participants. For he does nothing else but gather information and pass it along; it's a total headquarters for the exchange of opinions and rumors. The only people who go there are ones who should be locked up.[50]

Lukeš's apartment, although not exclusive, hosted a large contingent of reform Communists who had been expelled from the Party. Less than a mile away, there was another meeting place with a somewhat different character: Jiří Kolář's table at the legendary Café Slavia. Long before 1968, the poet and artist Kolář had "presided" over this table; it was, again, not an exclusive grouping, but over time had developed into an institution whose predominant tone was set by a group of poets and literary critics who had either never been in the Party or had broken with it long before 1968: Jiří Kolář, Jan Vladislav, and Josef Hiršal, as well as Václav Černý, who became its unofficial head after Kolář was exiled while attending an opening of his artwork in West Berlin. The translator and literary critic Jiří Pechar remembered his first visit in 1976; he was beckoned over to the table by his former professor, Černý, and he got into a heated argument with Kolář about the interwar avant-garde. Černý suggested they resolve the matter with a duel outside the city; Kolář responded by inviting Pechar to become a regular visitor to the table. In their memoirs, both Pechar and Eva Kantůrková write that the table's visitors grew more numerous and diversified after Charter 77 was drafted, as the table became an informal gathering place for Charter signatories.[51] Café Slavia was a no-man's-land between the regime and oppositional intellectuals; it was under heavy, more or less open surveillance by police (with help from the waiters), but they tolerated the get-togethers and *de facto* discussion groups of banned writers, artists, and scholars, if only because they could keep an eye on them. Intellectuals, in turn, could meet there and speak with relative freedom, as long as they were careful not to divulge secret and privileged information that might be of genuine use to the police.

There were many such meetings, some of which approached the frequency of what we might call salons—informal but regular centers of intellectual life, where a range of people could come together and discuss politics and culture freely. Historians have yet to map out all the various mini- and proto-salons that developed in the early 1970s in cafés, private apartments, cottages in the countryside, pubs, and other private and public spaces, but there were many, many more. The apartment of Jiří Němec and Dana Němcová on Ječná Street in Prague's Old Town became a headquarters and crash pad for members of the music underground.[52] Lederer met every Saturday with a group of five or six other former Communists who had been involved in the Coordinating Committee of Creative Unions.[53] The editorial boards of some of the key political and literary journals of the 1960s continued to meet even after their magazines had been shut down—another phenomenon of the "shadow world." The former editors of *Literární noviny*, ironically calling themselves "Orphans," gathered regularly: "The persistence of this strange community of people, connected with 1968 and the editorial board of *Literární noviny*, broken up and reassembled so many times, is amazing. A marketplace of reports, news, and gossip, fiery debates, the tragicomedy of individual fates."[54] In the intense, compact intellectual life of Prague, blessed with a host of exceptionally charismatic and enterprising individuals, there was often a fine line between a series of occasional dinner parties and a concerted effort to institutionalize independent intellectual life. At the other end of the spectrum, however, were different types of meetings that clearly strove to be more than just informal gatherings. These included "underground" or "apartment" university lectures, at which fired professors like Patočka might hold seminars for students who had been rejected from university because of their political background;[55] or the writers' meetings at Ivan Klíma's apartment during 1970 and 1971, where each month a different writer would read a work in progress and receive comments.[56]

For some time after 1969, the various informal groupings of friends and colleagues often sustained, as if by inertia, the postwar division in Czechoslovak culture between Communists and non-Communists. Lederer wrote: "When I take stock, I can see that a decisive majority of my friends in the state of exclusion were former Communists." This may have been natural—many former Communists had a lot in common. They had worked together on reform in the 1960s, had undergone similar screenings and expulsion in the Party purges, and were going through the long process of breaking with an ideology that the invasion, it seemed, had definitively discredited. One of Lederer's friends, Petr Pithart, himself a former Communist, thought that the reprisals after 1968 actually widened the gap between former Communists and non–Party members; "the excluded did not understand that only *for them* was the situation fundamentally new," whereas non-Communists were used to the "principle of exclusion" and were simply "playing, once more, a game they knew well." In Pithart's book *Osmašedesátý* (*Sixty-Eight*), he reproached former Party members for thinking they had been singled out for persecution, or that they needed to reconstitute a "party of the excluded" in order to take up a leading position in Czech culture once again. Rather, he said, their task was to realize that they were simply the latest in a long line of people who had been expelled and excluded—and that in the past, they themselves had taken part in the excluding.[57]

Pithart's criticism certainly reflected real resentments and fault lines within the community of people who shared a joint enemy in the normalization regime. On the other hand, the common trauma and common enemy had brought together many people who once maintained some reserve toward each other. Indeed, one of the most important centers for intellectual life had gone some way toward overcoming the principle of exclusion: the many meetings and discussions of friends at Hrádeček, the countryside cottage of Václav Havel and Olga Havlová. The Havels began to hold "miniature writers' congresses" here, with various groups of writers—both former Communists like Kohout, Vaculík, and Klíma, and nonmembers or those expelled long ago, such as Jan Vladislav, Josef Vohryzek, and Josef Hiršal. "These people all had very different pasts," said Havel in 1986, "but the differences of opinion that had once separated them had long since ceased to be important."[58]

But in either case, Pithart's comment reflected one of the weaknesses of the various "salon" groupings, which is that they effectively depended on personal relationships and face-to-face contacts. As lively and critical as these social groupings may have been, they lacked what might be called a "virtual" component—both an openness to potential new voices, and an ongoing sense of identity and organized activity. They existed when they happened to be meeting, but in the early 1970s, for the most part, they did not lead to larger initiatives or organized activity. Like the meetings of orphaned editors, they were often an extension of the cultural journals and intellectual life of the 1960s, which persisted as a "phantom limb" in these gatherings. One of the necessary stages in building these groupings into some kind of larger, coordinated oppositional community was ongoing communication, criticism, and discussion. And one of the most important steps in developing a more conscious, and self-aware, community came in 1973, when Ludvík Vaculík founded the first samizdat publishing house.

Reading in the Samizdat World

The word *samizdat* came from Russian; literally, it means something like "self-publish" or "self-publishing," and it can refer to a vast range of nonofficial or underground publishing activities. As often happens when a foreign word is borrowed and catches hold in another language, it named a phenomenon that no Czech word seemed properly to express; long debates tussled over terms like *neoficiální* ("unofficial"), *ineditní* ("out-of-edition" or "unpublished"), or *nezávislá* ("independent") literature, and many others, but it was *samizdat* that ultimately caught on.[59] Earlier versions of Czech samizdat go back to World War II, when plenty of information was passed around illegally in clandestine publications, although samizdat as a specifically *literary* phenomenon is generally dated to the late 1940s and early 1950s, when a small group of writers around Egon Bondy and Ivo Vodseďálek created Edice Půlnoc (Midnight Editions).[60] They typed their poetry in just a few copies; their aim was not really to set up a clandestine distribution network, but mainly to preserve their work for the future, so that it existed in more than one copy and was more likely to survive. Typewritten copies of banned literature circulated in the 1950s, although not in any organized or consistent fashion. Jiří Kolář and Václav Černý were arrested in 1952, for example, when police found a copy of Kolář's unpublished collection *Prometheus's Liver* during a house search of Černý's apartment. Jan Zábrana remembered how many "young nonconformist Prague intellectuals" in the 1950s tried their hand at amateur translations of another taboo author, Franz Kafka, which they passed around or read at get-togethers of friends: "I must have seen or heard some Kafka stories in twenty different translations circulating in manuscript form."[61]

As liberalization gradually proceeded in the 1960s, samizdat became less necessary for two reasons. Not only were state publishing houses more willing to publish more provocative literature, but the more provocative authors were willing to publish their work with state publishing houses, rather than keeping it "in the drawer" and waiting for better days. Some texts still circulated in typewritten copies, sometimes in the thousands—for example, the speeches at the 1967 Writers' Congress, after censors prevented the proceedings from appearing in print. But by 1968, and until the reestablishment of censorship in 1969, it was possible to publish almost anything.

It wasn't until the early 1970s that samizdat publishing really took off. In part, this was because the publishing bans of the 1970s were often more aggressive than those of the 1950s. For example, many writers who could not publish their own work in the 1950s, but had still been able to support themselves by translating or writing children's literature under their own names, now found themselves frozen out of *all* publishing possibilities.[62] At the same time, as the extreme repressiveness of the 1950s softened and people were allowed more private space in which to maneuver, it became easier to produce samizdat, at least on typewriters, and to organize larger-scale publishing operations.[63] A breakthrough came in 1973, when Ludvík Vaculík and others founded the first samizdat publishing house, Edice Petlice (Padlock Editions). Vaculík describes its beginnings: "What was to become a major cultural undertaking started when Ivan Klíma needed to get the manuscript of his *Lepers* typed out. Trying to save some money, he had it typed in several copies that he then sold to interested parties. There turned out to be more of them than there were copies." A state publisher had just returned Vaculík's own manuscript of *The Guinea Pigs* to him, so he decided to do the same thing. At first he simply had copies of his novel typed on regular-size A4 paper (just a bit bigger than the American 8½-by-11 sheet) and stapled them together. Then he began to have them bound in the smaller A5 format. The enterprise gradually grew and Vaculík christened it "Padlock Editions" in an ironic reference to an official series called *Klíč* (Key).[64] Edice Petlice would eventually publish 367 titles from a striking range of Czech and Slovak writers—novelists, poets, playwrights, philosophers, historians, and essayists.[65] One of its most significant early initiatives was Vaculík's annual anthology of Czech and Slovak "feuilletons"—short personal essays, often with a political slant, by dozens of different banned writers, who came together under one cover in an early example of how samizdat was forging virtual communities.

In the 1970s, samizdat relied on mechanical typewriters. Mimeograph machines were rare, and were easily monitored by the state, as was the stencil paper they used. (Computers, dot matrix printers, and even memory typewriters had the potential to completely change the world of samizdat, but they were scarce until the last few years of Communist rule.) The most common way of "printing" samizdat was to interleave thin pieces of paper—onionskin or "airmail paper"—with carbon paper, and then to feed the resulting stack of sheets into the typewriter. The force of the keystroke would impress the ink from each sheet of carbon paper onto the following page. Depending on the typewriter and the typist, you could make eight, ten, or twelve copies at a time, sometimes even more—the first copies, of course, would be the darkest, and they could be quite faint by the time you got to the tenth or twelfth. An "edition" of a given book might run to several dozen copies, with the original being typed three or four times.

A pillar of every samizdat publishing operation were the "copyists" or typists who produced these carbon copies. Most, but not all, of them were women. For Petlice, the "first and chief copyist" was Zdena Erteltová, a former librarian who had been fired after 1968, and who copied 190 of Petlice's titles and some 400 overall. Typists were generally paid according to the going rates in an official publishing house (five crowns a page, in the late 1970s and early 1980s), but they did not have an employer's stamp in their identification booklet; Erteltová, for example, was detained for "parasitism." There were many other copyists, equally courageous and dedicated, such as the former radio and television journalist Otka Bednářová, who would be arrested in 1979. Being a copyist took a great deal of courage, consistency, and coolness under pressure, especially since police activities were often directed against the technical and production side of samizdat—typists, binders, organizers—rather than the authors themselves. Typing was, of course, loud, and hard to hide from the neighbors; a professional typist might want to keep a legitimate commercial order in her desk drawer in case she was interrupted. Good copyists were in short supply, and usually had more than enough work to keep them busy.[66]

One of the forces shaping samizdat was the existence of laws against spreading subversive publications and operating a business without a license. It was legal to type up a few copies of a novel and give it to your friends to get their comments and advice; it was illegal to start your own publishing company without state permission. Samizdat existed in the world between these two extremes, and this position generated some curious paradoxes. In Edice Petlice, authors would sign the title page of each typed copy of their work, both signaling its authenticity and affirming its status as a personal copy or authorized "manuscript." The name of the edition did not appear, nor were books in the series numbered, in order to lessen the appearance of an organized publishing house. Each copy was marked with a formula to the effect that no further copying of the manuscript was permitted—a ban that many readers, of course, cheerfully ignored. One of the standard formulae, *Výslovný zákaz dalšího opisování rukopisu* (Further Copying of this Manuscript Expressly Forbidden), was a bit of a joke, since its acronym, VZDOR, means "resistance" in Czech. Vaculík worked out a system where different copyists would use different formulae, with "v.z.d.o.r." reserved for the original copyist, and formulae beginning with the word *Autor*—for example, "The author does not desire any further copying of this manuscript"—used for copies typed by the author himself or herself. As so often in the world of samizdat, however, these formulae could simply be copied by other people, so they are not always reliable guides.[67]

In the early years of samizdat, Edice Petlice was the most significant publishing operation. In Jiří Lederer's book of interviews, *České rozhovory (Czech*

Conversations), conducted in 1975 and 1976, both Lederer and his interlocutors use the terms "Petlice literature" and "samizdat" almost interchangeably. With time, however, a number of other publishing operations took their place alongside Petlice. The two most important ones began in 1975. Edice Expedice (Dispatch Editions) was founded by Václav Havel; he ran it with the help of his wife Olga and brother Ivan, both of whom took charge of the enterprise when Václav was in prison. Expedice brought some new innovations. It declared itself openly as an "edition," and rather than the author's signature, each copy was signed by the publisher: "Copied for himself and his friends by Václav Havel." Olga signed when Václav was in prison. In 1981, both Olga and Ivan would be detained for several days, although not actually jailed, for their work on Expedice; the charges hanging over them would cause a two-year break in Expedice publishing, but the edition started up again in 1983 and survived until the fall of Communism. Petlice focused on Czech prose; Expedice included poetry, plays, philosophy, and translations as well. It represented a shift toward a consistent layout and binding—the first 119 books, until Olga Havlová's and Ivan Havel's detainment, were published in a characteristic black binding, sometimes with a gold EE stamped on the spine. Each book in the series was numbered; overall the effort was to present, at considerable risk, the impression of a regular publishing venture. (Edice Petlice books, by contrast, did not contain any references to Petlice itself.) Ultimately, 232 books came out in Expedice.[68]

A second important venture founded in 1975 was Edice Kvart (Quarto Editions), founded by Jan Vladislav with significant help from Jiří Kolář and František Kautman.[69] Vladislav, born in 1923, was a poet and critic who had been unable to publish after 1948; he had also been kicked out of the university, where he was preparing his doctorate under Václav Černý. (He would finally complete it twenty years later, again under Černý, when both were allowed to return to the university during the Prague Spring—shortly before both were forced to leave again.) During World War II, he had worked in the library of the Agricultural Academy in Prague; the library had a printing press in the basement, where Vladislav spent long hours during air raids. Among other things, he learned how to bind books from the resident bookbinder. This experience would stand him in good stead thirty years later.[70] Like Expedice, Kvart revealed a visual and functional "division of labor" in the world of samizdat that was to be a harbinger of the even more highly developed publishing world of the 1980s. It also revealed how the enterprise of samizdat began in a world of face-to-face contacts before reaching out to more and more readers. Writing in 1992, Vladislav said:

> Even if Petlice was the most important undertaking of its kind, it was lim-
> ited, especially at the beginning, to a relatively narrow circle of authors
> around its organizer Ludvík Vaculík. [. . .] Petlice arose in a circle that was
> originally held together quite narrowly by personal and ideological bonds
> [. . .]. In discussions around Jiří Kolář's round table at Café Slavia, as well
> as elsewhere, there surfaced again and again the need to supplement Petlice
> with another series.[71]

Vladislav is oblique in discussing this point, but the subtext is clear: most of the authors who published in Petlice in the first few years, 1973–1975, were former Communists who had been able to publish officially in the 1950s and 1960s—when Vladislav, for example, was a banned poet who had to translate for a living. The core authors and editors of Kvart had all been banned long before the 1970s. Nevertheless, all three editions, Petlice, Kvart, and Expe-dice, collaborated closely, and it would be wrong to ascribe a clear ideological bent to any of the series. Karel Pecka published a novel in Petlice in 1974, for example, and by 1975 it had begun publishing many authors who had been banned or disadvantaged in the 1950s—Kolář, Havel, Patočka, Kliment, and Vladislav himself.

The differences between the editions were more of format, editing policy, and aesthetic program. Similar to Expedice, Kvart published genres that Petlice didn't handle—especially poetry and philosophy, as well as translated literature, which Petlice did not publish at all. In general, Kvart was more focused on intellectually demanding poetry and philosophy, as well as on the French cultural sphere. Vladislav eventually began to produce books in a "square" format, by cutting the edges off a piece of A4 paper—hence the name Quarto. Vladislav also paid attention to aesthetics, striving to produce beauti-ful books; eventually he began to bind them himself, since it was too risky to take them to professional binderies. He did not have a paper cutter and had to cut each page by hand.[72] "There were not just practical and aesthetic reasons for the name Quarto Editions and the new format," wrote Vladislav in 1991; "its very appearance sought to indicate immediately that there was more than one unofficial edition, to make their existence seem less interesting and so to distract the attention of the appropriate repressive institutions."[73] This attempt was not successful, but does indicate an important differentiation that was taking place inside the samizdat publishing world.

At the same time, Kvart cooperated closely with Petlice, Expedice, and other editions, trading titles back and forth. While all three operations worked hard on editing, Kvart would often take extra care to produce critically accurate editions of poetry and criticism, an endeavor that in some ways prefigured the interests of one of the early samizdat scholarly journals, *Kritický sborník* (Critical Almanac), which Kvart began publishing in 1981. In the chaotic world of samizdat, in which it was often difficult to distinguish between sanctioned and unsanctioned copies, *Kvart* was an early recognition of the need to produce "critical editions" of texts as well as to work out the definitive versions of works that had been widely copied and circulated—for example, Jaroslav Seifert's well-known poetry collection *The Plague Column*. Vladislav was an effective editor, publishing ambitious projects such as a two-volume edition of Baudelaire's letters, which he selected and translated, or an anthology of the French poet Henri Michaux, for which he had chosen the poems in consultation with Michaux himself. These were highly sophisticated undertakings (some of them had been completed in the 1960s but had not been allowed to be published), complementing Petlice and the other publishers with an effort to continue broadening the horizon of Czech samizdat readers and develop editorial projects that one might not have expected under the straitened conditions of samizdat publishing.

Samizdat was expensive. Anyone could type up copies of a work using carbon paper, of course, but running a full-scale Edice or publishing venture entailed many costs—mainly for paper, binding, and typing. Since the thin paper used was not always available, it was necessary to keep a supply on hand if you didn't want books to be published with paper of varying quality and hue. Typewriters had to be bought and fixed; white-out could be hard to come by.[74] Publishers had to scrupulously avoid making a profit, so as to avoid criminal charges for running an illegal business. Copies were usually sold at cost; this still made them roughly ten times more expensive than officially published books, which were heavily subsidized by the state. On the other hand, samizdat was often in greater demand.[75] Even so, Vaculík wrote that he generally ran at a deficit "that was inevitably created through lost books, vagaries of the postal services, police interventions, and bookkeeping errors."[76] Ultimately, Edice Petlice and many other samizdat organizations were helped greatly by financial support from abroad. In particular, the Charter 77 Foundation, set up in Sweden by František Janouch after his emigration, proved crucial in funding samizdat—both in paying for production costs and supplying more advanced technology, as well as creating "stipends" that might go to banned, and unemployed, authors.

Samizdat was also time-consuming. Running a publishing house is a lot of work under the best of circumstances, but it's an entirely different proposition when you can't use your telephone, your driver's license has been confiscated, and you are binding the books yourself. Vladislav estimated that each book took "ten full days of intensive work, reading and correcting typescripts, as well as manual work to do with binding. Apart from that there was a lot of traveling to be done, picking up manuscripts and delivering the finished product. When you take into account that I published 120 volumes, that makes 1,200 working days, or three full years. Nobody can do this sort of thing all his life because you really must devote all your energies to it while you are doing it."[77] Vaculík, too (who didn't bind his own books, but ran a much larger operation than Vladislav's), found it difficult to maintain his own writing activity. Petlice "was taking up all my time," he wrote about the 1970s, "and I was broke. I wasn't even managing to read others' manuscripts and work on them. And one ought not get the impression that there are many writers who are willing to take a careful pencil to a colleague's manuscript and correct the typing errors and punctuation. [. . .] I remember once bringing a certain author a parcel of copies of his manuscript and asking him to take them to the binders himself. 'Why me?' he replied, taken aback. That made me realize what a crazy situation I was in. People actually thought I was being paid for what I did."[78]

To the actual work must be added exhausting and time-consuming interrogations with the police—regular monthly ones for Vaculík—as well as the efforts necessary to hide manuscripts while they were in production. Vladislav never had a house search, but was openly threatened with them by the police, and so had to be prepared. He also faced more serious threats, which intensified during 1979 and 1980. Eventually, the pressure on Vladislav became so great—he was subjected to body searches and threatened with physical violence, his daughter in Canada was denied a visit to come see her parents, and the police tried to frame his wife for theft—that he decided to emigrate.

If producing samizdat was different from a regular printing operation, so was *reading* samizdat different from reading a printed book. For one thing, it could be hard on the eyes—the paper was thin, often translucent, and if you got a copy that had been at the back of the stack in the typewriter, the ink could be faint. (Expedice offered a discount on the eleventh and twelfth copies.[79]) For another, samizdat texts often had many typographical errors. Even the best typists were bound to make mistakes, with speed and accuracy posing competing demands. Typists, editors, and authors might all end up writing in corrections in blue ink, by hand. Characters that couldn't be typed, such as Greek letters in an essay on Plato or Aristotle, would also be written in. If we often think of reading as a process of getting lost in the intangible message of a text—the logic of an argument or the "fictional dream" of a novel—samizdat was always reminding you that you were holding a physical object in your hands, an object with its own history of past production and past readers, and its own presence in time and space. The book might just be a copy of some original, but it also had the aura of a unique existence with its own individual history. The "material reality" of a samizdat book was thus evident—although it was a copy, at least in a run of ten or twelve, it also carried signs of its own production.[80]

This basic fact had a number of implications. Miroslav Červenka described one of the essential paradoxes of samizdat. Binding a samizdat book, paying attention to layout, providing a table of contents, even using A5-sized pages, all testified to the author's and publisher's desire to present a work as finished and definitive: "A bound book sends a message from its author: 'This is how I wanted it, and I neither want to, nor can, interfere with what is presented here.'" (To see this point, just compare a samizdat book with, say, a folder full of loose-leaf pages, which would encourage a reader to think about what could be changed.) But in the vast majority of samizdat typescripts, this sense of finality was constantly being disrupted "by the inaccuracy, mistakes, and thus demonstrably unfinished nature of the copies."[81] Reading samizdat meant switching constantly back and forth from definitive to provisional, from spirit to matter, from text to world.

The paradox of the "unfinished finished text" also created a philological nightmare, in which it was often impossible to determine what the author's final version of a text was. Červenka compared the copying process to the game known as "telephone" in the United States, or as "silent post" in Czech or German, in which one person whispers a phrase to another person, who whispers it to another, and so on, to the end of the chain; the final version is invariably wildly different from the original. "For me," he wrote in 1985, "the reading of every samizdat text is, above all, a torture chamber of conjectures; that is, I am constantly dealing with the task of restoring the correct wording." Červenka issued a plea for stricter standards in the production of samizdat books. Corrections should be scrupulously written into every typed copy, with some kind of signal as to which changes come from the editor and which from the author; the copyist should make corrections while pages are still in the typewriter, immediately after mistakes arise. After the copies are typed, both the editor and the author should compare each one with the original, and then collate their findings. It was an "unforgivable sin" to handwrite corrections on some copies and not on others. Accuracy was more important than how nice the finished product looks, argued Červenka: "A smooth typescript with the mistakes left in is like a home that has been kept neat on the outside, but has a shameful mess in the drawers and closets. Beautifully typed nonsense is still nonsense."[82]

Červenka was well aware that these suggestions were a bit utopian. Samizdat was hard enough to produce without worrying about creating a critical edition of every text. There was always a tension between the desire to publish well-made, carefully edited books and the desire to generate as many texts as quickly as possible. The same tensions were evident in decisions about what to publish in the first place. Editors like Vaculík certainly did reject manuscripts they didn't like, but these decisions could be fraught—at some level, he and a few other people were effectively making a decision for the whole national literary culture, not just for a single publisher. Vaculík wrote about the novel *To Live Once Again*, published based on the posthumous papers of Eduard Valenta: "Was it complete? [. . .] Who was to assess its worth? What sort of work was it? It was certainly interesting enough to merit a decision by some future publisher or critic. It was therefore necessary to do something to keep it in existence and publicize it."[83] Here, Petlice expressly served an archival function, where the samizdat edition was a halfway house between a private manuscript and a novel published in a free and open, fully functioning public sphere.

Overall, there was a wide spectrum of practices, from the relatively exclusive and critical editing of Kvart, to Petlice's attempt to publish as much and as widely as possible, to the simple practice whereby an individual person at home, lacking any contacts with a samizdat publishing house or even with the larger world of dissent, might copy a text that he or she liked and thought should be circulated—so-called "wild samizdat," which might have plenty of mistakes and deviations from the original, but could more effectively serve the purpose of simply getting some form of the text into as many hands as possible. A 1989 samizdat volume of poems by Svatopluk Karásek, who had emigrated and was in Switzerland at the time, contained the following anonymous editorial note: "This collection of poems by Svatopluk Karásek [. . .] is published without his knowledge (the reason: the folly of this era). It is neither a selection of his work, nor a complete collection of his poetry. The goal was rather to assemble the available 'material.'" The editor went on to acknowledge the kinds of problems that made Červenka cringe: "For practical reasons, problems related to the layout and ordering of the poems could not be consulted with the author; nor could some questions about punctuation marks, etc."[84] A literary critic who was used to interpreting enjambments and comma placement would simply have to adapt.

Samizdat was marked not only by different forms of reading, but also by the varied types of reading communities that built up around the samizdat text. Just as the samizdat text stood in for an intangible master-text while constantly reminding readers of its own physical existence, the interpretive community of a samizdat text was both bounded and unbounded, finite and infinite. Samizdat was not "downloaded."[85] You got it from a specific reader and passed it on to another one. In this sense, samizdat still worked to some extent through face-to-face contacts; it was a bit like a club that you could join by invitation only, or only once you had established your trustworthiness or "oppositional" credentials. Likewise, in passing samizdat on to other readers, you had to be sure you could trust the next reader in the chain. Samizdat readers thus were generally aware of the communication channels surrounding them. This was clear in the instructions that samizdat journals used, for example, in order to solicit submissions. The underground journal *VOKNO* asked readers to send in articles using the same channel through which they had received their copy of the magazine.[86]

At the same time, by its very nature—like all literature—samizdat created a wider, unbounded community of readers. In reading samizdat, one was joining a larger culture, whether one saw that culture as "underground," "literary," "national," or in some other terms. The material text one held in one's hands had been held by unknown readers and would make its way through unknown channels into the future. In this sense, samizdat embodied some of the paradoxes of the underground and dissident publics that we will examine more closely in Chapters 4 and 6. It simultaneously modeled an abstract, universal reader and a very grounded community of actual readers, a public that was both open to all and was inhabited by specific people.

An essential characteristic of samizdat reading communities was that much samizdat was borrowed. This, too, affected the reading experience, in that you often had access to a copy for a relatively short time. It was common to get a novel, poetry collection, or work of philosophy for just a day, two days, or a week. Within that time, you might want to share it with your own friends as well, so that networks of borrowers and sub-borrowers developed. "When I buy a copy of a book, I put it on my bookshelf, thinking 'I'll read it when I have time'—which could be in five years, or never," wrote the literary critic František Kautman, "whereas, if I've borrowed a manuscript for the week, I have to read it right away."[87] This could lead to intense and memorable reading experiences, as you might call in sick or stay up all night in order to finish a book that you needed to pass on at an appointed time and place within a few days. On a Saturday in December 1976, Pavel Kohout was engaged in a "speed-reading" of Aleksandr Solzehnitsyn's massive memoir *The Oak and the Calf*, "which we had to hand off on Monday to the next in the relay of readers," when Havel pulled him outside for some of the early discussions about drafting Charter 77.[88] As one literary critic wrote about Milan Kundera's *The Unbearable Lightness of Being*, which circulated widely in an edition published by Sixty-Eight Publishers in Toronto and smuggled into Czechoslovakia: "It traveled from hand to hand. I myself had less than 24 hours to read it: I borrowed the Sixty-Eight Publishers edition from a friend at three P.M. on Wednesday, and I had to return it to him in front of the university dining hall on Thursday at one. I made it; in those days, the nights were long, especially the ones spent reading."[89] In this context, it is worth remembering that samizdat handoffs were part of a larger culture of appointments and meetings that was considerably less fluid than it is today. This was, of course, in the days before cell phones and e-mail; many people did not even have telephones. If you needed to meet someone in front of the dining hall at one, you couldn't just call them up and tell them that you still had a hundred pages to read and would prefer to meet the next day. And for those samizdat readers who were under police surveillance—not an insignificant subset, either in numbers or importance—it was sloppy, and perhaps dangerous, to arrange meetings by phone.

If you didn't borrow samizdat, you might buy it; then you had to figure out where to put it. Some people accumulated large collections, but if you were liable to have your house or apartment searched, it was not wise to hold on to a lot of samizdat. Fear and caution both played a role: samizdat could get you in trouble, of course, but you could also lose your library. Many people stored samizdat in the basements or attics of uncles, grandmothers, or friends who were less politically active and so less likely to have a house search. As Eva

Kantůrková wrote, after police confiscated dozens of samizdat journals from her bookshelves in a 1988 search, "I could have reproached myself that I didn't hide them at someone else's place, but that's an insoluble conflict. When you have them at home, you can lose them; when you leave them with someone else, you fret over your helplessness and lack of freedom."[90]

The Warrant against Culture

In *Czech Conversations*, his book of interviews with banned writers conducted in 1975 and 1976, Jiří Lederer frequently asked about the role of Edice Petlice. His interlocutors tended to see it as both a vital "testimony to continuity" and, ultimately, an inadequate substitute for genuine cultural life. Alexandr Kliment said that it was "a testimony that culture arises from its own sources, not on the basis of the state's political line," but he also lamented that it could never provide authors with the ongoing dialogue and criticism they needed if they were not to become "eccentrics." He saw Petlice books as similar to shoes, clothing, and eggs in a barter economy: good, necessary, and reliable things, "but it's not a currency." Even Vaculík said that samizdat and the whole world of unofficial culture was a "substitute circulatory system" for the social body, adding, "The intensity of culture and its saturation of the Czech space have ceased to correspond to population density."[91] These remarks on Petlice indicate a larger fact about the self-understanding of intellectuals in the mid-1970s. Rather than thinking of themselves as a proto-opposition or as laying political groundwork for an alternative to the Communist regime, they saw themselves as carriers and preservers of Czech culture in the face of the intellectual devastation of normalization. This was not a passive position, but it had not fully developed the conceptual framework for formulating an oppositional platform. Indeed, Lederer's interviewees often saw samizdat culture in personal terms, as a form of sustenance—a way of nurturing themselves as writers through contacts with other people's stories and with a national literary tradition. In the West, samizdat was invariably seen as an expression of resistance; for many writers and readers in Czechoslovakia, it was also a sign of subjugation—another phenomenon of the shadow world.

Václav Havel was among the first to develop a more far-reaching framework that would understand unofficial culture as an almost explosive force, one that politics meddles with at its own peril. Havel's first major statement of this idea came in a remarkable open letter that he wrote to Gustav Husák in April 1975. Havel accused Husák of issuing a "warrant against culture," and he articulated his criticisms with such force that they continue to dominate discussions of normalization to this day. But he begins by posing difficult questions about the resonance of high culture—questions that were clearly on his own mind and had contributed to his feeling of malaise in the early 1970s. Did a country really suffer that much from restrictions on its cultural life? Wasn't it presumptuous to assume that a few banned writers were so significant? Havel begins by pretending to assume a "plebeian" or "anti-intellectual" position, conceding that the banning of cultural journals after 1969, for example, might seem of little consequence: "The wheels of society continue to go round even without all those literary, artistic, theatrical, philosophical, historical, and other magazines [. . .] How many people today still miss those publications? Only the few tens of thousands of people who subscribed to them—a very small fraction of society." Nevertheless, the effect goes "infinitely deeper," even though it is hidden. Literature, theater, the arts—high culture, broadly understood—is part of a system by which "society becomes aware of itself." Banning a journal, for example, "is an interference, hard to describe in exact terms, in the complex system of circulation, exchange, and conversion of nutrients that maintain life in that many-layered organism which is society today." Havel continues, in a passage that—although written before dissent had a name—is essential for understanding dissent more generally:

> It is easy to show that the real importance of knowledge, thought, and creation is not limited, in the stratified world of a civilized society, to the significance these things have for the particular circle of people who are primarily, directly and, as it were, physically involved with them, either actively or passively. This is always a small group, in science and scholarship even more than in art. Yet the knowledge in question, conveyed through however many intermediaries, may in the end profoundly affect the whole society, just as a politics that takes into account the nuclear threat physically concerns each one of us, even though most of us have had no experience of the speculations in theoretical physics which led to the manufacture of the atom bomb. That the same holds for knowledge in the humanities is shown by many historic instances of an unprecedented cultural, political, and moral upsurge throughout society, where the original nucleus of crystallization, the catalyst, was an act of social self-awareness carried out, and indeed directly and "physically" perceived, only by a small and exclusive circle. Even subsequently, that act may have remained outside the

apperception of society at large, yet it was still an indispensable condition of its upsurge. For we never know when some inconspicuous spark of knowledge, struck within range of the few brain cells, as it were, specially adapted for the organism's self-awareness, may suddenly light up the road for the whole of society [. . .].[92]

Havel deploys a wide range of "multiplier" metaphors to convey why cultural factors exert a deep, invisible, and lasting influence. They are a "nucleus of crystallization," a "catalyst," a "spark," and flashes of light that temporarily reveal the landscape. Elsewhere he speaks of culture as a vitamin—a tiny portion of our diet, which is nevertheless essential for survival—or a mesh or net that unravels when a single thread is cut. All of these metaphors are getting at the basic idea that the purges of cultural and intellectual life had affected many more people than just their direct targets.

I think it would be difficult to overestimate the importance of this passage. It gets at several questions of grave concern to nearly all the people who would, just one and a half years later, form the core of dissent and sign Charter 77. One could consider Havel's account to be elitist, but he had taken the important step of giving intellectuals a way to think of their own isolation as something more than a personal catastrophe or an attack on a small group of people. Many banned novelists and poets *did* think of themselves as much better than the writers who had staffed the new, official Writers' Union. And many banned novelists and poets *were* much better. But the real question was not who was better—not the persecution of the country's intellectual elite— but rather: how does the attack on culture affect society as a whole, even people who never go to the theater or read a novel?

What allowed Havel to make this shift in self-perception? In part, he is writing as a person of the theater—someone for whom even the text of a play is an inert substance that can only be brought to life through its performance in a living world of actors, directors, and theaters. A samizdat novel read by only a dozen people could still—by Havel's own theory—have a major effect on society at large; a play that is never performed cannot. What's more, the "interconnection" of culture—as a mesh of many threads—may also be more apparent in the theater, where the banning of a director, playwright, or actor can directly affect an entire group of artists. It is notable that in *Disturbing the Peace*, Havel mentions three events that helped him break out of a period of malaise lasting from 1969 to 1975. One was the letter to Husák itself; the other two had to do with the reception of his plays. In 1975, an amateur theater group put on a single performance of his play *The Beggar's Opera* at a pub in Horní Počernice; knowing that the regime would not allow any encores, Havel invited about three hundred friends and was able to see one of his plays performed for the first time since 1969. The third event was the wide social resonance of his one-act *Audience*: "For example, I once picked up a hitchhiker and, without knowing who I was, he began to quote passages from that play. Or I'd be sitting in a pub and I'd hear young people shouting lines from the play to each other across the room."[93] These are classic examples of Havel's sense of how culture works "below the surface," circulating through society in unseen ways and reappearing at unpredictable moments. For all these reasons, the destruction of culture in the world of theater may have been more apparent to him than it would be, say, to a banned lyric poet. It is no accident that a number of actors and playwrights—Havel, Kohout, Pavel Landovský—would play such a prominent role in the beginnings of Charter 77; their sense of staging and performance was tied to a larger sense of culture as a living, breathing force.

Back in November 1968, when Jiří Lederer had given his speech at the meeting of the Coordinating Committee of Creative Unions, he had said: "Scientists, artists, and journalists are—whether they want to be or not—the main hope of our citizens. Every conversation with them—in workshops, in laboratories, in lecture halls—insistently reminds of this, again and again. [. . .] We will not take on the role of saviors, but we shouldn't give up the role of experimenter and pioneer."[94] These optimistic words would lose their force in the ensuing months and years. Having lost their public tribunes, "scientists, artists, and journalists" also lost the prestige that had allowed them to play a leading role in the Prague Spring. They also lost their self-confidence and self-awareness as a group of public intellectuals pursuing common goals of reform and liberalization during the 1960s. Dissent would emerge from their shadow world, but it still didn't have a name. If we step back and look at the state of oppositional circles—it is difficult to know what else to call them—around 1976, we can see a number of questions that would have to be answered before they might coalesce into a group that was conscious of its own political identity in a way that interlocking circles of intellectuals, no matter how active or imaginative, were not.

The first was the question of high culture and the intellectual more generally. Would banned writers enter into dissent *as* writers—as representatives of a suppressed national culture—or in some other capacity? How could the concern for high culture, with its necessarily elitist overtones, become a vehicle for a more broad-based and political dissent? Normalization had turned many "intellectuals" into "workers"; for the first time, many writers were holding nine-to-five jobs doing hard manual labor, and many had come into contact with a whole new set of friends and attitudes. Would dissent be an intellectual affair or would it somehow reach more broadly into all the levels of society?

A second question was the relationship between reform Communists, mainly those who had been expelled from the Party in 1969 or the early 1970s, and people who had never been in the Party to begin with, or had "seen the light" much earlier, for example, after 1956. There were many fault lines here. One was a disagreement over tactics and political futures. Some reform Communists still thought that the path out of normalization would lead to a replay of the Prague Spring—the Party would still be in charge, but once again in the hands of enlightened modernizers. Others had been so thoroughly disillusioned by 1968 (and more especially by 1969) that they were no longer interested in the idea of socialism with a human face. And still others had never put any faith in reform Communism to begin with. Any dissent built around a reform Communist platform would drive away many potential leaders and active members. What were the alternatives?

Another fault line, often more personal, traced a circle around former Communists who had held positions of power, or leading roles in journalism and cultural life, in the 1950s and 1960s, while millions of others had been disadvantaged by their class background, their refusal to join the Party, or the fact that they were in prison. For many in the 1970s, it was increasingly clear that Pithart's "principle of exclusion," according to which some people were privileged merely because they were Communists, was the most poisonous factor of Czechoslovak culture and politics since World War II. Even Havel, who tended to emphasize the unity rather than fault lines of dissent, nevertheless made clear allusions to it from time to time—as in "The Power of the Powerless," when he mentioned that the principle of exclusion "lies at the root of all our present-day moral and political misery."[95]

What ideas and institutions would bring together, say, Pavel Kohout, who had been an enthusiastic Communist in his teens and twenties, with Karel Pecka, who had spent the same years in the uranium mines, or indeed Havel, who had avoided arrest but had not been allowed to attend university because he came from a wealthy family? On one hand, these potential divisions should not be overstated. One of the things that had happened in the early 1970s was

that a great many potential rivals had become friends; magnanimity, tolerance, and solidarity overcame bitterness about past political mistakes. On the
other hand, any kind of common platform would have to overcome the awk-
wardness latent in František Janouch's reference to "socialist intellectuals" and
a "group of former party members as well as non-members" that we mentioned
at the beginning of Chapter 2. On what terrain could such a diverse group of
people come together and reimagine themselves as a community?

Underneath the traumas and dramas of intellectual life between 1969 and
1976, another movement had been quietly taking shape—one built around
working-class youth culture, and rock music, rather than the samizdat texts
of Edice Petlice, the proto-salons and café tables of Prague, and the agonized
discussions about what should or should not have been done in 1968. This
movement, the music underground, had a completely different set of idols,
ideologies, and dilemmas. It also had a spiritual leader, Ivan Martin Jirous,
who was just as aware as Havel that culture lives through performance. Most
of the intellectuals we have mentioned in this chapter had hardly any idea of
the underground's existence, or of how it would shape their lives.

4

Legends of the Underground

The standard account goes like this: In September 1976, the trial in Prague of a nonconformist psychedelic rock band, The Plastic People of the Universe, became one of the catalysts for the drafting of Charter 77. The band was accused of "disturbing the peace" and portrayed by the Communist regime as a group of long-haired, foul-mouthed, drug-using delinquents; but many Czech intellectuals, foremost among them Václav Havel, correctly perceived the trial as an attack on freedom of thought and creativity. The band, after all, had no interest in politics and just wanted to be left alone to play their music in their own way; the state's attack on them, in Havel's stirring formulation, was "an attack by the totalitarian system on life itself, on the very essence of human freedom and integrity."[1] Havel helped mobilize writers, artists, philosophers, and other opposition intellectuals into a strong show of support for the band, and by December 1976, their meetings to protest the trial had evolved into something larger: the drafting of Charter 77, a document calling on Czechoslovakia to recognize the basic human rights it had solemnly (and, of course, hypocritically) agreed to uphold when it signed the Helsinki Accords in 1975. The trial of the Plastic People had galvanized the opposition, convincing everyone of the "indivisibility of freedom" and making it clear that no compromise with the Communist regime was possible.

Is that what really happened?

Well, not exactly. Czech and English sources alike commonly refer to "the trial of the Plastic People," but in fact there was no such thing. Of the four defendants, only one—Vratislav Brabenec, the saxophonist—actually played for the band. A second, Ivan Martin Jirous, was not a musician at all; he was the Plastic People's artistic director, but to call him a member of the band does not really capture his importance as an organizer, theorist, and cult hero of underground circles. A third defendant, Pavel Zajíček, belonged to another band, DG 307. DG 307 shared a member with the Plastics, Milan Hlavsa. But Hlavsa was not put on trial. The fourth defendant, Svatopluk Karásek, was associated with the music underground but was not a member of the Plastic People, DG 307, or any other band—he was a Protestant minister and folksinger in his own right, whose spiritual "Say No to the Devil" had given the underground one of its rallying cries.

So "the trial of the Plastic People" was not really a trial of the Plastic People. What's more, it wasn't the only trial of the music underground in 1976. Three young men—Karel Havelka, Miroslav Skalický, and František Stárek— had already been put on trial in Plzeň in July 1976. They were prosecuted for organizing a lecture and concert, at which Jirous had spoken and Karásek had played with another folksinger, Karel "Charlie" Soukup, the previous December. They received sentences ranging from eight months to two and a half years, which were later reduced on appeal. Both the July and September trials were the result of a large-scale police raid that had begun on March 17, 1976. During a three-week period, nineteen people were arrested, including all the members of the Plastic People, and many more besides.[2] Only two members of the Plastics, however—only one of them a musician—were actually put on trial.

Contemporary sources did not start calling this event "the trial of the Plastic People" right away. Protests and essays from the summer of 1976 still speak of the "campaign against the Czech underground," for example.[3] In a July open letter, Věra Jirousová spoke of "the arrest of twenty young musicians."[4] An Amnesty International report from September 1976 was titled "Trial of Czech Non-Conformist Artists."[5] As Václav Havel walked out of the courtroom after the trial, he met an acquaintance who asked him how he was doing: "I replied, none too logically, that I had just been at a trial of the Czech underground."[6] None too logically, but at least, for now, accurately.

The folksinger Karásek was the first to be dropped from the abbreviation. In a 1998 interview, he remembered thinking, even before the trial: "What am I doing here, when it's called the trial of the Plastic People?"[7] In December 1976, Jan Patočka, who would become one of the first spokesmen of Charter 77, wrote a text called "On the Matter of The Plastic People of the Universe and DG 307."[8] DG 307 was the next to go; by the summer of 1978, in "The Power of the Powerless," Havel was speaking of "the trial of young musicians around the group the Plastic People."[9] In 1985 and 1986, as he was composing *Disturbing the Peace*, his book-length interview with the journalist Karel Hvížďala, he would refer simply to "the case of the Plastic People" and "the excitement around the Plastics."[10] H. Gordon Skilling begins his 1981 account by referring to "the trials and convictions of a group of rock musicians and their supporters," but later switches over to "the case of the Plastic People."[11] Today this is common usage. A standard account of the 1989 revolutions writes: "The immediate impetus that led to Charter 77 was the arrest and trial of members of a rock music group called The Plastic People of the Universe. [. . .] Despite the international outcry, the Plastics were convicted."[12] The useful shorthand has caught on, ultimately displacing a more accurate description. In a transmogrification familiar to anyone who has studied dissent or the underground, an anecdote has become history.

Does it really matter? The Plastic People were just a recognizable abbreviation for the music underground more generally—what is at stake in specifying whether or not all the band members were put on trial and whether or not all the defendants were members of the band?

In fact, the shorthand can be seen as a symptom of the larger tendencies, discussed in Chapter 1, to view dissent as a political strategy and a transnational philosophical movement, shaped by international factors such as the Helsinki Accords, rather than as a set of local decisions and practices. The "trial of the Plastic People" has always provided some useful narrative excitement to liven up these accounts, but remains little more than local color: it is seen as a historical accident, a catalyst helping a more sophisticated, intellectual opposition to coalesce.[13] But the ritualized reference to the "trial of the Plastic People" does not account for the influence of the music underground on Czech dissent; in fact, it does just the opposite, obscuring how underground artists and thinkers joined in the larger project of articulating an oppositional identity in the 1970s. In fact, the underground played a far more interesting and important role, helping to explain how Czech dissidents developed forms of organization and self-identification around which they could mount a more effective opposition to the regime. The underground provided models of oppositional behavior built around feigned naïveté, as well as a critique of consumerist culture that did not distinguish between Communism and capitalism. It also revealed the value of self-mythologization in forging and maintaining an oppositional identity. These contributions, I will argue, are elided when we speak simply of a "trial of the Plastic People." But to understand how these distortions arose, we'll first have to dig a bit below the surface.

The Plastic People Go Underground

Who were the Plastic People? Before they appeared on the radar of Czechoslovakia's banned writers, they had a history of their own.[14] Of course, following the life of any rock band (on either side of the Iron Curtain) can be complicated. Just as a person's identity remains the same even as all the cells in his or her body change, so a band can remain a band even as its members and styles are constantly evolving. The Plastic People went through many stages and groupings, with different people fighting over the band's direction and style (or, if you will, its soul) at different times.

The band was formed in September 1968 by four teenagers from the Prague district of Břevnov, and its real *spiritus movens* was seventeen-year-old bassist and singer Milan Hlavsa. At the mention of September 1968, one is tempted to add "just a month after the Soviet invasion of Czechoslovakia" or "as Soviet soldiers took up their posts around the country" or something like that, but the suggestive juxtaposition is misleading; all evidence suggests that the band members were not yet thinking politically. (Hlavsa was seventeen during the Prague Spring, and later recounted his surprise at seeing Russian soldiers on his way to rehearsal one day in the winter of 1968–1969.[15]) Current and future generations of Czech historians can be grateful that Hlavsa discarded one of the band's early names, New Elektric Potatoes.[16] "Plastic People" itself comes from a Frank Zappa song; depending on whom you ask, the band added "of the Universe" either because a UFO had been spotted above Prague or in the spirit of its early fascination with cosmology and astrology, in particular the mysticism of Cornelius Agrippa.[17]

The Plastics enjoyed early success, winning a prize at a Prague "Beat Salon" in May 1969 and attracting the attention of the two men who would become their joint managers, Pavel Kratochvil (former manager of the successful group Olympic) and Jirous, an art historian who had been involved with The Primitives Group, one of Prague's first "psychedelic" bands. (*Psychedelická* in this phase referred not to mind-altering drugs—in general, alcohol was the underground's intoxicant of choice—but rather to the skillful use of pyrotechnics and other scenic tricks during performances, something The Primitives Group had been famous for. The Plastics, however, would outdo them on this score.[18]) Jirous and Kratochvil represented two alter egos of the band's early history, one of them a path not taken. Kratochvil was an adept promoter who helped the band arrange a string of concerts, established their professional status under the official Prague Cultural Center (*Pražské kulturní středisko*, or PKS), and secured them expensive instruments and equipment as well as prime practice space in Kinský Palace on Prague's Old Town Square. Jirous, their "artistic director," was dead set against commercialization, which he saw as the spiritual and artistic death of any band. For all his stubbornness, he proved to be a more adept maneuverer than Kratochvil, and—given the band's eventual fame—ultimately a better promoter. He was also more in line with the band's desires. When Kratochvil scored a major media coup, arranging to get the band's color photograph on the cover of the popular magazine *Květy*, Jirous was furious. He saw *Květy* as "a collaborating magazine" and "the avant-garde of the so-called normalization process,"[19] and he cancelled the deal.

Similar frictions multiplied over the next year or so, as PKS tried to exert control over the rock scene. Czechoslovakia wasn't the only country to try to bring its scruffy rock bands in line, offering professional status and practice space in return for a few small concessions: wearing shorter hair, dressing nicely, and using Czech instead of English band names, for example. "You could not imagine a better barometer of the age," wrote Jirous; for him, these sorts of compromises were anathema, and he was convinced they would lead inexorably to ever more severe restrictions on music played, censorship of lyrics, and so on.[20] The members of the Plastics were of a similar mind-set; bolstered by Jirous, they refused to make such accommodations, and in 1970, the band broke its ties with the "official" world of Kratochvil and PKS. Their professional status was revoked, which had a number of repercussions: they had to return their expensive instruments and give up their practice space, and the members had to get jobs now that they were no longer professional musicians. Later in the year, Jiří Kabeš joined the band on violin and viola; the Canadian Paul Wilson also joined.

At this early stage in their careers, the Plastic People—again like many beginning bands, East and West—were still playing a lot of covers, particularly from the Velvet Underground, with a few of their own songs mixed in. (Lou Reed, after all, started out playing Chuck Berry covers.[21]) Some of the Plastic People's earliest songs, written by Michal Jernek, speak of "Velvet Valley," "velvety, underground pavilions," and a "velvet underground." As a teenager, Hlavsa was enchanted by the Velvets' famous "banana album" recorded with Nico while Andy Warhol was the band's producer; Hlavsa said he thought Warhol was the lead singer, and the band later gave Jirous the nickname *Varholec*. The Plastics' brilliant adaptation of the Velvet Underground is laced with ironies. The American band that spoke most openly about drug use—even calling a song "Heroin" was problematic in the America of the late 1960s—was picked up by the alcohol-based Prague music scene. Frank Zappa's Mothers of Invention, another inspiration for the early Plastics, was one of the Velvet Underground's archrivals.[22] By 1973, however, the band was shifting steadily toward a repertory of its own songs, sung in Czech. This in part reflected a natural maturation in which the musicians mastered different genres while developing a style of their own. It also reflected Paul Wilson's amicable departure from the band and the arrival of saxophonist Vratislav Brabenec. With a background in jazz, Brabenec began to push the band in new directions musically.[23] The turn to Czech lyrics was also shaped dramatically by Jirous's meeting with Egon Bondy.

Bondy, born in 1930, was a poet and philosopher who had been one of the pioneers of Czech "underground" literature *avant la lettre*, immediately after the Communist takeover of Czechoslovakia in 1948.[24] In the harsh conditions of the late 1940s and early 1950s, he had written subversive poetry in a style he called "total realism," mixing fragments of Communist discourse with scenes from everyday life. He reproduced it in just a few copies for a small circle of like-minded writers—some of the first Czech samizdat, also *avant la lettre*. In the 1950s, Bondy began to study philosophy—everything from Marx to Nietzsche to mysticism—and decided to finish high school and enroll in evening studies at the university, while supporting himself as a night watchman at the National Museum. He eventually would complete a PhD in philosophy, and in the 1960s he turned from poetry to philosophy, writing books on Buddhism as well as his major work, *The Consolation of Ontology*.

Bondy was skeptical of the Prague Spring, finding more inspiration in the New Left and the small group of Czech radicals like Petr Uhl, who placed themselves to the left of the Communists, in the vicinity of Trotsky and Mao. The 1970s found Bondy, like so many others, frozen out of the official world; having qualified for a disability pension, he ceased all official publishing and found himself back in a counterculture that he had never really left, and with a penumbra of legend already accumulating around his name—or, rather, names. "Egon Bondy" was really Zbyněk Fišer; he had first adopted his pseudonym for a 1949 samizdat poetry anthology called *Jewish Names*, for which all the contributors had taken Jewish-sounding pseudonyms—both a safety measure and a protest against official anti-Semitism.[25] Bondy held on to both his names—he published his philosophical works in the 1960s as Zbyněk Fišer—and eventually began to play on the alter ego he had developed. The title of one of his first poetic texts in the 1970s, *Diary of a Girl Who Is Looking for Egon Bondy*, gives an idea of the half-earnest, half-zany way in which he perpetuated his own legend. Jirous, who met Bondy in 1969 or 1970 at a psychiatric clinic (they shared a doctor), wrote: "I had known Bondy's work for quite a few years, but I had hardly been able to imagine a living person behind this legendary figure."[26]

Jirous and Bondy hit it off immediately. Bondy lent his apartment on Nerudova Street, just below Prague Castle, to the Plastics when they had no place to practice. Above all, the meeting of minds between Bondy and Milan Hlavsa would lead to a string of remarkable Plastic People songs that set Bondy's poems to music. Eventually, the Plastics would record a whole album of "Bondyovky" with the English title *Egon Bondy's Happy Hearts Club Banned*; many of their later songs were adapted from Bondy as well.

Every successful rock band has a shorter or longer period that seems to define its character and its success, when the personalities and musical styles of band members click. For the Plastic People, this period was roughly 1973 to 1976, when the band's lineup was Milan Hlavsa on bass, Jiří Števich on guitar, Vratislav Brabenec on saxophone, and Jiří Kabeš on viola and violin, with considerable intellectual inspiration from Jirous and, via his poems and presence, Bondy. Characterizing the band's legality in this period is not an entirely straightforward task. Until 1975 or so, the Plastics were neither official nor unofficial, nor even semi-official, but semi-unofficial—neither fully tolerated nor systematically harassed by the police, a status that gave their performances an undeniable frisson and intensified the audience's feelings of freedom and solidarity. Nevertheless, they played freely and openly in clubs in Prague and, increasingly, in smaller cities and towns. These concerts were legal and registered with the authorities; sometimes, they were even sponsored by government organizations such as the Socialist Youth League, which had somewhat more room to maneuver in smaller towns and venues. (For a long time, it is true, police threatened to hit Jirous with the charge of running an illegal business; this line of attack was eventually dropped, however, when he was picked up on other charges.)

At the same time, however, it was clear that the band was becoming one of the focal points for a larger grouping of nonconformists, many of them artists and musicians, but many of them also just working-class youth who enjoyed the solidarity and liberating atmosphere of the Plastics' concerts. (As in other spheres of Czech society under Communism, the designation "working-class" is not entirely meaningful; some undergrounders were young people who had been kicked out of high school or university, while others had never wanted to apply, or never bothered to.) These were the people who grew into the "underground"—in addition to the Czech *podzemí*, the English loan word was also used, and "undergrounders" were sometimes called *androši*. Even if the exact borders and numbers of the underground were, and still are, difficult to define—the largest Plastics concerts may have had a few hundred people in the audience—it was becoming more and more identifiable.[27]

It is probably worth recalling here the crucial function of long hair in this context as a clear marker of difference between "us" and "them," one of the semiotic indicators of belonging to an (or "the") underground subculture. As in other countries, long hair was a serious issue in the sixties and seventies. It was often the flash point of struggles at home between parents and children, as well as between young people and the police. For both the secret and regular police, *vlasatec* ("long-hair") was a *terminus technicus* used even in formal police reports; young men were often chosen for harassment or even arrest on this basis alone. Long hair clearly marked young people as nonconformist; perhaps more important, it also marked them as wanting to mark their own rebelliousness. It could also make it more difficult to find work, not a trivial problem in the 1970s when the alternative could be a charge of "parasitism." Conversely, getting one's hair cut short, after having worn it long, was a symbolic defeat and hence was fraught with emotions for many people. "Hair in general," said Hlavsa, "was a problem back then."[28]

In the early years, run-ins with the police were not inevitable at Plastic People concerts, but they were not uncommon, especially when some ornery policeman was looking for a fight. By 1974, these kinds of clashes were becoming more routine. Indeed, the increasing police harassment of the audiences at Plastic People concerts was both a sign of the underground's growing cachet and a catalyst of the very solidarity and self-definition the state was trying to suppress. A turning point in the relationship between the band, the underground, and the regime was the so-called "České Budějovice massacre" on March 30, 1974. At a concert in Rudolfov, just outside of České Budějovice, police with dogs appeared before the Plastic People began to play and directed the audience to leave. Police herded people outside, often using force, and drove them through an underpass toward the train station, where trains were waiting to cart them back to Prague. Inside the underpass, many people were beaten, some bloodily; dozens were arrested and many young people were subsequently kicked out of school or otherwise sanctioned. Several people were eventually put on trial and convicted.[29]

The recent examination of police archives by Pavel Ptáčník suggests that the police action itself was not necessarily meant as a policy signal. Jirous's account of the subsequent trial makes it clear that local officials were genuinely surprised by the size of the crowd, and by the fact that people had come to the concert from far away; officials chose a hard-line response without a great deal of forethought.[30] The band itself was not arrested. Nevertheless, České Budějovice became a milestone on both sides. As Jirous wrote, "the regime had thrown down the gauntlet" and there was to be no more accommodation with the government.[31] Over the next few years, the Plastic People and other underground bands would play under increasingly difficult conditions, with an ever more visible police presence at their concerts.

As repressive measures increased, however, so did the underground's self-confidence. On September 1, 1974, a celebration of a wedding in Postupice doubled as a large-scale underground concert, with performances by the Plastics, DG 307, and others. This was also the first time Karásek played at a concert of the underground—shortly before, two people had come to him ("only much later did I find out that their milieu was called the underground") and invited him to perform. He would soon become a familiar face at concerts.[32] The Postupice wedding was called "The First Festival of the Second Culture"; the name clearly marked the underground's consciousness of setting up a world apart from the official structures of the regime. Perhaps the high-water mark, and in some ways swan song, of the underground came on February 21, 1976, at the Second Festival of the Second Culture in Bojanovice. This large celebration, with performances by some dozen bands (even Bondy sang), seemed to go smoothly. The absence of police was, by this time, conspicuous, but it was also simply a calm before the storm. The police raids beginning on

March 17, 1976, were far more than an attack on the Plastic People. Indeed, this "campaign against the underground" was a long-prepared and well-thought-out attempt to stifle the activities of a specific group of nonconformist youth. It was also a qualitatively new kind of intervention. The "classic" phase of the underground ended with the March–April raids, at which point the state's *modus operandi* shifted from harassing concert audiences to arrests and imprisonment of musicians and organizers.

Invalid Siblings and the Third Czech Musical Revival

This brief narrative overview of the Plastic People and the underground has yet to clearly define the impulses and motives that shaped the underground's identity. One of the puzzles of the underground is the way it coalesced, from 1972 to 1976, in a kind of dialectic of external police harassment and internal self-articulation. Much of this self-articulation took place in the music of the Plastics, DG 307, and other bands, but it was also shaped decisively—given a context and a story—by two of the most important texts of Czech culture in the 1970s.

On November 2 and 3, 1974, Bondy read his new novel, *Invalidní sourozenci*, to a spellbound crowd at a pub in Klukovice on the outskirts of Prague. *Invalid Siblings*—the title will take a bit of explanation—is a bizarre but good-natured postapocalyptic romp, one of the great cult novels of the 1970s. The action takes place centuries in the future, when a cataclysm has submerged most of the earth in water, leaving only a large island that is home to two (Czech-speaking) cities, the Federation and the Allies. The inhabitants of this island live comfortable lives devoted primarily to oblivious consumerism; their governments periodically lob nuclear weapons at each other, at which point everyone scurries into underground shelters until the all-clear is sounded, a new period of détente begins, and they can return to the surface to resume their mindlessly materialist lifestyles.

Bondy's novel articulated a recognizable critique of Czechoslovak society in the 1970s, one we have already encountered in slightly different form in later texts like Havel's open letter to President Husák or Milan Šimečka's *The Restoration of Order*. Even more striking about *Invalid Siblings*, however, was Bondy's characterization of the small group of *invalidní důchodci*. In normal discourse, this term would refer to people who had retired early because of an accident or disability, and were now living on a disability pension. In Bondy's novel, the *invalidní důchodci* are a group of nonconformists who scorn the materialistic pursuits of the cities and live their own lives in the countryside, often as vagabonds and squatters. They have been granted a disability pension by the government, which sees this as the easiest way to get them out of its hair. Although they are not simply idealized in the novel—a few are annoying and unpleasant—they tend to be lovable, scruffy, creative, generous, and alive to the charms of solidarity. The novel's protagonists, A and B, are half siblings (which doesn't stop them from sleeping together); the word "siblings" in the title, however, also referred more generally to the underground community with its atmosphere (and ideology) of family-like familiarity. They appreciate the good things in life, like a concert, an exhibition of "invalid" art, or an afternoon at the pub with their friends. They tend to stay on the margins and out of trouble, but they are also periodically beaten up by the police, known as the *postiženci* (handicapped or afflicted—many of them do have various physical disabilities).

Bondy's reading of his novel took place after České Budějovice, but it still reflects a kinder, gentler phase of underground–state relations, in which Bondy gave free rein to his weirdly warmhearted sense of humor, without the bitter desperation that inflects much of his poetry from the same period. The whole idea of a disability pension for undergrounders is part fantasy, part reflection of the fact that many in the underground did work at various menial and dead-end jobs simply as a way of freeing up maximum time and energy for concerts, happenings, and other creative pursuits; some, indeed, had a disability pension, like Bondy himself. The Keystone Cops "disabled" police are more comical than anything else—a nuisance, but also a joke—although the silent, stalking war machines of the two cities are genuinely chilling, and the novel does have its dark side. Nuclear war was never far from Bondy's mind in the 1970s; many of his works, particularly *Leden na vsi* (January in the Village, 1977) and *Afghanistán* (Afghanistan, 1980), contain stunning visions of apocalypses and postapocalyptic societies, and *Invalid Siblings* likewise ends when the Federation and the Allies have one war too many and wipe themselves out, rather to the invalids' bemusement. But the novel has a hopeful ending in which the protagonists A and B have a child, harbinger of a new society.

Bondy's reading of his novel entered immediately into underground folk-lore. Underground culture, especially in its early phases, displayed a marked preference for oral rather than written culture. Its primary forms of communication were music, word of mouth, and direct contact at concerts; it did not develop its own samizdat editions until later in the 1970s—the magazine *Vokno* (Window), for example, which began in 1979. It is fitting, then, that one of the underground's defining texts was presented at a public reading, which itself became an underground legend. *Invalid Siblings* gave a name and a story to the identifiable phenomenon of a growing underground culture. In a way, the novel was about the reading of the novel; listeners marveled as they realized that they were attending just the sort of gathering of "invalids" that the novel described. Pavel Zajíček of DG 307 was at the reading and wrote:

> invalid siblings—e.b.—2 evenings in K[lukovice].—me drunk and mejla too
> e.b.: "it doesn't matter that you're drunk, the main thing is that YOU'RE
>   HERE. after all it's a wonderful gathering of invalids . . ."
> inv. sib.: it is a dream—it's about us—it's a fairy tale—we are in it[33]

Zajíček was not alone in thinking "it's about us." With flair, self-irony, and good humor, the novel had bestowed an identity on this alternative community. One of its most amusing turns was the role given to Bondy and the Plastics themselves. Although the protagonist B was clearly a Bondy alter ego, the novel is set in a distant future when Egon Bondy himself has become national poet; the "invalids" celebrate his birthday and recite his poetry at national holidays. A and B also find a magic boat that takes them to a heavenly world, where they witness a concert of "six wild men" playing a song that at first seems similar to "the roar of mammoths in heat," until an incredible melody emerges that, "like a psalm, united the musicians and their listeners into a single body." "This," says B., "is how I always imagined the Plastics must have played at Egon Bondy's funeral!"[34]

Bondy's novel, in other words, not only provided the underground with a myth about itself; in another self-reflexive turn, this novel about an underground, centered around a mythical poet named Bondy, was read in a performance that cemented the "real" myth of Bondy as a constitutive figure of underground culture. Bondy's own self-legendarization was an encouragement to the rest of the underground to do the same. What's more, it articulated the desire of the "invalids" to step outside of society, and it managed to do so without being shrill or self-important. With his strangely light touch, Bondy had captured a tone of easy opposition that Charter 77, and Czech dissent more generally, would never really manage to perfect.[35] In fact, it is useful to compare Bondy's texts of the early 1970s with Havel's letter to Husák—both made a similar critique of normalized Czechoslovakia as a consumerist society that had sacrificed higher aspirations, whether political, artistic, or spiritual, to the pursuit of an uncomplicated life. Havel's letter, circulating in samizdat, rocked many circles with the force of revelation. For the underground, however, it was a familiar complaint. (Which text was more influential among Czech readers is a still an open question, and a good one.)

Perhaps the only real weakness in Bondy's characterization was that his labels—"invalids," "retired people"—did not really catch on, perhaps for obvious reasons. It took a short, programmatic, and combative text by Ivan Jirous to do that, a manifesto called "Report on the Third Czech Musical Revival," written between prison terms in February 1975. Jirous's "Report" has also become legendary, and rightly so—not only for its rhetorical mastery, but also because it was just the right text at just the right time, written by just the right person: an account of the underground, captured at the peak of its arc, when it had fully coalesced as a conscious movement but was already starting to undergo the systematic police persecution that would eventually force it into entirely new, and unrecognizable, forms. Jirous's text circulated in samizdat, but according to Hlavsa, it also percolated through the oral culture of the underground, as Jirous "began to devote himself to spreading the word. He gave lectures in various cities, read from the 'Report' and played our recordings. He had a lot of success."[36]

Jirous begins with an account of a December concert in Líšnice, near Prague. He depicts undergrounders walking together from the train station to the concert "across a half-frozen marshy meadow," and compares them to the fifteenth-century Hussites going off into the countryside to hear the word of God preached in Czech instead of Latin, outside the official churches. It is an effective image, imbued with winter nostalgia, simultaneously forlorn and appealing, idyllic and frustrated. Jirous was alive to the romance of small groups held together by music and the spoken word; the comparison to the Hussites works on many levels, evoking a ceremonial self-separation from society in the name of moral purity, as well as the notion of "preaching in the vernacular," of producing art in a form that people can understand. One of the most important words in Jirous's manifesto is the verb *oslovovat* ("to address, speak to, connect with")—emphasizing neither the artist nor the listener but that mystical space of communion in between the two.[37]

Jirous's "Report" goes on to describe the underground and articulate its goals, motivations, and hatred of the "establishment." It gives a mini-history of the Plastic People, DG 307, and other bands, with accounts of particular concerts that were already becoming legendary (in part thanks to this very text). Jirous is careful to define the underground not as a particular style of rock music but as a *duchovní postoj* (spiritual stance). This stance is defined largely as a desire to step outside of a corrupt society, in order to seek authentic values within a small group of like-minded people. Jirous uses the term *druhá kultura* (second culture) to talk about underground writing, music, and performance. In his final section, he suggests that "the underground is an activity of artists and intellectuals whose work is unacceptable for the establishment, and who are not patient and passive in this unacceptability, but who try with their work and their stance to destroy the establishment." In the West, the underground faces a constant threat of being "swallowed"—co-opted or bought off—by the "first" or "official" culture of the establishment. In Czechoslovakia, however, the first culture rejects the underground entirely: "Nothing that we do can please the carriers of official culture, because it is useless for creating the impression that everything is in order." Therefore, Jirous continues:

> In the West, the goal of the underground is directly to destroy the establishment. The goal of the underground here is to create a second culture. A culture that will be completely independent of the official communication channels, societal recognition, and the hierarchy of values that are controlled by the establishment. A culture that cannot have as its goal the destruction of the establishment, because it would thereby drive itself into its embrace.[38]

There is a productive tension here—one wants both to destroy the establishment and to ignore it—which became one of the formative contradictions for the whole underground experience. It is contained in the two values that Jirous highlights in the same concluding section of his essay: *zběsilost* (madness or rage) and *pokora* (humility): "Anyone lacking these qualities will not be able to stand living in the underground."[39]

Underground Primitivism and Self-Mythologization

Bondy's and Jirous's characterizations clarify the impulses underlying an "underground" identity: a complex mixture of anger, humility, disgust, scorn for establishment materialism, and the desire to escape from a corrupt system. These impulses would all become important as the underground encountered the intellectual opposition I looked at in the last chapter. In his accounts of the Plastic People from 1976 on, Havel would draw on these impulses to paint the band as pre-political—young people who only wanted to play the music they liked, had "no political past" of their own, and were not interested in political debates. The question of the supposedly apolitical nature of the underground, however, is far more complicated. We can understand it better by considering two more constituent elements of underground culture.

Separating oneself from the standards of a corrupt society also means overturning aesthetic canons—these are just another way of smuggling in the values of the establishment. Jirous therefore emphasizes that *everyone* has the ability "to express himself through an unrepeatable, individual act of creativity." Quoting the nineteenth-century French proto-surrealist Lautréamont, who said, "One day, everyone will make art," Jirous agrees that even the untutored or uneducated can be artists. In fact, he sees "openness and lack of suspicion" toward all sorts of creativity as a defining mark of the underground. Rather than "technical perfection," it prefers "authenticity and honesty of expression."[40]

The rejection of technical skill belongs to a set of underground values that we might call "primitivism"—that is, a conscious rejection of refined, polished, or civilized art in favor of the raw authenticity that comes from untutored performance.[41] Jirous quotes one band as saying: "Tuning up is a luxury of bourgeois music." Primitivism, of course, is a long-established tendency in art and art history, perhaps most associated with things like Picasso's love of African masks or the disarmingly direct paintings of Henri Rousseau. It has often been associated with racial and racist stereotypes, for example of "native art." In the underground, primitivism was occasionally expressed in ethnic categories, but it was far more commonly tied to madness, lack of artistic training, or Dionysian states of intoxication—all three of which were then tied to a notion of "authenticity," a rather ill-defined value but something that everyone (thought they) knew when they saw it.[42]

There is thus a tension in underground culture between the idea that underground musicians were good artists and the idea that it didn't matter. Jirous calls the Plastics' music "a polished artistic form,"[43] but he is not above the occasional primitivist anecdote—one of the most memorable is a story of how Brabenec was expected to play at a concert but had drunk himself into a stupor. He was hoisted on stage and Jirous stuck a saxophone in his hands, whereupon he played brilliantly: "You could clearly see that he was drunk through and through, that the music was emerging, independently of his condition, directly from the inside."[44] Stories of madness were also common currency in the underground—the primal one being Jirous's meeting with Bondy in a *blázinec* (madhouse). The band name DG 307 means "Diagnosis 307"; according to Jirous, the band members thought this was the diagnosis for schizophrenia, although in fact it refers to a range of post-traumatic and stress disorders—all the better. Even the brainy and occasionally pedantic Jirous was known almost universally as "Magor"—madman or nutcase.

Underground primitivism took many forms. Martin Machovec discusses a number of *insitní* or indigenous poets who were, or portrayed themselves as, various kinds of idiot savant, holy fool, or *lidový vypravěč* (storyteller of the people)—poets such as Milan Koch or Fanda Pánek, who wrote singsong verses of both real and deceptive simplicity. Jirous's poetic masterpiece from the 1980s, *Magor's Swan Songs*, plays consciously with an exaggerated simplicity of rhyme and expression ("This constant stress I'm living in, / Lord— what keeps me from giving in?"). Primitivism was also tied to the prestige of oral culture in underground circles, which persisted even as underground samizdat gained strength in the late 1970s. Jirous "wrote" his *Swan Songs* in prison, composing the collection in his memory, since prisoners were allowed to write just one letter home every three weeks; a transcription of the poems was smuggled out, at great personal risk, by his fellow prisoner Jiří Gruntorád. The poems circulated spontaneously in samizdat, in various configurations; the whole collection was first published abroad, after Jirous's release.[45] The underground poem was closely associated with the nursery rhyme and the folk song; conversely, the Plastic People would put many written poems to song, such as the work of Bondy or the poet Ivan Wernisch, himself a master of primitivism.[46]

Primitivism also explains why many underground writers and musicians cultivated an image of exaggerated simplicity or working-class salt-of-the-earthiness. Bondy had a PhD in philosophy, and another cult underground writer, Bohumil Hrabal, had a law degree and was widely read in nineteenth-century German philosophy, but both at times cultivated the image of an "earthy" or working-class man of the people who was not afraid of vulgarity or vulgarisms. Bondy wrote many poems, some of them genuinely disgusting, about various bodily functions. Some of this "primitive" art was an aesthetically sophisticated simulation; some of it was "genuine"; but part of the point is that this distinction is difficult to make in an environment that attributes aesthetic value to the rejection of established norms (whether these norms be social, moral, or aesthetic). The tension between "rage" and "humility" appears again here, the artist in his Dionysian trance expressing both emotions at once.

All such primitive art was tied closely to ideas of "authenticity," "genuineness," and "truthfulness," probably the supreme values in this phase of underground culture. These terms may require some discussion, if only to clarify that they had no particular philosophical grounding. "Authenticity" is itself a problematic term, often a self-serving one, and notoriously difficult to define with any philosophical rigor; in its underground usage, it remained a largely intuitive conception. It did not involve any reference, say, to existentialism or Heideggerian philosophy. Nor was it, essentially, a political idea; although one would be hard put to find "authentic Communists" in underground discourse, this was because Communism was associated with an even more nefarious force, the "establishment." Communist or capitalist, the whole world of official art and culture was seen as having sold out to the "establishment," with its conventional aesthetics, its petit bourgeois fear of sex and dirty words, and its rampant consumerism. The only way to deal with it was total rejection. Jirous was fond of referring to the title of one of Karásek's spirituals, "Say No to the Devil": "As soon as the devil (who today speaks through the mouth of the establishment) places his first condition—cut your hair, just a little bit, and you'll be able to play—it's necessary to say no. [. . .] The establishment can only put the screws on someone who wants to be better off than others. Its talons are too short to reach someone who wants to live better—not in the sense of material security, but in the sense of searching for and following the truth."[47]

Alongside primitivism, a second key feature of underground culture was its tendency to generate legends and myths about itself. In an insightful meditation, Martin Putna offers a "topography" of underground culture in which he discusses the underground concert as a kind of *Gesamtkunstwerk*, an overwhelming experience that has to be perceived directly or participated in—you have to be there: "Seeing, hearing, and experiencing Sváťa Karásek as, surrounded by cops, he plays 'In Heaven There's a Throne in a Stable'—that's not the same thing as seeing and hearing Sváťa Karásek play the same song under 'normal,' unmarked conditions, and that's not the same as hearing a recording of Sváťa Karásek, and nothing at all like reading the lyrics of a Sváťa Karásek song."[48] One can also think here of Egon Bondy's two-day reading of *Invalid Siblings*, which clearly made a greater impression than the sum total of private readings of the novel could ever have supplied. This emphasis on "being there" ties into what Putna calls "self-mythologization." Putna here speaks of "underground writing," but the phenomenon he describes actually points to the importance of oral culture in the underground's formative phase:

> Every report on an arrest, release, or emigration is a historical event that is the subject of intensive communication and that has to be recorded as well [. . .]. Historical events soon change [. . .] into legends and can even become founding myths. The founding myth of the whole underground in Bohemia is, of course, the story of the Plastic People, their trial and the rise of the Charter, but other myths are added on [. . .]. In the underground method of writing, then, current information, communication, and creation *sensu stricto* all mix together.[49]

Putna's excellent point can be expanded further. Inside the underground, legends function as a kind of surrogate participation—they heighten the sense of being present at something you didn't actually experience—but they also function as a means of communication with the fringes of the underground and with the outside world as well. An underground exists both as an identifiable, potentially "numerable" group of people, held together by their own stories, and as a set of rumors, myths, and legends that "spill over" from their immediate carriers into an indeterminate space surrounding them. That is, underground legends are not merely a form of *internal* communication or an epiphenomenon generated by close contact and heightened solidarity under persecution; they are also a primary way such groupings interact with the surrounding world, reaching out to prospective members and simultaneously, by a closely monitored feedback function, confirming the group's own identity. Legends are a form of public text that make an underground seem both open to new members and closed in around an identifiable set of gestures and ideologies. Without its legends, the underground would be little more than a sect; with them, it is a sect that, potentially, everyone can join. Legends are thus crucial to the way in which the underground portrays itself as simultaneously welcoming and close-knit.

These legends encountered a number of crucial readers outside the underground. One was the police, who were just as interested in delineating underground culture, and identifying its main protagonists, as Jirous was. The police, and the state more generally, were not only major consumers of underground legends, but also helped generate them by spreading rumors of their own. In 1976, for example, Czechoslovak television broadcast a "documentary" called *Attack on Culture*, portraying the underground musicians as dissolute and antisocial drug addicts, and spreading remarkable stories—naked orgies, animal sacrifice, using dead rats instead of drumsticks. Such stories function as myths even for listeners who know they are false. When *Rudé právo* wrote that the underground bands had "organized fraudulent public performances that degenerated into orgies,"[50] this could become a kind of humorous counterdefinition, a sign that the underground was pushing the establishment's buttons.

Of course, such uncomprehending reactions on the part of the establishment went hand in hand with police surveillance and harassment. But rather than imagining a clear and consistent police surveillance of a well-defined and clearly articulated group, we should conceive of a dialectic of mutual self-definition, often marked by chance and error, in which police and members of the underground responded to each other's actions and provoked each other to a clearer recognition of their own sense of mission. In August 1974, the secret police had intercepted a personal letter and learned about the upcoming "First Festival of the Second Culture" in Benešov. They suspected the concert would be used for "enemy provocations." This same report, however, does not seem fully informed—for example, it refers to "Miroslav" (instead of Milan) Hlavsa and Egon "Boudy," without even realizing that they are connected with the Plastic People. In the end, the local secret police in Benešov allowed the wedding and concert to take place, contenting itself with checking people's identifications and making a list of participants; it reported that no disturbances or dangerous activities had taken place. Only after the concert did state security begin to compare the attendance list with names from the disturbances in Česke Budějovice, and start to put together a clearer sense of a specific underground community. And only in October 1974 did a police report speak of "examining the character of this group with the goal of verifying whether it is an organized grouping of persons carrying out hostile activity against the ČSSR."[51]

These considerations suggest some of the limitations of a sociological approach to the underground. As with samizdat, where we can never really track down the exact circulation of particular typed texts, we must read the underground legends without, ultimately, having a clear sense of their spread or reception; nevertheless, we must also remember that imagined circulations were just as important as real ones. The legends about Bondy, Jirous, and the Plastic People were both *descriptive* of an underground environment and *constitutive* of a cultural identity. We can be sure, however, that for at least some readers, the image these legends projected was as important as any real activities "on the ground" (or under it). And even more important than this reality could be the reception and creation of these legends by various groups of readers—in some cases by the police, in others by one reader alone.

Havel Reads the Underground

The regime was not expecting the sudden response that its arrest of nineteen members of the underground provoked. On April 9, a protest letter was sent to President Husák by Jan Patočka and four other writers, Josef Hiršal, Jiří Kolář, Jindřich Chalupecký, and Zdeněk Urbánek. Two months later, on June 12, five more writers—Václav Černý, Václav Havel, Ivan Klíma, Pavel Kohout, and Ludvík Vaculík—signed a proclamation linking their own fate to the underground's. "If young people with long hair are going to be condemned for their unconventional music as criminal delinquents today, without awakening wider notice, then it will be all the easier tomorrow to condemn any other artists for their novels, poems, essays, and pictures—and then it won't even be necessary for them to have long hair as a photogenic decoration for the criminal charge." This protest mentions "The plastic People" and DG 307, but seems under the misconception that all the arrested people were musicians. After the July trial in Plzeň of Havelka, Skalický, and Stárek—who were not musicians, but had organized a concert—there was a better sense of what was going on. The same group of five writers, joined now by Patočka, philosopher Karel Kosík, and poet Jaroslav Seifert, sent an open letter to German writer and Nobel Prize winner Heinrich Böll two months later, on August 16, 1976. This letter does not mention the Plastic People, but speaks of the remaining defendants as "fourteen young people [who] will stand before a court not for their political opinions, activity or ambitions, but—if it can be so described— simply for their relationship with the world."[52]

A moving force behind these protests was Václav Havel, and the August letter already bears strong traces of the interpretation of the trial he would develop over the next few years. Havel's interpretation and, indeed, deployment of the underground was courageous, compassionate, strategically brilliant, and highly problematic. Havel was not the first writer to enter the fray on the side of the underground, but he was the most deeply engaged, and his decision was a daring one. The underground was a world apart from Havel's circles, which were shaped more by his role in the cultural elite of the 1960s. It was more working-class, highly creative but often without formal education, and often anti-intellectual. It had few points, or people, in common with the groups of writers, philosophers, actors, artists, and intellectuals around whom the whole idea of dissent was coalescing in the mid-1970s.[53] It was Havel and his wife Olga, however, who were able to use their many friendships, charisma, and growing authority to mobilize support for the underground.[54] This was not an obvious decision to make; Havel had to trade in some of the moral capital he had just acquired with his open letter to President Husák, in order to help a group of people who often seemed to spit in the face of public taste.

Havel, in turn, had come to the underground primarily through a meeting with Ivan Jirous. When they met in March 1976, the two hardly knew each other. In the mid-1980s, Havel nicely recreated his initial, somewhat "square" and naïve understanding of Jirous and the Plastics:

> Occasionally I would hear wild and, as I discovered later, quite distorted stories about the group of people that had gathered around him, which he called the underground, and about the Plastic People of the Universe, a nonconformist rock group that was at the center of this society; Jirous was their artistic director. I understood [. . .] that Jirous' opinion of me was not exactly flattering either: he apparently saw me as a member of the official, and officially tolerated, opposition—in other words, a member of the establishment.[55]

Jirous, writing in 1980–1981, described their meeting as follows: "I interrupted his introduction. 'We actually know each other, we met at the opening of Vyleťal's exhibit. That was when I explained to you that you were basically a paid agent of the regime.'"[56] Despite the rocky start, the two hit it off. Jirous played scratchy tape recordings of underground music and gave Havel a copy of his "Report"; then they went to a pub and stayed out until five in the morning, talking nonstop.[57] Two of the most charismatic figures of Czech culture had discovered each other, and their intense, all-night conversation—the kind many of us have only a few times in our lives—would rechart Czech culture and the fortunes of European Communism. Just a week or so later, Jirous was arrested along with many of the musicians he had played for Havel. Havel, that is, was fresh off his meeting with Jirous and barely knew him, or anyone else from the underground, when the police raids put nineteen of them in jail. His decision to drum up support for them, then, was a leap of faith, and an expression of genuine and farsighted tolerance and respect.

The initial shows of support for the arrested musicians give the impression of intellectuals rallying around a youth culture and an "entire younger generation" that they don't entirely understand. In the August letter sent to Heinrich Böll, the eight signatories (three of whom, Černý, Kosík, and Patočka, included their academic titles after their names) framed themselves as speaking for people who couldn't speak for themselves. They focused on two main arguments. The first was that, if the state could persecute these harmless private citizens (this time they did not mention the defendants' long hair), then it could persecute anyone. The second was that the signatories felt this injustice "with particular intensity, because we cannot rid ourselves of the impression that these people are being treated so harshly partly for us—this is, just because they are less able than we to look for solidarity to their colleagues abroad. [. . .] [W]e refuse to accept the status of some sort of prominent 'protected species' and silently to accept the fact that others, less 'protected,' can be tried like criminals without the cultural world taking notice."[58] This was magnanimous, and there was some truth to it, but it also reflected an unnecessary internalization of Jirous's critique that Havel and his colleagues were just part of the establishment. After all, several of the eight signatories had suffered quite a bit in the 1970s, often without awakening much sympathy abroad. One can almost sense that, by protesting against their role as a protected species, the eight future "dissidents" were beginning to define this role and even to assume it.

Havel, however, was eventually able to formulate a more persuasive defense of the musicians that framed the protest in more universal terms. The experience of actually listening to the Plastic People clearly made a big impression on him, and he was the first person who was really able to articulate this experience in a way that spoke to a larger community of opposition intellectuals. Nevertheless, he understood the Plastics in his own way; their "translation" into a more philosophical idiom came at a price:

> Although I'm no expert on rock music, I immediately felt that there was something rather special radiating from these performances, that they were not just deliberately oddball or dilettantish attempts to be outlandish at any price, as what I had heard about them before might have suggested; the music was a profoundly authentic expression of the sense of life among these people, battered as they were by the misery of this world. There was disturbing magic in the music, and a kind of inner warning. [. . .] Suddenly I realized that, regardless of how many vulgar words these people used or how long their hair was, truth was on their side. Somewhere in the midst of this group, their attitudes, and their creations, I sensed a special purity, a

shame, and a vulnerability; in their music was an experience of metaphysical sorrow and a longing for salvation.[59]

One of the striking things about this account—Havel wrote this in the mid-1980s, when he had fully worked out his interpretation of the trial and the Plastic People's role in the formation of Charter 77—is how it translates Jirous's combative claims about the underground into a more anodyne and accessible language of metaphysical desperation. Above all, it picks up the "primitivist" ethos articulated by Jirous, but translates it into a philosophical vocabulary that could be more understandable and palatable to the circles of writers, journalists, political thinkers, and philosophers who were gradually coalescing into a full-scale "dissident" movement. The drunk saxophone virtuosos and naïve poets of the underground had now become bearers of "metaphysical sorrow" (no matter how obscene their lyrics might be); the values of "genuineness" and "authenticity," which had remained largely untheorized in the underground and were seen simply as a refusal to negotiate with the establishment, were now being translated into Havel's language of existentialist angst (and in the process acquired an air of philosophical sophistication that they probably didn't deserve). But we can still hear rage and humility in the undertones of Havel's description.

Here is where we must approach Havel's account more skeptically. In order to frame the Plastic People and the underground in this way, Havel saw them as members of an innocent youth culture—uncompromised, uninterested in the corrupt world of "politics," and in a real sense inarticulate. They were able to write songs with an "inner warning," but not able to articulate a systematic critique of the society they lived in. In his brilliant essay "The Trial," written shortly after the September trial at which all four defendants were convicted, Havel wrote:

> What did Ivan Jirous and his friends in the dock wish to be? Certainly not heroes who, like Dimitrov, would rise from the dock to become prosecutors and condemn the world that was trying to condemn them. I doubt they had any other aim in mind than persuading the court of their innocence and defending their right to compose and sing the songs they wanted.[60]

This account emphasized an imposing purity, but also homogenized the diverse phenomena of underground culture into that simple, innocent desire to "live in their own way."

Havel's accounts of the trial would ultimately elide many important tensions. Age, for one thing—Jirous was thirty-one when arrested, Brabenec and Karásek both thirty-three. Havel himself was just thirty-nine, going on forty, when the trial took place. Referring to the "trial of the Plastic People" helped reinforce the image of young rockers, eliding over the inconvenient fact that three-quarters of the defendants were over thirty. Religion also drops out of Havel's account, although Brabenec, Jirous, and Karásek were all devout, and their spirituality informs their writings and their work. Karásek, in fact, was a Protestant minister who had been labeled undesirable and denied permission to preach by the government—hardly the position of a political innocent. Havel's portrait of metaphysical anguish is a convenient, and secularized, simplification.

The "metaphysical reading" of the underground also reinforced a number of larger theses that Havel was developing, over the course of the 1970s, about an authentic, existential truth that exists before and beyond politics. Havel repeatedly formulated the idea that the "young" musicians "had no political past, or even any well-defined political positions. They were simply young people who wanted to live in their own way, to make music they liked, to sing what they wanted to sing, to live in harmony with themselves, and to express themselves in a truthful way."[61] Their protest was a cry of despair directed against a corrupt society, not a move in a political game. But here, too, the reality is more complicated. It is true that the Plastic People were not a political band in the sense, say, that they didn't sing overt "protest songs." But some of Karásek's spirituals, like "Say No to the Devil" or "There's a Throne in Heaven," come close, and another folksinger who had been arrested and almost came to trial, Karel "Charlie" Soukup, sang satires that explicitly mocked Communist ideology and language, even as they were tied into a larger, recognizably "underground" critique of mindless consumers who have no sense of the transcendental.[62] Speaking of the "trial of the Plastic People" is a convenient way of leaving Karásek and Soukup out of the picture, and provides a false picture of underground music with much of its social commentary and oppositional edge blunted. But even the Plastic People flirt with politics in their lyrics, especially in the songs they adopted from Bondy— songs like "Tractors" or the lyric "Mír mír mír / jako hajzlpapír" (Peace peace peace / like toilet paper), for example, satirize the language of Communist propaganda. In fact, Havel's "apolitical" reading of the Plastic People conveniently pushes Bondy out of the picture as well, although he had a long and complicated political past of his own.

These simplifications begin to make clear why the phrase "trial of the Plastic People" caught on. The Plastic People were a useful metonymy for the

underground as a whole, but above all they were a useful label for a particular *vision* of the underground—Havel's vision of pre-political, metaphysical
distress—even as the actual defendants at the trial represented a much more
diverse and complex cross section of oppositional thought. It's as if the mystical tag "of the Universe," added to the band's name way back in 1969 (when
it was still officially sanctioned and even pampered) now became a marker of
the depth of their anguish. (It's a useful thought experiment to ask whether
Charter 77 would have emerged from the trial of the New Elektric Potatoes
or the Lumberjacks.) For that matter, what happens if we call Brabenec not
a "young person who just wanted to make music," but, say, an "accomplished
jazz saxophonist" or a "respected jazz musician"? What if we called Jirous "an
antiestablishment art historian who had lost his job when the normalization
government shut down the journal he wrote for," or Karásek "a Protestant
minister who had been denied permission to preach for political reasons, and
whose folk songs were clever reworkings of American spirituals"? The one
defendant who best seemed to fit Havel's descriptions was Pavel Zajíček, the
talented twenty-five-year-old poet whose lyrics did echo the sorts of angst and
desperation Havel wrote about—but he belonged to another band. All of this
is strategically elided in the "trial of the Plastic People," which is, of course,
precisely why the phrase caught on.

But why did Havel frame the Plastic People this way in the first place?
How did the secularized and depoliticized version of the underground help
draw together such a wide grouping of people and launch the discussions that
led to Charter 77?

From Trial to Charter

The organized support of the underground scored some minor successes.
Nineteen people had been arrested in the spring, and three were put on
trial in July. The letter to Böll, dated August 16, spoke of a trial of fourteen people that would begin on August 30. But ten of them were released,
and the three sentences from July were all reduced at an appeals hearing on
September 3. That left the trial of Jirous, Karásek, Zajíček, and Brabenec on
September 21–23, 1976. And although all four were convicted, and not to
trivial sentences—Jirous got eighteen months, Zajíček twelve, and Karásek
and Brabenec eight—their punishments were not as harsh as the prosecutor
demanded.[63] It seemed natural to continue efforts that been so successful, and

over the next few months, as the undergrounders served their sentences, the people who had come together in their defense continued to talk—conversations that culminated in the drafting of Charter 77 in December. But what role did the underground and the trial have in these conversations? A number of possible explanations present themselves.

The first is that the trial was simply a catalyst that helped unify support for the Helsinki Accords. This, as I have argued, is the least persuasive account. It relegates the underground to a minor, formal role; effectively, it just uses the trial to supply the psychological richness and narrative drama that is otherwise missing from the "Helsinki Effect" account. A second type of explanation suggests that the underground gave the intellectuals a "shot in the arm"—a perspective Martin Machovec suggests when he writes that the regime's raid on the underground "unintentionally alerted the intellectual elite, which until that time had been considerably paralyzed, to the necessity of defense." Here, too, I would suggest that more depth is needed in an account of the "intellectual elite," which had its own forms of organization and motivation and was not simply a dead letter in the mid-1970s. When Machovec writes that "The rise of Charter 77 appears, in this light, as a direct result of the persecution of the underground community," this is correct as far as it goes, but it leaves out the other half of the story—the creative "appropriation" of the underground by Havel and other members of the "intellectual elite."[64]

A better explanation looks at institutional and organizational factors. All observers of the trial were struck by the fact that so many different kinds of people mixed together in the corridors of the courthouse—people who came to observe the trial, but were not allowed into the courtroom. As Havel wrote, "A distinguished, elderly gentleman, a former member of the presidium of the Communist Party of Czechoslovakia, spoke with long-haired youth he'd never seen in his life before, and they spoke uninhibitedly with him, though they had known him only from photographs." This mingling had both a human and a logistical dimension. For Havel, it meant a breaking down of psychological barriers: "no one bothered with introductions, getting acquainted, or feeling one another out. The usual conventions were dropped and the usual reticence disappeared [. . .]." Even in front of secret-police officers, "Dozens of things were discussed that many of us, in other circumstances, might have been afraid to talk about even with one other person."[65] But it also created new acquaintances and brought people together who might otherwise never have moved in the same circles. Karásek was struck by how many different kinds of people first met in the corridors of the court building: "undergrounders and Protestant ministers and Catholics and writers and Kriegel and Eurocommunists, and Havel came from Hrádeček, and they shook hands and exchanged telephone numbers. This particular affair called together people who had up to then been isolated, and something new arose there."[66]

The underground quickly became a blank slate, an "empty signifier" that could unite many different kinds of opposition intellectuals—reform Communists who had been expelled from the Party, Catholic and Protestant priests or intellectuals, "revolutionary Marxists" and the remnants of the student New Left, former political prisoners from the 1950s, and a whole spectrum of banned writers and academics, who themselves ran the gamut from ex-Communists to anti-Communists, and everything in between. In the words of František Stárek, one of the defendants from the July trial, the undergrounders "were just blank pieces of paper," whereas everyone else "had their own label [. . .]. Suddenly here was a phenomenon, a common denominator, that they could take a stand for."[67] This explanation is persuasive, except that it is missing one thing: it takes the "blank slate" conception of the underground for granted. In fact, this was an *interpretation* of the underground, brilliantly and persuasively formulated by Havel above all. One can imagine that if each of those people in the hallway could have sat down and had a talk with the brilliant, combative, controversial Jirous, they would not have come away thinking he was a "blank piece of paper."

But the underground did more than just provide an empty signifier, around which other people who did have "political pasts" could come together and temporarily put aside their conflicts. The underground contribution to the Charter, that is, should not be seen as limited to the immediate effects of the trial itself. As we have suggested, Havel's version of the trial both places the music underground in the limelight and, paradoxically, obscures its real significance. If we liberate the underground from those seductive labels—young people who just wanted to make music expressing their metaphysical anxiety—we can get a better sense of the ways in which it influenced, invigorated, and joined with the fledgling dissident movement.

First, we should note the larger confluence of the critiques of consumerist society—the similarity between the thinking of people like Jirous and Bondy, on one side, and Havel and Šimečka, on the other. In fact, several years before Havel's letter to Husák or Šimečka's *The Restoration of Order*, Bondy, Jirous, and underground music had formulated their attack on the materialism, banality, and lack of spirituality in normalized society of the early 1970s. The Chartists, indeed, had to rephrase this attack for public (and Western) reception, leaving out drugs and sexual promiscuity and instead emphasizing the political apathy of a population obsessed with Havel's question of which refrigerator or washing machine to buy. If the Charter did not frame itself as an attack on Communism, this was in part to bring a large contingent of reform Communists on board, but also because the underground had already framed its opposition to the "establishment" rather than to Communism *per se*. This stance, itself building on Western models, could circle back to Western society in a different form, via Charter 77. Havel would lay out this extension of the Charter critique to the West just a couple years later, in "The Power of the Powerless."

The underground (and the idea of "a trial of young musicians" or, later, of the Plastic People) also meshed with Havel's account of the political force of "pre-political" behavior. The idea of a pre-political realm was important to Havel's larger conception of truthful behavior—his faith that individuals have access to a sense of truth and lie that is uncorrupted by political calculations and compromises. But we can also trace its genealogy back to the primitivism of the underground—the idea of the innocent artist, uncorrupted by aesthetic training, being a kind of analogue for the ordinary citizen coming face-to-face with his or her own sense of right and wrong, uncorrupted by the compromises necessary to get ahead in normalized Czechoslovakia. In "The Power of the Powerless," Havel's famous greengrocer, who one day decides not to post an ideological slogan among his vegetables, is another variation on this theme. Here, the importance of having an "ordinary citizen" at center stage is unstated, but unmistakable—imagine how much force Havel's essay would lose if his hero were a philosophy professor who one day throws away his notes on dialectical materialism and decides to lecture on existentialism instead! It is a short step from here to the mock naïveté and performative innocence of Charter 77, pretending to believe that the state took its own laws seriously and was genuinely committed to the human rights it had endorsed at Helsinki.

A third element of underground philosophy was also picked up and transformed by Charter 77—the very ways in which a community in protest partially defines itself through legends and mythmaking, in an inevitable dialogue with regime repression. The early years of Charter 77 can, indeed, be understood as a dialectical process in which abstract claims about human rights entered into dialogue with thick descriptions of dissident life—in which arguments about universal values interacted with personal narratives about police repression and oppositional activities such as samizdat publishing. This third lesson of the underground will only become visible if we do not buy into Havel's "primitivist" image of young people "battered" by the world and radiating an inchoate anguish. Rather, we should pay attention to the extremely careful mythmaking skills of Jirous and Bondy, and ask how Charter 77 learned these skills as well. The creation of a founding myth in the "trial of the Plastic People" was itself an early sign that a new dissident community would be more than just an appeal to international treaties.

The influence of the underground can be seen in one more crucial decision made in the early days of dissent. To understand this decision, however, we must consider the discussions in December that led to Charter 77.

The Third Spokesman

The first of three meetings that would lead directly to the drafting and signing of Charter 77 was held on December 10 or 11 at the apartment of Jaroslav Kořán—a translator from English, and one of the four people who had been arrested along with Jirous back in 1973—on Tyršova Street in Prague.[68] It was organized by the historian Václav Vendelin Komeda, who as a less-high-profile figure had somewhat more freedom of movement; the others present were Havel, Mlynář, Kohout, and Jiří Němec. Petr Uhl, Pavel Bergman, Ludvík Vaculík, and Jiří Hájek joined the group at the following two meetings. As the initiative gained momentum, the "founders" consulted with friends, and impulses and ideas were gathered from many other people; Mlynář and Hájek, to some extent, communicated the ideas of a large grouping of reform Communists that had been discussing possible action for some time.

Havel is generally given credit for preparing a basic draft of a document on December 16. The final version, however, was worked over by many different hands and incorporated many deletions, additions, and changes. The first Chartists agreed that they would not elaborate as to who wrote which sections; Havel said that the Charter belonged to everyone, and Pavel Kohout said that he preferred "fumbling historians to arrested friends." It was only after the first meeting, Havel remembered, that the Protestant philosopher Ladislav Hejdánek alerted him to the fact that "our declaration might be based on the recently issued pacts on human rights. Parallel with that, but also after the first meeting, Mlynář came up with the same idea." Mlynář himself wrote that the idea of appealing to the pacts came "from the ranks of the opposition reform Communists." He also wrote that he formulated the paragraph saying the Charter would have no firm organizational structure. All accounts, however, agree that Pavel Kohout came up with the name *Charta 77*. The first discussions spoke of a "Committee," with a fixed membership, which would monitor human-rights abuses. Kohout's suggestion "Charter 77" was not only infinitely catchier and more inspiring; it was also tied to a more substantive point, that the Charter was not a fixed group of opposition intellectuals but rather—in Mlynář's words—a "broader movement that would constantly add new members and would not be understood as a human-rights committee."[69]

Kohout remembered the first meetings in Kořán's apartment, where "the smoke was so thick you could cut it, but we couldn't open the windows or the neighbors would call the fire department."[70] One thing that was immediately clear to the first organizers was that the Charter would draw together people of many different political opinions and political pasts. There was a significant contingent of reform Communist politicians, many of whom had been expelled from the Party but still had hopes of reforming the Communist system along the lines of another Prague Spring, but there were many others: writers like Vaculík and Kohout, who had moved on from the dreams of 1968; political prisoners from the early 1970s, including Petr Uhl, the former student radical who still spoke of "revolution" and placed himself to the left of the Communist Party; and Havel himself, never a Party member and someone who had always sought a way into politics for non–Party members. There were also Catholics and Protestants who approached dissent from a religious standpoint, as well as former political prisoners from the 1950s, like Karel Pecka.[71]

Given the diversity of potential signatories, the task of choosing a Charter spokesman would be difficult. The reform Communists seem to have agreed on Jiří Hájek, who had been Foreign Minister during the Prague Spring, but he hesitated to take on the role all by himself. Uhl remembers that while he and his wife Anna Šabatová were hanging up diapers to dry in their attic, where there were no listening devices, she suggested that there should be three spokesmen, including someone younger, like Havel. Havel agreed and thought this would "express the pluralistic nature of the Charter." But who would the third spokesman be? Later in the Charter's career, an informal rule developed according to which one of the three spokesman would be a reform Communist, one would represent religious currents in dissent, and one would be a non-Communist, often an intellectual or writer; but at this early stage, this tradition was not yet in place. (The role of religious figures in the Charter, never dominant, was not yet as pronounced as it would become later.) In fact, there were two obvious choices, elder "intellectual statesman" who had never been Communists and might lend the whole enterprise a certain dignity as well as a pedigree going back to the interwar First Republic: Václav Černý and Jan Patočka.[72]

Patočka, sixty-nine at the time, was a legend of Czech philosophy but was not particularly well known among all the Charter organizers. He had often held himself back from open political activity; quiet, modest, and measured, he had rarely sought the sorts of open confrontations that Černý seemed to enjoy. Černý, at seventy-one, was as fierce and fearless as always; his whole intellectual style was based on polemics; his conception of democracy was a vigorous battle of ideas. He had distinguished himself in the anti-Nazi resistance during World War II and had evolved into one of the most prominent anti-Communist intellectuals over the last thirty years. In their own ways, both seemed like natural choices, even if entirely different ones.

The choice of an elder spokesman would say a lot about the Charter itself. Havel, as well as Jiří Němec, supported the choice of Patočka and visited him several times to convince him. At first Patočka, too, thought that Černý was the obvious choice, so Havel:

> went to Černý and laid the cards out on the table. I told him Patočka didn't want to take the job without his blessing, because he thought that Černý was in line ahead of him, but that it was essential to get Patočka for the position precisely because his political profile was not as sharply defined as Černý's and therefore he could function more easily as a binding agent, whereas Černý, who was prickly and outspoken, might well have created a lot of resistance from the outset [. . .].

Černý agreed, without (in Havel's estimation) any bitterness, and Patočka became the third spokesman.[73]

Patočka would become so closely associated with the Charter, as will be seen in the next chapter, that it is difficult to think back to these early hours and days when its leadership could have taken a wholly different form. It did make some sense for Černý to cede to Patočka. The pressure Havel put on him may be seen as a function of one of the open secrets of the early Charter, which was that no one would benefit from friction between the reform Communists and the large group of signatories who had suffered greatly from the

Party's ministrations—whether political prisoners from the 1950s, priests and ministers who had been denied permission to preach, or people like Černý who been repeatedly singled out for punishment. The years leading up to the Charter had already seen great strides toward overcoming this latent split in Czech oppositional culture, but making a high-profile anti-Communist a spokesman could have complicated relationships internally—not to mention with the regime. Like most secular Czech intellectuals, Černý supported some form of socialism, but this was tied to a hatred, even a fury, directed at the Communist regimes of the 1950s and 1970s. Černý's memoirs, still unpublished, would eventually reveal just what heights of vituperation he could work himself into when describing his enemies. And just a few years earlier, Černý had been subjected to the television slander campaign using private conversations taped in his apartment, as well as to attacks in *Rudé právo*, which ascribed to him the wish "to hang Communists from the lampposts" in 1968; one can imagine what a gift to propagandists his appointment as spokesman would have been.

But Havel's choice of Patočka was also part of his larger conception of the Charter as a moral initiative, more than a political-civic one. Rather than a civic leader, Patočka was a philosopher who had worked extensively (among many other things) on Husserl, Heidegger, phenomenology, and ancient Greek thought, on questions of truth and authenticity. Havel's support of Patočka grew naturally out of his moral interpretation of the Charter, which in turn was closely tied to his "metaphysical" reading of the underground. Patočka himself seemed to enjoy an almost natural affinity with the underground; he knew some of its members through Jiří Němec and Dana Němcová, and already in December 1976 he had written a rather unusual essay imagining the Plastic People and DG 307 as "young cosmonauts," innocents who had landed on a corrupt planet and might possibly cure it of its ills. Patočka was glad "that we, the older ones, the ones who have fallen into our routines and have our own perspectives, used and worn, have the opportunity, indeed the necessity [. . .] to renew ourselves, not by some slavish parody, [. . .] but by communication with something that we ourselves do not produce."[74] Černý, by contrast—although he had signed the protest letters about the underground in June and August—was on uneasy terms with its art and music. In 1979, he would write an extremely dismissive criticism of underground literature, provoking a heated polemic that many took part in, including Jirous.[75]

An insightful account of the Černý–Patočka decision was written some fifteen years later by Eva Kantůrková, who thought that when it came to finding a "person who could give the Charter its basic spiritual impulse," the fundamental choice was not among Hájek, Havel, and anyone else, but between Patočka and Černý. She saw Černý as an Enlightenment rationalist who had imbibed the spirit of French liberal republicanism (he had gone to high school in Dijon in the 1920s, and French literature was always one of his first loves and research interests), whereas Patočka represented "a more lyrical, enigmatic line, looking for meaning rather than definition, respecting mystery and coming from a German rather than a French intellectual environment." Against the Communist conception of *homo faber*, of people defined by productive capacity and work, Černý placed "love and democratic responsibility," while Patočka represented "conscience, faith, vertigo, mysticism. [. . .] The tendency of heightened moral conflicts won out over the spirit of rational investigation, faith in reason, and the view from a distance."[76] Here, too, Kantůrková says, Černý was out of step with the underground's language of authenticity, epiphany, and direct access to truth. These are, we might add, the very characteristics encompassed in underground "primitivism," which was far more compatible with Patočka's language of transcendence than with Černý's cantankerous rationalism.

Kantůrková's is just one voice, but as this perspective tends to have dropped out of accounts of the Charter, it is worth recalling here. The only variable she leaves out of the equation is Havel himself, who played such a major role in presenting the underground to the first Charter organizers, framing the Charter in moral terms, and bringing on Patočka as an ally in this endeavor. In choosing Patočka as its spiritual leader, the Charter would also end up choosing Havel, his most effective popularizer and successor. Not all of these questions could have been clear in December 1976, when the spokesmen were being chosen; much would depend on Patočka himself, who would put his stamp on the Charter to a greater degree than anyone could have imagined. But it is worth pointing out that in this early decision about the Charter's spiritual profile, Havel's reading of the underground, allied with his moral and "metaphysical" reading of the Charter's purpose, won out across the board.

Signed, Sealed, and Arrested

By December 20, there seems to have been an agreement about the spokesmen and the definitive text of the document. The next question was how to gather signatures. It had been complicated enough to draft the document without attracting the attention of the police; gathering as many signatories as possible was an even more daunting task. It was carried out in sophisticated fashion. The week between Christmas and New Year's was chosen for collecting signatures; the intense activity and coordination would be camouflaged by normal holiday visits among friends and family. Some police, too, would be on vacation. In order to prevent the actual Charter from falling into the hands of the secret police, originally only a few copies were made; these were distributed to Havel, Mlynář, Kohout, Uhl, and a few others who were detailed to collect signatures. They would let a potential signatory read a copy and then take it back, to keep the Charter from entering into wider circulation. This strategy worked—although five of the original signatories were collaborating with the secret police, they were not able to get a copy beforehand.[77]

Signatories, then, did not actually sign a copy of the Charter itself. Instead, they wrote the following formula (with slight variations) on a note card: *Souhlasím s prohlášením Charty 77 z 1.1.1977* (I agree with the Charter 77 declaration of January 1, 1977), signed it, and printed their name, occupation, and address below. This allowed the gatherers to collect all the signatures without yet distributing copies of the document. Kohout suggested another function of this technique: "It fulfilled the psychological function of a kind of modern blood oath, so that no one could be misled into signing too easily, or could say they had been misled."[78] Vaculík was given the task of arranging for copies of the Charter to be made; the stalwart Petlice scribe Zdena Erteltová spent a good portion of her Christmas vacation typing. The plan was to "publish" the document on January 6 by mailing copies to the Federal Assembly as well as to all the individual signatories, who would thus receive their copies once there was no longer anything to hide. Kohout arranged for the text to be sent abroad through diplomatic channels—Wolfgang Runge, a press attaché for the West German embassy, got the text to the journalist Hans-Pieter Riesse, a former Prague correspondent for the German radio station Deutschlandfunk, who had been kicked out of Czechoslovakia in 1974. Riesse performed the near-miraculous task of getting the text to major world newspapers and, more important, of convincing them not to publish the text until January 7.[79]

The secret police had realized something was up as early as December 10, when their listening device in Kohout's apartment picked up a conversation with Havel and discussions of an upcoming meeting of writers and political figures, but they could not put together all the pieces in time. (As historians Petr Blažek and Radek Schovánek suggest, it was much easier to analyze material from a bugged phone line than from a bugged apartment; in the latter case, police had to go through hours of tape, piecing together fragmentary conversations.[80]) But surveillance of Kohout's apartment on January 5 did pick up a mention that some "texts" were going to be transported the following day.

A little before noon on January 6, after licking the stamps for over 240 envelopes with copies of the Charter for the original signatories, the actor Pavel Landovský, Václav Havel, and Ludvík Vaculík pulled out into the snow-covered streets of Prague to mail the copies and deliver the original to the Federal Parliament. (Vaculík was not planning on accompanying them, but had some shoes he needed repaired and asked for a ride to Wenceslas Square.) Landovský thought he recognized an Alfa Romeo parked outside as belonging to the secret police; three more cars began to follow them as they reached the main thoroughfare, Lenin Street.

What followed next is material for oral rather than written history. It would pass into legend largely thanks to the inimitable storytelling skills of Landovský, a brilliant raconteur.[81] As he told the tale to journalist Karel Hvížďala some ten years later, he hit the gas and was speeding through downtown Prague at over seventy miles an hour, more and more police cars "with ten-foot-long antennas" joining them at each intersection. Landovský pulled sharply into a side street that hadn't been salted; two of their pursuers fishtailed and collided, giving them a few precious moments. "We drove over a small rise and there, as if we had summoned it, was a mailbox. I stopped, Vašek [Havel] flew out of the car with a bag full of the Charter [. . .]. Vašek crammed the letters with the Charter into the mailbox, you can't imagine how long it takes, but he managed to mail the one bag in which there were about forty letters." Then the police reappeared and they were off again; Landovský ran a red light back onto Lenin Street and then turned down Gymnasijní Street, where two police cars appeared in front of them; when he tried to back up, two more blocked them from behind. In Landovský's spirited retelling:

> In a moment there were maybe eight cars in the street, and about twenty guys rushed out of them at us. I just locked all the doors from inside, so they couldn't get to us so easily. I said to Vašek Havel: "See, now they'll pound away at the car, get a bit tired, and when they start pounding us, it won't hurt so much!" And Vašek replied with a memorable sentence: "What a way to start a struggle for human rights!" The enraged cops outside had calmed down a bit and instead of pounding the car, they began slapping their secret police ID's against the window. Vašek Havel remarked: "Pavel,

it looks like these gentlemen really are from the police," and because he was convinced that we weren't doing anything wrong, he unlocked the door next to me and suddenly all I saw were the soles of his shoes. They grabbed him and pulled him out like a rolled-up carpet, like a piece of pipe. All I saw were the shoes. I didn't open the door myself, on the contrary, I entwined my hands in the steering wheel, then suddenly I saw the soles of Vaculík's shoes, he was flying out along with the bags he held in his hands. They passed him over their heads like a log and he disappeared into another car. I held on to the steering wheel like a leech, but somebody unlocked my door from the other side so they could get to me, and they started to tear me loose and shout: "In the name of the law, in the name of the republic!"

Landovský had not appeared on television or film since 1972, and he had been forced out of Prague's *Činoherní klub* theater, his last refuge, in 1976. But he was still a famous actor, and as a crowd gathered around the scene, someone shouted: "Look at this, Mr. Landovský is making another movie!" The police had brought along a cameraman who was filming the whole thing.

> Only now did the police realize that other people were there. But they reacted quickly, shoved a kid inside my car, maybe thirty years old, slammed both doors, the kid pulled out a gun, released the safety and said "Okay, follow them!" and so we started moving. After a few meters, he put away the pistol and I hear beside me: "Holy shit, this is really screwed up! [. . .] We've been on alert since two A.M. What did you guys do, rob a bank or something?" [. . .] I said: "Look here, kid, all we were doing was taking a petition to parliament, we didn't do anything wrong. So you'll get me a carton of Spartas and a toothbrush, because I didn't expect that turning in a petition was going to be a crime. Promise me!"

And, as Landovský tells it, the policeman showed up at his interrogation and handed him a toothbrush, toothpaste, and *half* a carton, at least, of Sparta cigarettes. Landovský, Havel, and Vaculík were released late that night, and the story of their Hollywood car chase began to spread.

Landovský's version is surely richly embellished, especially after ten years of tellings and retellings. Sticklers for the truth may prefer to go by the secret-police file on the arrest (where, however, they won't find any mention of the collision of police cars that allowed Landovský to lose them for a minute).[82] But as we are unlikely to get any definitive version of the events, we might instead think about the ways in which the Charter, before the proclamation had even been proclaimed, was beginning to generate an oral history of its own. Two days later, on Saturday, January 8, Jan Vladislav, the publisher of

Edice Kvart and another of the Charter's first signatories, described the event with undisguised fascination in his diary (the italics are his):

> When Václav Havel, Ludvík Vaculík and Landovský set out from the Urbáneks' apartment in Pavel's old Saab [. . .] men from the StB began to *chase* them in four or five unmarked cars. They went after them until, somewhere down by Dejvice, they victoriously *caught* them. And if the whole affair had been run according to the rules of a normal police raid and not the script of an espionage film, a single car with markings from the traffic police would have been enough; Landovský could have hardly done anything else besides stop when it directed him to. But then the guardians of order would not have been able to demonstrate how dangerous were the conspirators, and how valorous were they; and so it happened that Landovský managed, his car surrounded in the middle of an intersection, to jump out and call for help as if he were being attacked. I'm selling what I bought; I wasn't there. In any case, all three were arrested.[83]

Vladislav's entry is fascinating because it shows the story as it is being born. We don't know whom he heard this tale from—perhaps Havel or Landovský himself, who had been to his apartment for lunch just three days earlier—but he is well aware that it might have been embellished. In any case, just as important as the arrest was the tale that arose around it, and the way that the police had cooperated in generating a good story—a story that, within Charter circles, rapidly became famous, as did Havel's ironic lament, "What a way to start a struggle for human rights!" We may be forgiven for not believing every last detail, but on this occasion accuracy was hardly the most important thing; what *was* important was that a Czechoslovak opposition was now generating legends of its own.[84]

5

Everything Changed with the Charter

One of Ludvík Vaculík's talents, honed over decades of journalism in radio and newspapers—as well as years of writing with the censor at his back—was to phrase his observations in such a way that they balanced on the edge between quirkiness and universality. Vaculík's writing is full of formulations that at first seem odd but, on closer inspection, express complex thoughts with precision and clarity. He had composed what were arguably the three most important protests of the preceding ten years: his speech at the 1967 Writers' Congress, one of the early salvos of the Prague Spring ("Power is a uniquely human situation. It affects both rulers and ruled, and threatens the health of both"); the Two Thousand Words manifesto ("Truth, then, is not prevailing. Truth is merely what remains when everything else has been frittered away"); and the Ten Points manifesto of August 21, 1969 ("Socialism wasn't threatened here; what was threatened was the position of the people who had been ruining it for the last twenty years"). All three texts boasted a wealth of complex and subtle ideas, expressed in fresh and arresting language. "A nebulous thought," Vaculík once wrote, "cannot hope for a precise sentence. Writing a precise sentence about a takeover of the state is almost the same as drawing up a plan for such a takeover."[1] Over the years, Vaculík had established his calling as a civic stylist, a writer who was able to articulate issues of public concern, questions that were in the air, while still stamping them with his own personal perspective and unusual phrasing.

As soon as you start reading the Charter, you begin to get the sense that Vaculík didn't write it:

> On 13.10.1976, there were published in the Codex of Laws of the ČSSR / no. 120 an "International Pact on Civil and Political Rights" and an "International Pact on Economic, Social and Cultural Rights", which had been signed on behalf of Czechoslovakia in 1968, confirmed at Helsinki in 1975 and which came into force in our country on 23.3.1976. Since that time our citizens have had the right and our state the duty to be guided by them. The freedoms and rights of the people guaranteed by these pacts are important factors of civilization for which, throughout history, many progressive forces have been striving and their enactment can be of great assistance to the humanistic development of our society.[2]

One hates to say it, but the language of the Charter is uninspiring. It is earnest, methodical, and plodding. Although Havel wrote an initial draft, changes and additions were made by many different hands, and the result is unwieldy. It is full of nebulous thoughts, such as "important factors of civilization," "throughout history," and "many progressive forces," just to name a few in the first three sentences. It contains numerous pleonasms such as "forced to live in constant danger," "carry out in the realm of its activity," "unacceptable threats," "work and live freely." There is hardly a striking rhetorical device or colorful turn of phrase in the whole text; the prevailing tone is studied emotionlessness, with little pathos, anger, or excitement. And although it is incomparably more clear and concise than the standard fare of Communist political texts—whether Party directives, *Rudé právo* editorials, or May Day speeches—it is still marked inescapably by bureaucratic Czech and even patches of jargon, such as *pokrokové síly* (progressive forces) or *humánní vývoj* (human/humanist development).

And yet the text *is* inspiring. This is largely because of the modest but forceful tone, speaking clearly and matter-of-factly without trying to be flashy or clever. The Charter's own ethic of solidarity is encoded in its legalistic, unexciting style: the point was to fashion a neutral language in which violations of international pacts could be articulated without strained melodrama, and without smuggling in any ideological commitments that might dissuade signatories. This was the only way to bring together such a diverse grouping of people. In the electrified atmosphere of the Prague Spring, over a hundred thousand people had been eager to sign on to Vaculík's Two Thousand Words; in the dull, muffled world of normalization, a quirky or unusual text would have felt too complicated, risky, and off-putting. Even the clumsy and circular formulation "Charter 77 arose from the background of the solidarity and friendship of people who share concern for the fate of the ideals to which they have linked their life and work" studiously avoids specifying just what those ideals were. For the most part, the text contents itself with a negative delineation of what the Charter is *not*: "Charter 77 is not an organization, it has no statutes, no permanent organs and no organized membership," nor is it "a base for oppositional political activity." The main positive program comes in the third-to-last paragraph, and remains formal and noncommittal. The Charter:

> does not want to lay down its own programmes of political or social reforms or changes but to engage in the spheres of its activity in a constructive dialogue with political and state power, especially by calling attention to various concrete instances of the violation of human and civil rights, to prepare documentation on them, propose solutions, submit various general proposals aimed at deepening these rights and guaranteeing them and to act as intermediary in cases of conflicting situations which can evoke wrongful action, etc.[3]

Nevertheless, for all its "and so forths" and "et ceteras," this unlikely text completely rewrote the script of oppositional activity in the Czech lands. For the first time in Czechoslovakia, dissent had a name, and a new word, "Chartist," entered the political vocabulary. Even the word "signatory" alone now evoked an air of political opposition—after the Charter, no one had to ask what it was a signatory had signed! Varied activities that once would have languished in isolation suddenly belonged to a larger grouping of "dissident" activities, a larger social movement aimed at dialogue and openness. The popular singer Marta Kubišová, banned from performing since 1970, said in a 1980 interview: "Until the Charter, I consistently and intentionally ignored all domestic politics. On principle I didn't sign civic petitions; I suffered from the fear that my signature would be seen as some kind of yearning for glory. I signed Charter 77 spontaneously. It gave me the feeling that it was possible to sing again."[4] Many other signatories echoed her enthusiasm; but their excitement did not seem to feed off the *language* of the Charter, and it is striking how few people can recite any lines from this, perhaps the most important political text of postwar Czechoslovak history. The Charter was, in fact, *missing* something, a deeper expression of its own inspiring power. Where would it find this moral force?

Patočka's Imprint

Two days after the car chase, Jan Patočka sent a letter to the Federal Assembly with a copy of the Charter. If you want the original, he wrote politely, you will have to get it from the secret police. That same day, he finished an essay called "What Charter 77 Is and What It Is Not (Why Right Is on Its Side and No Slander or Forcible Measures Can Shake It)." As he would tell the police when he was interrogated three days later, he wrote this text because he thought that "a deeper philosophical meditation on the Charter" was necessary—"in my opinion," he said, "it was necessary to add to the Charter an account of my personal conception of its deeper moral meaning."[5] Patočka's comment reflects the strengths and weaknesses of the Charter's initial text—the very formalism and universalism that made the text widely acceptable also left an oddly flat impression. In the remaining two months of his life, one of his main accomplishments was to breathe philosophical life into the Charter; he did so in two texts that would turn the Charter into much more than an appeal for the government to uphold its own laws.

"What Charter 77 Is and What It Is Not" picks up on the negative delineations in the initial Charter proclamation, but also articulates a clearer sense of what the Charter *does* stand for. In order to head off any regime objections, the original proclamation was at pains to specify that the Charter was not an "organization": "Charter 77 is not a basis for oppositional political activity." Patočka clarifies this idea, seeing it less as a defensive gesture than as an appeal to higher values transcending the instrumental rationality of politics. By refusing to be an organization, the Charter had stepped outside the world of power calculations: "participants in the Charter do not act out of any interest, but out of *obligation* alone, out of an injunction that stands higher than all political commitments and rights [. . .]." Above the sphere of human interests and competition, of behavior aimed at getting ahead or defeating an opponent, there is a moral sphere—"there exists a higher authority" to which we are bound by our conscience. Human rights are an expression of this authority:

> The concept of *human rights* is nothing other than the conviction that states, too, and all of society are placed under the supremacy of moral feeling; that

they recognize something unconditioned, above them, something weighty and sacrosanct (untouchable) even for them; and that, by their own powers with which they create and secure *legal* norms, they intend to contribute to this goal.[6]

We can guess that such language—not explicitly religious, but clearly open to religious interpretation—might have dissuaded many of the original signatories. But Patočka, as indeed he told the police, was articulating a "personal conception" of the Charter, not issuing a document in his capacity as spokesman. In fact, the copy of the essay in Patočka's interrogation file contains a revealing handwritten note by his fellow Charter spokesman Jiří Hájek, who had read and commented on Patočka's draft on January 8. Hájek was reluctant to abandon the more legalistic language of the Charter itself: "It is a citizens' initiative resting on article 29 of the Constitution of the ČSSR and drawing the attention of the organs of power to problems associated with the execution of the directives of international pacts, and of commitments taken on by the government of the ČSSR in Helsinki [. . .]," wrote Hájek. "But if this is going to be the personal declaration of Prof. Patočka, and not a joint one, I have no comments at all."[7] In other words, Hájek would have liked to guide this essay away from the language of conscience and morality, but concluded that it was Patočka's own viewpoint and not an official Charter document. Nevertheless, Patočka's formulations would be far more influential than anything formally issued by the Charter itself.

Patočka's second essay, "What We Can Expect from Charter 77," is written in livelier, more specific language than his first essay. It gave the Charter what would become one of its unofficial slogans: "There are things worth suffering for." Written in March, the essay reflects the regime's apopleptic response to the Charter, and poses the question of what the Chartists can hope to achieve against "the almost incalculable resources" of power. Has the Charter just made things worse by calling down the wrath of the regime on everyone, even those who previously had some room for maneuver? Patočka replies that submissiveness and servility never improve anything, whereas the Chartists, by retaining their confidence as well as their decency, "had won more sympathy at home as well as abroad than we had dared to expect. That in itself is an important result: innocence and decent behavior are also a powerful factor of political reality." But, Patočka asks, "How long do you think you will have the sympathy of your own people if you aren't able to help them with something other than paper protests?" Somewhat paradoxically, Patočka suggests that the main "result" of the Charter has been to expose how far the Helsinki Accords are from being fulfilled—to expose the hypocrisy of détente. (He refers to "*disappointment* in a *false* relaxation of tension.") It is a strange, even circular reflection—almost as if Patočka were saying that everyone expected the Helsinki Accords to be little more than a sham, but it took the Charter to reveal just how ineffective they were, giving courage to people at home and abroad to voice their criticisms. Above all, writes Patočka in a passage that would be frequently (mis)quoted, one of the Charter's goals was to demonstrate "that people today once again know that there are things that are also worth suffering for. That the things for which one may suffer are the things worth living for."[8]

This phrase, shortened to the idea that "there are things worth suffering for," would become a kind of slogan, or even in-joke, for many Chartists.[9] When Havel gave the phrase a prominent place in a 1986 speech, the philosopher Petr Rezek lampooned it mercilessly as a misreading that reduced Patočka's thought to banality. As Rezek demonstrated, Patočka was not simply saying that suffering is, sometimes, worth it—you wouldn't need a philosopher to tell you that. Rather, Patočka meant there are specific things that we should suffer for, and indeed went on to specify these things: the qualities that distinguish true art and literature from mere routine and craft. Chartists like Havel tended to ignore the specific context of the statement and reduced it to a moral platitude; in so doing, Rezek argued, they were really diverting our attention from the causes we suffer for to the suffering itself—from the Charter, for example, to our own noble sacrifices in its name.[10]

What Patočka said, however, was not just that certain things are worth suffering for, but also that the Charter had helped make people *aware* of this obvious truth, had brought this idea out into the open, where it might influence people's behavior once again. If the behavior of states should change as a result, that's fine; but "The Charter never intended to act in any other than a pedagogical fashion." It did not want to force people to behave a certain way, but rather to set an example that might help them "educate themselves."[11] Indeed, Patočka's own estimations of the power of the Charter remained conservative. In the two short months he was able to observe and guide it, he conceived of it more as a shining moral exemplar than as a functioning institution. He understood that it needed a clearer moral basis if it were to inspire its members, but he did not live long enough to grapple with the question of what institutional forms could secure this basis.

In the stressful late winter and spring of 1977, Patočka was working hard, and like other Chartist leaders, he was subjected to "vicious press attacks and repeated police questioning."[12] On January 14, Havel had been arrested; he would remain in detention until May, which left only Patočka and Hájek to carry out the work of the Charter spokesmen. On March 1, Patočka was confined to bed, with chronic bronchitis, but when a group of Dutch reporters came to see him and suggested he meet with the visiting Dutch foreign minister Max van der Stoel, he agreed to go. Vaculík wrote: "I was surprised how quickly he changed out of his green dressing-gown into his Sunday best: dark suit, white shirt, tie, and above them his ruddy, energetic, and in the past few weeks perceptibly younger face."[13] The meeting with van der Stoel enraged the government, which considered it "unparalleled interference" in Czechoslovakia's affairs; police came to Patočka's apartment on March 1 and 2, and on March 3, he was called in for a daylong stay at the police station. After returning home that night, he woke up with chest pains, palpitations, and trouble breathing; a doctor was called, and he was taken to the hospital. After several days of treatment, he was feeling well enough to write two more texts in his hospital bed—"What We Can Expect from Charter 77" and an interview with *Die Zeit*—as well as to read and sign Charter documents 7 and 8. On the eleventh, however, he fell unconscious, and despite a brief improvement he died on March 13.

Tracing some of the Western accounts of Patočka's death offers a lesson in the distortions of dissident politics. Tom Stoppard's account from the summer of 1977, written for the *New York Review of Books*, is still careful and restrained: "Weakened by frequent and lengthy police interrogations, compounded by influenza, Patocka suffered a heart attack on March 4. [. . .] On March 13 he died." But in May, the great linguist Roman Jakobson, in an appreciative obituary in the *New Republic,* had already (knowingly) laid the framework for a martyr-narrative, saying that Patočka suffered heart trouble and was admitted to the hospital "after undergoing 11 hours of harsh police interrogation in two days." Years later, Richard Rorty, in another *New Republic* article called "The Seer of Prague," transformed this into a scene from a hackneyed spy novel: "By accepting that role [of Charter spokesman], and by serving as a courier carrying Chartist literature and messages around Prague, Patočka was inviting brutal treatment from the police. Three [sic] months after the publication of the Charter, on March 13, 1977, he died of a brain hemorrhage while being interrogated." This is inaccurate, to put it mildly, although the implication that Patočka was beaten or tortured to death under interrogation has been widely repeated. Such accounts, exaggerating the martyrological aspects of Patočka's death, do no service to his memory, although they do testify to the way that even critical intellectuals create dissidents in the image of their own preconceptions and yearnings.[14]

What does seem clear is that Patočka, already sick in bed with bronchitis, did not hesitate when offered the chance to meet with the Dutch foreign minister, beginning several days of intense activity and police harassment that were, if not brutal, certainly exhausting and stressful, and contributed to his death. Writing about the first days of March (which, of course, he did not know would be his final days), Patočka himself was modest and guarded—qualities that may be more inspiring than the overheated account that has him dying during a brutal interrogation. In an account of his March 1 meeting with the Dutch foreign minister Max van der Stoel, Patočka paints himself as a patient and undemanding visitor who went to visit the minister at the instigation of Dutch reporters—almost a supplicant, who waited in the Hotel Intercontinental until van der Stoel's official state meetings were over. Patočka also made it clear, in his final interview for *Die Zeit*, that his interrogations were, in the main, quite civil, although he mentions that he got into a "'discussion' that was actually a quarrel" with the "gentlemen from the Ministry of the Interior" who came to his home late on March 1 and again on March 2.

According to the police report from March 3, Patočka was called in so as to keep him from attending a reception at the West German embassy, and was held by the police for ten hours, from 11:00 A.M. to 9:00 P.M., including a two-hour lunch break and a nap, under the false pretext that a high-ranking official would be willing to discuss the Charter with him. The police report makes a point of emphasizing that Patočka was dealt with considerately "so as not to disturb the fiction that he was voluntarily spending a long time in the Ministry of Interior building." In *Die Zeit*, Patočka described his daylong interrogation thus: "The third day there came a summons, allegedly to [meet] a person from the 'leadership,' who however never appeared but left me to argue with one of my visitors from the previous day."[15]

It is conceivable that Patočka was treated harshly on March 3 (and that both he and the internal police report, for different reasons, chose not to mention this) but the written evidence does not seem to provide much support for this theory. Another point may be more important: as the accounts surrounding Patočka's death ten days later would reveal, the Charter was already creating the background for an oppositional community that could nurture, and be nurtured by, myths of its own. On March 16, Vaculík wrote a stirring tribute in which he said Patočka died "from the fatal disease of civil liberty, respect for the law and statesmanlike wisdom [. . .]. He died, a Czech in Europe. There can be no doubt that had he not stood up for his convictions he need not have died."[16] Patočka's death, further, was difficult not to see in connection with Jan Palach's—not just for the similarity of their names, but also for the common themes of self-sacrifice and the appeal to conscience. Jan Zábrana, who never associated himself with dissent, nevertheless wrote in his diary: "The line is clear: Hus, Komenský, both Masaryks, the boy Palach, and now Patočka." On March 24, in what is hard not to read as a reference to Palach's self-immolation, Ladislav Hejdánek wrote: "We do not feel sorrow and disappointment, but it is suddenly as if we were holding a torch that has been passed on to us."[17] Hejdánek's reading of Patočka's death as a moral appeal struck a chord with the whole community of Charter signatories. The Charter itself perceived Patočka's death less as an example of police brutality than as an example to be lived up to, and a sign of how important their own struggle was. This was, indeed, a myth of sorts—not in the sense of being inaccurate, but in the sense of bestowing a self-identification on a larger community, of presenting its beliefs to the outside world, and of inspiring it to further cohesiveness and activity.

What may speak most impressively to Patočka's wisdom and moral authority, however, is that he himself had created the framework for such a "reading" of his death. His own essays from January and March understood the Charter as a commitment to a higher authority, rather than as a mere political calculation. On these very terms, he should not be seen as a victim, a martyr, or the combination of the two that took hold in Western accounts. His brilliance lay elsewhere. Patočka articulated a civic commitment whose strength bore no relation to political calculation or expected consequences. He had recognized quickly—and during a stressful and distressing time, when he was being slandered daily in the press—that the Charter needed to account for suffering and self-sacrifice in its own narrative, that it needed a "deeper moral meaning." That deeper meaning allowed his death to serve as an example to others, rather than as mere evidence of the cruel stupidity of the Communist regime. Without realizing how little time he had to spare, he had articulated a moral framework in which his own death made sense.

To Sign or Not to Sign, Part I

Let us return for a moment to the original situation of the Charter's first signatories in December 1976, well before Patočka's death or his efforts to imbue the Charter with a moral meaning. What sorts of considerations went into the decision to sign the Charter, or indeed not to sign it?

Today, if you want to launch a petition, you can put up a website and start sending e-mails to likely signatories. If you have enough money, or devoted supporters, you can pay or persuade people to stand on street corners asking for signatures. Of course, neither of these options was available to the Charter. Like any samizdat, it had to circulate through private channels, relying on previously existing contacts and personal initiative. The Charter did, however, have one thing in common with any modern petition: your decision to sign or not often had a lot to do with the circumstances under which the petition reached you. With its neutral, legalistic language, the Charter generated the fiction of a free, equal public sphere in which everyone could read the text, weigh the issues involved, and make a considered decision about whether to sign or not. Indeed, the heroic narratives of dissent that I criticized in Chapter 1 tend to assume a clear channel between the Charter and anyone reading it—as if the text could, indeed, be downloaded in identical copies into the conscience of each individual, who would then decide whether or not to sign. These narratives turn the signing of the Charter into a deed of conscious, concerted heroism based on a full understanding of the risks and principles involved.

The reality, of course, was different. By the very nature of samizdat circulation networks, the first group of signatories—241 in all[18]—would end up, to a large extent, consisting of a relatively small, interlocking network of friends, colleagues, and acquaintances living largely in Prague and Brno. (This network would expand with time, of course, but—as we shall see—signing the Charter was a completely different decision for the first signatories than it was for the roughly 1,650 people who came later.) In reality, the decision to sign depended on a host of variables, some of them quite random. In December, the Charter did not yet have anything like the moral gravity it would acquire after Patočka's death; to many it seemed like just another petition, which need not call down earthshaking retribution, and the initial signatories had little idea of how many people they were joining.

As we might expect, some decisions to sign seem not to have involved much deliberation at all. In a 1995 interview, Josef Vohryzek, a literary critic and translator who would become a Charter spokesman in 1987, remembered his own signature. One day he happened to run into Havel on the street in Prague. "And he said to me, hey, we've drawn up this thing. Read it and sign it if you want." Even before seeing the text, Vohryzek said he "definitely" wanted to sign. They walked a few blocks to Pařížská Street, where Havel had parked his car, and they drove to a gas station where they would not be so conspicuous. Then Havel gave Vohryzek the text to read. "And I read it and I thought it was just great. I remember how, where it said the Czechoslovak parliament had ratified the Helsinki. . . , I said, are they really that brazen, that they ratified it? And he said, yep, they ratified it."[19] Vohryzek's memory captures the sense of informality that accompanied some Charter signatures (and, incidentally, reveals once again that the Helsinki Accords were not even on the radar of many signatories).

Other signatures were more structured. In Brno, Jiří Müller invited the historian Jaroslav Mezník over to his apartment and conducted the entire conversation silently, in writing. He gave Mezník a piece of paper asking if he would be willing to remain silent about a text he was going to show him; Mezník nodded. Then Müller gave him a copy of the Charter with written instructions to read it carefully; when Mezník raised his head from his reading, Müller gave him a further paper asking if he would like to sign the Charter or not, or if he would like some time to think it over. Mezník wrote that he would sign immediately. Müller then gave him two pieces of paper—the first contained instructions about what to write on the second, which was blank. "Only later," wrote Mezník in his 2005 memoir, "did I learn what had preceded this"—that UN human-rights pacts had acquired legal force in Czechoslovakia, and that "several Prague dissidents" had decided to use them as an avenue for criticizing the regime.[20]

As these two examples suggest, there were different kinds of communication between the Charter and the potential signatory. Sometimes these channels could be "jammed" or otherwise distorted. Mezník trusted Müller, in part because they had been political prisoners together in the early 1970s, in part because he conducted the signing so carefully. A different case was that of Eva Kantůrková, who heard about the Charter in December, but from an unreliable person—this was one of the reasons she didn't sign until January, after the first wave of persecutions had begun.[21] In fact, there were plenty of good reasons not to sign the Charter. Many people did not want to cause trouble for their families, and others knew they could never withstand the pressure the police would inflict on them. There were a host of other people who did not sign, in 1977 or later, because they were too valuable to oppositional circles for other reasons. Vaculík says that he pulled Jiří Gruša's name from the pile of signatory cards because Gruša was working on a number of samizdat projects—including an almanac of banned writers, *Hour of Hope*, to be published in 1978 on the tenth anniversary of the invasion—and Vaculík didn't want these projects to be shut down. Gruša agreed, and simply asked that his signature be "published" at a later date—it was revealed on October 10, 1978.[22] Václav Benda, who had already been involved in the campaign of support for the music underground and had suffered in the 1970s for both his political and religious beliefs, didn't sign at first; not only did he have five children, but his apartment on Charles Square in downtown Prague was a useful meeting place that hadn't yet been compromised. In mid-January, soon after the persecution campaign against signatories began, he added his name out of solidarity.[23] Perhaps the most noteworthy long-term "non-signatory" was the sociologist Jiřina Šiklová, who since 1972 had been the lynchpin of an extensive operation to smuggle banned texts in and out of the country. Šiklová's courageous activity provided a crucial link with major émigré journals and publishing houses abroad; her signature on the Charter could easily have destroyed the whole operation. "[I]t would have been stupid to sign it officially," she said in a 2005 interview. Eventually, after her arrest in 1981, she did sign, but since she continued to help with foreign communications after she returned from detention, her signature was not published in the Charter documents until 1989.[24]

Even if we don't include the large group of people who made a considered, often quite sensible decision that the costs of signing outweighed the benefits, a host of more subtle reasons could play a role. A consideration of four potential signatories who eventually decided *not* to sign the Charter may give a sense of the issues involved.[25]

Jaroslav Putík, whose diary we have quoted several times, was a natural candidate for Charter signatory—once a reform Communist and a journalist for leading journals of the Prague Spring, he was now a banned writer surviving on translations. He first mentions the Charter in diary entries from the end of 1976. He heard about it in December, shortly after his daughter Martina married a Danish man and was preparing to move to Denmark. Putík's first diary entry about the Charter is worth reproducing at length, for it gives a sense of the impression someone might have about this document before it had a name. (Putík calls it a *listina*, a word meaning document, deed, title, or indeed charter or bill of rights.)

> An unexpected thickening of the atmosphere. People are talking about a joint signature of a *listina* of freedoms; Havel, Professor Patočka, Hájek and some others are behind it. I don't have much of a desire for this; I could let myself be persuaded, but luckily no one is forcing me. But there's a whole tangled ball of problems here. Problem number one. Martina is getting reading to leave for Denmark. If I sign, they can cancel her trip or definitely make it very complicated. If I sign, we will never get to Denmark, and Martina will hardly be able to come home. And so my adage (or Jiří Kolář's, actually) has caught up with me: If there were no children, there would be lots of heroes in Bohemia! Problem number two, more serious than problem number one: to sign means to set out on a political path. This is a gauntlet thrown in the face of the regime, which will of course get its revenge, and from one action there logically flows another and another—ad infinitum, including all the consequences that are easy to imagine. But I don't have political ambitions; I have no desire to play this game, and no illusions about it. Our conspiratorial tactics are comical and it's impossible to doubt that everything is shot through with agents and informers. I didn't come alive, politically, until the Prague Spring, but even then the proper élan was missing. We, the generation of '45 and '48—we simply can't be involved in everything. We used to think we were the happiest generation under the sun; for a while we even believed it, then we opened our eyes (1956), then we believed again, and then again didn't. Hasn't there been enough of this? We'll see how things develop. If possible, I'll stick to my writing, even if it's unclear what will come of it.[26]

Putík's decision had several dimensions. If he signed, he and his wife might not see their daughter again, or at least not for a very long time. But his distaste for signing clearly goes deeper, and taps into a straightforward desire not to shape his identity around political involvement. Putík's ironic cynicism and a weariness with his own political past kept him from wanting to get engaged again; he sensed that it was more important to him to write, even if he couldn't publish. His skepticism continued into 1977 and beyond. Although his diary entries are supportive of the Charter, he repeatedly voices the suspicion that it may be a regime provocation, in which some signatories must be playing a "double game" and "Mother Police" is "making politics for us."[27]

Putík's decision not to sign also had to do with the people he was talking to. In his next entry, he mentions a visit from the poet Jan Skácel, who lived in Brno: "From what he says, it seems that the [Communist] Party in Brno is still courting him, just as they are [the poet Oldřich] Mikulášek. He hasn't said no to them clearly enough, and so they maintain their—futile—hope that he may be persuaded, that he'll repent a bit and everything will be fine. As for signing the 'Listina,' he has the same qualms as I do. I have a feeling that he came to Prague just to clear up how he should proceed—even if, in principle, he is clear: he won't align himself on either side."[28] Like Putík, Skácel did not sign the Charter and avoided opposing the regime too publicly, while still maintaining his own personal stance of internal opposition. Putík would continue to maintain close ties with many Chartists, and mingle respect for their cause with frustration at their self-importance and taste for conspiracy. ("When I hear ever more about the naivetés of our dissi-movement, an image appears on my retina: schoolchildren on a field trip, marching against an armored division. . . ."[29]) In the main, he saw the Charter as a somewhat esoteric, courageous, but rather self-satisfied subset of a much larger oppositional culture. At one point he notes: "Dinner at Eva Kantůrková's in Košíře. I was expecting a get-together of banned writers, but it was actually a meeting of the Charter."[30]

Jiří Pechar was, by his own account, a bit of a loner, and even something of an autodidact. In his university years after World War II, he faced the enviable dilemma of having to choose between two seminars that met at the same time: Václav Černý's course on Spanish literature and Jan Patočka's lectures on pre-Socratic philosophy. He chose Černý, and began a career studying Romance languages, translating French literature, and writing on literature and philosophy, while staying on the margins of official academic circles. After the Communist takeover in February 1948, he went to the Party office to turn in his membership card; this demonstrative resignation could have attracted unwelcome attention, but the official in charge was too busy and told him to come back later. This was one of many chance events that would shape his life; he left the Party, less conspicuously, a short time later and embarked on a career of editing, research, and translation in which he managed to keep a low profile, not compromising his beliefs but also avoiding confrontations that would force to him take an outspoken stand. He joined the Czechoslovak

Writers' Union during the Prague Spring, but after it was liquidated in 1971, "there did not exist a single organization of which I was a member," as he wrote in his 2009 memoir *Život na hraně* (Life on the Border).

Pechar was a regular at Jiří Kolář's table in Café Slavia. "One day in 1976," writes Pechar, "I arrived at the café when only Jan Vladislav, Josef Hiršal and Václav Černý were sitting with Kolář at his table. Hardly had I arrived when Černý turned to me: So, have you signed? I didn't know what they were talking about: it was a signature of the Charter, which was just then being prepared. I certainly wouldn't have refused to add my signature on Černý's bidding, but Kolář, Vladislav, and Hiršal immediately declared that I shouldn't sign, since the regime was allowing me to publish my translations: they were of the opinion that the only ones who should become immediately involved were those for whom any kind of literary activity was impossible." Indeed, Pechar had recently "covered" Vladislav's translation of a history of Renaissance art. Characteristically, Pechar concludes: "And because Černý ultimately agreed with their opinion, the decision in this question was made about me, without my having the opportunity to take up any position myself."[31]

Pechar invites us to think that, under other circumstances, he might have signed—if a different group of people had happened to be sitting at the table when he walked in, for example, or if he had been alone with Černý when he first heard about the Charter. At the same time, of course, he *did* decide not to sign, and this was a position in and of itself, which he articulated as a kind of life philosophy: he would keep writing books under his own name in samizdat; would remain friends with Charter signatories, even if he were pressured to break off contacts with them; and would continue to behave as if he expected his freedom of conscience to be respected.[32] But he wouldn't needlessly provoke the regime by, say, refusing to vote in elections. He avoided the worst repressions in the 1970s, received minimal attention from the secret police, and was even able to make several visits to France in the 1980s. When French philosophers began visiting Prague as part of the Jan Hus Association's lecture series, Pechar did not attend the lectures themselves, but he did meet openly with the visiting professors (a welcome opportunity to practice his French with the likes of Jean-Luc Nancy, Philippe Lacoue-Labarthe, and Étienne Balibar). He published in samizdat, including essays on the works of banned authors, but was also able to publish a slim volume, *Questions of Literary Translation*, with an official publishing house in 1986. Pechar continued to test the limits of the position he had chosen for himself, neither looking for trouble nor avoiding it, neither compromising his beliefs nor taking a public stand on them. Signing the Charter just was not part of his program. As with Putík, a confluence of factors—character, chance, and the company one keeps—combined to make signing seem unnecessary, while still leaving open many possible civic stances toward the regime.

Like his good friend Vaculík, Ivan Klíma had been a visible public figure during the Prague Spring. He was a well-known contributor to *Literární noviny*, and during the 1967 Writers' Congress he, too, had made an inflammatory speech, for which he was duly expelled from the Party. After the invasion, he had secured a teaching position at the University of Michigan and had spent much of the 1969–1970 school year in Ann Arbor; his decision to return into what would surely be a difficult situation made a big impression on his friends back home. "Ivan Klíma has returned from the USA; everyone is amazed," wrote Putík in his diary.[33] The regular meetings of banned writers that Klíma held at his apartment in 1970 and 1971 were a major event for the people involved. Klíma's own writings were banned at home, but his plays were performed in the West, and he had published two novels in English translation in 1970; William Styron, Arthur Miller, and Philip Roth all came to see him when they visited Prague in the 1970s. He was close friends with many banned writers and others on the regime's blacklist, and he made no effort to hide his opposition to the normalization regime. He was among the initiators of Edice Petlice, and one of the first to publish there. When Havel drew up a "short list" of eight likely signatories for Pavel Kohout to approach in December 1976, Klíma was on it—he seemed like an obvious choice.[34]

And yet he didn't sign. Like Pechar, Klíma returned to this question in his memoirs; unlike Pechar, he framed the decision as his own. Once again, as he tells it, particular circumstances played a role. At a parent–teacher conference in December 1976, Klíma and his wife Helena met with their daughter's homeroom teacher, who told them that, unfortunately, she could not recommend their teenage daughter for further study, even though she was a gifted artist. It would be better if she spent a year or two working in a factory, after which the factory itself could recommend her for art school. The unstated but obvious problem was her parents' political stance. Klíma continues:

> Soon after that, Helena's college classmate Jirka Dienstbier suddenly turned
> up at my place (I knew him from the days when I taught at the University of

Michigan and he and his wife visited us on their way to the northern U.S. or maybe to Canada). Jirka was an unusually sharp and clever observer, but I think, at that time, somewhat less skeptical than I. His vital optimism was on display now as well. He said that some of our common friends had prepared the text of a petition that basically repeats the main principles of the Helsinki declaration [. . .]. The petition demands nothing more than that [our] government really fulfill what it promised to fulfill with its signature. And he added with an almost malicious pleasure that he really couldn't imagine how they could object to such a petition. And he pulled four typewritten pages out of his briefcase so that I could read them as well.[35]

Klíma balked as soon as he got to the Charter's third paragraph, when it began to detail human-rights violations. "I said that if any of the authors thought our regime was going to conduct a dialogue with them about these most sensitive matters, they were mistaken." The government, he said, would "go crazy." He hesitated, worried that his signature would completely bury his daughter's chances of going to art school. He presents himself as a bit frightened, but worldly wise, and his account stacks the deck against the irrepressible Dienstbier, who comes off here sounding naïve. The Charter's deadpan pretense to inoffensive legality is likewise exposed as silly and transparent. However this scene actually played out, Klíma's account is useful in reminding us how much circumstances could play a role. (One wonders why a closer friend was not sent to present the initiative to Klíma—or perhaps Dienstbier meant to catch Helena at home and found Ivan instead.) Characteristically, however, Klíma does not spare himself in his account. When the teacher informed them that she could recommend their daughter for further study after all, he felt ashamed. "I was stunned at how quickly the StB had decided to let me know they noticed the absence of my signature [. . .]."[36]

Klíma explained his decision as follows:

> I didn't sign the Charter; perhaps it surprised my friends, but no one ever asked me why; no one ever considered me a traitor because of this. After all, everyone has the right to act according to their own decision and deliberation, and everyone knew that I don't like to sign texts that I haven't written (or at least helped to write) myself. More than once I explained that if I am going to get in trouble anyway, then it's better that it be for my own texts.[37]

Klíma's account leaves some unanswered questions—if no one asked him why he didn't sign, then to whom was he explaining himself? Would he have signed under different circumstances, or if he had been included in the meetings to draft the Charter? Nevertheless, Klíma's own doubts were quite different from Putík's or Pechar's. Unlike Putík, his failure to sign was not tied to any reticence about the signatories themselves; unlike Pechar, it was not tied to any reticence about exposing himself to persecution, something that Klíma did quite regularly. Klíma's failure to sign undoubtedly saved him from some police harassment, but it opened him up to other kinds of chicanery; misled by his failure to sign, the secret police tried to break him off from the Charter community, inflicting a complicated game of blandishments and threats on him.[38] Klíma's decision not to sign may be a reminder that some of our deepest, most essential decisions can be made without consciously articulated reasons—or it may simply suggest that, for some dissidents, it did not make much difference whether they actually signed the Charter or not.

Elžbieta Ledererová was from Poland, and would become one of the few Charter signatories born in another country. When she met her future husband, Jiří Lederer, in 1963, she was working as a television reporter in Warsaw. She moved to Prague in 1966; in 1968, as Czechoslovakia became a less and less reliable member of the Communist bloc, her Polish employers broke off all contact with her, but she was able to find work as a translator with the Prague Information Service. She and Jiří had a daughter in the fall of 1969, just a couple months before Jiří's first arrest in January 1970. Elžbieta took various jobs to supplement Jiří's meager income as a freelance journalist—his income was limited by publishing bans and, more drastically, by his two arrests in 1970 and 1972. By 1973, she had lost her translator's position.[39]

In his own memoirs, Jiří Lederer describes one of those typical holiday meetings at which the Charter was signed, stylizing it as a two-act play:

> On December 26, a large group of guests appeared at our cottage. [. . .] The first act of our meeting was devoted to a group reading and discussion of the Charter 77 declaration—and then we all signed it; we aligned ourselves with its ideas, and so we made a free decision about our future fate. There must have been this kind of atmosphere at the gatherings of the Czech Brethren during the Counter-Reformation, when they were being persecuted. [. . .] The second act, lasting long into the night, was filled with a banquet and stormy debates. How good we all felt! Someone proclaimed: Next year things will start moving—it will be easier to breathe! For the majority of us, those words characterized our mood, the hopes associated with the Charter. . .[40]

In 1979, Elžbieta told a rather different story when Eva Kantůrková asked about her signature:

> There's a kind of funny story connected with that. We had guests at our cottage, and I was cooking bigos. That's a Polish dish, cooked by hunters; it's nutritious, filling. It's a winter dish that has to last for a while; it's better each time you heat it up again. They say it's best after two weeks. You have to drink something with it; it's served hot. I'll invite you over the next time I make it. So I was cooking bigos and you have to keep stirring it, because it can easily burn and stick to the pan. Our guests were sitting at the table, they were talking about something, I kept running off to stir, I would yell to them: wait, stop talking until I get back, but they kept talking and talking and I kept stirring and stirring, until they left and Jirka says: "And you didn't manage to sign." That doesn't matter, I said, your signature was also on my behalf. Then they put Jirka in jail and I realized that it really did matter whether I signed or not, so I signed.[41]

It would be a bit too easy to read this event as the marginalization of a woman's signature of the Charter. This would not be a wild misinterpretation; it is true that wives sometimes had less "access" to signing the Charter than their husbands. For example, when Pavel Kohout returned from the late-night meeting to prepare the Charter signatures for parliament, he revealed to his wife, Jelena Mašinová, that they had taken her name off the list so it wouldn't look as if they were "padding" it with the "relatives of signatories." She made him get out of bed at 2:00 A.M. and go back to return her name to the list, a punishment he fully deserved.[42] Jiří Müller, the former student activist and political prisoner who was one of the mainstays of dissent in Brno, mentioned in a 2004 interview that his wife had twice attempted to sign the Charter, but her signature had never been published. Of all the Charter signatories, Müller was one of those most aware of the importance of couples; his success in organizing samizdat publishing and underground lectures in Brno had a lot to do with his choice of stable couples who could handle the pressure. Nevertheless, he remembers having discouraged at least one Charter spokesman from publishing his wife's signature—a decision that flowed precisely from his conception of the couple as a single signatory: "My wife signed the Charter twice, but [her signature] was never published. And it bothered her. It didn't bother me, because I felt very strongly that someone had to take care of the children. But it bothered her."[43]

While some women were certainly held off from signing the Charter, the decision not to sign was often their own. I see no reason to doubt that

Ledererová simply made her own decision not to sign with the first group. Her signature was published in May 1978, and she certainly could have signed before then if she had felt more strongly about it. What *is* revealed in her description is that signing was not always an individual decision. While many couples signed the Charter—for example, Zdeněk Mlynář and Irena Dubská, František Vaněček and Dagmar Vaněčková, Jiří Němec and Dána Němcová, to name just a few—it often made sense for just one family member to sign. For many writers who did not hold a full-time job, for example, their spouse was the family's breadwinner, and if both had signed, they would have been left without any income. "I didn't add my signature," remembered Madla Vaculíková, "because someone in the family needed formal employment so that we could have health insurance and receive state allowances for our children [. . .]."[44] This logic was common. In other words, one spouse might not sign in order to make it possible for the whole family to survive the signature of the other spouse.

Ledererová's own response, however, suggests also that she considered her husband's signature to be valid for both of them. We should keep this in mind even as we note that, of the 241 original signatories, only forty-two were female. In many cases, we should think of the signatory as the "spousal unit," where one partner continued working in order to support the family, or simply decided that a second signature wasn't necessary. In most cases, the "signing partner" was the man, but this was not always the case—Eva Kantůrková signed, for example, while her husband Jiří Kantůrek, who had been a prominent television journalist and reformer in the 1960s, did not. Anna Marvanová describes reading over the text with her husband; communicating with hand gestures (they avoided speaking in case their apartment was bugged), they agreed that she would sign.[45] Nor do we necessarily have to read the failure to sign as some kind of "moral sacrifice," in which both partners wanted to sign and one had to hold himself or herself back. In fact, we can certainly imagine that the decision of one partner to sign actually took some of the pressure off the other.

There is a final point to be made about the decision to sign the Charter: it looked entirely different for the first group of "December signatories" than it did for everyone else. The first group had a pretty good idea that they might get in trouble, but they had no clear sense of just how the regime would respond; the Charter, after all, was simply a call for dialogue that might conceivably have disappeared among the dozens of open letters, petitions, and appeals that had been written since the early 1970s. Some even thought it was too mild.[46] It was clear that the Charter would get more signatures than previous initiatives had, but no one really knew just how many people were signing until all the cards were in—Havel was amazed when Mlynář turned up with over a hundred signatures, "which took my breath away."[47] This is a remarkable admission that reveals just how much variation there was in the first signatories' understanding of the enterprise. Their exact expectations are probably forever lost in the fog of hindsight, but it does seem safe to say that no one quite expected such an immediate and savage response. Writing several years later, Lederer recounted a visit to Vaculík shortly after Christmas in 1976. Vaculík asked: "What's going to happen after the Charter comes out? Do you think they'll start arresting people?" Lederer replied: "They might not go that far, but they're going to holler and there will be interrogations."[48]

Nevertheless, they did know that *something* would happen. Perhaps the most eloquent prediction came from Jan Patočka himself, who commented—in an uncharacteristically laconic, and uncharacteristically colloquial, formulation: "Make no mistake. This time it's gonna explode."[49]

Failures, Usurpers, and a Lying Pamphlet

The regime response to the Charter was unexpectedly vicious, even hysterical. It was carried out on a number of planes, of which we might identify three: a legal response, a mass media campaign, and police harassment and repression of signatories.[50]

At its meeting on January 7, the Central Committee presidium appointed Husák himself with the task of drawing up a response to the Charter.[51] On January 11, the presidium sent a resolution to representatives from the Justice ministry and the prosecutor's office, stating that "Charter 77 is an anti-state, counter-revolutionary document; a platform for the creation of a bourgeois party" and that it was "prepared in collusion with foreign countries." The resolution asked for a legal characterization of the "charter" with an eye to associating it with particular crimes: could it be considered an illegal organization? Could it be characterized as the crime of "damaging the republic's interests abroad," under paragraph 112 of the legal code, or as "illegal printed matter," in which case its distribution could be punished?[52] On January 14, the regime's legal luminaries issued a joint answer.[53] The result may have been a foregone conclusion, but it also gives a sense of how the regime viewed the Charter. It was, indeed, an "illegal organization," since it was a unified community of people who shared a common goal and had distributed tasks and functions (such as the spokesman's role) among its members; this left it open to prosecution under article 98 ("subversion of the republic"). The question of "damaging the interests of the republic abroad" was a little more complicated; the Charter certainly did do such damage, but in order to convict anyone of this crime, it would have to be demonstrated that he or she had actually participated in, or made possible, distribution in other countries. Finally, the Charter was characterized as "illegal printed matter," so that distributing it in print, or even "reproducing the content of 'Charter 77' for at least two persons," could be classified as a crime under paragraph 100 ("incitement"), provided it could be demonstrated that the activity had been carried out "because of hostility toward the socialist state and social administration of the republic." The federal chief prosecutor further complained that the Charter was in violation of the Helsinki Accords, which had enshrined a right of nonintervention in the internal affairs of signatory states. The "internationalization" of the Charter, framing it as a foreign-sponsored and foreign-funded initiative, was thus an important part of the regime's legal attack—portraying a petition from its own citizens as a foreign intervention.[54]

One might ask whether these legal decisions were really that important. Once the regime had decided to persecute the Chartists, there was little doubt that it would find the paragraphs it needed to prosecute them. What's more, the legal charges against the Charter were quietly dropped in November 1980, when state police decided that the document had not gained as many supporters as originally feared and that its influence had gradually diminished. Persecution of Charter signatories, of course, continued apace and even intensified after 1980, so the fact that formal charges were dropped suggests that the original legal response was more an element of its larger "public relations" campaign against the Charter than a necessary prop for its repressions.

Nevertheless, the prosecutors' decision, though a foregone conclusion, was still important. Although the police often ignored the laws and the courts interpreted them in perverse ways, Czechoslovakia was not a lawless state. Even where the laws existed merely to provide a framework for repression, they provided a framework nonetheless.[55] Havel analyzed this question at some length in "The Power of the Powerless," explaining why bureaucratic forms of control are so invested in the appearance of legality. Communist Czechoslovakia was not "some ephemeral dictatorship run by a Ugandan bandit," in which a tyrant could act on his most brutal whims; it was, instead, a complex bureaucracy, "permeated by a dense network of regulations, proclamations, directives, norms, orders, and rules." Laws were needed to regulate all these complex relationships, and could not simply be ignored if the system was to function. The law played a double role. First, it acted as an "alibi," creating "the pleasing illusion that justice is done, society protected, and the exercise of power objectively regulated." Up and down the chain of harassment, police officers, prosecutors, judges, and even government ministers could absolve themselves of guilt by telling themselves they were simply following the letter of the law. More generally, the complexity of the modern bureaucratic state meant that the law operated as a form of "ritual communication" that "enables all components of the system to communicate, to put themselves in a good light, to establish their own legitimacy." When the Chartists appealed to the law, they revealed that it was an empty ritual, but by the same token, they forced "all those who take refuge behind the law to affirm and make credible this agency of excuses, this means of communication, this reinforcement of the social arteries outside of which their will could not be made to circulate through society."[56]

Every Chartist had stories of moments when the law seemed to spring into action. Sometimes these were merely bizarre glitches. Jiří Muller described how, on his release from jail, the warden wanted to confirm that he had taken all his possessions with him; Muller answered that he had everything but a pair of dirty socks he had left in the cell: "the next day I got a bag with the holey socks inside. This means that the prison warden had gotten an order that I was to be released along with everything that belonged to me; there were not to be any complaints, any problems."[57] But more generally, there were certain protocols that had to be followed. A house search, for example, could be successfully delayed if the paperwork was not in order or if a civilian observer had not been brought along to countersign the search protocol. One of the most common legal quirks was the rule that suspects brought in for questioning could only be held for forty-eight hours; after that, they must be formally charged or released. Police would get around this by taking people in for a "forty-eighter," releasing them, and then detaining them again as soon as they had walked out the door of the station or the gate of the prison.

These short circuits rarely led to any substantial relief or freedom; they are important to remember mainly because the legal landscape of persecution formed an important part of the Chartists' interactions with the police and the courts, and hence of their daily lives. Many Chartists became familiar with the various paragraphs of the legal code and the lengths of prison sentences associated with various crimes; samizdat texts circulated with directions on how to behave during a house search or interrogation.[58] Of course, many Chartists still ended up in situations where police used violence or ignored the laws altogether. In fact, the first few minutes of an arrest or interrogation often involved uncertainty as to whether this particular encounter would be "legalistic" or whether all bets were off. When the laws were being followed, though, the legal code provided a set of rules for conducting arguments with the police and the courts; some Chartists fought hard battles over every legal concession.

As a defensive weapon, too, the law was a double-edged sword. From the regime's point of view, dragging the Chartists into endless legal battles was surely one of the more refined ways of harassing them—not just a side effect of the tenuous rule of law, but an essential form of regime repression. In some cases, for example, prolonging a court case by carrying it through the appeals process (during which the original sentence was often affirmed or even lengthened) merely intensified the uncertainty and anguish of arrest and detainment. But in order for this harassment to work, the laws did have to have some validity, and occasionally had to work as checks on the police and the courts. This could happen, for example, in cases where a judge or policeman did not have specific orders covering a specific eventuality. And the whole legal structure, corrupt though it was, multiplied the number of nodes and fissures where a more courageous judge, sympathetic clerk, or even a less vindictive secret-police officer could nudge things in a more promising direction.

A second element of the regime's response to the Charter was a well-orchestrated campaign in the mass media. On January 12, *Rudé právo* published a four-column editorial entitled "Ztroskotanci a samozvanci"—a title that needs a bit of explanation, but could be translated roughly as "Failures and Usurpers." These insults were recycled from the show trials of the 1950s—Husák had been called a *samozvanec* in his day—but they also took on new meanings in the 1970s. The attack in *Rudé právo* began with a long description of the "crusade" of the forces of imperialism, the bourgeoisie, and "international reaction," which were attacking Communism "in an effort to put the brakes on the process of their own inescapable demise." In the West, these forces deployed a wide range of strategies—from discrimination against Communist workers to espionage and repression—but they also looked abroad, where they recruited "émigrés as well as various *ztroskotanci* living in Socialist countries, those who, because of their class or reactionary interests, because of vanity, megalomania, renegadism, or their notorious lack of character, pliably lend their names, even to the devil." The *ztroskotanci*, that is, were the dregs of society, people who had failed to become productive members of socialist society and so were willing to sell themselves to foreign bourgeois schemes, "including the fabrication of all kinds of pamphlets, letters, protests, and other trivial slanders." These "political corpses" ran the gamut from hostile émigrés and the remnants of class enemies inside socialist countries "all the way to various criminal and asocial elements." An example of one of their fabricated pamphlets was the "so-called charter 77" (regime propaganda consistently printed "charter" with a lowercase *c*), presented to "certain Western agencies" on the orders of "anti-Communist and Zionist centers."[59]

Two photographs on the same page depicted the world of productive work that the monsters of the Charter were attacking. Right below the editorial, two men in work clothes were shown on the factory floor, surrounded by machinery; one was kneeling on the floor and turning the dials on a control board. According to the caption, they were being aided in their work by "an increase in the productivity of labor and the development of socialist competition." In a second photo to the right, a blonde woman in a white lab coat poured a clear liquid into a large glass beaker while a man and a woman, also in white coats, consulted with each other next to a tangle of glass tubing and rubber hoses. (The liquid was a drink called "biokys," using "certain non-traditional bacteria, with important nutritional qualities, arising from lactic acid fermentation"; judging from the smile on the scientist's face, it must have been rather tasty.) These images of productive and focused labor, the "everyday work" of dedicated Communists, contrasted clearly with the villains of the editorial. In particular, the "technical intelligentsia" in their laboratory were prominently featured in implicit opposition to the failed philosophers and writers who signed the Charter.

"Failures and Usurpers" set the tone for the regime's view of the Charter. It boiled down to three theses. First, the Charter was an international initiative, ordered up by foreign imperialist and "cosmopolitan" capitalists—here, as in the legal response, the idea that the Charter was a foreign initiative was important because the Helsinki Accords clearly prohibited intervention in another country's internal affairs. Second, the Chartists were not full-fledged, productive members of society but rather *ztroskotanci*—failures, dregs, and renegades; their own inability to fit into society (itself the result of their class background or political heresies) made them ripe for exploitation by the enemy. And, finally, the Chartists were *samozvanci*—"usurpers" or literally "the self-proclaimed," people who—whether out of megalomaniac delusion or cold calculation—claimed to speak for society as a whole, when in fact they represented their own narrow, bourgeois, and elitist interests.

The editorial was just the beginning of a massive media campaign, carried out in newspapers, on radio, and on television. Throughout the country, in factories, offices, schools, and universities, workers were summoned together and told to sign various condemnations of the Charter, sometimes called the Anti-Charter. Since the press never published the Charter itself, most of these people had little idea what it said; their only sense of its content came from the rabid and overheated rhetoric of the Party's propaganda machine. Many who did not even know what the Charter *was* now got in trouble for refusing to sign a condemnation of something that hadn't even read, or simply for asking to see a copy before expressing their opinion.

Every day *Rudé právo* contained front-page articles condemning the Chartists and reprinting angry letters from workers' groups as well as individuals—many of these supposedly spontaneous outpourings of protest merely reproduced the rhetoric, word-for-word, of "Ztroskotanci a samozvanci." On January 18—just to take a random sample of the types of things the Chartists were reading about themselves, and everyone else was reading about the Chartists—a front-page caption in *Rudé právo* proclaimed:

A UNIFIED VOICE FROM OUR ENTIRE HOMELAND
PEOPLE FROM THE ASH HEAP OF HISTORY HAVE NO
    PLACE AMONG US
WE REJECT THE ATTACKS AGAINST SOCIALISM

The article underneath reprinted resolutions sent in by factory workers, miners, and various organizations, as well as individual statements by academics and others. These statements are full of typical Party jargon, hammering home the same talking points over and over again. A protest resolution with "hundreds of signatures" proclaimed: "We have cut ties forever with subversives and apostates of the likes of Hájek, Mlynář, Kriegel, Havel, Patočka, Vaculík and others. These gentlemen have no right to speak for us [. . .]." The chair of the Czechoslovak Writers' Union called the Charter "a voice from a distant planet. [. . .] This is an individual hostile gesture, and all we can do is condemn it." Workers from a bus company in Slovakia wrote: "We are outraged by this pamphlet that crudely slanders the Czechoslovak Socialist

Republic. [. . .] Its authors come from the class positions of the defeated bourgeoisie and reject socialism. Their goal is to break the unity of the socialist
community and the world-wide proletariat."[60] These condemnations, accusing
the Chartists as a group, were actually among the less savage; a special subset of the media campaign consisted of attacks against individual signatories,
often revealing details of their private lives and accusing them of being in the
pay of foreign governments. The Czechoslovak press filled literally dozens of
pages with these sorts of articles, which were reinforced daily by attacks on
radio and television.

On January 28, 1977, heading to see Jiří Kolář at his table in Café Slavia,
Jan Vladislav noticed that the street outside was full of official cars. Across
the street, in the nineteenth-century building of the National Theater, hundreds of prominent actors, popular singers, writers, and other intellectuals
and celebrities were gathering together for a televised display of loyalty to the
regime. The prominent actress Jiřina Švorcová read out a long "Proclamation
of Czechoslovak Artistic Unions," which was then signed by the assembled
luminaries.[61] The proclamation, which would also come to be known as the
"Anti-Charter," was a long assemblage of platitudes about the magnificent
work of socialism and the dreams of generations fulfilled by both manual
workers and "workers of the spirit" or "cultural workers" (otherwise known
as artists). It called for international cultural cooperation in the spirit of Helsinki, and it ended with a brief but unmistakable reference to a certain group
of traitors "who—in their uncontrollable pride, conceited superiority, or self-
interest, or even for base financial reward—tear themselves away and isolate
themselves from their own people, its life and true interests, wherever in the
world they should be—in our country, too, there has been found a small group
of such renegades [*odpadlíků*] and traitors—and with implacable logic become
the tools of the anti-humanist forces of imperialism and, in its service, the tribunes of subversion and national conflict."[62] The word *odpadlík* literally means
someone who has "fallen away," a renegade or apostate; in "The Power of the
Powerless," Havel would offer this word, perhaps with the Anti-Charter in
mind, as a Czech etymological equivalent of the foreign borrowing *dissident*.[63]

A third element of the regime's attack on the Charter was police harassment and repression. Overall, the persecution of signatories was more targeted, energetic, and vindictive than the retributions against expelled Party

members after 1969. The Charter set off another round of firings and demotions; many signatories who thought they had hit bottom were pushed even further down the employment ladder. The ranks of parking lot attendants, stokers, and window washers were further swelled by a new influx of intellectuals; even in these low-paying jobs, Chartists would continue to be harassed. The journalist František Vaněček had been an editor at *Rudé právo* from 1961 to 1969, and had refused to participate in the Party screenings. He was fired and worked as a parking lot attendant in the 1970s. After signing the Charter, he was fired once again. He found work as a bellhop and assistant at the Hotel Internacionál, which was so full of spies, black marketeers, and prostitutes that he called it a "branch office of the Ministry of the Interior."[64] Eventually he was offered a better position as the hotel's storeroom manager, but when he was told that there was no need to carry out an initial inventory of the hotel's supplies, he suspected he was being set up for charges of theft. Wisely, he quit. After several more positions he found work, like so many others, in a boiler room.[65]

Charter signatories were subjected to a wide range of everyday harassments. Police would call them in the middle of the night, every night, or simply turn off their phones. (The Bendas' telephone stopped working because, they were told, of a "defect in the cable" that was not fixed for eight years.) If a signatory's identity booklet had the slightest defect, a scratch or a tear, they might be forced to get a new one, and subjected to all kinds of petty bureaucracy along the way. Many had to retake the driver's test in order to keep their license. When they drove somewhere, they were often followed and stopped—they might be given breathalyzer tests, for example, or have their drivers' licenses taken away under various pretexts. Vaněček mentions that he avoided driving whenever possible, although he did hide his typewriter in his car, parked far away, when he was preparing for a house search.[66]

These petty harassments were, in fact, at the bottom of the scale. Police inflicted a wide range of punishments. Nearly every Charter signatory was brought in for interrogation, sometimes repeatedly.[67] Many were also subjected to house searches, and some signatories grew used to hiding compromising materials away each evening in case the police came during the night. Many were vilified in the press, and some received verbal threats (including anonymous hate mail). Chartists were also subjected to surveillance—sometimes surreptitious, sometimes conspicuous. Surveillance operations could be extensive; over a four-day period in November and December 1977, for example, Ivan Dejmal was followed by a total of thirty-two agents, using twenty-three different cars, under the command of six superiors. A single "surveillance squadron" might have a dozen people in three to six cars for a shift of five or eight hours.[68] High-profile Chartists like Uhl, František Kriegel, or Ladislav Hejdánek were often subject to a special regime, with police officers stationed outside their apartment building, or even apartment door, all day and night. As always, unpredictability was part of the routine: the officers might turn all visitors away, simply let them in after checking their papers, or, sometimes, take them to the station for questioning. Uhl reported that some visitors forced their way in, even with police officers grabbing their arms and sleeves, but then were left in peace once they were inside; at other times, only three people were allowed in at any one time.[69]

Nor were police above arranging assaults. After an interrogation on May 16, 1978, Ivan Medek was told by an "elegantly dressed" agent that he would be driven home; in the street outside, he was seized from behind, stuffed in a car, bound and blindfolded. After an hour's drive, he was dragged out of the car through the mud, punched in the solar plexus, and left alone in the middle of the forest and the middle of the night. He wandered an hour before finding a town. Bohumil Doležal was subjected to a similar scenario a week later: the police driving him home left him in the middle of a Prague street, where another group of five men chased him down and dragged him into a car. He was bound, blindfolded, and driven outside of Prague, where he was beaten, kicked, punched in the stomach and left in the forest in the middle of the night. Doležal walked some ten miles to Příbram and caught the 5:45 a.m. train back to Prague.[70]

A number of women signatories were accused of prostitution or forcibly hospitalized, purportedly for fear they would spread venereal disease. In August 1978, Zdena Erteltová, not a Charter signatory but known to the police for her work as a Petlice copyist, was forcibly hospitalized after she refused to report on whose literary works she had been typing. She was held in the hospital for fourteen days, during which she underwent an operation and was not allowed to call her family or a lawyer.[71] In 1979, spokeswoman Zdena Tominová, arriving home at her apartment building around 10:00 P.M. one night, was confronted by a man with a nylon stocking over his head. He threw her to the sidewalk and beat her head against the pavement; she was hospitalized with a concussion.[72] In a particularly harsh wave of violence in the early 1980s, when many Chartists were singled out for special treatment in an effort to make them emigrate, beatings became less uncommon, as did death threats and physical violence during interrogations. Charlie Soukup, Václav Malý, and others were beaten during interrogations. The singer, writer, and artist Vlastimil Třešňák had matches stubbed out on his wrists; he was told that if he didn't emigrate, he might be hit by a truck.[73]

As the writer Alexandr Kliment aptly remembered: "The state police were, for the most part, primitives, but they could do an excellent job of blackmailing and harming" people.[74] Refined forms of chicanery and harassment form a special chapter in the annals of repression, and reveal just how much time and energy the police could expend in "working over" one of their charges. On March 30, 1978, the children of the historian Karel Bartošek found a coffin outside their front door, with their father's name on it. A similar "joke" had been played twice on Libuše Šilhanová the previous year: while her husband was away at their country cottage, workers from a funeral home had visited her, saying they had instructions to pick up his body.[75] Perhaps the most absurd and complicated drama was inflicted on Pavel Kohout, who received an anonymous letter on July 11, 1978, threatening him and his family if he didn't pay 500,000 crowns; he was to go to the 8-km marker of the Benešov highway at 8:00 P.M. the next day to receive further instructions in a blue Nivea cream tin. He was warned of harsh measures if he told the police. Kohout, a playwright and actor who had a flare for staging spectacles, entered into this charade with a certain verve and an awareness of his own role as actor in a strange drama, but the whole affair was also exhausting and frightening. At one point police discovered a bomb, or something they said was a bomb, underneath his car; at another point, when his wife, Jelena Mašinová, drove to meet him, she found the brake lines had been cut. The absurd and cruel harassment culminated in the poisoning of their dog.[76]

Threats, of course, were often stronger than their execution, and placed Chartists and their families under enormous stress. A house search or interrogation often served not only to gather information but—even more—to upset, irritate, humiliate, and provoke. Vaněček noted that a house search "demands great self-denial if you are to remain calm and not cause an incident with the police."[77] If a Chartist could be provoked into insulting or even striking an officer, this was an added bonus. The early years of the Charter saw a number of instances in which Chartists "fought back." On January 10, 1977, Mašinová was arrested—it would be more accurate to say abducted—by policemen on Hradčanské náměstí, just in front of her apartment near Prague Castle. She bit one of her assailants, leading to assault charges that hung over her for the next two years; the threat of her trial was one of the reasons she and Kohout emigrated. Jan Šimsa, a Protestant minister, shoved a policeman who was manhandling his wife during a house search in 1978; he was jailed for assault. In the fall of 1978, Jaroslav Šabata was picked up for questioning when he attempted to meet with Polish dissidents on the Czechoslovak–Polish border; when an StB officer roughed him up, Šabata slapped him, and also ended up going to jail.[78]

These different incidents may give a sense of the wide variety of stresses and dangers involved in police harassment. The StB were both crude and inventive, and they had a great deal of time and manpower to expend. Facing them did not mean simply deploying conscience and courage against a set of known threats. Rather, it involved nerve-wracking standoffs in which uncertainty and anguish played as important a role as open force. And the pressure was not just psychologically, but physically taxing; some dissidents who were morally robust but physically frail ended up crumpling, physically or morally, under the stress. "Police repression" thus encompassed threats, violence, and fear, but also systematic attempts to irritate, anger, humiliate, and confuse. It was not only a test of courage, but also a test of levelheadedness, patience, even intelligence and imagination. Sometimes the second test was much more difficult than the first.

To Sign or Not to Sign, Part II

The massive anti-Charter campaign and police repression immediately changed the equation for those considering whether or not to sign. Some who had held back from the first "wave," like Benda and Kantůrková, now signed quickly to show their solidarity. Some people learned about the Charter from friends or foreign radio broadcasts, but most of the Czechoslovak population heard about the Charter for the first time only thanks to the regime's media campaign. For some it opened up new possibilities of protest, at the same time as it raised the stakes of any kind of oppositional activity. Signing now meant joining a group as much as taking a moral stand. And now that everyone had a clearer sense of the sacrifices involved, signing the Charter also meant convincing the spokesmen, or whomever your "contacts" in the Charter were, that you knew what you were doing. Patočka is said to have simply refused the signatures of students, since they would surely get expelled; he thought it was more important that they finish their studies and then make the decision when they were a bit older.[79] Even in the case of older "candidates," existing Chartists sought to help them make an informed decision about whether to sign or not. The case of Václav Malý, a twenty-six-year-old priest who lived in the town of Vlašim about an hour from Prague, is instructive. Malý had finished his theology degree and had been ordained as a priest in 1976, and he had received official permission to practice in August. He quickly got into trouble with his superiors, among other things for leading prayers in Patočka's memory. Malý knew one of the original Charter signatories, Ivan Medek, and told him that he wanted to sign. Medek arranged a meeting with the Protestant philosopher Ladislav Hejdánek, another member of the first group of signatories, and at first they tried to dissuade Malý from signing: "They discouraged me from it; they asked if I had taken into account the fact that I would lose the possibility of working as a priest, if I had thought it over carefully. I said yes, so then they accepted my signature." After repeated threats, Malý finally lost his official permission to work as a priest in January 1979.[80]

Potential new signatories had to weigh a number of different factors. Unless they were already connected by friendship or acquaintance to the "main" Charter circles, they had to realize that they would not have the network of moral and logistical support that existed in Prague or, to a lesser extent, in Brno. Regional issues came to the fore. Signing the Charter was far riskier if you lived in a small town, since there were fewer dissidents to keep the police occupied. Another instructive case is that of Jan Urban, who came from the family of a prominent reform Communist (and former ambassador to Finland); in 1977, he was a high-school teacher in the town of Prachatice. Although he did not sign the Charter until much later, he immediately ran into trouble in January 1977 for refusing to sign the Anti-Charter and was fired from his job. In his words, "In the whole district there were three of us dissidents and the department of the StB working on us had eleven people; they had to carry out some sort of activity, so—interrogations and things like that."[81]

As Urban's comment suggests, the decision to draw the regime's attention to oneself looked very different depending on where one lived. The Charter itself was an overwhelmingly Prague affair—of the original 241 signatories, some 90 percent lived in Prague or a nearby suburb, with most of the rest in Brno. This was understandable, given that the signatures were collected over about a two-week period, in all secrecy; the networks of signatories mirrored

preexisting groupings of families and friends, and there simply wasn't time to
secure signatures all over the country. People in Prague, especially those who
already knew some signatories, could count on safety in numbers—not only
was police attention divided among a greater number of people, but one could
expect camaraderie, logistical help, and moral support from those who had
already signed. This support network might not make a huge difference when
the brunt of police repression was coming down on you, or when you were sitting alone in an interrogation room, but it was a massive advantage compared
to the situation in other parts of the country. In northern Moravia, around the
mining city of Ostrava, the government was less unpopular than in Prague—
miners were well paid, and their work was so exhausting and dangerous that
they had little time for civic initiatives.[82] There were just a few Ostrava natives
among the first group of signers, and within days they were feeling the full
force of house searches, dismissal from work, and interrogations. Petr Uhl's
March 6 report on the state of the Charter says that there were fewer than
ten signatories from Ostrava, and that they "are exposed to a level of police
monitoring and repressions that is not usual in other regions"; some of the
January signatories were interrogated even before their signatures had been
published.[83] Many were also pressured into emigrating, which thinned the
ranks even further. In Ostrava as in other regions, signatories were routinely
subjected to a level of harassment—including threats and inducements to col-
laborate with the police—that only the highest-profile Chartists in Prague
were subjected to.

   Similar problems can be said to apply, *mutatis mutandis*, to Slovakia, where
in addition a number of other factors helped keep the number of Charter
signatories down to some thirty or thirty-five Slovaks overall, some of whom
lived in Prague.[84] It is important to remember that there were other forms of
opposition besides the Charter—in Slovakia, where religious feeling was generally much stronger than in the Czech lands, the so-called *malé spoločenstvá*,
small groups of people who gathered for discussion and worship, were an
important form of local organization that was oppositional in tone but did not
enter into the kind of "civic" dissent that characterized the Charter. (In this
respect, the "Slovak question" is linked to the larger story of religious dissent,
which overlaps with the Charter but in many ways forms a separate story.)
Nevertheless, other factors came into play in Slovakia, and it is worth pausing
on why the Charter—as Slovak newspaper *SME* put it in 2007—"sounded
foreign" to Slovaks.[85]

Havel's own discussion of the choice of the first spokesmen for the Charter betrays the fact that, while there was some effort to represent different "constituencies" among the signatories from the very beginning, there was apparently little or no discussion of how to bring the Slovaks on board—an all-too-typical oversight in Czech cultural circles. Although there were a few prominent Slovaks among the early signatories—the political scientist Miroslav Kusý, the writer Dominik Tatarka, and the historian Ján Mlynárik, for example—the Charter had no Slovak spokesperson until 1990. What's more, the Charter failed to win (or perhaps to ask for) Dubček's participation. In a 2007 article, Kusý writes that Zdeněk Mlynář tried to contact Dubček in November 1976, but failed. According to Kusý, Dubček later told him: "I could have been one of the founders of the Charter, but not just one of its signatories."[86] In his own autobiography, Dubček wrote: "I am occasionally asked why I did not sign the charter myself. The question results mainly from a lack of understanding of the difference between Czech and Slovak realities. The charter was a Czech response to the situation. In Slovakia, we agreed with virtually every idea in it, but we had our own ways to support these ideals."[87] The failure to secure a Slovak spokesperson was just one symptom of the larger failure to address Slovak concerns. The Charter itself did not mention the federalization of the country or other specifically Slovak questions; there was no Slovak version of the text included in the original "publication"; and, as Kusý points out, although there were official Charter documents about the situation of the Hungarian and Romani minorities, there were none about questions of Czech–Slovak relations.

Aside from a traditional Czech lack of interest in Slovak questions, there were other reasons, some of them structural, that Slovak intellectuals may not have been interested in the Charter. A main reason seems to be that the purges in the early 1970s had been somewhat softer and less vindictive in Slovakia, and so had not created the same large class of "underemployed" intellectuals as they had in the Czech lands. Slovak intellectuals often had somewhat more room for maneuver, and more to lose in terms of publication and travel possibilities; once the Charter was seen as "marked" by its Czech origins, it would make even less sense to invite persecution for the sake of this distant initiative, even if one wholeheartedly supported it. In this sense, the scarcity of Slovak signatories reminds us of the Charter's institutional limitations; it was not *just* a moral appeal with infinite reach, but also a network of friends and contacts that was primarily based in Prague and radiated outward, ever weakening, from there. By the time it reached Bratislava, it was less an appeal than something happening somewhere else.

Ladislav Hejdánek's *Letters to a Friend*

The "Slovak question" points to a more general issue. Was the Charter an abstract, universal appeal accessible to all, or a loosely organized group of specific people held together by friendship and kinship as well as by political solidarity? In Slovakia, the answer was obvious, but even in the Czech lands, this basic ambiguity would shadow the Charter for its whole existence. One of the first people to recognize the dilemma, and to try to turn it into a strength, was the philosopher Ladislav Hejdánek. When Hejdánek sat down in February 1977 to begin writing a letter to a fictional young friend who wanted to sign the Charter, he may not have realized that he was penning the first in a series of dozens of letters that would circulate widely and would become one of the most important internal histories of the whole Charter movement. Hejdánek's letters, both articulating and reporting on debates within the Charter while still reflecting his own positions, were a crucial form of internal communication in the early months of the Charter. They were prescient in formulating questions and ideas that would become prominent in Charter discussions in the years to come.

Hejdánek, born in 1927, graduated from university in 1952 but was unable to find work after graduating. Although he sympathized with the left, he did not join the Party and, worse from the Communists' point of view, he was a Christian. He had little hope of finding a job commensurate with his abilities. He worked as a mason and digger before he finally secured a position as a clerk in a research institute. In 1968 he was finally able to take up a position in the Philosophy Institute, only to be fired in March 1971. In 1972 he was arrested in connection with the summer political trials and was detained for eight months; he was freed on amnesty in 1973. He found part-time work as a night watchman in the National Literary Archive, where he was put on a succession of six-month contracts, and after signing Charter 77 he ended up, like so many intellectuals, as a stoker. And like so many intellectuals, he searched for his calling outside of his day job; throughout the 1970s, he organized several ongoing seminars in his apartment, for students of philosophy and theology, including those who were dissatisfied with their official university courses.[88]

Hejdánek's organization of these apartment seminars helps explain the form he chose for his letters to the Charter community. The first one, dated February 10, 1977, begins:

> Esteemed and dear friend,
> I understand very well your confusion, caused by my refusal to accept and pass on your signature, just as I understand well your rage at the manner in which newspaper, radio, and television [. . .] are trying to stir up as much mud and filth as possible around the whole affair. But consider yourself whether your active participation would make any sense: above all, you would be immediately expelled from the school that, after three years of waiting, you've finally been accepted into.[89]

Hejdánek's fictional addressee is a male student, probably in his late teens or early twenties, who has had trouble getting admitted to university for political reasons—perhaps because his parents are political "undesirables," perhaps because he himself said or did something in high school that put a black mark on his record. This student has sent his signature to Hejdánek, asking him to pass it on to the Charter spokesmen. (As Hejdánek's letters use the familiar *Ty* rather than the formal *Vy* form of address, we can surmise that he has known this student a long time, probably since he was a child or adolescent.) The student is politically aware enough to have secured a copy of the Charter and to want to sign, but is not so close to Charter circles that he is informed about its background; we can assume that his parents are not signatories. The letters, then, fashion Hejdánek as a link between the Charter and the outside world, indeed, as a kind of spokesman. Initially, he responds with reservations: "After all, society needs educated, informed, and experienced experts—and not people who may have behaved courageously one time, but otherwise don't accomplish anything." Hejdánek assures the student that he still has "many weeks and months" in which to make a decision; in the meantime, "we could try to clear up some serious questions of a more general nature."[90] This "clearing up" constitutes the first cycle of Hejdánek's letters—the visible half of his correspondence with this unknown student, framed as a series of lessons that would either dissuade him from signing the Charter, or turn his signature from a rash and hotheaded impulse into a well-considered decision.

Hejdánek surely thought carefully about how to present his series of meditations—why not write informal feuilletons, philosophical essays, or "situation reports" from inside the Charter? His choice of the genre of "letter to a friend" immediately encodes several important assumptions. Hejdánek seeks to explain the Charter to a sympathetic, interested, and not fully informed observer; this position, in effect, codified the new situation that the first signatories had found themselves in during January 1977. The Charter was now surrounded by "barriers to entry" that had not existed in December, and that any subsequent signatory needed to consider; further, it was no longer simply a human-rights initiative but was now a bounded group of people, joined by conviction and persecution. At first Hejdánek did not know what to call this group; in the first letter he speaks of "Chartists" but puts the word in quotation marks. By mid-March the quotation marks have disappeared.[91]

The choice of a student (someone who is willing to be lectured, but also to make critical, even impertinent comments in reply) is a clever one. It allows Hejdánek to move back and forth among several registers—now assuming a fatherly tone as he initiates his young friend into the Charter's internal debates, now launching into more abstract discourse and implicitly treating his interlocutor as an equal who is capable of following philosophical argument. The letters give Hejdánek a platform to talk about himself and expound his own ideas and positions at length, while still reacting to implied criticisms. We never see the student's letters, but they seem to pose frequent questions about Hejdánek's views and beliefs. Each letter begins by referring to such questions: "Thank you for your letter. I read it with interest and I must confess that it inspired me once again"; "I am quite glad that you asked me to say a few words about Professor Jan Patočka, who recently died." Hejdánek often uses his interlocutor's presumed questions as a way of interrogating his own earlier positions, circling back to previous letters: "you reproach me for having brought up the theme of revolution without having actually said anything about it"; "it was almost a source of amazement to me that, among the range of questions and themes you've proposed to me in the last few weeks, there was nothing related to Christianity, which I have mentioned more than once. Now that you've touched on it, I understand why you hesitated for so long. I hear a great deal of skepticism in your question [. . .]." Over time, Hejdánek fashions his fictional addressee into a friendly but independent-minded interlocutor; the title of the whole cycle, *Letters to a Friend*, guarantees that, even as potential conflicts arise, they will be resolved in an atmosphere of civil debate.

The letters are thus much more than a sounding board for Hejdánek's own ideas. Although his voice remains the most important one, the letter genre sets up a genuine dialogue, in which ideas are constantly tested against likely objections and questions. As he specifies in the seventeenth letter, from July 17: "For when I sit down to write you, I don't spend a long time thinking through every formulation, I hardly correct what is already written, I don't want to write a tractatus. So nothing in my sentences should be considered a definitive, final wording—everything is really just a contribution to a discussion."[92] A "friendly" audience, willing to deliberate along with him, is both the starting point and end point of these letters, which are meant to raise more questions than they answer, and to inform about ongoing debates as well as intervene in them.

Indeed, over the course of the letters Hejdánek develops a conception of the Charter that embodies this idea of dialogue. He thereby begins to revise Patočka's own crucial formulations from the beginning of 1977. Here we might recall Patočka's "What Charter 77 Is and What It Is Not," which insisted that people need "a moral foundation, a conviction that is not an affair of opportunity, circumstances, and expected advantages." This foundation does help society function properly, but in the end morality does not exist simply in order to help society function; it exists in order for a person to be a person. Patočka hoped that these ideas, "tested by the painful experience of many decades," would "pierce, in their clarity, into the consciousness of all." This last phrase is an odd formulation—in Czech, it reads "ujasněně pronikly do vědomí všech"—with connotations of enlightenment and epiphany, of a sudden, self-explanatory understanding that enters into one's consciousness from outside. Patočka saw the Charter as the self-evident expression of a higher morality that would begin to operate in the world merely by being expressed.[93] In this vision of morality, we might say that "the message is the medium"—it reaches each person through its own sheer force and clarity.

Hejdánek moves away from Patočka's self-evident message toward a much different conception, built around a still inchoate but unmistakable sense of an informed Charter "public," engaged in dialogue and reasoned debate. In the letter of August 18, he describes this public in hesitant, frequently qualified phrases that nevertheless clearly set the terms for a new way of understanding the Charter:

> In a situation where all public opinion had once again been banished and driven out of our society, so that it was in fact replaced by "secret opinion," there have appeared the first signs of an integration of individual and group initiatives in a kind of oasis—not very large, thus far—of independent public spiritual, cultural, and even political (more precisely: non-political

political) life and thought, in which a small, for now, but distinctive and gradually growing number of people are making use of their freedom [. . .].

It's true that Hejdánek remains beholden to the notion of a higher truth that cannot be countermanded ("something to which every opinion, teaching, etc. must also appeal, and to which it must leave the last word"), but at the same time, he is moving toward a dialogic conception of freedom in which "we need others, at least as listening partners, even if they don't agree." The Charter needs a "mutual solidarity" that "does not lead to uniformity."[94] This is not the solidarity of a common moral appeal, but rather the solidarity of "an 'open' community without precise and accentuated borders, from which people are not, cannot be, and surely will not be excluded as long as [. . .] they remain in fundamental solidarity alongside those with whom they disagree (which does not at all mean that they will muffle their disagreement)."[95]

Hejdánek's letters thus preserved the spirit of Patočka's higher moral calling while still recognizing a fact that had become increasingly clear since Patočka's death: there were, and would continue to be, serious differences of opinion within the Charter itself. Originally the Charter avoided fashioning itself as an "organization" in order to sidestep the repression that would inevitably have greeted an opposition party. The regime's hysterical response had rendered this defense irrelevant. Hejdánek realized, however, that there were now other reasons to avoid any clear organization; the more any particular set of opinions became identified as an official Charter position, the more internal tensions would threaten to break it up. What was needed was a shift from the discourse of moral appeal—from "the message is the medium"—to one of open discussion, in which moral decisions are shaped by dialogue and mutual respect.

In the final letter, Hejdánek "discovers" that his student friend has decided to sign, after all: "In closing, I would also like to write that I have already discovered that you did add your signature below the Charter. I don't know what kept you from telling me."[96] The rhetoric of this sentence is precise: Hejdánek doesn't know when his student-friend actually did sign, nor does he reveal when exactly he found out. There is an appealing self-irony here, as the would-be teacher discovers that his student has long ago assimilated the lesson, disagreed with it, and moved on to other things. But the more important point is that it doesn't matter: the purported dialogue between someone inside the Charter and someone outside has changed imperceptibly into an intra-Charter dialogue, and no one was any the wiser. This is precisely Hejdánek's larger point: the Charter's public discourse is not that of some interest group but rather is accessible to all.

> [T]he signature alone is most definitely not the question, and it is not even the most important thing. To act and live in the spirit of Charter 77 is quite possible even without a signature. [. . .] The goal of the Charter is not to gain as many signatures as possible, but to convince as many people as possible that they can and should behave toward the state as free, courageous citizens, and above all that they can and should behave toward their fellow citizens as friends, companions, comrades.[97]

Voices of the Charter

Hejdánek's letters informed their readers about events and debates within the Charter community, but they also helped create that community. One of the themes of this book is the way oral and written texts both circulate certain ideas and create the "circulatory system" of a social grouping—a network of interlocking contacts, finite but unbounded, that is essential to a community's self-definition. Just as Patočka had met a need by providing the Charter with a moral foundation, the important innovation of Hejdánek's "letters" was to suggest a model for a self-constituting discourse that would allow the Charter to form itself as a deliberating public, rather than let itself simply be defined as an object of state persecution. This is precisely why Hejdánek wanted to transcend the question of who had actually signed the Charter and who had not.

In other words, circulating texts serve at least a double function. On one hand, they communicate information among members of the group and thereby help identify a specific set of people who share this information and thereby belong to the group. On the other hand, they reach unknown readers and thereby create a "virtual" community whose borders are unclear. Samizdat circulation networks, for example, reinforced personal contacts among people who handed texts off to one another, but also encouraged them to imagine a community of readers radiating out from the material world of these circulating texts. The lack of clear boundaries is essential: the circulation of material texts, hard to keep track of in itself, both creates a specific community of readers who are connected to each other and yet creates the impression (or illusion) that this community is potentially open to all.

The original proclamation of the Charter had little to say about the circulation of information. It talks about "carrying on a dialogue," "drawing attention to," "preparing documentation," "suggesting solutions," but it offers no forum or medium in which to do so. This was, of course, understandable—it was hard enough to keep the Charter secret and arrange for 241 signatures without launching into plans for some kind of internal samizdat operation. Nor could the Chartists fully imagine how vicious the media attack against them would be, effectively shutting down any hopes for public dialogue. Nevertheless, it is fair to say that the Charter, at first, did not have a clear idea of what kinds of information it wanted to circulate, and how it wanted to do so. For example, Havel's notes from a January 3 meeting, in which the future activities of the Charter were discussed, mention four possible types of documents, but do not seem sure about how they would be circulated: "At the center of its work (although not its only task) should be the preparation of documents, which would then be handled according to circumstances." These documents might consider specific cases of injustice, which "could be written up, so that there would be a reserve of prepared materials; whether, when, and how each document is published is another question."[98] This lack of concern for questions of circulation is striking.

A system of official proclamations did take shape relatively quickly—statements were signed by the spokesmen and given the status of official Charter documents. By the end of June, the Charter had issued nineteen such statements (including the original proclamation itself). These included reports on the persecution of signatories, open letters to the Federal Assembly and other government organs, an obituary for Jan Patočka, and the periodic lists of new signatories, as well as a new "genre" that would become one of the Charter's most important activities: reports on issues of pressing interest to Czechoslovak society, usually issues that had been silenced in the state-run media. At first these focused on specific human-rights violations. Charter document 4, for example, issued at the end of January, described discrimination against students who were not admitted into high schools and university because of their own political statements or those of their parents. Document number 10 from March 8 highlighted problems in the social and economic sphere—for example, low work morale, unequal pay for women, and the failure of unions to support the rights of workers. Document 13 from April 22 discussed freedom of conscience and religion. Preparing these documents would eventually evolve into one of the Charter's most important activities, and they would form the most important subset of the nearly six hundred statements the Charter published by 1989. These reports were always signed by the Charter spokesmen, although their complexity and scope generally made it quite clear that they had been written by someone else. In fact, they were frequently drawn up over several months by teams of people—not just Charter signatories, but often sympathizers inside the "official structures" who had access to economic and sociological data and were quite eager to participate, albeit anonymously, in the Charter's own activities.

Such documents, however, could not serve all the needs of a growing community starved for information and a clearer sense of its own identity. Above all, the Charter documents maintained a studied, subdued, and matter-of-fact tone, as well as legalistic diction. The Charter strove for a neutral, third-person voice that would not be open to accusations of distortion or sensationalism. The many reports detailing police repression remained vague about particular instances of violence and harassment. Above all, these statements feel *official*, as if they were a bureaucratic instantiation of the whole "the message is the medium" approach—a suppression of rhetoric that was meant to allow injustice to speak for itself. The vast majority of the Charter documents, even stretching into the 1980s, are written in what I would call an organizational "spokesvoice"—professional, reasonable, just a bit stiff and formal. Some examples from document 8 ("Overall Report on State-Organized Actions and Slanders against Charter 77 and Its Signatories") may give a sense of this tone:

> From 21 to 24 January, the writer Karol Sidon was detained by security organs for more than a hundred hours; because he was not accused within forty-eight hours, it is necessary to conclude that his personal freedom was illegally restricted for more than forty-eight hours. On 21 January the personal freedom of Jaroslav Suk was seriously violated: members of the police used force and then searched his house and prepared a sample of the typeface of his typewriter. [. . .] A series of acts of repression and defamation against Pavel Kohout was accompanied by dozens of threatening letters whose content is capable of awakening the fear that their addressee will be physically destroyed or seriously injured.[99]

The "spokesvoice" was a recognizable strategy, and probably a good one. The Charter did not want to issue overwrought statements that could be accused of scandalmongering or exaggeration, especially when the repressions were so outrageous that no particular emphasis was needed. Its own reputation for fairness and neutrality—well earned over the course of many years of these objective reports—was far more important than any particular outrage.[100]

Nevertheless, it is not surprising that, within a number of weeks, other types of texts had begun circulating that gave a more personal, lively, and narrative view of life within the Charter. Hejdánek's letters were one such text, and crucial because of it—when new spokespersons were chosen in the fall to replace Patočka and Havel, Hejdánek was a natural choice. Ludvík Vaculík, too, weighed in quickly. For years he had been writing regular "feuilletons," short, quirky personal essays that formed something like a chronicle of his life in the 1970s; in the first days of the Charter, these, too, circulated widely and provided a more personal perspective. His first "post-Charter" feuilleton, entitled "A Cup of Coffee with My Interrogator," quickly became a classic description of the strange pseudo-politeness and veiled threats that reigned during the Chartists' interrogations—this was just the kind of perspective that was absent in the official Charter documents. Václav Havel was in detention from January through May of 1977, and again from the end of January through March 1978, but he found time to write a number of feuilletons that gave a more personal view of questions affecting the Charter—descriptions of his own arrests, an account of his relationship with Patočka, meditations on the legal code (particularly the statutes on "disturbing the peace" and "parasitism"), and others. Ultimately, such feuilletons would become an important genre of the Charter, and the yearly collections of feuilletons that Vaculík had begun putting together in 1976 evolved into something close to an annual anthology of Charter essays, encouraging many other dissidents to experiment with this first-person voice.

We might say that if the Charter documents provided the neutral, third-person narration ("he," "she," "they") of the Charter's "spokesvoice," then Vaculík and Havel gave the Charter its first-person "I," while Hejdánek gave it its second-person "you" as well as a sense of incipient dialogue. What was still missing, however, was a sense of the Charter's first-person plural—a diversity of voices coming together to create a larger public discourse. This would be provided, above all, by the closest thing the Charter had to a newspaper—*Informace o Chartě 77* (*Information on Charter 77*), known to all as *INFOCH*.[101]

Information and the Charter

On February 12, Petr Uhl sat down and wrote his first "Zpráva o Chartě" ("Report on the Charter"). This was, at the time, an unknown genre.[102] What should such a "report" look like, what tone should it take, and from whose point of view should it be written? Would it be angry about persecutions, and accusatory toward the state and the police? Would it make demands, or just report instances of persecution? "For four weeks now," Uhl began, "Václav Havel, spokesman of Charter 77, has been detained, along with the signatories František Pavlíček, a writer, and Jiří Lederer, a journalist. Together with the director Ota Ornest, who is not a signatory of Charter 77, they have been accused of the crime of subversion of the republic, or of damaging the republic's interests abroad." Uhl chose a tone that was neither emotionless nor sensationalist, presenting information without demanding a response—a style without exclamation points that lists facts one after the other, without "plotting" them or structuring them for effect. In effect, he had taken up the tone of a relatively objective newspaper article, informative and low on pathos, but not eschewing descriptive details. It was a happy choice. Uhl would write seven more "Reports" between February and October, fashioning an informal bulletin that reported regularly on Charter activities and above all on the persecution of signatories.[103]

In many ways, Petr Uhl was the ideal person for this job. A veteran of the student New Left, he called himself a "Trotskyist," "revolutionary Marxist," or "ultra-leftist," and his political sympathies lay with the revolutionary working class. Indeed, at the end of his first report he departed from his neutral tone to suggest that working-class support was essential to the Charter, even if workers' interests were expressed only "inadequately and, at first glance, marginally" in the Charter's goals.[104] Nevertheless, Uhl quickly abandoned such outbursts, presumably realizing that they went against the very spirit of openness that reigned elsewhere in his reports. In the end, Uhl's major contribution to the Charter was not ideological but organizational; it was precisely his status as an outlier on the Charter's political spectrum that made it possible for him to become a neutral voice and neutral editor. Because he represented the tiny "Trotskyist" minority among the Charter signatories, he was not seen as being allied to any of the major groupings such as the reform Communists, religious dissidents, writers and artists, or the underground. The perception of neutrality was helped by his personal friendships with a wide range of signatories and his genuine commitment to the idea that the Charter was open to all.

In the summer of 1977, a number of Charter signatories initiated discussions about the Charter's future, drawing in part on a text written by Uhl's father-in-law, Jaroslav Šabata. In the fall, a poll of signatories was arranged, in which about two hundred people were asked whether they would like to have a Charter news bulletin, as well as whether they were satisfied with the institution of Charter spokesperson. (At that stage, after Patočka's death and with Havel in detention facing trial for much of the year, Jiří Hájek was carrying on much of the work himself.) About 80 percent agreed that the number of spokespersons should be increased again to three, and that the job should be held on a rotating basis for one year at a time; but only 35 percent wanted a news bulletin.[105] Historians have not really explained these numbers, and it is difficult in any case to speak about the representativeness of a poll carried out under such difficult conditions; it is possible that a news bulletin was seen as too much of an extravagance, requiring a sophisticated distribution network and a list of subscribers, to whom it might pose further risks. Nevertheless, Uhl decided to formalize the publication of his situation reports and launched a new periodical, *Informace o Chartě 77*, widely and affectionately known simply as *INFOCH*. Beginning with the fifth issue in 1979, published on April 10, Uhl added a formula to the front page of each issue, below the table of contents: "Published by an independent editorial group of Charter 77 signatories," followed by his own name and address.

In a 1998 remembrance, Uhl said, "The idea of writing situation reports came automatically, because my wife and I had been making regular contributions with this type of report to the Berlin quarterly *Informační materiály* for the previous five years, ever since our release from prison at the end of 1973."[106] Uhl's wife, Anna Šabatová, born in 1951, was also crucial to the success of *INFOCH*. She had been picked up, along with her father and brothers, in the major wave of arrests in November 1971. At the time, she was in her third year of college, studying history and philosophy. Šabatová received a three-year sentence, but was released after two years, about the same time as Uhl finished his own four-year sentence. Uhl had met Anna's father and brothers in prison; soon after his release, he traveled to Brno to visit them, and met Anna for the first time. They were married soon after—in part with an eye to possible future jail terms, in which they would not have visiting rights unless they were husband and wife. Šabatová and Uhl must be counted as one of the most active and effective husband-and-wife teams in dissent. In 1978, both were founding members of VONS, the Committee for the Defense of the Unjustly Prosecuted, which I will discuss in the next chapter; in 1979, when Uhl was arrested and sentenced to a five-year jail term, Šabatová stepped up to an even more active role. (During this period, not only was her husband in jail, but her father too; as "second-time offenders," both were sentenced to stricter regimes, and she was allowed to see them only once every six months, for just an hour.) Both Uhl and Šabatová had been subject to extensive surveillance and intimidation since signing the Charter. In a 1980 interview with Eva Kantůrková, Šabatová mentioned some of the harassment she had dealt with: "A month ago they kicked in our door. Yesterday there was security in the building; they checked the ID of everyone who came in against their list, and took everyone who was coming to see us to the station. [. . .] Before, everything was mediated through Petr. I have two children and the police correctly deduced that I didn't have much time for anything else."[107] But Šabatová did find the time to keep *INFOCH* alive for five long years, continuing to publish it for the entire time Uhl was in jail. Starting in November 1979, Šabatová added her own name to her husband's on the front of each issue.[108]

INFOCH's first issue, dated January 14, 1978, was printed in several dozen copies, which were then copied further; it came out at two- to four-week intervals. It evolved fairly rapidly into a clearinghouse for news events about the Charter and its signatories. The core of each issue were the official Charter documents, most of which were published in *INFOCH*, as well as detailed reports about the harassment and repression of individual signatories. Uhl also wrote and published short notices about new samizdat publications (a feuilleton by Vaculík, a new "letter to a friend" by Hejdánek) and brief reports of happenings within the Charter. While these various reports were written in the Charter spokesvoice or Uhl's own "editorial voice," *INFOCH* also opened its pages to individual members. Every issue contained a selection of open letters, interviews, announcements, polemics, declarations, feuilletons, and miscellaneous other articles, written by a wide range of signatories. Václav Benda's essay "The Parallel 'Polis,'" for example, appeared in the June 20–30, 1978, issue. *INFOCH* became a favored forum to place an open letter—the very first issue contained Pavel Kohout's open letter to the Minister of the Interior, complaining about an attack by two secret policemen against Ladislav Hejdánek on January 6, 1978, the anniversary of the Charter's "publication." Even if one wrote a complaint to a government official without circulating it as an open letter, one could still post a notification about it in *INFOCH*, including a summary of questions or demands.

INFOCH provided a forum for more personal and individual voices. There were interviews with new Charter spokespersons and other prominent Chartists, for example. A substantial subset of individual reports constituted

accounts of encounters with the police. These reports were not just announcements; they were stories. Freed from the objectivity of the spokesvoice,
some of them were minor masterpieces, in various genres both tragic and
absurd. When Andrej Stankovič was hauled off in his slippers by police, Olga
Stankovičová wrote an ironic description of the case with strong resonances,
conscious or not, of Kafka's *The Trial*; since the policemen had failed to show
their identification, she concluded, or rather pretended to conclude, that her
husband had been kidnapped, and she reported this crime to the police. In
January 1979, after Šabata was convicted for slapping a policeman, a report
of the trial was written up by his daughter Anna and Zdena Tominová. They
reproduced the trial from memory as best as they could, and their account is
impressive for its controlled emotion:

> Jaroslav Šabata was led into the courtroom in handcuffs, a bit pale, but
> clearly calm and determined. [. . .] After the main proceedings were over,
> Anna and [Šabata's son] Jan were allowed to speak briefly with their father
> right in the courtroom, and Tominová was at least allowed to press his
> hand. Šabata definitely did not give the impression of being a broken man;
> one could see that he clearly felt his moral victory, which in any case had
> illuminated this otherwise gloomy and embarrassing picture of our judicial
> system throughout the proceedings. Šabata is looking forward to meeting
> all of us again; "Well, here we go again: I'll see you in a few months," he
> said with a smile.

Tominová also reproduced Šabata's entire closing defense from memory: "If
any inaccuracies have crept in, it is the result of the imperfection of human
memory and Zdena Tominová apologizes to J. Šabata in advance."[109]

Such reports achieved a pathos and intimacy that was inaccessible to the
more formal reports of the Charter. In fact, all these examples represented a
new kind of voice in the world of the Charter—neither the spokesvoice nor
the somewhat livelier but still formal "editorial" voice of Uhl, but rather a
mosaic of many different speakers. *INFOCH* thus varied the public face of the
Charter and lent a new status to personal experiences—a way of presenting
them in one's own words, but as events of interest to the Charter community as a whole. The "public" that read these reports was still small, of course
(although *INFOCH* did make the journey abroad, and became an important
source of information for Western historians like Skilling and publications
like *Index on Censorship*), but *INFOCH* gave it a chance to be addressed *as a
public*. It provided a way of speaking for oneself, but in a forum where one's

words entered into wider connections and implicitly addressed society as a whole. Historians have tended to read *INFOCH*, if at all, as a neutral source of information; it is, indeed, still one of the best sources for consistent and detailed information about the history of Charter 77. But it is not just a transparent well of information; it was an institution in its own right, one that shaped internal communications within the Charter and helped it evolve from a series of documents signed by the spokespeople into a living, breathing, debating community of its own.

The existence of such a community was something entirely new. In *A Carnival of Revolution*, his insightful work on the Central European opposition movements of the 1980s, Padraic Kenney writes that "Czech opposition had not changed much for the two decades before 1988. There had been new issues raised—like ecology, or peace—or political programs advanced, but the forms and tactics of dissent remained largely what they had been even before the advent of Charter 77. What Charter 77 added was a platform for new participants and new ideas, and a resource for new opposition."[110] In fact, the Charter was a resource so radically new as to constitute a reimagination of what opposition was. For its initial signatories, Charter 77 was an intellectual earthquake, shaking up the world of opposition activity—which, indeed, only now coalesced into something called "dissent." The Charter drew disparate ideas into a network of unified discussions, helping dissidents understand themselves as part of a larger movement with a name and a mission. Under interrogation or during a house search, Chartists could now see themselves as writing a chapter in the larger story of Czech dissent, rather than as just tossing another pebble of suffering into the bottomless pit of police persecution. Like the underground before it, then, the Charter assembled individual fates into a larger whole, creating one of the essential elements of any lasting oppositional community—a set of myths and legends that define oppositional identities. These identities were shaped by the Charter's own activities as well as an intensity of targeted repression that was entirely new in Czechoslovakia in the 1970s. Also like the underground, then, the Charter was defined by a dialectic of police repression and self-articulation, but its internal debates and communication channels were far more active and widespread. Not only did it provide the moral framework for an organized opposition movement, uniting diverse strands of thought and behavior, but it also led to new forms of solidarity, including the "political samizdat" represented by the Charter documents and *INFOCH*, which should itself be seen as a new form of activism.

The Charter shaped a moral appeal, proposed a unitary identity, defended itself against the new levels of persecution it had evoked, led to major new initiatives in samizdat publishing, and fostered new contacts (some friendly, some frictional) among a wildly diverse group of individuals. It remapped the landscape of protest, creating a world of ideas and practices that no future opposition could ignore.

6

The Public of the Powerless

Who was Charter 77—and dissent more generally—talking to?

The question is surprisingly hard to answer. The signatories themselves would talk about it for the entire life of the Charter, and historians continue to discuss it today. In September 1977, in a letter to spokesman Jiří Hájek, Eva Kantůrková wrote:

> all the amazing energy that the Charter signatories have put forth, as well as the danger they have undergone, is too concentrated inside their own circle and has little effect on the public [. . .]. At present, I think it's more important that the wider public find out the Charter has taken up some cause, has stood up for someone against the authorities, etc., than for it to win such a fight against the authorities.[1]

But who was this wider public?

There was a whole range of answers. Certain passages in the Charter itself set up the idea of a "dialogue" with the state—an idea that rapidly came to seem quixotic. "No dialogue with the servants of anti-Communist centers," proclaimed *Rudé právo* on January 21, 1977.[2] The regime saw the Charter as speaking to foreign governments—as a "slander" that would blacken Czechoslovakia's good name abroad. More constructively, many dissidents perceived the Charter as a universal appeal, supporting human rights or framing a philosophical discourse that strove to be available to all. We saw this in Patočka's idea of a moral appeal, in which the message was the medium; this reading also underlies the Helsinki narrative of dissent discussed in Chapter 1. Conversely, others argue that the dissidents were their own main audience. In the parallel-polis narrative, their internal debates are interpreted as a political good in and of themselves (although there nevertheless remains the burning question of just how they are supposed to influence the world outside). Skeptics, however, criticize the "dissident ghetto" for conducting a self-obsessed and neurotic monologue. One version of this criticism was the regime's two-pronged attack on the Charter as a "hostile organization" (a discrete group with its own interests), and on the Chartists as *ztroskotanci* and *samozvanci* who claimed to speak for all but were merely overcompensating for their own miserable failed existences. Another, more reasoned, version is the recent injunction of historians to look at the everyday life of "ordinary people," who had little to do with organized dissent and in many cases had not even heard of the Charter.

We can start to get beyond this impasse by thinking more generally about the idea of the public sphere of dissent. Kantůrková spoke matter-of-factly of a public as if it were the world of people "out there," beyond the circle of Chartists, but we might also ask whether, and how, dissent structured *itself* as a public. To approach this question, it will be useful to consider one of the genres from which Charter 77 itself evolved.

The Age of Open Letters

František Janouch wrote that, in 1970, "open letters were coming into fashion."[3] He was right, although the term *otevřený dopis* (open letter) needs to be unraveled, as it encompasses several possible genres, as well as various contradictions. The open letters of the early 1970s were rarely that "open" in the sense of being well publicized—they were a weak substitute for the editorials or exposés a journalist might write if he or she actually had access to newspapers, radio, or television. But the word "open" does suggest a readership broader than the letter's ostensible addressee. In general, open letters are addressed to someone other than they are written to, and they are sent to someone other than they are addressed to.

To some extent, open letters evolved as a genre from the many "private" letters that intellectuals were sending to state officials in the early days of normalization. These letters could often do little more than convey anger; many of them relied implicitly on the sender's prestige. They evolved from the more personalistic view of political activity that dominated the 1960s, when battles over what could be printed, for example, were argued out during long negotiations with censors, and when prominent journalists often had direct access to high-ranking politicians. In August 1969, for example, Havel sent a prescient but futile private letter to Dubček, encouraging him to speak out in favor of the reform process and against the invasion. This was not an open letter—it was not published in Czech until 1989—but rather an appeal from one Czechoslovak to another, from a cultural and intellectual leader to a political one; as such, it relied implicitly on Havel's own prominence. "It is not my intention to be a self-appointed spokesman of the people," he wrote. "But if anything is certain, it is that most Czechs and Slovaks today think as I do. It's hardly possible to think otherwise."[4] In April 1970, two days after Czech television broadcast the "documentary" montage of conversations taped in the apartment of Václav Černý, Ludvík Vaculík sent a protest letter of his own to the chief prosecutor, calling the broadcast "an insult to all lawfulness, the legal sensitivity of citizens, and human dignity, and therefore an insult to you." Six weeks later, Vaculík received a brief form letter in reply: "With respect to your notice of 24.4.1970 I convey that it was transferred for further measures to the appropriate military prosecutor's office with reference to reg. 14 para. 1 letter b/ of the crim. code."[5] This was the last he heard. In fact, such letters were almost always ineffective—the best they could hope for was to be fed into the state's bureaucratic machinery, which might eventually spit out a form letter in reply.

The early "open" letters represented a shift in rhetorical strategy. They were often still addressed to a state official but sent, at the same time, to Czechoslovak or even foreign newspapers in the hopes of forcing a response. Two letters written by František Janouch in 1972 may illustrate how things were changing. Janouch was incensed when Charles University posted a directive from the Ministry of Education stating that the university could not publish work by people expelled from the Communist Party. Janouch first sent the usual protest letter to the chief prosecutor, pointing out that this directive was at odds with both the criminal code and the constitution. But he then went on to send a *second* letter, this time an open one, to the Minister of Education. First he notified him that his activity was against the law, and said he had asked the chief prosecutor to take appropriate action. "But," he continued, "I am writing this open letter to you in another connection, for the problem

I have described has a moral and ethical side in addition to the legal one." Janouch asked what would happen if a scientist made a discovery that could save lives or alleviate suffering, but had been expelled from the Party—would his discovery be silenced as well? Janouch sent this letter, not just to the Ministry of Education, but also to the largest Prague daily newspapers as well as about thirty other academics.

Janouch received no reply from the Minister of Education, but he did get a short private letter from another Czech scientist, Otto Wichterle, inventor of the modern hydrogel contact lens and one of the initiators of Two Thousand Words. Wichterle admired Janouch's persistence and his efforts to logically "deduce" particular civil rights from the constitution and legal code. But he also found these efforts naïve and, in a letter laced with melancholy humor, suggested that such deductions could only make sense in a region "where the laws of grammar and logic" still applied. The words of the constitution no longer meant what they used to, even if Janouch was still clinging, "through inertia," to the older meanings. "I would be happy to join your resistance," wrote Wichterle, "if I didn't recognize its futility. Maybe it would be more dignified to accept any further blows in silence."

What is most interesting in Wichterle's response is the way he read Janouch's letter—as the public announcement of a legal argument. Wichterle had not yet registered the new rhetorical situation of the open letter; meanwhile, Janouch was already shifting genres from a private complaint, sent through proper channels, to a more broad-based appeal. And as Janouch had specified ("I am writing this open letter to you in another connection"), the "openness" of the letter had more to do with its moral and ethical aspects than its legal ones. In other words, the very fact that Wichterle had seen a copy of this letter was more important than anything it actually said; the appeal was no longer to technical legal considerations (as in the "private" letter to the chief prosecutor), but rather to more universal ethical ones. And in this respect, the open letter was more successful: Janouch discovered that it was circulating in hundreds of copies across the country; a police interrogator told him that it had been published abroad; and a year later it was mentioned in *Der Spiegel*. The letter had reached an audience "over the head" of its actual addressee; this was, of course, the point, and only the mention of the earlier notification sent to the prosecutor makes this letter a hybrid genre, somewhere between a formal complaint from a prominent private citizen and an open letter aimed at a wide readership.[6]

Open letters became one of the favorite genres of protest writing by the mid-1970s, and they gradually grew more sophisticated in their rhetoric and terms of address. They also began to turn increasingly to an audience abroad. In 1975, for example, not only did historian Karel Kaplan write to the Party presidium, film director Věra Chytilová to president Husák, and Jiří Hájek to the Federal Assembly, but Pavel Kohout wrote to Heinrich Böll and Arthur Miller, and Vilém Prečan to the World Congress of Historians in San Francisco. After U.N. Secretary General Kurt Waldheim came to Prague to receive an honorary law degree, Vaculík wrote him an ironic open letter asking him if he was aware of the lawlessness of the regime. When police confiscated a thousand-page manuscript from philosopher Karel Kosík during an apartment search in April 1975, Kosík sent an open letter to Jean-Paul Sartre.

These letters were crossing over from simple public protest into a more precise rhetorical strategy, one that sought to create two kinds of larger communities. Any open letter involves a writer, an addressee, and an imagined community of readers who will (presumably) agree with the points the writer is making. Open letters to Western intellectuals, such as those to Sartre, Böll, and the historians' congress, *included* the addressee in their imagined community; they sought to associate the letter-writer with a larger, usually European, cultural or intellectual heritage. They became more diverse in style and tone, aimed consciously at presenting a Czechoslovak dilemma to a foreign audience. A second type of open letter, aimed at the government and the architects of normalization, *excluded* the addressee, delineating a potential community of reasonable readers from whom the addressee had supposedly separated himself. These tended to be directed "inward," primarily toward other Czechs and Slovaks, although a foreign audience could be in the back of the writer's mind. The most important example of such a letter was also the most famous open letter of the 1970s, written by Václav Havel to President Husák in 1975. In Chapter 3 I talked about this letter's invocation of high culture as a political force; it will be useful to return to it briefly to understand how it encodes a conception of a public sphere, as well as the contradictions built into the open-letter genre.

Havel begins his letter by suggesting that, to a superficial observer, Husák seems to have won the support of the Czechoslovak population: people "commit themselves to numerous output norms which they then fulfill and overfulfill; they vote as one man and unanimously elect the candidates proposed to them; they are active in various political organizations; they attend meetings and demonstrations; they declare their support for everything they are supposed to."[7] The problem, of course, is that this outward agreement is merely a sham, covering up the "real inner state" of society. Behind the façade lies the moral crisis of selfish materialism, political apathy, and fear—the three pillars of the regime. "In the foreground, then, stands the imposing façade of grand humanistic ideals—and behind it crouches the modest family house of a socialist bourgeois."[8] Toward the end of the letter, however, Havel does sketch out his sense of what more genuine public life might look like:

> Where there is, in some degree, open competition for power as the only real guarantee of public control over its exercise and, in the last resort, the only guarantee of free speech, the political authorities must willy-nilly participate in some kind of permanent and overt dialogue with the life of society. They are forced continually to wrestle with all kinds of questions which life puts to them. Where no such competition exists and freedom of speech is, therefore, of necessity sooner or later suppressed [. . .] the authorities, instead of adapting themselves to life, try to adapt life to themselves. Instead of coping openly and continually with real conflicts, demands, and issues, they simply draw a veil over them. Yet somewhere under this cover, these conflicts and demands continue, grow, and multiply, only to burst forth when the moment arrives when the cover can no longer hold them down.[9]

This passage says a great deal about how Havel conceived of the public sphere at this time. Rather than seeing it as a place where people come together to debate (and thereby to constitute themselves as a political body), he understood it largely in "informational" terms, as a way of conveying the true moral state of society to its leaders. Thus, when social pressures finally do burst (as they did in 1968), Havel's letter uses imagery, not just of energy exploding into the open, but of new information appearing: "long-denied mysteries" come to the surface, "life is now one huge surprise," and "to our amazement, we find that nothing was the way we had thought it was." The two metaphors of the "veil" and the "cover"—one hiding reality, the other pushing it down—merge together and, to some extent, express the same thing.[10]

Like many of the open letters of the 1970s, Havel's rests on the borderline between two genres: a personal appeal from a prominent cultural figure to a political leader, and an attempt to go behind that leader's back to address a nascent community of like-minded people. The first genre is still evident in the ending of the letter, which closes with an appeal directly to the president: although no leader rules alone, and the public is also responsible for the state of society, Havel tells Husák, "you have the chance to do much toward at least a relative improvement of the situation." As Pavel Landovský astutely commented: "at that time everyone, without saying it, had hidden away somewhere the thought that Husák, as president, should be the sounding board [*rezonér*] of any complaint and that he could somehow moderate the whole horrible atmosphere!"[11] At the same time, of course, Havel clearly meant for his diagnosis of society's ills to resonate broadly among ordinary people—in this sense, the letter was not meant for Husák at all. As Havel told Jiří Lederer shortly after sending it, "That letter is the type of text that becomes itself, acquires meaning and substance, only through the response to it. Without any resonance, it would be [. . .] whistling in the wind, a defeat, an embarrassment."[12]

Havel's own position thus also combines two genres—that of the scolding prophet and the public spokesperson. He ends the letter: "As a citizen of this country, I hereby request, openly and publicly, that you and the leading representatives of the present regime consider seriously the matters to which I have tried to draw your attention, that you assess in their light the degree of your historic responsibility, and act accordingly." It is worth pausing over Havel's phrase "openly and publicly" *(otevřeně a veřejně)*—what is the difference, actually? In fact, the letter's bifurcated "mode of address" is encoded in this somewhat odd locution: the letter is both "open" (it is not anonymous, its writer has nothing to hide, and is unafraid) and "public" (addressed to a larger political community and its representatives). This, the most successful and lasting open letter of the 1970s, embodies the form's contradictions, one might even say its paradox: by speaking directly to a public representative, the letter-writer assumes a representative role and speaks to society as a whole. Tellingly, the official reaction was to try to redefine the community of the letter's readers; Husák's secretary replied to Havel that the president would not answer him, because Havel had leaked copies of the letter in advance to the foreign media. The implication was that the letter was really directed at the country's imperialist enemies abroad, and Husák could have nothing new to say to them.

Public Addresses

One tradition of discussing the public sphere draws on the work of Jürgen Habermas. It asks how private individuals can "come together as a public" in order to discuss, as equals, questions of common concern; one of its essential prerequisites is that arguments are considered on their own merits, rather than based on the prestige of the person who made them. In the ideal case, such free, open, unconstrained debate among equals allows people to constitute themselves a political body, an enlightened public that can bring the political order into harmony with the moral order. In reality, of course, public life rarely attains this ideal—much of Habermas's discussion of the concept was devoted to considering how European public spheres had fallen short—but it still enabled a tradition of public debate that *responds* to the ideal and strives to become more free, open, and equal.[13]

In the Communist countries of Central and Eastern Europe, of course, there could be no question of full-scale public debate. In theory (Marxist theory), the "bourgeois" public sphere was merely a cover for class interests; in practice, many voices were systematically silenced while others were privileged, for example, by Party membership and access to the Party press. But our discussion of open letters points to a different conception of public life— one that does not rely on widespread public debate, but rather emerges from particular texts, statements, proclamations, letters, and announcements. The rise of samizdat had helped bring many texts to a broader group of people, but there were still too few of them to justify speaking of an open and free public sphere in Habermas's sense. Rather than drawing from a tradition that seeks to evaluate the quality of debate in the public sphere, we might find it more useful to consider a theory that tries to define as clearly as possible the public of a particular text.

Michael Warner has suggested a useful approach to this question in his work on publics and counterpublics.[14] Warner asks what the difference is between any bounded group of people (such as the crowd at a concert or opera) and "a public," a group of people that sees itself as a structured, open entity, engaging in public rather than private discourse. One of Warner's key insights is that a public "comes into being only in relation to texts and their circulation."[15] That is, membership in a public is not determined by some external, "essential" characteristic such as race, gender, ethnicity, or nationality. In order for a group of people to become a public, something more is required— open interaction, a mode of "public address." A public can be seen as a group of people who are addressed by a particular text and who have access to that text—they may read it, or hear it on the radio or at a political meeting.

For Warner, the idea of public discourse only makes sense if we can imagine it taking place among people who don't know each other. Publics are not just cliques or groups of friends; the discourses that construct them are more open and welcoming. This also means that "the address of public speech is both personal and impersonal." If we are to belong to this public, we must perceive its speech as being addressed to us, almost as if to a familiar friend—but we must also understand that it is addressed to strangers as well, who have access to the speech even though they do not know the speaker. Warner knowingly builds his whole idea of a public around a paradox: "how can this public exist before being addressed?" Public speech is aimed at a group of people, but this group is constituted by the speech itself: "We say it in a venue of indefinite address and hope that people will find themselves in it."[16]

Warner's discussion of publics resonates with the concerns of dissent and the ways in which texts like Charter 77 might address a well-defined, yet unbounded audience. When the Charter said it was "a free, informal, and open association of people of different convictions, different faiths and different professions, who are linked by the desire, individually or jointly, to insist on the respecting of civil and human rights in our country and throughout the world," this was a much more effective articulation of a public sphere of signatories than any of the open letters in the previous few years, which had styled themselves rhetorically as an appeal from one person to another, even as they had hoped for a wider audience. Seeing Charter 77 as a "public-generating text" elucidates why it was so much more ambitious than the earlier open letters, and why it seemed to pose such a threat to the regime. The Charter not only imagined an oppositional discourse into existence; it consciously framed this discourse as a *public* one, rather than as the speech of a particular oppositional group. Anyone could sign the Charter; ultimately, of course, few people did, but that did not affect the kind of public the Charter was generating. For the same reason, we can see why the regime devoted so much of its legal and rhetorical energies toward demonstrating that the Charter was a bounded organization of *samozvanci* ("usurpers"). The idea was to present it as a finite group of people, an "organization," rather than a conceptual framework for a much broader public discussion. For the regime, the Charter was not a public organization, but merely a private organization pretending to be public.

For the historian who is trying to recover a past public, Warner's approach is particularly congenial because it gives us a framework for interpreting the written traces that a group—Charter 77, for example—leaves behind. This approach does build in a bias in favor of written texts as opposed to, say, rumors or word of mouth; it turns our attention away from groupings that rely on oral rather than written culture to articulate their identity—groupings like the Czech music underground in the 1970s, for example. But it also helps explain why Charter 77 could achieve a kind of "public" existence that the underground never could—in passing from a largely oral to a largely written culture, a grouping acquires many more potential forms of address with a broader reach. This is not to say that the underground had no written culture, or that the Charter was not shot through with rumors, hearsay, and urban legends, but rather to say that the characteristic modes of address and public existence of each group were different. Jirous's "Report on the Third Musical Revival" was a written text, but also one that he personally "delivered" to many small gatherings of the underground. The Charter, on the other hand, encouraged the sense that its primary existence was in the documents it issued.

A single text, of course, can hardly generate a full-blown public on its own, or at least not for long. Publics are defined, Warner suggests, not only by the forms of address in their constitutive texts, but also by a "circulation of discourse" over space and time. Again, this discourse simultaneously addresses people known and unknown; a polemic, for example, will be written not merely as a response to a specific opponent, but also with an eye to all the other people who will read it. This circulation creates a sense of a public that occupies a certain social space and has its own history and "an ongoing life." Here, too, it is instructive to think of the Charter in terms of this creation of "an ongoing space of encounter for discourse."[17] How to get from the single text of the Charter to a lasting discussion and self-renewing initiative? There were the official Charter documents, but to some extent they simply kept reduplicating the Charter's initial gesture, even as it was expanded to new fields and problems; they did little to create a sense of an ongoing conversation. Many Charter documents were, indeed, based on a process of intensive discussion among experts and smaller groups of signatories, but the goal was to present the document itself as a considered statement, not as a working paper that was still waiting to be finalized. And the discussions themselves were often conducted in private, so as not to endanger sympathizers at academic or government institutes who had access to valuable data but did not want to publicize their support.

This is why *INFOCH* was so important. It created a sense of an ongoing, cross-referential field of discourse. By placing the official Charter documents into a world of larger texts, where they would coexist with open letters, personal essays, announcements, and polemics signed by individuals or ever-shifting groups of signatories, *INFOCH* was able to "relativize" the finality of the Charter's official statements, inserting them into a much larger field of ongoing discussion in which the Charter's "spokesvoice" played an important role, but not the only one.

For Warner, the texts that define a public are able to address us as both friends and strangers—they incorporate us into a group while maintaining the feeling, the sensation, that we are being addressed as strangers and are responding to an appeal that could theoretically be addressed to anyone. Warner speaks of "recognizing ourselves as strangers" inside a public.[18] For those who signed the Charter, I think, there was just this sort of double feeling—of joining a very particular group of people, to be sure, but also of allying with a group of strangers who wanted to talk about public affairs in a more free and open way. The "double vision" of the public text is, of course, a matter of the text's own language as well. Any text makes some presumptions about its audience. It is written in a particular language, and so at the very least it assumes a public that speaks this language. For example, the very fact that the Charter was written in Czech, without a parallel Slovak version, is itself a symptom of the factors that discouraged an effort to bring in more Slovak signatories. But the audience of a text is far more than a question of the national language it is written in. Any text has a certain style, uses a particular vocabulary, appeals to well-known symbols or arguments, and so on. Thus, even as a text raises the fiction of universal openness, it is "weighted" toward a particular kind of listener: "In addressing indefinite strangers, a public address puts a premium on accessibility. But there is no infinitely accessible language, and to imagine that there should be is to miss other, equally important needs of publics: to concretize the world in which discourse circulates, to offer its members direct and active membership through language, to place strangers on a shared footing."[19]

Another reason Warner's framework is so useful for historians and literary scholars who work closely with the textual traces of the past is that it formulates so many suggestive questions we might pose to these traces. Above all, it suggests we look for the markers of "self" and "other," "friend" and "stranger," "known" and "unknown," that are so crucial to constituting a public text. Or, if we consider one final formulation of this double vision: "From the concrete experience of a world in which available forms circulate, one projects a public. And both the known and unknown are essential to the process. The unknown element in the addressee enables a hope of transformation; the known, a scene of practical possibility."[20] Warner's contrast between a "hope" and a "scene"— an aspiration for broader change, and a specific community that will foster these aspirations—is a key to understanding the competing visions of dissent.

The Parallel Polis Revisited

Although the Charter was marked by debates about its audience, its public, and the proper sphere of its activities during its entire existence, the years 1978–1980 saw a particularly intense discussion of these questions. In Chapter 1, I briefly discussed Václav Benda's idea of a "parallel polis." Western historians and political theorists, who turned to this essay as a positive program for dissent, often ignored the fact that it was responding to a very clear sense of crisis within the Charter. Benda himself, without ever retreating from this essay—in fact, he saw developments in the 1980s as fulfilling the trends he had pointed to in 1978—repeatedly emphasized that it was something of an improvisation, tied very specifically to the situation in 1977 and 1978.[21] Benda's essay referred to the "schizophrenia" built into the Charter's position: it knew very well that the government was illegitimate, but it pretended to take the authorities at their word. Benda thought this rift was untenable, and had merely been papered over by the "moral and ethical" approach of Jan Patočka. By 1978, however—a year after Patočka's death, and months after the regime had decided to try to ignore the Charter rather than vilifying it in the mass media—this approach was no longer working. Benda argued that the "abstract moral stance" embodied in Patočka's approach might cause "an ecstatic sensation of liberation," but this excitement "cannot be sustained for more than a few weeks or months" and must give way "to disillusionment and deep skepticism." His idea of a parallel polis was meant to propose a different sort of activity that might mobilize people, as well as provide needed support to Chartists who were feeling demoralized. It was fine for Charter documents to draw attention to "genuinely urgent problems," but it was just as important to propose "parallel civic activities that would enable improvements to be made in the given state of affairs."[22]

Benda argued that the parallel structures must go well beyond the Charter itself: "sooner or later they must become autonomous, not only because they don't fit into the Charter's original form and mission, but because were they not to become autonomous, we would be building a ghetto rather than a parallel *polis*."[23] But it is not really clear what the force of this argument is. Why would parallel structures be more like a "polis" if they were able to cut free from the Charter? And might you be building a ghetto even if the structures *were* autonomous—wouldn't the threat of isolation still hang over them? The term "polis" is suggestive, but certainly the parallel structures don't begin as a full-blown polis—and until they reach that stage of development, just what are they? To many, they would indeed look like a "ghetto" or perhaps an exclusive club open only to a privileged few.

The "parallel polis" makes the most sense if we see it as a stage in the internal debates of the Charter, rather than as a full-blown program of its own. Benda's wisdom consisted in articulating a post-Patočkan view of dissent that would no longer place so much weight on moral questions and would broach the issue of institutional life. In terms of the "double vision" of publics offered by Warner, we could see the parallel polis as an effort to revitalize the Charter as a "scene of practical possibility" rather than as a "hope of transformation"—indeed, the whole thrust of the new strategy was to postpone the question of transformation to a later date, until the possibilities for change had acquired some reality on the ground.

Nothing in Benda's account suggested that anyone would be excluded from the parallel polis; indeed, one of his goals was to open up the parallel structures beyond the circles of Charter signatories. At the same time, the whole "parallel" metaphor makes it unclear just how far, if at all, the polis can intersect with official structures, and it does seem fair to say that Benda was seeking to revitalize dissent as a known space for friends, rather than an unknown one for strangers. The question was how far the Charter could veer toward either extreme before it began to lose its psychological and institutional coherence. When would the fear of isolation, the sense of a ghetto, become just as demoralizing as the "schizophrenia" of the moral appeal?

From Dialogue to Self-Defense: VONS

On January 28, 1978, a large group of Chartists began to arrive at the neo-Renaissance National House on Náměstí míru in downtown Prague, where the union of railway workers was holding its formal ball. Although the Charter had nothing in particular to do with the railway workers, a number of Chartists felt there would be nothing wrong if they attended the ball themselves—after all, it was open to anyone who had bought a forty-crown ticket, and why should Charter signatories feel that they were banned from such activities? They put on their formal wear and prepared for a night on the town.

For many, the ball turned into one of the first real fiascoes of the Charter. Secret police found out about the plan, and they came out in force to turn away the signatories. When Pavel Kohout arrived, "a man with a mouse-like face" took his ticket, stuffed two twenty-crown bills in his vest pocket, and told him: "The workers do not wish to dance alongside enemies of socialism!"[24] A few Chartists got in, but most were denied entrance into the ballroom; as more and more began to gather in the lobby, policemen linked arms and forced them out the lobby's one narrow doorway. A couple blocks away from the National House, Havel saw Pavel Landovský talking to two policemen; when Landovský was arrested, Havel said he would accompany him as a witness to the fact that Landovský had done nothing wrong. At the police station on Bartolomějská Street, Havel found out that, in fact, he had been arrested too, along with Jaroslav Kukal, an electrician who had signed the Charter in January 1977. They were held for nearly two months.

The ball exemplified the "schizophrenia" that Benda would write about soon afterward. Some felt that it was perfectly legitimate for a Charter signatory to do anything that other citizens could do; it was then the regime's business to decide whether it would persecute them or not. Others thought it was foolish to provoke a police response such as attending the ball had done. It was fine and good to pretend the regime took its own laws seriously, but was it worth going to jail to demonstrate that the laws were a rhetorical fiction? And it was one thing to go to jail because you had defended human rights; it was something altogether different to go to jail because you wanted to waltz. Petr Pithart asked scathingly if a signature beneath the Charter was also "a commitment to have fun together? Are we going to go on excursions together? To marry amongst ourselves? To root for the same soccer team?" He called the idea of going to the ball a "sadly ridiculous abasement."[25] Even Havel, who defended the decision to attend the ball, highlighted the absurdity of the whole affair in his droll account of his arrest. For several days and nights of his detention, including a string of interrogations, he was still wearing formal attire.

Whether or not the decision to attend the ball was a wise one, it had far-reaching consequences. As early as 1977, different groups of Chartists had been discussing the need to create a committee that would spread information about political prisoners and call for their release. In February 1978, a group met at the Bendas' apartment and decided to found a Committee for the Release of Václav Havel, Jaroslav Kukal, and Pavel Landovský, also known as the Committee for the Three, which announced its existence in an open letter on February 17, 1978; the announcement was reprinted in the February 7–28 issue of *INFOCH*. These efforts seemed vindicated when the three were released a few weeks later, and plans were drawn up for a more lasting enterprise, to be called *Výbor na obranu nespravedlivě stíhaných*, or VONS: The Committee for the Defense of the Unjustly Persecuted. It issued its first statement on April 27, 1978, saying that it had been founded "in the spirit of Charter 77" in order to "monitor the cases of people who are being prosecuted in the courts or imprisoned for displays of their convictions, or have become the victims of the arbitrary behavior of the police and the courts. We will inform the public of these cases and, as far as we can, help the people affected."[26]

VONS was careful to put some distance between itself and the Charter, mainly to protect the latter. In the original VONS discussions, three possible relationships to the Charter were considered: it might simply be part of the Charter; it might be completely separate; or it might be *v duchu Charty* (in the spirit of the Charter) or *na půdě Charty* (on the basis of the Charter).[27] "In the spirit" won out, suggesting that VONS would be allied with the Charter but would act independently, in both administrative and philosophical terms, and would not necessarily implicate the Charter in everything it did. Nevertheless, VONS must be seen as the most important development in the institutional life of the Charter since the massive repression of January 1977.

Where the Charter had, at first, paid relatively little attention to questions of information and publicity, this was an explicit concern of VONS from the very beginning. It had a number of functions—preparing legal information for political prisoners, providing moral support and material aid for prisoners and their families, and sending representatives to monitor trials. But one of the first goals the founding members discussed was the drawing up and publication of communiqués about political prisoners; "informing the public" was given pride of place in its founding statement. The communiqués were not only circulated within Czechoslovakia, but also transmitted—generally read over the telephone—to friends abroad, like Vilém Prečan, who could both archive them and circulate them further.[28]

In this sense, the history of VONS and *INFOCH* must be seen as closely intertwined. Not only were *INFOCH* editors Petr Uhl and Anna Šabatová also founding members of VONS, but Uhl (along with Václav Benda) was most involved in drawing up VONS's so-called *sdělení*—the "announcements," "messages," "communiqués," or "statements" containing biographies of political prisoners, along with information about their arrests, trials, and sentencing. *INFOCH* then published these announcements; indeed, the VONS communiqués became a regular part of *INFOCH*, taking up significant space in each issue and helping to shape the overall character of *INFOCH* as a bulletin that devoted much of its attention to arrests and political prisoners. The listing of *sdělení* in the table of contents of each issue of *INFOCH*, indented under the rubric *Výbor na obranu nespravedlivě stíhaných*, often took up an eighth or quarter of the page and visibly outweighed the Charter 77 documents themselves. VONS and *INFOCH* thus existed in symbiosis—one of VONS's major goals was to put information about political prisoners into circulation; and, as I argued in the previous chapter, one of *INFOCH's* major functions was to provide its readers with the stories and debates that gave "life" to the Charter's existence. If *INFOCH* hadn't existed, VONS would have had to invent it; if VONS hadn't been founded, *INFOCH* would still have served as a clearinghouse for information about political prisoners.

Although Benda himself was one of the guiding spirits behind VONS, there was nothing "parallel" about it. It was based on intersection, indeed confrontation, with the regime—more specifically, with the police and the courts. But even if it wasn't parallel, did VONS undertake the kind of activity that could pull the Charter out of the "malaise" that Benda had diagnosed? In fact, the activities of VONS, shaped by the considerable courage of its members, posed a number of new questions to the body of Charter signatories. On the one hand, it was admirable that VONS was standing up for people who had been harassed and arrested; on the other, this very activity raised the specter of a vicious cycle in which repression called forth protests, which called forth further repression, and so on. In drawing attention to the plight of those arrested—and how could it do otherwise?—was VONS reorienting the Charter around the question of police and legal persecution? Without intending to, did it risk turning away from the Charter's original goals of dialogue with the regime and its plans to draw up documents calling attention to a range of social problems, not just those having to do with persecution and harassment? In early 1979, Luboš Dobrovský estimated that "repressions against the Chartists had concentrated a considerable part of Charter 77's activity on self-defense." People were following these self-defensive activities rather than reading the Charter's documents, and rather than thinking about signing themselves.[29] Not everyone agreed with Dobrovský—there was a great deal of discussion, for example, about just how effective the Charter documents were—but he was not the only one to raise such concerns.

It would be a distortion to blame VONS alone for these shifts in perspective. In some ways, VONS was merely the most organized and visible instantiation of a division within the Charter between those who were willing to take greater and greater risks, and a larger group that did not want the Charter to become the arena for an ever-intensifying confrontation with the regime. VONS was only part of this equation. In the minds of many Chartists, it was associated with other forms of "extreme" or radical protest; for example, a surprisingly common tactic (and one rarely talked about today) was the hunger strike. The first years of *INFOCH* are littered with announcements of such strikes. On June 28, 1978, in response to Jan Šimsa's arrest, Miloš Rejchrt announced a hunger strike in an open letter to the chief prosecutor. After four days, the strike was taken up by Dana Němcová, her daughter Markéta, and then Svatopluk Karásek, who all held the strike for two days each, in an (unsuccessful) effort to attain Šimsa's release.[30] Ladislav Lis, after a long sequence of police harassments culminated in his arrest on a ridiculous charge of stealing public property (he had let his sheep graze on the grass of a railroad embankment), held a ten-day hunger strike.[31] The October 1978 issue of *INFOCH* carried extensive information about a ten-day hunger strike called by philosopher Julius Tomin to protest the fact that Petr Uhl's and Ladislav Hejdánek's apartments were being guarded constantly by police. Eventually, Zdena Tominová reported, over twenty-five Chartists joined the hunger strike for a day or more.[32] At Christmas 1978, Dana Němcová reported on a thirty-hour hunger strike to be held from noon on December 23 to 6:00 P.M. on December 24 in solidarity with three young men in Brno, Petr Cibulka, Libor Chloupek, and Petr Pospíchal, who had been sent to jail for circulating Charter materials and hosting a folk concert with the singers Jaroslav Hutka and Vlastimil Třešňák.[33] The hunger strike may have been "safer" than, say, actually trying to observe a trial, since it did not involve a direct confrontation with the police or the courts, but it definitely felt like a more radical form of protest, with elements of exhibitionism, than did an open letter or philosophical essay. In a June 1977 feuilleton, Tomin recorded Vaculík's reproach: "Do you know how many people in the world are hungry? There's nothing philosophical about it."[34] Especially the longer strikes, such as Tomin's, helped associate this tactic with a more radical wing of Charter activity.

The more radical protests taking shape in 1978 and 1979 helped pose the question, once again, of who the Charter's audience was. When a hunger strike was announced in *INFOCH*, or in an open letter to the chief prosecutor, who was actually being addressed? Who was expected to join? Were these "public-generating texts" of the sort Warner describes, or simply announcements of individual actions, as if someone were running into battle and shouting over their shoulder for others to join them? As the Protestant minister Jakub Trojan pointed out in a 1979 essay, the Charter was not "born primarily out of the confrontation with power, and so power does not determine our opinions and positions."[35] But what did?

In fact, the question was becoming acute even before Trojan's essay. Since Patočka's death, no one had really stepped in to provide dissent with a moral and philosophical grounding that could advance beyond Patočka's initial formulations, including working out institutional "defense" mechanisms that might provide dissent with an organizational structure. Benda had taken a first step by shifting attention from morality to institutions, but some moral-philosophical grounding for these institutions was still needed. At the same time, even as intellectuals sought clearer forms of self-definition and characterizations of their own community, they found themselves labeled "from the outside" with a word they had hardly used before 1977. In the summer of 1978, Václav Havel decided to take on these problems.

The Greengrocer's Sign and the Brewer's Tale

In the Introduction, I spoke briefly about Havel's famous opening lines: "A specter is haunting Eastern Europe, the specter of what in the West is called 'dissent.'"[36] (Actually, he uses the term *disidenství* [dissidence], which has gradually given way in both Czech and English to the more sonorous *disent* [dissent].) Since at least the late 1960s, the Western press had used the words "dissent" and "dissidents" to refer to opposition intellectuals in the Soviet Union, and occasionally in Czechoslovakia, Poland, and other Warsaw Pact countries as well. As I mentioned in Chapter 1, however, the word itself was not a significant part of the self-consciousness of either opposition or regime. For example, the word hardly appears at all in the conversations Jiří Lederer conducted with banned writers (most of whom would sign the Charter) in 1975 and 1976. Pavel Kohout says he first heard the word in 1973 or 1974 from a German visitor,[37] but one finds it rarely in texts from before 1977.

In fact, this specter established itself in Czech discourse at exactly the same time as Charter 77. In its internal documents, the regime began using the word overnight—realizing, not without a certain grim satisfaction, that, like its big brother the Soviet Union, it now had dissidents of its own. The Chartists themselves acknowledged the term while trying to discourage its use. One of the earliest usages of the term in this context came in a secret internal communiqué of the West German embassy from December 30, 1976, written by Wolfgang Runge, a press officer at the embassy who played a key role in smuggling the text of the Charter, via diplomatic courier, to West German radio. Runge emphasized the wide range of people who signed the Charter, from ex-politicians, artists, and intellectuals to workers: "This is meant to demonstrate that the signatories are not to be understood as 'dissidents,' but as a representative sample of the whole population."[38] As Runge was friends with Pavel Kohout, who also gave him the text of the Charter, we can imagine that this information about the intentions of the Chartists came from Kohout himself.

The word also appears in the interrogation protocol of Jan Patočka, at one of the few moments where Patočka—instead of simply refusing to answer—dictated a carefully worded reply into the protocol. When asked about how the Western media had responded to the Charter, Patočka said he appreciated the fact that it had been mentioned on Western radio stations as well as by Arthur Miller, but he was concerned that "the signatories of Charter 77 are labeled as dissidents and also as followers of Dubček, which I consider to be a fundamental error and misunderstanding."[39] In one of its first official documents, the Charter also thanked the Western media for their support but rejected the label of "dissidents." Here, too, the fear seemed to be that the term "dissident" was restricted to intellectuals and reform Communists from 1968; the Charter document emphasized that it also included workers and people who simply felt the need to speak out. "Charter 77 therefore deserves to be spoken of as a civic initiative rather than as a group of dissidents."[40]

All these early usages of the word indicate that it was closely tied to the Western reception of the Charter, and to the signatories' own ambivalent relationship with the Western press. Media attention was crucial to the Chartists, and for the most visible ones like Havel, it provided a certain degree of protection; but it also meant, invariably, a simplification of their identity, one designed for Western consumption. In the first days of the Charter, the main fear was that Westerners would think "dissidents" had to be intellectuals or reform Communists. By 1978, however, Havel had already come to a deeper understanding of the dangers of the word. In an interview with an Austrian newspaper in March 1978, he said that in the past some people had ended up being in the position of "professional dissidents" or "so-called 'dissidents,'" but that the trial of the underground and then Charter 77 had succeeded in erasing the distinction: "we no longer divide ourselves into dissidents and the others."[41] Havel realized that the term itself was a problem, no matter what it meant, because it set up artificial barriers between the Charter and the rest of society. In this interview, in March 1978, he still seemed to hope that the word might simply go away. A few months later, as he wrote "The Power of the Powerless," he had clearly decided that such an approach was no longer viable. Rather than simply reject the term, he suggested that it be accepted as an inevitable side effect of the dissidents' behavior, but at the same time he wanted to explain, definitively, why they themselves dislike the term. Havel took the word as a teachable moment, an occasion to meditate on just what dissent was.

"The Power of the Powerless" tends to be read as a timeless and definitive statement of dissident morality, but in fact it reflected other recent developments in Havel's thinking. Three years earlier, in 1975, his letter to Husák had still suggested that the state's rulers could cause, and fix, society's problems. By 1978, he had shifted his attention from the rulers to the ruled, looking at the way power is exercised in post-totalitarian systems. "Post-totalitarianism" is Havel's coinage for the kind of regime Czechoslovakia was in the mid-1970s—resting less on the ostentatious depredations of uniformed thugs than on a more subtle stifling of individual initiative and civic solidarity. The letter to Husák had understood citizens as the helpless victims of an external power structure, and had emphasized the fear everyone feels before the ubiquitous state police, "the hideous spider whose invisible web runs right through the whole of society," which "can intervene in one's life at any time, without his having any chance of resisting."[42] By contrast, "The Power of the Powerless" approaches power from a different angle, asking how people are brought to participate in their own subjection.

The centerpiece of Havel's analysis is the now-famous anecdote of a greengrocer who places a sign in his shop window that says "Workers of the world, unite!" In much the way that the French theorist Roland Barthes had deconstructed advertising slogans of the bourgeois public sphere in his 1957 classic *Mythologies*, Havel carries out a semiotic analysis of the greengrocer's message, trying to find the hidden structures that give it meaning. Surely the grocer could not care less whether the world's proletarians unite, nor is he trying to convince anyone that they should. The greengrocer puts out the sign because he is expected to, because he might get in trouble if he didn't. The sign thus has a different, hidden meaning: "I, the greengrocer XY, live here and I know what I must do. I behave in the manner expected of me. I can be depended upon and am beyond reproach. I am obedient and therefore I have the right to be left in peace." Or, in other words: "I am afraid and therefore unquestioningly obedient."[43]

Of course, says Havel, the greengrocer would never hang a sign with this latter message in his window. He needs to be given a "higher" reason for his behavior; and this reason is provided by Communist ideology. Rather than admitting his fear, the greengrocer can easily convince himself that he is merely expressing an idea about the workers of the world—why shouldn't they unite, anyway? Ideology is an "alibi"; it helps the greengrocer hide from himself the fact that he is scared, and even hide from himself the fact that he is hiding something from himself. Putting out the sign, in fact, is just one of many obedient acts he performs every day: "At trade union meetings, after all, he had always voted as he should. He had always taken part in various competitions. He voted in elections like a good citizen. He had even signed the 'anti-Charter.'"[44]

The sign in his shop window, then, is a display of the system's power, but it is far different from a public spectacle—say, a show trial, military parade, or public execution. In fact there is nothing of the spectacle about it. Its strength relies on the fact that people hardly notice it; they are much more interested in the size and color of the tomatoes. The force of the sign, and of all such minute displays of obedience, comes from its multiplication; the very reason people don't read the greengrocer's slogan is that there are hundreds of such slogans "in other shop windows, on lampposts, bulletin boards, in apartment windows, and on buildings; they are everywhere, in fact. They form part of the panorama of everyday life." People may not notice each individual sign, but they "are very aware of that panorama as a whole." And while they may not act in a way that helps the workers of the world unite, they do act according to the dictates of ideology. The panorama of banners, signs, and slogans "tells them what everyone else is doing, and indicates to them what they must do as well, if they don't want to be excluded, to fall into isolation, alienate themselves from society [. . .]."[45]

Ideology for Havel is something halfway between false consciousness and a bad conscience. It makes the bitter pill of our own conformity easier to swallow, sweetening it with high-sounding words (or, more often, depriving it of any flavor whatsoever through the bland bureaucratic jargon of propaganda), but it never fully convinces us; deep down we know that we are deceiving ourselves. Havel calls this state of self-deception "living in a lie." Three years earlier, in his letter to Husák, Havel had portrayed this alienation as a retreat inward, into a private sphere where one renounced any higher values. In "The Power of the Powerless," he now sees it as a split personality, a crisis of identity itself: the line between ruler and ruled runs through each person; living in a lie means sacrificing one's true needs and desires to the artificial ones of the system.[46]

The (somewhat hazy) contrast between the true needs of "life" and the artificial needs of the "system" is one of the keystones of Havel's argument, and is essential for understanding how he wanted dissent to relate to society at large. Havel paints a picture of a dualistic world in which "life, in its essence, moves toward plurality, diversity, independent self-constitution, and self-organization," while "the post-totalitarian system demands conformity, uniformity, and discipline" in order to perpetuate itself as smoothly as possible. Ideology provides the system with internal coherence and an internal "communication system," one that increasingly replaces reality with empty rituals. Havel speaks of the system's "fundamental automatism": individuals are dehumanized and anonymous; their only importance is to fulfill their prescribed roles within the rituals of ideology. A judge, for example, is not expected to decide a case on its merits, but only to hand down a predetermined decision that has already been communicated to her by the Ministry of Justice. A philosophy professor is not allowed to present his own ideas about texts that interest him, but only to repeat clichés about the class struggle and the means of production; his students, in turn, are mere receptacles for this information, which they are supposed to ingest without thinking. Ideology thus creates a world of appearances that are cut loose from reality; indeed, they *suppress* reality—uniqueness, individual creativity, self-realization, freedom, and all the diverse aims of "life" that do not fit in with ideology's false image of the world.

The idea of "living in a lie" would have been quite familiar to Havel's readers. Husák's rule was founded on a number of obvious lies—most notably, that the Soviet invasion had been "fraternal assistance," the Prague Spring "a counterrevolution." These lies had become institutionalized in the Party purges, in the questions asked on job applications, and in the mass media, but they were still quite recognizable. Indeed, one of Havel's brilliant rhetorical tricks in this essay is to begin by discussing the quite intuitive idea of "life in a lie" and only subsequently to deduce from it the more debatable notion of "living in truth," which is, at first, simply defined as the opposite of living in a lie: "Individuals can be alienated from themselves only because there is something in them to alienate. The terrain of this violation is their authentic existence. Living the truth is thus woven directly into the texture of living a lie. It is the repressed alternative, the authentic aim to which living a lie is an inauthentic response."[47]

These authentic aims are located in what Havel calls the "hidden sphere"— the sphere of people's true needs, which their vigilant dissimulation screens from the view of the post-totalitarian system. This accounts for the "explosive and incalculable political power" of living in truth: one person's act of independence inevitably sets an example for others, revealing the possibility of a different form of life, sowing seeds in this "hidden sphere." Because it is hidden, this sphere is all the more dangerous; the revival and recovery of the truth takes place in "semidarkness," almost invisibly, and so when it finally comes to light it will be too late for the regime to repress it. When everyone is pretending to obey, it is impossible to tell how close people are to a breaking point where they will finally recognize their own alienation and try to repair it.[48]

This sense of incalculability, the inability to tell how far our own influence reaches, is one of Havel's most cherished ideas. In Chapter 3, I talked about the "multiplier" metaphors Havel used in his letter to Husák, such as the vitamin or the spark. In "The Power of the Powerless," he adds several more: "the fifth column of social consciousness," in which one's own soldiers are hidden among the enemy; "a bacteriological weapon [. . .] utilized when conditions are ripe by a single civilian to disarm an entire division"; or, more simply, the final straw (in Czech, the "last drop" that makes a cup run over).[49] But there is a major difference. In the letter to Husák, Havel was speaking about the hidden force of *high culture*—banning a magazine, for example, could do unpredictable, long-term damage to society, far beyond the few hundred readers who might be directly affected. In "The Power of the Powerless," the leverage metaphors apply to *anyone's* attempts to live in truth. Nothing better illustrates Havel's massive shift in perspective between 1975 and 1978, a shift that, for many people, made dissent possible. No longer was opposition the purview of a group of intellectuals and former politicians who were seeking to recover lost power and prestige. Through the encounter with the underground and the early discussions about Charter 77, dissent had expanded outward. For Havel, it was now a way of life accessible to anyone.

But how can someone tap into this "hidden sphere" to release the power of the "real intentions of life"? Although Havel is often charged with holding a naïve conception of absolute truth, he actually traces a whole spectrum of ways of living in truth. A first step might come when, one day, the greengrocer decides to stop putting up slogans, voting in sham elections, or suppressing his true feelings at political meetings. These first attempts at living in truth are "confined to not doing certain things," "a mere negation of living with a lie." They are invaluable, but they remain inarticulate and unorganized: "in its most original and broadest sense, living within the truth covers a vast territory whose outer limits are vague and difficult to map, a territory full of modest expressions of human volition, the vast majority of which will remain anonymous [. . .]: you simply straighten your backbone and live in greater dignity as an individual." But when these small acts of self-respect begin to articulate themselves, they may become something more, the "independent spiritual, social, and political life of society." Havel gives various examples of independent life, some of them returning to the sphere of culture (writers who publish in samizdat, historians who organize private seminars, clergymen who "try to carry on a free religious life," whether or not they have been deprived of their office), but also many others (workers who try to form independent unions, people who complain about injustice, young people who live "in the spirit of their own hierarchy of values").[50]

For Havel, the people called "dissidents" are merely a small subset of this much larger independent life of society, "the proverbial one tenth of the iceberg visible above the water":

> if the independent life of society, externally at least, can be understood as a higher form of living within the truth, it is far less certain that "dissident" movements are necessarily a higher form of the independent life of society. They are simply one manifestation of it and, though they may be the most visible and, at first glance, the most political (and clearly articulated) expression of it, they are far from necessarily being the most mature or even the most important [. . .].[51]

Here we can finally see why the idea of a "dissident" is so problematic for Havel. Not only are dissidents merely a tiny subset of a much larger social phenomenon, but they are a subset chosen according to arbitrary criteria. This is why Havel's definition of "dissident," which he gives in section 13 of his essay, feels so jury-rigged and *ad hoc*—it is meant to be. In fact, he doesn't even define the term but merely tries to mark how it is used: "It seems that the term is applied primarily to citizens of the Soviet bloc who have decided to live within the truth and who, in addition, meet the following criteria [. . .]."[52]

There are five such criteria, which are worth examining just to show how arbitrary they are. Dissidents are, first, people who "express their nonconformist positions and critical opinions publicly and systematically," and therefore are well known in the West; second, they have acquired a certain prestige in their own countries, and so are protected from the worst persecution; third, their work is political in that it reaches "beyond the narrow context of their immediate surroundings or special interests to embrace more general causes"; fourth, although they need not be professional writers, they are "writing people," "people for whom the written word is the primary—and often the only—political medium they command"; and fifth, whatever their actual professions (physicist, sociologist, actor, worker, singer), they achieve recognition in the West as activists rather than because of the work they do in their own fields. Havel mentions that he is not seen abroad as a playwright who is also a concerned citizen, but as a dissident "who almost incidentally (in his spare time, perhaps?) happens to write plays as well."[53]

"Dissent" thus covers a small subset of the social activities that preserve independence, freedom, and creativity (the "aims of life") inside the post-totalitarian system. In a strange way, then, the limited Western conception of dissent threatens to "cover up" the hidden sphere just as post-totalitarian ideology does. Another of Havel's complaints is that the Western definition only covers a small subset of what "dissidents" themselves actually do. But perhaps the most serious problem is that the Western definition makes dissent seem like a conscious choice or even "a special profession, as if, along with the more normal vocations, there were another special one—grumbling about the state of things."[54] Indeed, one reason Havel chose a worker, and not an intellectual—a greengrocer, and not a poet or physicist—as his protagonist was to suggest that the independent life of society was open to far more people than just a narrow class of Western-anointed "dissidents."

Here we can see how "The Power of the Powerless" emerges very clearly from the crisis of the Charter, a year and a half into its existence—from the fears that it was becoming a closed interest group. Like Benda, Havel recognized that the regime's manic repression of the Charter had destroyed its original hopes to address society as a whole; subsequently, the regime's attempt to silence and suppress the Charter had left many wondering if it could have any effect at all. But unlike Benda, Havel wanted to return to Patočka's original moral appeal in order to deepen and expand it in a way that would make "living in truth" seem more widely acceptable and, indeed, necessary. Indeed, although Havel does endorse Benda's idea of "parallel structures" in section 18 of his essay, the moral appeal remains dominant in his argument, as is evident in his dedication of the essay to Patočka, whom he quotes at several key moments. Ultimately, Havel's "return" to Patočka is not really compatible with Benda's attempt to move onward from a politics of moral appeals to one of grassroots institution-building. Rather than imagine parallel dissident structures, Havel wanted all his readers to think about their own participation in the system, and hence their own ability to change it. He also wanted them to stop thinking of dissent as a political calcula-tion, and to start recognizing it as a straightforward expression of their own immediate interests.

Havel tells another story in order to illustrate this point. It is the story of the brewer Š, and because it has received relatively little attention compared to the more famous fable of the greengrocer, it is worth quoting at length:

> In 1974, when I was employed in a brewery, my immediate superior was a certain Š, a person well versed in the art of making beer. He was proud of his profession and he wanted our brewery to brew good beer. He spent almost all his time at work, continually thinking up improvements, and he frequently made the rest of us feel uncomfortable because he assumed that we loved brewing as much as he did. In the midst of the slovenly indiffer-ence to work that socialism encourages, a more constructive worker could not be imagined.
>
> The brewery itself was managed by people who understood their work less and who were less fond of it, but who were politically more influential. They were bringing the brewery to ruin and not only did they fail to react to any of Š's suggestions, but they actually became increasingly hostile toward him and tried in every way to thwart his efforts to do a good job. Eventually the situation became so bad that Š felt compelled to write a lengthy letter to the manager's superior, in which he attempted to analyze the brewers' difficulties. He explained why it was the worst in the district and pointed to those responsible.
>
> His voice might have been heard. The manager [. . .] might have been replaced and conditions in the brewery might have been improved on the

basis of Š's suggestions. [. . .] Unfortunately, the precise opposite occurred: the manager of the brewery, who was a member of the Communist Party's district committee, had friends in higher places and he saw to it that the situation was resolved in his favor. Š's analysis was described as a "defamatory document" and Š himself was labeled a "political saboteur." He was thrown out of the brewery and shifted to another one where he was given a job requiring no skill. [. . .] By speaking the truth, Š had stepped out of line, broken the rules, cast himself out, and he ended up as a subcitizen, stigmatized as an enemy. He could now say anything he wanted, but he could never, as a matter of principle, expect to be heard. He had become the "dissident" of the Eastern Bohemian Brewery.[55]

The brewer's story serves a double purpose. First, it shows that people do not *decide* to become dissidents; you don't just choose one day "to take up this most unusual career. You are thrown into it by your personal sense of responsibility, combined with a complex set of external circumstances." But second, the story of the brewer reveals how difficult it is to remain inside the official structures and still do good work that makes a contribution to society. The brewer was a bit more honest than the greengrocer, who, after all, had been willingly going through the motions of obedience and had even signed the Anti-Charter. One might have thought the brewer's position was a tenable response to normalization, a way station between hanging up Communist slogans and stepping into open opposition. Couldn't one imagine small-scale, positive work that would improve one's local conditions without antagonizing the government? And couldn't a job well done, in and of itself, actually end up being a blow to the regime?

Havel felt a pressing need to dispose of this idea. The problem was not with small-scale work, *per se*, but rather with the idea that honest and creative people could *avoid* a run-in with the regime. On the contrary, says Havel, a run-in was inevitable; it flowed inevitably from the very nature of "post-totalitarianism," an all-encompassing system that pushed everyone inexorably toward greater anonymity and uniformity. This is the lesson of the Brewer's Tale.

Earlier, I suggested that Havel chose "ordinary people" like the greengrocer and the brewer because he saw dissent, along the lines of the underground and Patočka, as a straightforward decision to live in the truth. (It might be a *difficult* decision, but in Havel's telling it rarely seems *complicated*—it is always moral, rather than logistical.) Locating dissent in ordinary occupations is also tied to the larger question of the public of Charter 77: if dissent is open to brewers and greengrocers, then the Charter is speaking implicitly to all of society, not just to a few brave intellectuals. "The Power of the Powerless" presents dissent as maximally open—Havel is speaking to a world of strangers and asking them to step into the unknown. He is more concerned with the hope of transformation than with the scene of practical activity, more concerned with an inspiring call to action than with a description of what that action would look like. Indeed, this is one way of understanding the brewer's tale: no matter how much people try to make themselves at home in the post-totalitarian world, they will end up being "thrown" into dissent by their innate honesty and creativity.

Along with this implicit appeal to ordinary people, Havel also insisted that the world of dissent was closely tied to "everyday life," one of the key categories of "The Power of the Powerless." Havel repeatedly turns to everyday life—in Czech, *každodennost*, literally "every-day-ness"—as a way of making dissent seem more down-to-earth and intuitive. Thus, Havel rejects explicit political programs because they do not speak to people's "everyday concerns"; he wants to rebuild political life from the roots up, so that it corresponds to what people really need and want. In the beginning, this political life won't even look political; Havel calls it *pre-political*, and it will emerge from "the everyday human world, the world of daily tension between the aims of life and the aims of the system." Dissidents, in turn, are not political animals but pre-political ones; if the government fears them, it is not because they form "an alternative power clique," but "because they are ordinary people with ordinary cares, different from the rest only in that they say aloud what the rest cannot say or are afraid to say."

At the end of his essay, Havel sketches out a vision of political renewal meant to apply to both East and West, both Communist and democratic society. Having defined normalization as a "post-totalitarian" society, he now begins to speak of a "post-democratic" society as well, in which Western consumerism and technocratic capitalism may find a new spirituality. He hopes that political life will be reconstituted by small, informal, local groupings of people that "emerge, live, and disappear under pressure from concrete and authentic needs"—groupings that resemble the dissidents' initiatives of post-totalitarian Czechoslovakia. In this sense, dissent may point to possibilities that are not yet clear in the democratic West; Havel asks "whether right here, in our everyday lives, certain challenges are already encoded, quietly waiting for the moment when they will be read and grasped."[56]

The most striking fact about "The Power of the Powerless"—and one that is visible only if we read it in context—is that it does not mention VONS. This is highly unusual. Not only had VONS emerged from the effort to get Havel himself released from prison after the railway workers' ball; not only was Havel a founding member of VONS; but by October 1978, when Havel dated his landmark essay, VONS was a well-established presence, having issued some forty-five communiqués. Even more puzzling, Havel devotes a whole section, number 16, to the idea of "defense," mentioning the Polish Committee for Social Self-Defense (usually known by its Polish acronym, KOR) and clarifying that Charter 77 was "clearly defensive in nature." But he fails to bring up VONS at a moment when it would have been natural and quite expected.[57]

Instead, Havel sought explicitly to justify the "defensive character" of the Charter with one further reference to "everyday life." The defense program might seem "minimal, provisional, and ultimately negative," since it offers no positive program of its own. Havel disagrees, saying that the post-totalitarian system cannot simply be countered by an alternative political program. The defensive program, far from being minimal, was actually more effective at superseding politics as usual:

> defending the aims of life, defending humanity, is not only a more realistic approach, since it can begin right now and is potentially more popular because it concerns people's everyday lives; at the same time (and perhaps precisely because of this) it is also an incomparably more consistent approach because it aims at the very essence of things.[58]

Defense is a way of staying close to everyday life and thus of seeking a more fundamental transformation.

This may be inspiring, but it remains strikingly unclear. Chartists had voiced many criticisms of the "defensive strategy," but not because it was minimal or provisional. On the contrary, VONS symbolized a type of activity that was maximalist, radical, and threatened to generate a cycle of protest and repression that would make dissent into a photographic negative of the secret police. Havel's pointed reference to "people's everyday lives" here seems to be an implicit attempt to frame the "defensive" activities of VONS as somehow closer to people's real needs. But his failure to actually mention VONS seems an implicit acceptance of how difficult this argument was to make. VONS, indeed, may have been one of the clearest examples of what Havel called, without a hint of overstatement, the "cruel paradox" of dissent: "the more some citizens stand up in defense of other citizens, the more they are labeled with a word that in effect separates them from those 'other citizens.'"[59] Nothing represents this cruel paradox as eloquently as the absence of VONS from "The Power of the Powerless."

Havel's deployment of the category of everyday life raises two interesting lines of questioning. First, we can return to the question of the type of public constituted by Charter 77. A skeptical reader of "The Power of the Powerless" would note that it is long on "hopes for transformation" but short on descriptions of "the scene of practical politics." Everyday life and other terms like "concrete," "authentic," or "true" needs are a shorthand that allows Havel to avoid discussing actual civic initiatives; we might ask if the term "everyday life" here has any meaning other than as a vague existential hope for some ill-defined authenticity or immediacy of political life. Yet one of the most active initiatives within the Charter seemed to be pushing people away from the concerns of daily life and tying their fates ever more closely to the repressive choices made by the regime.

A second set of questions asks about the Charter's relationship to its larger public, those "other citizens" it might potentially address and draw into its discussion. Havel suggests that the defense of everyday life could be a more popular form of dissent—but what would such a defense look like? What was the everyday life of dissent, actually? As I mentioned in Chapter 1, the everyday experiences of the average Chartist didn't have much in common with the daily lives of the vast majority of Czechoslovaks. They were shaped far more by harassment, employment difficulties, sanctions against one's spouse and children, and—for the major contingent of dissident intellectuals—the inability to publish one's writing or work in one's chosen field. In the summer of 1978, when Havel began writing "The Power of the Powerless" at Hrádeček, he was under frequent surveillance by the secret police; they erected an observation booth on stilts resembling a Soviet moonwalker right outside his house, vandalized his car, and accompanied him whenever he left the house, even when he walked his dogs in the forest. What happens to everyday life when such things occur every day? In reporting on his house arrest, Havel insisted that his own situation was quite bearable, but that he was writing about it because "my harassment illustrates the general situation and should not be kept a secret."[60] But did his harassment really illustrate the general situation? Under such conditions, was it possible for a dissident to meditate on the everyday life of society as a whole?

The Courage Debate and "Dissi-Risk"

In the final months of 1978, Havel's theses would be debated even before "The Power of the Powerless" had begun to circulate widely in samizdat—a clear sign that he had articulated questions and dilemmas that faced many others besides himself. On December 6, 1978, Ludvík Vaculík wrote a short feuilleton called "Notes on Courage," addressed to Karel Pecka on his fiftieth birthday. On December 31, Petr Pithart voiced similar arguments in a feuilleton called "The Shoulders of a Few." These two essays set off a major debate, punctuated most furiously by Václav Havel's open letters to each author. A samizdat edition on the controversy, called simply "Discussion," numbered twenty-one entries from seventeen different authors. The debate was an open acknowledgment of major fault lines running through the Charter community.

Vaculík's feuilleton, "Notes on Courage," was a meditation on what kinds of actions were worth getting arrested for. He began by mentioning the people arrested in 1971 for circulating flyers encouraging Czechoslovak citizens not to participate in the elections. Vaculík suggested that "it is hard to be locked up for something that will have ceased to excite anyone even before your sentence is up"—a harsh comment for the many Charter signatories who had been jailed in the early 1970s. Vaculík then turns to Karel Pecka, jailed in the 1950s. Pecka's courage lay, not in surviving imprisonment in the uranium mines, but rather in how he put his life back together after getting arrested "more or less by accident" as "a young, immature person." While wondering aloud "where are the decent limits of such reflections?" Vaculík clearly suggested that the Charter might be asking too much of people, alienating those who can never hope to be so heroic:

> Most people are well aware of their own limits and refrain from actions whose consequences they would be unable to bear. [. . .] An instinctive fear of hunger prevents a healthy and sensible person from feeling sympathy for someone who, in his own and the general cause, goes on a hunger-strike. A matter of life and death? The sensible person gets cold feet and tries to find a way of dissociating himself from it at least a little.

Under these circumstances, the actions of the Charter might look like "the increasingly heroic actions of an increasingly diminishing platoon of fighters," less and less relevant to the majority of people.[61]

Rather than heroism, Vaculík appealed to "the integrity of the ordinary person" who believes "that decent behaviour will find a decent response."

Vaculík closed by returning to the still-burning question of the difference between the 1950s and the 1970s, asking which was worse. He suggested that, under normalization, "the main brunt of the attack is not directed so much at heroes as against what we used to consider the norm of work, behaviour and relationships." Heroes were needed less than people who would try to maintain standards of professionalism, honesty, and hard work, even on a small scale:

> Under the circumstances, every bit of honest work, every expression of incorruptibility, every gesture of goodwill, every deviation from cold routine, and every step or glance without a mask has the worth of a heroic deed. [. . .] While heroism frightens people, giving them the truthful excuse that they are not made for it, everyone can bravely adhere to the norm of good behaviour at the price of acceptable sacrifice, and everyone knows it.[62]

Vaculík was careful to temper his criticism of the Charter itself. Although he pointed out the negative effects of too much heroism, he also suggested that if anyone didn't like the Charter's activism, they "should withdraw quietly and undemonstratively and not hamper the work of those who are left." Three weeks later, on New Year's Eve, Pithart finished his feuilleton called "The Shoulders of a Few." It was directed much more clearly at the Charter's active members, although Pithart did not name any names. In any political grouping, argued Pithart, there will be an "active minority" that is simply more interested in politics than the rest of the members. It may seem natural for this minority to take the community's affairs onto its own shoulders, but Pithart was trying to think through why that might be dangerous. In fact, "being less concerned about politics belongs to life, or actually that's what a decent life is, and good politics secures such a life" for the passive majority. But, said Pithart, an "active minority" inside the Charter had diverted attention from things that really matter to politics for politics' sake: "a handful of enthusiastic, self-sacrificing, risk-loving, fervent, impatient, in short, radical—often against their own better resolutions—people took into their own hands a cause that was supposed to be common." To the obvious reply—if you don't like the way things are being run, do it yourself—Pithart suggested that an active minority always has different interests from the passive majority. It is more concerned "with proving its own truth against power, than with the common interest of the nation."

Pithart reproached the unnamed minority for wanting more and more, and achieving less and less: "Who today knows about their good work? According to a law of internal development in any small circle of initiates, they are more and more consumed by their own internal problems and conflicts." Similarly to Vaculík, but with a much more pointed criticism of the Charter leadership, Pithart suggested it would make more sense to pay attention to "our everyday life, rather than to sacred freedoms." In a more or less explicit repudiation of the whole Helsinki interpretation of dissent, Pithart relegated "the paper world of constitutions, declarations, and international pacts" to the sidelines, seeking instead to foster something "more basic, something like an uncertain inner claim on those rights and freedoms, which, in any case, are unequivocal only in the logical sense." Against the logical clarity of Helsinki, that is, Pithart wanted to pay more attention to personal responsibility and "the overall quality of human relations."[63]

Vaculík and Pithart both knowingly crossed certain lines in their essays. Vaculík dared to suggest that some Chartists were going to prison for things that weren't worth it. Underneath his arguments one can hear a repudiation of the Patočkan formula that some things are worth suffering for. Some things, Vaculík seems to say, aren't. One can, perhaps, also faintly hear questions such as whether Jaroslav Šabata's altercation with a police officer at the Czechoslovak-Polish border was worth two years in jail, or whether the surveillance of Hejdánek's apartment warranted a ten-day hunger strike. Pithart ruffled even more feathers by accusing the Charter's most active members of leading it astray, without stating clearly whom or what he was talking about, such that his own essay seemed to be consumed with the "internal problems and conflicts" he was complaining about. (In fact, many observers assumed his main target was Petr Uhl.[64]) In the end, Pithart's language may have uncomfortably recalled the regime's own "usurpers" rhetoric.

There was much to reproach in both essays, but they deserve credit for openly facing a question that was becoming more and more important to many Chartists. Was the Charter turning into Vaculík's "increasingly diminishing platoon of fighters" or Pithart's "small circle of initiates"? How would it recognize when its own interests had become a world of their own, rather than a symbol of universal aspirations? Was it more concerned with living in truth, whatever that might mean, than with reaching the people around it?

Of the many replies—most of which ranged from doubtful to outright dismissive—the most striking came from Václav Havel, who circulated two surprisingly angry open letters in response. Without mentioning "The Power of the Powerless," finished a few months earlier—he may have been frustrated that neither Vaculík nor Pithart seemed to have read it—Havel circled around

234

a similar set of arguments. No one *chose* to be a dissident. Where Vaculík suggested that people should calculate whether a given action was worth getting locked up for, Havel replied that the regime arrested some and didn't arrest others, based on its own cynical calculations, not on the intrinsic merit or influence of particular deeds. People don't go to prison because of their own ambitions, but "because of the indecency of those who lock people up for writing novels or making tape recordings of unofficial singers!" Given the regime's incalculability and fundamental indecency, it was foolish to base one's own sense of right and wrong on how the police would react to one's behavior. "None of us decided beforehand that we would go to prison; what's more, none of us decided that we would become dissidents. We became them, without even knowing how [. . .]."[65] It's useful to remember that, the last time Havel was arrested—at the railway workers' ball in January 1978—he had not even realized he *was* arrested until he arrived at the station. Thinking he was going to testify to Landovský's innocence, he had instead been thrown in a cell.

Havel's replies were cogent, but his vehemence revealed that both Vaculík and Pithart had touched a sore spot.[66] Havel finished his reply to Vaculík by saying that he "resented" him for "not telling the truth." As for Pithart, Havel welcomed an open discussion about the Charter's problems—but "your feuilleton is not a contribution to such a discussion." He accused Pithart of settling some obscure personal accounts and dressing this up "in a cloak of 'politological' meditations." These were harsh words (especially coming from the famously polite and mild Havel), but we can imagine why he was so angry. By any account, Havel belonged to Pithart's "active minority," and, having served two jail terms since January 1977 (one of them for the railway workers' ball, which by Vaculík's lights surely "wasn't worth it"), he was certainly justified in seeing "Notes on Courage" as touching on his own behavior. And he surely must have felt frustration with these two reform Communists who themselves had never been in jail. In his reply to Vaculík, he mentioned, "Some of us have been in this tough and depressing confrontation with the secret police for two years [i.e., since Charter 77], some for ten years [since 1969], and some their whole lives"—a not-so-veiled reference to the fact that, whereas Vaculík and Pithart had once been Party members, Havel himself, and many other Chartists, had been suffering from the attentions of the regime long before normalization began. Havel was normally cautious about raising the divisive issue of Party membership in public discussions; the fact that he let this comment slip shows just how agitated he was.

At the same time, despite his effective arguments, Havel may have missed the point of both feuilletons. Both Vaculík and Pithart were trying to articulate a certain disillusionment with the Charter and indeed with the whole conception of dissent it had come to embody. Perhaps they had been unsuccessful in naming this disillusionment, but it still existed, whether or not Havel said it made sense. A number of people did speak up in their defense. Anna Marvanová actually suggested that Vaculík had not gone far enough. She thought the Charter leadership needed to do more to draw on the experiences of less active signatories: "after all, 'activity' and 'impassioned commitment' are definitely not protection against errors, let alone false paths."[67] A woman who signed herself only as A.R. also thanked Vaculík for trying to step outside the circle of dissidents and address everyone else. Where Havel accused Vaculík of "not telling the truth," A.R. told him: "And so this time you are telling the truth, a certain truth, even if it speaks to someone else besides Václav Havel [. . .]."[68]

Perhaps the most effective reply came from someone writing under the name of Jan Příbram.[69] Příbram wrote quite simply that Pithart's feuilleton "is, as far as I know, the first published text to write about what is usually called, in private conversations, the 'crisis of the Charter.'" Police repression had maneuvered the Charter leaders into a difficult position, forcing them "to take up positions and make decisions before these decisions are able to mature on their own." This was a recipe for radical behavior. Příbram accepts this, indeed is thankful for it, but thinks it would be naïve to ignore the resulting "polarization." Those who like conflict will naturally take the lead, while the public they are trying to convince "becomes a mere observing audience." The most active are like "an isolated avant-garde" that has become separated from the main army; unable to admit that they are lost, they blame the others for remaining far behind. Příbram was not unsympathetic toward the "active minority"—people like Havel, he thought, were "despairing," in part because they could never erase the suspicion that they were acting merely to win "a martyr's palm." But for just this reason, he welcomed Pithart's feuilleton and hoped that it would lead to more discussion.

The whole "courage debate" was a bit chaotic, for several reasons. For one thing, it was the first major airing of some troublesome questions. It was undeniable that a few active members had helped change the Charter's profile, and that VONS was raising a whole new set of concerns. But it was painful—and bordered on the tasteless—to criticize VONS members for the work they were doing. A second source of confusion was the mix of genres involved. Vaculík's and Pithart's original essays were feuilletons and subscribed to fairly specific genre rules: rather than logical, structured disquisitions, they were fast-moving pieces that painted narrative scenes and sought to interpret them concisely. This type of feuilleton was a long-established genre in Czech journalism and literature—in fact, one of its appeals had always been the way it straddled the boundary between journalism and literature. As a rule, the feuilleton seeks to raise questions rather than answering them; suggestive rhetorical questions are common, and the whole operates at a level of generality that can be provocative. An expert feuilletonist like Vaculík knows how to play on the frequent shifts between the general and the specific, such that his reader often doesn't know whether he is making a serious proposal or simply following the twists and turns of his own state of mind.

Some of the replies were feuilletons in turn, remaining at a similar level of suggestiveness. Others, like Havel's, were open letters, boiling Vaculík's and Pithart's ideas down into a few theses, which were then refuted. If Havel got so irritated at the vagueness and sloppiness of his opponents' arguments, it may also have been because he misread their genre, treating provocative rhetorical questions as if they were carefully thought-out theses. Luboš Dobrovský made this point in an open letter to all three: Havel had unfairly "radicalized" Vaculík's and Pithart's arguments in restating them, while Vaculík and (especially) Pithart had raised good questions in a somewhat sloppy and careless way. Other entries in the debate played with different genre conventions. Jiří Gruša subjected Vaculík's feuilleton to a lengthy "semantic analysis" in which he traced the meanings of Vaculík's words back to entirely different contexts, ultimately suggesting Vaculík had strayed too close to endorsing collaboration with the secret police. Dobrovský then wrote another open letter to Gruša, who replied to him in turn. Josef Zvěřina, a priest who had been imprisoned in the 1950s, wrote an "anti-feuilleton" discussing his time in prison and suggesting that courage is never as clear-cut as Vaculík seemed to think. ("A hero is someone who gets into a situation he can't get out of.") Jaroslav Suk, in an astute reply to Pithart, ended with a P.S. that speaks volumes about the state of intra-Charter communications: "I deny the latest piece of gossip that has reached me: I am alleged to have quarreled with my good friend Petr Pithart."[70] A.R. suggested that "after ten years in the absence of polemic, people have a desperate need for some." In the Charter, a group of intellectuals had been granted a rare "moment of understanding without words," but unfortunately they couldn't stop talking.[71]

Another source of confusion was that both sides were in broad agreement about the goal of bringing dissent into closer contact with society at large. They both thought "small-scale" acts of honesty and courage were important; Havel simply wanted to emphasize that these acts would pull you inexorably toward a more open opposition, while Pithart and Vaculík thought that people might well persist in such behavior while never getting near a real-life dissident. But it took some time for all the participants to realize where, exactly, their disagreements lay. In fact, the debate on courage was not actually about courage, but about the ways dissent was interacting with the rest of society. It was not about the greengrocer; it was about the brewer.

Both Pithart and Vaculík eventually developed their initial feuilletons into more sophisticated arguments. Pithart would write a number of controversial essays over the next ten years, pursuing a similar set of ideas: the dangers of separating off the Charter into a separate world with its own customs, rules, friendships, and standards. (His own attempts to make dissent less demanding were all the more striking in that he himself had served for years as one of the major contacts for sending banned literature abroad, as well as for receiving shipments of émigré journals and literature—a very risky, but less visible form of dissident activity.) One of Pithart's major statements on these issues came in an essay called "Disi-rizika" (Dissi-risk), dated February 28, 1979. By this time—two months after finishing "The Shoulders of a Few"—Pithart had read "The Power of the Powerless," and now he took aim at, among other things, the story of the greengrocer. What was the real significance of the slogan in the vegetable stand? For the greengrocer and his customers, its importance was negligible. "For us, for intellectuals, it is probably greater: words and slogans matter a great deal to us. But must we always be so cursedly literal?"

Pithart pointed out that for the intellectuals of dissent, "Our protests are above all verbal, and that's natural. But that isn't the only valid and effective form of criticism! We are, in part, people of the word and so we have an unavoidable feeling that what isn't expressed doesn't count. Doesn't exist. We suffer from a mania of explicitness; what's more, our words always reckon with power as their most important partner: as their main addressee [. . .]." In Pithart's estimation, dissident intellectuals had a hard time understanding non-verbal protest. One of the most unpleasant questions for dissent was thus the question of "small-scale work." Of course it could get you into trouble if you framed it as a protest against the regime, but who was doing the framing? Such protests were the obsession of intellectuals, not of people who were genuinely trying to improve their surroundings but felt no need to turn their good work into a universal critique of the system. "Sometimes," wrote Pithart, "I have the feeling that we would most like to take a well-made product and write on it: Let no one pass by without noticing what a blow the regime has suffered here."[72] Although Pithart takes explicit aim at the greengrocer, his real target should have been the brewer Š, and we can see what a Pithartian critique of this story would look like: Why in the world does the brewer need to write a *letter* to his superiors? Is he really so naïve as to think that will do any good? (Here Havel's "primitivism," his fascination with the brewer's naïve sincerity, is clearly on display.) Is the brewer really unable to work around his bosses and get something done despite their incompetence? Isn't that what capable subordinates with hopeless bosses do all over the world? Rather than answering such questions, Havel's Brewer's Tale had adroitly sidestepped them. But Pithart was looking for a different way to understand dissent, in terms of the ordinary work of ordinary people striving to improve their communities and local environments, rather than as a protest, parallel polis, or moral appeal.[73]

Ludvík Vaculík would take yet a different approach, but his reply was somewhat longer in coming.

Dreams of a Dissident

In 1968, during the Prague Spring, an employee of the Ministry of the Interior telephoned the Vaculíks. He informed Madla Vaculíková that their apartment was under surveillance: "There's a microphone, five millimeters in diameter, in the room you call 'the big room.'" He gave her the names and addresses of agents who had ordered the surveillance and installed the device from the attic above. Vaculíková also discovered their phone was bugged. The days when the secret police would warn their own victims, however, were soon over. Eventually the Vaculíks had listening devices in all the rooms of their apartment—devices that, they discovered after 1989, could even pick up conversations in the corridor and by the elevator outside. There was a camera stationed across the street, and one of the apartments in their building (they lived on the sixth floor) was taken over by the police as a headquarters for listening to them. As a result, for some twenty years between 1968 and 1989, they avoided talking about important things and wrote them instead on a slate; if they wrote anything on paper, they flushed it down the toilet.

For the regime's most prominent opponents, these were standard measures, and they indicate how the private and "everyday" lives of not just Charter signatories, but also their families, could become distorted by police surveillance. In a 2002 interview, Vaculíková remembered perhaps five major house searches "where they threw everything into disarray and carried off boxes full of things," but says that most of the time the police came to their apartment when they weren't home: "For everything that happened in our apartment, for example if I couldn't find something, I blamed the StB [. . .]." Once, when the Vaculíks went on vacation, they were openly followed by two StB agents as soon as they walked out the front door: in the tram, at their cottage in the countryside, even when they went swimming. Vaculíková estimated that, at times, forty people were involved in tailing them.[1]

Ludvík Vaculík's affair with Zdena Erteltová—herself a courageous woman who eventually became a pillar of Edice Petlice, and withstood harrowing abuse from the regime—was particularly hard on his wife, especially when she was simultaneously fending off the police. She encountered agents in various guises and locales. The StB officer in charge of their case, who always identified himself with the (presumably fake) names of Martinovský or Matura, forced Vaculíková out on walks in the countryside, or took her to cafés, and tried to persuade her to either divorce her husband or inform on him. Vaculíková could handle Martinovský. Eventually, she says, she got used to him and "I would enjoy having a vodka or coffee with him." But the attention was unpleasant and the constant game with the police was tiring. Once she was interrogated by a young policemen who looked exactly like their son Jan—this was the kind of psychological warfare the police were adept at, and when they picked out a family like the Vaculíks for twenty years' worth of special attention, the pressure was rough. "What are you—a saint?" one interrogator asked Vaculíková, after telling her about another one of her husband's lovers. One day, Radio Free Europe broadcast a commentary that was attributed to Vaculíková, although she had not written it. She was called in for interrogations several days in a row; the police told her the false report had been manufactured by Petr Uhl and wanted her to accuse him of lying. She refused. Finally, the police showed up at her workplace and screamed at her, telling her she should weigh the consequences of her refusal, and "think of her children." Vaculíková, who was not accustomed to using foul language, replied with a mild obscenity—"and in fact, from that day on, I wasn't interrogated again."[2]

Vaculík was not a saint, but he was a good writer. From a working-class background, he had joined the Communist Party in his youth, but his firm principles and unwillingness to keep quiet had quickly begun to get him into trouble. He established himself as one of the leading reporters of the 1960s,

first for the radio and then for the legendary *Literární noviny*, reliably formulating a fresh and unprejudiced view of the realities of Communist society. In
1966, his novel *The Axe*—the story of a young man coming to terms with the
legacy of his father, a dedicated Communist and strict patriarch—had been
one of the harbingers of the Prague Spring. Although in the West it has not
received as much attention as Milan Kundera's *The Joke*, published a year later,
it is equally subtle and daring.

Since 1969, however, Vaculík's writing seemed to have lost its stride. He
would later speak of "ten years of non-writing." His novel *The Guinea Pigs*,
written as the screws were tightening in 1969 and 1970, is a peculiar and
depressing morality tale about a bank clerk who becomes so fascinated by the
defenseless passivity of his family's pet guinea pigs that he begins to torture
them. It showed Vaculík's usual stylistic flair and quirky humor, but left many
readers at a loss. Since then, Vaculík had limited himself to writing feuilletons—he had composed dozens of these short essays, mixing philosophy,
politics, and everyday life, and had come to inhabit the genre in a way that
only a few other Czech writers had, before or since. But for all their brilliance,
the short essays seemed themselves to pose the question of why Vaculík hadn't
written another novel, something that would capture the whole world of normalization the way his short pieces seemed to capture particular moments.
Vaculík was also devoting a great deal of time and effort to running Edice
Petlice and editing the many manuscripts he received. If Petlice had, to a large
degree, kept Czech unofficial culture alive in the early 1970s, it had also kept
Vaculík so busy that he had little time for writing of his own.[3]

Just like his wife, Vaculík had suffered from the attentions of the police.
As the author of Two Thousand Words, he was immediately put on the list
of public enemies after 1969. He was interrogated and almost arrested after
drafting and signing the Ten Points manifesto for the first anniversary of the
invasion, but the regime apparently did not feel confident enough to stage a
major political trial at that time. Nevertheless, the charges were never formally dropped and continued to hang over Vaculík. In April 1975, in a wave
of house searches of opposition intellectuals, police confiscated photographs
that Vaculík had taken several years before. He and his lover had photo-
graphed each other lying nude on gravestones, in the poses of *ginants*—the
recumbent statues on medieval tombs. For two years, the StB blackmailed
Vaculík, threatening to expose the photographs unless he emigrated, or at
least shut down Petlice.[4] For two years he refused, and he continued to refuse

through the week of interrogations that followed Charter 77. On January 21, 1977, the photographs were published in the Saturday paper *Ahoj*, accompanied by an indignant attack on Vaculík and the Charter. Later the pictures were also broadcast on television.

The publication of the photographs was an act of unusual cruelty. They were not meant for public viewing; they were difficult to explain; they publicly exposed Vaculík's infidelity, as well as an unconventionality that would outrage many people; and last but not least, at a time when the Charter was under heavy fire, they could potentially be seen even by Vaculík's friends as stupid and reckless. In our own media-saturated culture, when moments of indiscretion can be filmed, viewed by millions, and then forgotten as soon as the next YouTube video goes viral, it is worth pausing to reflect on what a scandal the pictures would have caused, and how difficult they were to deal with. The photographs were the biggest shock since the television broadcast of surveillance tapes from Václav Černý's apartment in 1970.

The affair of the photographs, which both Vaculík and his wife have discussed openly and in detail since 1989, is worth reviewing here for several reasons.[5] It demonstrates just how nasty the StB could be, and just how much trouble the Charter could cause for the friends and family of signatories. Not only Vaculík, but also his wife and lover suffered greatly, of course, from the publication of the photos. The episode also casts a great deal of light on the Charter's fledgling, but impressive, solidarity. Vaculík immediately received support from his friends, including a letter from Petr Uhl. The writer Karol Sidon, who at the time was working at a newsstand, cut the offending pictures out of every copy of *Ahoj* he received, and was detained for four days as punishment.[6] Perhaps the most impressive response came from none other than Jan Patočka. Patočka, who certainly had plenty of other things to worry about in the last week of January 1977, went to visit Madla Vaculíková the day the photographs were published, to make sure she was all right. She hadn't yet seen them, and when he realized she didn't know, he said nothing and simply arranged to come back the next day.[7] Patočka also wrote the Vaculíks a letter in which he condemned the publication in no uncertain terms. When he had first heard about the confiscated photographs, he wrote, he thought Vaculík should give in to the regime's blackmail; now he realized that Vaculík's refusal was "the only possible solution." It had taught Patočka a "lesson" for which "I am most genuinely bound in gratitude to you. We cannot give in to violence, even when it appears in the shroud of a supposedly 'moral' indignation [. . .]."[8]

Patočka had immediately grasped what was at stake—not the regime's staged outrage, nor merely solidarity with a friend. Showing impressive humility—with thanks for the "lesson" he had been taught—Patočka gave his blessing to Vaculík's principled, albeit somewhat reckless, stubbornness. It was a wise and magnanimous decision from the Charter's moral authority.

Last but not least, the whole affair had an important effect on Vaculík himself. "This event," he wrote twenty years later, "had a lifelong effect on me—an instructive and encouraging effect. Once I had made the decision to preserve my honor intact, even with my sins—that is, to defend my soul even with its spots—everything that came afterward was much easier. I had given the enemy proof that not even the worst would get to me, and it really seemed to me as if they had taken note of my persistence."[9] Martinovský was transferred off their case, perhaps because the photographs failed to achieve the desired effect. Vaculík himself had been a guinea pig in a strange experiment by the regime; having withstood extremes of both surveillance and exposure, he had nothing left to hide. Strengthened by this experience, Vaculík was ready to embark on one of the Charter's most revealing self-examinations.

And yet he still seemed to be having difficulties writing. He touched on the photograph affair in a few places, but only obliquely. His feuilleton on courage, from December 1978, had sparked off a wave of protests, in which many of his good friends took him to task for tactlessness or even cowardice. At the beginning of January 1979, he made one of his occasional visits to Café Slavia and stopped by Jiří Kolář's table. Kolář told him: "When you can't write, you should write about why you can't write! Record what you see, hear, and what occurs to you. You've worked out the style for it in your feuilletons, and they're outstanding!"[10] Three weeks later, on January 22, Vaculík rolled a sheet of paper into his typewriter and began typing: "Last night, I don't know why, I couldn't sleep."

Up Late Writing about Sleepless Nights

Those words would launch a yearlong project and 466-page manuscript, consisting of almost daily entries about Vaculík's life from January 22, 1979, through February 2, 1980. He eventually published this work in Petlice as *The Czech Dream Book: Dreams of the Year 1979*; the subtitle carefully refrains from specifying the genre of this half diary, half novel. With a typical paradox, he began his "dream book" with a sleepless night, but the book does end with a dream, in which Vaculík and many of his friends—Ivan Klíma, Jan Vladislav, Karel Pecka, Karol Sidon, and others (including those in jail and abroad)— gradually gather on a train to Brno in a fantasy of Chartist solidarity. The conflict between the everyday harassments of normalized life and the vision of something better—between sleeplessness and dreams—is the central axis of the book.

Vaculík's daily entries cover a wide range of topics. At one level, this is a book about dissident politics. Thanks to his work in journalism and in Petlice, Vaculík knew a wide range of writers, both Chartists and those who hadn't signed, and—also thanks to Petlice—he spent a great deal of time visiting them, either to pick up or drop off manuscripts. His diary entries record numerous conversations about the Charter, the Communist regime, forms of protest, and everything that the Chartists referred to laconically as *poměry* (the conditions). Many pages in the early entries are devoted to the debate about "Notes on Courage," which was just getting going at the time. Vaculík received Havel's reply ("an eloquent transcription of him shaking his head in amazement") on January 26; a few days earlier, he had been asked about the feuilleton at his monthly interrogation with a certain Major Fišer, the StB officer who had replaced Martinovský-Matura and who was, noted Vaculík ironically, the only person "I am completely unable to confuse and who believes in my good character [. . .]."[11]

Vaculík also describes in detail the various logistical, administrative, and editorial tasks he had to perform in order to keep Petlice running: reading and editing submitted manuscripts, delivering them to "copyists" like Erteltová, Miroslava Rektorisová, and Otka Bednářová, dropping them off at the bookbinder's, arranging for authors to sign the finished copies, and so on. There are also encounters with the police: monthly interrogations, surveillance, and other brushes with authority, including the traffic violations known to every Chartist. (Vaculík was told to change his license plate number, which apparently carried unpleasant connotations: AO 19–77.) Interwoven with these accounts of harassment is an ongoing polemic against those who emigrate— including several of Vaculík's friends who emigrate during the course of the year—leaving behind an ever-smaller group of people to create the conditions for a normal life under normalization.

During 1979 two events, in particular, mobilized the Charter community, and they are also reflected in *The Czech Dream Book*. The first was a major regime crackdown on VONS. In May and June, fifteen of the seventeen members were arrested; in October six of them were put on trial, and five—Havel, Uhl, Benda, Jiří Dienstbier, and Otka Bednářová—went to prison. A second event—less important in the scheme of things, but the object of much publicity—was the expulsion of Pavel Kohout and his wife Jelena Mašinová. In 1978, they had been given permission to leave the country when Kohout was offered a yearlong position at Vienna's Burgtheater. On October 4, 1979—three weeks before his year was up—Kohout and his wife drove up to the border crossing, bringing along their friend Margarethe Schell (the Swiss actress, and mother of Maximilian Schell); the trip was timed to coincide with the return of a Czechoslovak parliamentary delegation from Vienna. Kohout would, indeed, preempt any coverage of the state visit; he and his wife were turned back and soon afterward their Czechoslovak citizenship was revoked, unleashing a wave of protests in the Western press.[12]

Vaculík describes the reactions to both events in dissident circles. He himself gathered signatures for a petition of writers protesting the exile of his friend Kohout, and he gave an interview to West German television about the case. But Vaculík seemed less enthusiastic about protesting the arrest of the VONS members; in an extension of his arguments in "Notes on Courage," he refused to be drawn into the round of protests and petitions. "As always, in my mind I circle around the unattractive idea of doing something, at least in my own name. But I've moved away from solo performances; I'm afraid to get back on the merry-go-round of annoyances, now that I've managed to free up some time and attention for writing and thinking about things more broadly, and when I have so many unfulfilled plans."[13] It is not clear that he planned on attending the actual VONS trial, but in any case, when he opened his apartment door the day before it took place, he found two police officers sitting in the hallway. The next day, they told him he would not reach the courthouse if he tried to attend. He went to the doctor's instead. Although he does mention gathering signatures before the appeal of the convicted VONS members in December, Vaculík also records his and others' skepticism about the protests—as well as Eva Kantůrková's reproaches for failing to take more decisive action.[14]

As much as he remained an opponent of the government, Vaculík longed to break out of the restricted world of political opposition. This desire was already apparent in "Notes on Courage," and in *The Czech Dream Book* we see it again and again. "Consistent opposition to injustice will make a person an outlaw by profession. For he has no time or energy for anything else.

It's a cyclotron!" The metaphor is carefully chosen; for Vaculík, dissent risks becoming an ever-accelerating motion in the same direction—and, what's more, in circles. More than once Vaculík considers stopping all his Petlice activities so he can devote himself to his writing: "For years I've been bothered by the realization that instead of working I walk, carry, talk, paste, cut. Instead of writing I read other people's concoctions, edit, correct, and negotiate for authors who don't even know whether a period comes before the quotation mark at the end of direct speech, or the other way round."[15] And at some point during the year, the *Dream Book* itself becomes more important than any other forms of opposition. As Vaculík wrote in a September 1980 letter about his book to Major Fišer: "These days once again I'm hearing about the steps taken by your non-literary institution against the spokespersons of Charter 77 and the members of VONS. You know that I belong among those people, even if I have decided based on experience for a different kind of activity and of coming to terms with the conditions. That is, by the way, the subject of my book."[16] Ultimately, Vaculík reminds himself, "didn't I assign myself a year of restraint to finish writing this dream book?"[17] As these comments reveal, *The Czech Dream Book* is much more than an attempt to portray the political life of dissent, much more even than the diary of a dissident.

First of all, Vaculík describes much of his "dissident" activity in down-to-earth, unenthusiastic terms. Jiří Pechar called the book "a kind of de-glorification of dissidence."[18] For example, Vaculík characterizes work on a special issue of the exile journal *Svědectví* as drudgery—a constant chasing around Prague trying to catch the editors at home—rather than glamorous political resistance. But even more important, most of the *Dream Book* is devoted to other affairs entirely. Vaculík writes at length about everyday activities that have nothing to do with Petlice or Charter 77 *per se*: daily chores, the weather and changes of the seasons, visits with friends, shopping, excursions. Vaculík and his wife spend many weekends at their country cottage in Dobřichovice outside Prague, and he devotes many pages to taking care of his garden, pruning trees, picking apples and cherries, and so on. This gives the work an intimate connection to the passing seasons, suggesting a different timetable from the hectic urban and political calendar of active Chartists in Prague.

Vaculík's dreams constitute a second thread in the book's composition. A dream book is one containing descriptions of common dreams and their interpretations. In this strict sense, Vaculík's diary is not really a dream book.

Although he describes at least one of his dreams every few days, he rarely offers his own interpretations of them. Rather, the dreams function as a disorienting device (at the beginning of each entry, it is often unclear whether he is describing a dream or a real experience), as well as a running commentary on the diary, an implicit expression of his desires and anxieties. Sometimes the dreams' relevance to the events of Vaculík's waking life is obvious—and even though this is often the case with dreams, their conspicuous appropriateness led some of his readers to suspect that he was making them up. Also unlike a true dream book, Vaculík often comments on why he *isn't* having any dreams; further, there are times when he seems to interact with them: "I knew it was a dream—a silly one," he says of one nightmare, "and I didn't give a damn how it turned out. The dream, when it recognized that it wasn't bothering me, simply stopped."[19]

Perhaps the most important layer of the book's many-layered construction is Vaculík's relationships with three loves of his life—his wife Madla and two lovers, Zdena Erteltová and a younger (thirty-seven to Vaculík's fifty-two) married artist whom Vaculík calls Helena. The latter affair is the most intense, culminating at the end of August, when Helena and her husband emigrate to Austria. Vaculík has still not fully recovered from this loss when his diary ends five months later. His wife Madla—who, many readers agreed, is one of the most beautifully drawn characters in the book—knows about these affairs and, despite a few harrowing fights that he depicts obliquely, seems resigned to them.

Vaculík's open description of his love affairs was one of the most provocative aspects of the book, but Vaculík also caused controversy by describing, in great detail, his meetings and conversations with friends, many of them well-known writers and dissidents like Klíma, Kantůrková, Gruša, Černý, and others, who appear in the novel under their own names. (One notable exception is Václav Havel, who was under house arrest for the first half of the *Dream Book*'s year, and was then arrested and imprisoned in the VONS trial.) Vaculík talks about his stopovers at Café Slavia, where Kolář's table is "draped with dissidents like a summer hive with bees."[20] He records many conversations, writing them out as direct speech, as if he were transcribing them directly—even though he is clearly quoting from memory later that evening or the next day. There are debates about literature and politics, gossip, quarrels, flirtations, speculation about other people, and a number of drunken dinner parties. He is also open about voicing his disappointments, even anger with his friends and acquaintances. He is annoyed with Eva Kantůrková throughout much of the book, at one point referring to her "hind" leg and portraying her as overeager and presumptuous. A more oblique case is Otka Bednářová, with whom Vaculík had had a falling-out; at the beginning of the year, he reveals his frustration with her refusal to join a 1977 protest letter signed by forty-nine women in support of Zdena Erteltová. By the time Vaculík published his *Dream Book*, Bednářová had been arrested, convicted in the VONS trial, and jailed, presumably in large part because of her work for Petlice; nevertheless, Vaculík chose to publish the critical remarks he had made about her in earlier entries. His frank comments, which could have been perfectly normal under normal circumstances, but in the context threaten to display an alarming lack of solidarity, provide a good sense of the kind of "de-glorification" he was engaged in.

Most of Vaculík's friends did not know they were "under surveillance" until late in the year, when he began to tell people about his writing project and showed at least some of them the passages in which they appeared, in order to get their permissions and reactions. These reactions were then included in his further entries, ultimately creating a kind of Escher-like house of mirrors in which he speaks about his willingness or unwillingness to make the edits his characters have demanded. Things got even more complicated when Vaculík gave the finished text to the people who appeared in it and asked them for their responses, which he then gathered into an anthology called *Hlasy nad rukopisem Vaculíkova Českého snáře* (Voices over the Manuscript of Vaculík's *The Czech Dream Book*) and also published in Petlice. The ongoing self-commentary of the book's community of characters led to some inspired interpretations; Jaroslav Putík, a fan of the book, noted that people were perceiving it as a kind of group therapy, "a brilliant application of the well-known methodology of Doctor Moreno and his psychodrama, in which actors release their stresses by talking with each other. And we cannot deny that the whole dissi-movement is neurotic." Jiří Pechar, writing at a time when just a few copies of the book were circulating, saw that readers' criticisms were an integral part of Vaculík's literary project; the book was like "the libretto of a performance that has not yet taken place."[21]

Whether they liked it or not, *The Czech Dream Book* supplied many dissidents with their most intense reading experience of the normalization years. Over and over again, the responses to Vaculík's work record all-day and all-night reading sessions, marked by strong emotions ranging from anger to amazement, even laughter and tears. Within this intensity, responses varied. Many readers entered into the spirit of the whole endeavor and read it as a novel, interpreting the "real" people as characters, and even appreciating the fact that Vaculík hadn't referred to them by pseudonyms, in which case readers would have spent hours trying to guess who was who. They also accepted that Vaculík's deftly sketched portraits would, of necessity, appear as grotesques and caricatures reflecting his own moods and frustrations, rather than as sympathetic portraits. To readers with some distance on the text, most of the portrayals may well seem quite sympathetic, uncovering surprising depths of gentleness and intelligence; even when Vaculík is being negative, he encourages the reader to spot his prejudices and omissions, and some of the "negative" portraits of others are really portrayals of Vaculík's own limitations. Karel Pecka initially had serious reservations about the book, but in a 1998 interview said he was glad that he hadn't written them down in 1980 for inclusion in Vaculík's *Voices* anthology: "with the passage of time, I appreciate his confession more and more. Today I give *The Czech Dream Book* an important place in the dissident literature of the 70s and 80s. I don't think there can be a better record of the atmosphere of dissent."[22]

Nevertheless, a significant minority of readers felt that Vaculík had gone too far by describing *any* real people under their real names; this was seen as an abuse of confidence and a manipulation of others' lives. Klement Lukeš thought it was simply immoral to offer such distorting versions of other people; Mojmír Klánský, despite finding the book beautiful, pointedly suggested that people need friends in order to step out of their solitude without having to worry that chance remarks will be broadcast to the world. Perhaps the harshest rejection came from Václav Černý, who saw Charter 77 as a common trust that Vaculík had violated; just because someone signed the Charter did not mean they agreed to having their privacy laid bare in one of Vaculík's novels. Vaculík's "ruthless manipulation" was a "denial of the spirit and meaning of the Charter."[23]

A further fear, often but not always tied to the first, was that Vaculík had given away too much about the inner workings of the Charter—secret means of transmitting messages, for example—and especially about Edice Petlice. Jiří Kantůrek was perhaps most upset on this score, asking: "How can you be so sure that your *Czech Dream Book* won't end up in the future as documentation in the indictment papers of a prosecutor against some of your friends [. . .]?" Others, like Milan Šimečka, thought there was nothing in the book the police didn't already know; Vaculík himself was fairly cagey, hiding or distorting any information that could cause trouble for others. Nevertheless, the book did have repercussions. Pecka recalled that his interrogator showed up at his trailer with a copy of the book and made the following absurd argument: "Look at what he's writing about you. [. . .] You see, that's the way they are. First they locked you up, then you made friends with them, and now they're kicking you again." In other words: first the Communists put you in a labor camp; then you joined a lot of former Communists in signing Charter 77; and now the ex-Communist Vaculík is making fun of you in his book.[24]

It didn't help that Vaculík presented Major Fišer with a complimentary copy of the manuscript at their monthly interrogation in September 1980: "[. . .] against my will you have somehow entered into my book: You claimed your place in it through your regular monthly summons to 'official discussions.' For that reason you have the same right [to read the manuscript] as the other characters [. . .] and I only ask you, like them, to tell me your opinion afterwards."[25] Major Fišer returned the manuscript a month later; although he didn't write up his thoughts, Vaculík took notes on their meeting: "He said that although he's not a literary critic, he thinks, based on what he's read by me so far, that 'I can do better.' I recorded a year of my life, it certainly must have been a lot of work, but my point-of-view is one-sided, that's not what life looks like in our country." Fišer seemed not to have much to say about the book, admitting only that "he didn't find out as much as the rumors circulating around it had led him to expect." As for using the information in the book against its author, Fišer merely warned Vaculík that some of the sentences, "taken out of context," could be construed as defamation of a representative of the republic and hence were "on the borderline of legality." Vaculík then tried, by alluding to moments in the book, to see whether Fišer had actually read the whole manuscript, and concluded that he probably hadn't.[26]

Fišer was, indeed, no literary critic, even though he had a professional interest in reading everything that Vaculík wrote. But several of Vaculík's detractors did criticize the *Dream Book's* literary structure, or rather lack thereof, arguing that it was merely a chaotic day-to-day record of events without the plot or structure necessary for a novel. It may have had some documentary value (albeit distorted); it had less literary value because, as a succession of disconnected entries, there was no drama. It was too distracted and scattered over too many themes and conflicts. The text is crippled, said

Eva Kantůrková (whose negative review rather charitably overlooks her unkind portrayal in the book), by "the method of diary entries, genuinely kept in real time. One more futile attempt to reprint a life right into a text."[27] Václav Černý asked skeptically: "And is Vaculík's book a *literary* text at all and not the diary of a year ripped out of his biography, a life *document*, whose rules and regularities are other than exclusively aesthetic [. . .]?" Černý called the book "a strange proto- or transitional form" without "its *own* beginning and its *own* end, [. . .] its *own* integrity."[28] The confusion of genre was also reflected in comments by some of the more sympathetic critics, who granted the *Dream Book* all the rights and privileges of a fictional text, yet felt compelled to correct Vaculík's facts. Josef Vohryzek specified that he was stopped by a police officer on foot, not by a police car, as Vaculík had him report during a meeting at Café Slavia.[29]

In the end, it would be just as naïve to assume everything in the *Dream Book* really happened as it would be to pretend it was a fictional text with no basis in reality. But the furor over the text's alleged fictionality or authenticity—and Vaculík had already muddied these waters when he chose his title and artfully refrained from further specifying its genre—obscured the more important question of just why he chose to write this kind of book, structured as short daily entries about everyday events. Vaculík had long been a master of the short form and feuilleton, but this was something different, precisely because it involved building a larger structure out of those smaller pieces. In the end, Kantůrková and Černý were right: Vaculík's diary had no traditional literary form to it, and it could have just as easily begun a day earlier or ended a month later. In looking at daily writing as a literary form, however, they failed to see it as a *practice*. They failed to ask what Vaculík gained from such an approach—why it precisely suited his aims—and how it might open a whole new world of first-person perspectives on the dissident community.

The Dissident Self

To understand what everyday writing meant for Vaculík, we must look more closely at his method in *The Czech Dream Book* and especially at his views of the self. This topic is conveniently raised in an underground university lecture he attends at the apartment of the philosopher Julius Tomin. The lecturer, a visiting professor from Oxford, presents her conception of a transient, unstable self. In Vaculík's retelling:

A person's self changes; in fact we have several selves at once, according to place, function and purpose. A fluid lifelong self is made up of partial ones that transcend themselves; memories are followed by memories of memories. [. . .] A personality must consciously cultivate itself and bring itself into order, if it is to resist the influences that want to break it up. Rather than something constant and delimited, then, a personality is a constant striving for firm unity. It is expressed in its development.[30]

Vaculík here provides a concise and precise statement of his own views about the self, and in effects suggests a guideline for reading *The Czech Dream Book*. Indeed, several important points follow from this emphasis on fluidity and development. The first is that consistency is not necessarily a virtue:

I don't understand people who renew their integrity by continuously casting out their older parts that don't fit. [. . .] [W]hoever foolishly sorts out their own past will be dull, and whoever cold-shoulders their constituent parts will be a schizophrenic. With a huge embrace, as far as I can reach, I want, as much as it's possible, to hold everything that once was mine, and I'll be healthy. Along with that I hope and ask that overall nothing more terrible will happen to me than having to drink drown, gobble up, and then lick up everything I've done.[31]

These remarks, among other things, provide a useful justification for keeping a diary, as a way of preserving one's past views. They also capture the way a typical Vaculík entry runs. Thoughts and ideas are occasioned by the random events of the day, and Vaculík tries to portray each of these events in its uniqueness, without forcing it into a larger explanatory context.

Thus, many entries begin *in medias res* and end inconclusively, without any fireworks, leaving the reader to draw his or her own conclusions. The entry for April 1, for example, is framed by two conversations. The first takes place between Vaculík and Madla at their country house, during a few free moments while they are waiting for the stove to warm up. Madla tells an anecdote from her work as a marriage counselor, in which two of her colleagues ignore a man in the waiting room, meanwhile complaining that they don't make enough money. "What would you say to that," she concludes. Vaculík replies tersely: "They're livestock, young, state-owned," and immediately moves on to a new paragraph about how he gathered wood and grafted three trees that afternoon. The entry ends with another conversation, at Karel Kosík's nearby cottage. This discussion, too, feels provisional: "They invited me over for tea, I didn't want to detain them or myself, Marie [Kosíková] brought the cups and teapot outside and we drank standing up in the wind." *This* conversation deals with Kosík's masterpiece-in-progress, a philosophical tome that he works on continuously but refuses to publish. In fact, they don't actually talk *about* the book, really, but rather Vaculík tries to needle clues about its content out of Kosík. The entry (and the conversation) end: "The tension is getting awful, Karel, about what you're actually writing."[32]

These two conversations, framing everyday chores in the garden and rooted in a particular time and place—waiting for the stove to warm up, drinking tea outside in the wind, talking about a work in progress—capture nicely the provisional feel of much of the thinking in *The Czech Dream Book*. Vaculík is less interested in constructing a definitive thesis about "conditions" in Czechoslovakia than he is in simply recording the daily wanderings of his mind. "I don't claim my thought is the truth about what is thought about; it's the truth about my thinking."[33]

This claim provides an important guideline for Vaculík as he edits his own manuscript. "In the morning I always read what I wrote the night before. So I recognize whether it's good. But I won't ever change much of it; I would erase the fluctuation of mood, energy, rhythm and truth." Later in the year, the editing becomes as much a daily activity as the writing, but Vaculík continues to opt for minimal intervention:

> I work on this manuscript almost every day, and I don't know where I should help it go. [. . .] Toward a more polished form, from which a more decisive impression would emerge, or back into doubts, hints, and mere feelings, into a fragmented style? In the first case, I would certainly find more truth, over which I would stand as a master, greater than it. In the opposite case, I might not even find or want to find truth. Let it be elsewhere, at least beside me, and I don't know how great it would be. I recall my intention for my writing to speak not only through its words, but also through its state, and in the end I leave it in its original expression. [. . .] Am I more interested in the reading of a future reader, or in my past life?[34]

Of course we can't know how much editing actually took place, but what is more important here is that Vaculík proposes an ideal of minimal self-editing. To this end he carefully records all his later interventions into the text (or at least creates the illusion of doing so) by drawing attention, in the appropriate place, to thirty or so changed or added passages. For example, in February 1979 he mentions his resolution to edit and publish his childhood diaries by the summer—a resolution that goes unfulfilled, and so immediately after, in parentheses, we find the following comment: "I am so disciplined that I'm not even crossing out this bit of stupidity as I retype a clean draft in 1980!"[35]

Everyday writing, for Vaculík, thus becomes a way of preserving a truthful relationship to his past ideas and views, as well as emphasizing the way his thinking is shaped by daily events. In the terms of the Oxford professor, it captures the idea that the self is made up of several selves, "according to place, function, and purpose," and is "expressed in its development." This theory of the self is also reflected in the content of the diary, the kinds of things Vaculík actually writes about. When he engages in self-examination or soul-searching, he is generally trying to find the best expression for his thoughts or feelings, rather than seeking to uncover hidden motivations; his stated goal is to express his personality in what he does and the way he writes about it, rather than plumbing the depths of his own soul to discover a true self. (In the same way, he offers little interpretation of his own dreams, preferring to let them speak for themselves.) Later Vaculík speaks of his diary as a method of *denní sebeúprava* (self-grooming, self-adjustment, or self-management), and, indeed, the self for him is something that has to be cultivated and taken care of, rather than interpreted and discovered.[36]

Finally, Vaculík's view of the self, and the way he displays it in writing, fits in well with what he calls his "yearning for reconciliation" and even a kind of complaisant conservatism. If the self develops naturally and organically from its surroundings and daily activities, it is difficult to find any leverage for radical change. Vaculík's own ability to encompass contradictions—"Sometimes I have two or three opinions about things, according to mood, state of health, according to context or recent experience. [. . .] People who can't have more than one opinion don't think; they just go"—is likewise an ability to empathize with other points of view, even opposing ones.[37] It is no accident that Major Fišer is one of the more likable characters in the book. ("Major (?) Fišer looked at it with swarthy silence in his heavy, tired face"; "Major Fišer is a little older than me, I'd guess he's also looking forward to retirement, he behaves politely, controls himself better than I do."[38]) At times Vaculík even seems to sympathize with the government, as in this conversation about emigration with the former radio journalist Oldřich Unger:

Olda said "[. . .] I want my children to be whole people, not to turn into wrecks corroded by the state, like we are."—"The worst thing," I said, "is that nobody wants that. I think that not even the government wants that."— "You're still the same old . . ." laughed Olda. But that is my conviction: The people who bear the particular day-to-day responsibility for the state must feel as troubled as we do, at least some of them, sometimes. That's why Pithart's idea makes sense to me. An evaluation of the conditions is one thing; how to behave in them is another. It's material for thought, whereas absolute negation doesn't leave anything to think about; the result is either resignation or escape.[39]

Are empathy and a yearning for reconciliation virtues suitable for a dissident? Vaculík concerned some critics with his remark that "I have a tendency to respect superiors and leaders, even the government [. . .]. Only a bad experience will place me in opposition, which I'm willing to abandon at every improvement from above."[40] Comments such as this seemed to reinforce the reservations expressed about "Notes on Courage"—didn't Vaculík really just want to abandon open opposition and sequester himself away to work on his writing? Despite his stubbornness, did he wield too little leverage against the state? And didn't his own failure to get arrested suggest that he just wasn't all that threatening? Josef Vohryzek, one of Vaculík's most astute critics, spoke of his "identification with the aggressor" and was bothered by his "ghastly conservatism," even as he noted that this tendency was "not always so completely infertile. It is individualist and, together with his stubborn eccentricity and expressive personality, forms a combination from which, sometimes, something unclassifiable emerges."[41] This kind of ambivalence was common in responses to Vaculík. On the one hand, he seemed a model of self-expressive freedom; on the other hand, he left his readers wondering how the bundle of contradictions he called a self was to relate to power, and what kinds of freedom and autonomy were available to it.

Havel Reads Vaculík

Václav Havel missed most of the debate about *The Czech Dream Book* because he was in prison. In February 1983, seriously ill, he was released—largely in response to a Charter campaign—and sent straight to the hospital, where "I spent the whole night reading *The Czech Dream Book* by Ludvík Vaculík, the pivotal work of that time, which everyone said I had to read first."[42] Havel's subsequent essay on Vaculík, "Responsibility as Fate" (dated October 1983) is one of the most inventive of the responses to the book ("a self-referential novel about the origin of a self-referential novel"),[43] but it also tries to bring Vaculík firmly back into the framework of Havel's own interpretation of truth and dissent. Havel recognizes that the *Dream Book* begins simultaneously with the furor over "Notes on Courage"—with Vaculík's expression of a desire to break out of the closed community of dissidents, a resolution "to step out of his role" and "once again be only himself, and only for himself." In Havel's eyes, however, the diary is built around the *impossibility* of taking such a step, and Vaculík never really escapes his fate. The diary's protagonist, "as it were unawares, by the by, somehow 'on the margin' and without any explanations [. . .] is not true to his resolution: he goes on writing petitions and gathering signatures, goes on organizing samizdat publishing [. . .]."[44] (Havel magnanimously, but also rather conveniently, overlooks Vaculík's own expressed doubts about the wisdom of protesting the VONS trial in which Havel received his prison sentence.) Rather than seeing this as one of the lasting contradictions in Vaculík's personality, however, Havel insists on viewing it as a kind of fall back into the truth, into the responsibility of an integrated personality: "It is just that human integrity of his, which feels permanently threatened by the role of 'dissident,' that forces him to carry out 'dissidence,' to be a 'dissident,' over and over again." Far from escaping dissent, Vaculík accepts "this burdensome and unpleasant fate"—and thereby "he can confirm and prove his human identity."[45]

This interpretation, as enthusiastic as it is, certainly doesn't do justice to Vaculík's book; rather, it reconceives the *Dream Book* to bring it line with Havel's own ideas of truth, selfhood, and everyday life. In "The Power of the Powerless," Havel had suggested that we can get back in touch with our true selves by returning to the basic needs and unpredictable impulses of everyday life. Ultimately, he hoped, the small communities of dissent, by drawing on everyday needs and experiences, could serve as a model for rejuvenating political life, potentially in the capitalist West as well as in the Communist countries. And although Havel could not really specify the mechanism of this rejuvenation, his main concern throughout the essay was with how dissent could reach out to society at large.

None of these ideas really resonates with Vaculík's work. In fact, Vaculík differs from Havel on each of three crucial questions, regarding the nature of truth and selfhood, everyday life, and dissent's relationship to its own public. We have already considered Vaculík's view of identity, which rejects the idea of a true self, one that can be discovered or restored, in favor of a self that is "expressed in its development," never attaining a definitive integrity. It is difficult to imagine Vaculík using a phrase like Havel's "confirm and prove his human identity." Vaculík's use of the diary and daily writing also helps highlight his differing conception of everyday life, which is always shot through with politics and corrupted by power. *The Czech Dream Book* is full of seemingly trivial events that acquire a political inflection. At one point, as some friends show him around the countryside outside Prague, he suddenly remembers the "conditions" of normalization: "I stopped paying attention at the moment they told me that it used to be a little wine cellar for hikers on the mountainside, with a view of the Vltava River: my thoughts caught on the wretchedness of conditions and life, when little wine cellars aren't allowed to be on a mountainside with a view of the Vltava."[46] Vaculík is reacting less to the wine cellar, or its absence, than to the idyllic calm and peacefulness it represents. This motif, the idyll violated by the "conditions," is a recurring one. The most important relationship in the book, for example—that between Vaculík and Helena—is colored by politics, even though they hardly ever talk about the government. The fact that both are married does not stop them from having an affair, but when she emigrates to Vienna, there is no longer any way for them to see each other. "In our country people cannot keep hold of any human relationship—between friends, relatives or lovers. A third power always works its way in. A monster that, on principle, opens wine bottles by shattering them against a roof beam."[47]

One more example will demonstrate just how far the "conditions" could reach. Vaculík tells how, at Christmas 1978, he sent a tape recording of the family's dinner conversation to his son Martin, who had emigrated to France. Given that their apartment was under surveillance, this could be seen as a rather grim joke. But Martin was even repulsed by the conversation itself. "It seems to me that you are rough, your humor is black, black, inhuman, on the border of dementia," he writes in a letter. "What has happened to you, have you gone crazy?" Vaculík continues, in his diary: "We haven't gone crazy, dear Martin, we've just worked out a way of behaving, probably the only one that lets us survive with honor in the local climate. It's a rough climate, not Czech and maybe fatal."[48]

Vaculík's Public

Vaculík's reservations about the liberating power of the self and everyday life lead to his larger disagreement about the public of dissent, and the way in which a dissident community might be conceived. With his vision of small,

pre-political communities at the end of "The Power of the Powerless," Havel
had suggested that local groupings of dissidents could create exemplars of
free behavior radiating outward into society and politics at large. (This vision
would become one of the underpinnings of the whole civil-society narrative
of dissent.) At the beginning of his diary, Vaculík also seemed to be thinking
about this question of "reaching" the rest of society, although he was more
skeptical about the potential role of dissident communities. In "Notes on
Courage," he had suggested that "Psychologists and politicians cannot expect
heroism in everyday life except when the whole environment is literally ion-
ized by radiation from some powerful source." In the absence of such "ion-
ization," Vaculík sought to promote a model of more realistic behavior that
would make lesser demands on a larger cross section of the population.[49] But
over the course of the *Dream Book*'s year, he seems less and less interested even
in these more modest demands. By the end of November, when a stranger
recognizes him and says, "We're all crossing our fingers for you," he thanks
her but, on his way down the stairs, adds: "How will we be able to tell?" In his
diary, he notes: "If they would only form a union, these finger-crossers!"[50] This
frustration reflects a more general turn inward, toward a deeper examination
of what the community of dissent looks like, and of the kinds of people who
inhabit it.

The changed perspective crystallizes in two important passages when
Vaculík reflects on his speech at the 1967 Writers' Congress and, more generally, his role in the events of 1968. In April 1979, going through his correspondence from 1967, he reflects on "the explosion of sympathy" surrounding
his speech. There was a widespread expectation that he would embark on
a political career, but, he says: "I was already trying to make it clear that I
intended to act publicly on the basis of a purely private right." His speech
at the congress was not meant to advocate a particular thesis, but rather to
provide an example of how everyone should talk: freely, openly, directly, like
a free citizen rather than a loyal Party member.[51] A second passage comes in
September; remembering his work for radio in the 1960s, Vaculík clarifies
his stance further: "So I didn't advocate my opinion and way of working;
it would be more appropriate to say that I displayed them. But their agreement with what other people were advocating led to my being counted among
them. Then people didn't understand why I wasn't willing to draw further
consequences from my agreement with them."[52] Vaculík's reputation as a rebel
and a troublemaker, although well deserved, led to exaggerated expectations

about his desire to clash with authority, or to organize other people for such a clash. His distinction between "advocating" and "displaying" his opinions suggests a political *performance* aiming at sincere self-expression, rather than at influencing others. Political influence, on this view, is an epiphenomenon of public activity, rather than its goal. And rather than building dissent around a harmony of values, Vaculík seems happier when he is deepening and exploring disagreement—especially if this might give others more space to express their own ideas. Havel thought Vaculík was trying to escape the "dissident ghetto"; it would be more accurate to say he was trying to get past that cliché, yet another of the external labels associated with dissent—labels that hid the richness of individual lives and friendships.

In this sense, *The Czech Dream Book* could be seen as a reminder that public spheres require private worlds. Here we might recall Habermas's early meditations on the bourgeois public sphere of the eighteenth century, where he paid close attention to the ways in which a growing public life had generated forms of private life, built around family and selfhood, as well. Literary forms such as the letter or the diary (later incorporated into the epistolary novel) were implicitly addressed to other people: "the first-person narrative became a conversation with one's self addressed to another person." Literature worked out forms of intimacy and self-reflection that could be discussed with others; this was part of a larger process whereby people saw themselves as taking their own personal perspectives into the debates of the public sphere, rather than letting themselves be defined by a public position or role.[53] Although Habermas proposed this account for a particular time and place—Western Europe in the eighteenth century—it points to general questions about the ways in which privacy and subjectivity enter into public life.

In fact, Charter 77 had created a new kind of public life without saying much about the types of selves and souls that would inhabit it. Patočka's formulations about the Charter's deeper meaning were a response to just this dilemma, but they remained unsatisfactory for many—in part because Patočka's own death had lent them such a mythical aura that they seemed inaccessible to mere mortals. (Vaculík, who had written two moving tributes to Patočka immediately after his death, hardly mentions him in *The Czech Dream Book*.) Now, the Charter was undergoing an almost inevitable development in which signatories worked out forms of self-reflection and self-understanding through first-person writing. In a sense, we could read the *Dream Book* as an implicit reproach to the thin and uninteresting notions of selfhood that had accreted around dissent in the first years of the Charter. Havel's conception of an identity crisis that could be healed by a return to the truth was inspiring, but it hardly corresponded to the richness and complexity of most people's beliefs, rationalizations, and self-deceptions. It was a lyrical and philosophical parable rather than a novelistic narrative; around 1980, a novel—or a dream book—may have been just what dissent needed.

Vaculík realized that the world of dissent was too busy straining for a public face and needed instead a more plausible account of its own inner life, and with this realization he took a decisive step away from the reigning Charter question about how to "reach" or "speak to" the outside world. He seemed to be saying: our own world is complicated enough; let's figure out where we stand in it, and let the rest take care of itself. Toward the end of 1979, after Havel was sentenced in the VONS trial, Pavel Kohout—now exiled in Austria—organized an event in his support: not a protest petition, but an evening of reading Havel's texts. He then proposed to organize a similar event for Vaculík—who was, however, lukewarm about the idea.

> It just isn't correct to demonstrate that we are all in agreement and how we're all the same—Kohout, Havel, Vaculík . . .—when we're not. I am with them, but I'm also a little bit separate; every person has to be. If we keep putting our unity on display, people will have an easy excuse: after all, that crew got what was coming to it. Not at all, gentlemen! This misfortune heads straight for those who are most various.[54]

Vaculík's thoughts here reveal that rejecting the external label means highlighting internal differences as well. And by trying to cut the bonds between dissent and its public, Vaculík wanted to provide the dissidents themselves with an example of how to free themselves from their political roles, as if he were asking the dissident "ghetto" to perform the same operation he had performed on himself in the 1960s—to "display" its positions rather than "advocate" them, to act publicly by a private right.

Vaculík thus brought to dissent a sophisticated treatment of performance and self-presentation. Gone was the idea that Charter 77 can beam its ethical message directly into someone's soul, or that a greengrocer's everyday behavior can transmit a straightforward commitment to a truth or a lie. Vaculík suggested that, like it or not, people must constantly struggle with their own self-presentation—as well as with other people's refusal to see them as they wish to be seen. He thus drew attention to the performative element in dissent, and to the risk that one's own ethical commitments might be perceived (even by other dissidents) as an act. Indeed, it is no accident that Vaculík's behavior often evoked charges of exhibitionism—of valuing attention no matter what the cost, of needing to put his private life on public display, and of putting the reception of dissent over and above its ethical content. But it would underestimate Vaculík's project to frame it merely as exhibitionism. For one thing, Vaculík's own meditations return consistently to ethical dilemmas, indeed, to the very dilemmas involved in valuing "display" over advocacy. For another, his self-presentation in the *Dream Book* can be seen as a response to surveillance—rather than becoming an object of the state's gaze, he decided to observe himself and then "turn himself in" to the police. If he thereby publicized his own private life, he did so on his own terms.

But there is a third way in which Vaculík moves beyond self-obsession and self-publication. Here it is useful to look, not just at the *Dream Book* alone, but at what might be called the whole *Dream Book* project: keeping a diary, folding other people's feedback into the daily entries, distributing the final version, soliciting responses, and then publishing them in a separate volume. All these activities together staged a dissident happening, of sorts, and created a sophisticated vision of a dissident public that was far different from that underlying "The Power of the Powerless." To understand the force of this happening, it may be useful to return for a moment to the music underground. In a strange way, *The Czech Dream Book* became something of a Charter counterpart to *Invalid Siblings*. Like Bondy, Vaculík turned himself and his friends into literary characters, and then presented the resulting work to them directly; like Bondy, he had turned a literary work into a public event, one that was about a particular community and simultaneously helped to define and consolidate that community. Vaculík, however, did not read his diary aloud to groups of friends, but rather distributed the finished manuscript, so they could read it in private, and then assembled their written responses. This would be a "happening" in print; Vaculík was a publisher, not an actor, stage manager, or artistic director of a rock band. The *Dream Book* thus transposes the oral legends of the underground—built around concerts, recitations, and other face-to-face performances—into the writing-based culture of dissent—built around considered and well-crafted responses to reproducible texts. As a corollary, the *Dream Book* is not a celebration of community and solidarity, as *Invalid Siblings* was, but rather an exploration of fault lines within a dissident community. Nevertheless, Vaculík had successfully staged an open discussion about the world of dissent. The result was a textured, fine-grained image of a living, breathing community, as well as a vivid sense of that community's genuine interest in the well-being of Czech culture as a whole.

A World Without Shadows

Vaculík's shift of perspective imagined another way into dissent—not through an ethical appeal, but through the portrayal of a specific, bounded community. Warner's notion of a public-generating text, which encodes specific readers in its language and references but also reaches out to a potentially infinite audience, is again useful here. To a large extent, the *Dream Book* stands or falls on how well it combines specificity with universality, on how well it communicates the sense of a bounded address to its own characters while still inviting outsiders into the discussion. Indeed, it is instructive to see how intensively the *Dream Book*'s first readers thought about its potential audience. Would the book be comprehensible to an outsider? To a foreigner? Was it gossip, aimed at people in the know—or did it communicate a deeper, more universal sense of life in Prague under the normalization regime? This was a question about dissent itself—indeed, it was the question that constituted dissent, and it was a question Vaculík wanted to force his readers to ask about themselves.

Two of the best responses to the *Dream Book* dealt with precisely these concerns. Tellingly, both came from critics who were closely involved with dissent but hadn't actually signed the Charter. The literary critic Milan Jungmann appreciated Vaculík's portrayal "of the relationships among individual 'dissidents,' [. . .] of the complex fabric joining people of such quizzical past fates, ideological starting-points, and current defensive postures, beneath which so many understandable and mysterious ambitions, needs, strivings, and desperations are in conflict." Thanks to Vaculík, an outside reader could now see dissent as "a free grouping of personalities" with all the range of human virtues and vices, as people who knew how to both help and undercut each other. "I think that many people on the sidelines who are yearning for idols will find their images [of the dissidents] battered, but that's a good thing. A reasonable person can only welcome such a portrayal that does not hide the human qualities of these individuals 'driven to the margins of society' without any political influence. . . ." Jungmann matter-of-factly accepted that the dissidents have no political power, and instead welcomed an effort to depict their human qualities, the diversity of their motivations and relationships.

Milan Šimečka approached the text from a similar perspective, thinking his way into the head of a foreigner who might wonder why the *Dream Book* doesn't "fall into the categories with which his favorite newspaper describes dissidence. Why is there so little violence, real violence with night-time interrogations and brutality? Why do those dissidents have so many private and human worries when they should be devoting themselves fully to human rights from morning till evening? Why doesn't the West appear here as the shining hope for all who are subjugated and oppressed?" Šimečka welcomed a "de-newspaperized" view that was not obsessed with ideology and the state: "[. . .] this point-of-view is the real path to salvation," he wrote. "If, of course, it's not too late."[55]

These responses, appreciating the book on its own terms, do not erase the objection that Vaculík had published personal information about his friends. The angry, disappointed responses of some of his readers suggest that this was a real issue, and one he never resolved. Šimečka defended Vaculík against the charge of "giving away" information to the secret police, presuming, like many others, that he hadn't told them anything they didn't already know; but he had less to say about whether Vaculík had betrayed personal confidence or manipulated his friends. It was one of the *Dream Book*'s most disapproving critics, Eva Kantůrková, who would analyze this question in a way that rose above simple questions of betrayal or trust.

Kantůrková was unenthusiastic about the *Dream Book* when it was published, and never lavished praise on it, but she did come to appreciate it as an example of a particular dilemma of dissident style—the need to reconcile public and private behavior. In 1980, she had published a book of interviews with women Chartists, mainly those who had been accused in the VONS trial, or whose husbands had been; the resulting work, *Sešly jsme se v této knize* (We Have Gathered Together in This Book), remains one of the most interesting and underappreciated documents of dissent. In her own memoir, published in 1994, Kantůrková mentions that she was criticized for publishing some of the interviews, in which her interlocutors spoke candidly about their personal lives. This criticism leads her to a meditation on the paradoxical relationship between public and private during normalization:

> In the events of that time, and in the actions of people in the Chartist community, there was a remarkable weightiness, as if people from that circle were not allowed to cast the shadows in which, somewhere else and in other circumstances, it would have been possible to hide a thing or two.

The regime even used quite personal things to discredit the disobedient; we were shaken by the blackmail [. . .] using edited surveillance from Václav Černý's apartment, and also, especially, by the printing of Ludvík Vaculík's private photographs. Openness was one of the weapons we had for protecting ourselves, the principle of publicizing everything. And it was partly for this reason that a kind of public responsibility developed, one that would be perceived as oppressive under free conditions; and I contributed to it—albeit involuntarily—with the book [of interviews].[56]

While not coinciding exactly with Vaculík's own ways of "publicizing everything," Kantůrková here points to the questions that Vaculík's literary project, as well as her own, might raise—questions that are far from the concerns of "The Power of the Powerless," or even the debate on courage. Elsewhere in her memoir, Kantůrková suggested that dissent was "a style of public behavior, worked out through frequent clashes of opinions, a deeply democratic style [. . .]."[57] The decision to reconcile public and private here runs through the creation and presentation of a style, rather than through public activity designed to bring the polis into harmony with one's own political conceptions. This point recalls Vaculík's conception of displaying his ideas rather than advocating them. But not having a shadow in which to hide, Kantůrková suggests, created an even starker form of individualism; publicizing one's own isolation was one way of creating solidarity. This was not the solidarity of small "prepolitical" communities, or of any kind of political action; rather, it was a gambit, an effort to put one's own behavior into question, and to show that one was willing to do so. Kantůrková suggested that dissent would ultimately be understood through the behavior of its individuals, and judged for its democratic style rather than its philosophy or its political effects.

By the end of the *Dream Book*, Vaculík had developed a sophisticated understanding of dissent as a form of self-expression rather than political action, always remembering that self-expression takes place in both a public and a private world. This understanding was not equally inspiring to all the Chartists, but it represented a serious alternative to the Havel–Patočka understanding. For Havel, dissent was a response to an identity crisis; the moral appeal to the truth would heal a split or corrupted identity. For Vaculík, selfhood was more a question of holding several contradictory ideas at once. For Havel, everyday life was an arena of existential purity, where people might discover their true needs and desires and rebuild political life from the ground up. Vaculík, on the other hand, saw daily life as a foundation on which he could fully appreciate the subtlety, contradictions, and internal conflicts of his own "identity," which in turn is never completely formed or discovered but is always caught up in a process of revelation and construction. Feeling that there is no true self buried deep within and waiting to find expression, Vaculík did not see the same opportunities as Havel did for creating an integrated self. But that did not make him feel manipulated or disempowered. In December 1980, when he finally got around to writing the preface for those childhood diaries he had failed to revise for publication while writing the *Dream Book*, he returned to the question of free self-expression:

> I used to take up my pen with the burden of censorship: it became my opponent, I trained my sentences on it. Expressing a thought was often only half my task; the other half was to overcome or get around its forbidden-ness. In this way my writing took on a kind of independent existence, not completely reflecting my real personal character and need, and it became an uncomfortable function for me, whose success in the end tasted bitter: it dictated to me its own continuation [. . .]. In recent years I began to gather the intention to resist. [. . .] I tore myself away from considerations and began to write the *Dream Book*. In a time of the worst possibilities of the word, in 1979, I wrote actually my freest text. It's about sixty percent free.[58]

Vaculík here speaks of his "real personal character," but also imagines writing as something "uncomfortable," even alien, both an agent of external forces as well as a means of self-expression. If he saw *The Czech Dream Book* as sixty percent free, this is a fitting comment on the precarious nature of dissident self-writing and its simultaneous negotiations with power, various publics, and itself.

Conclusion

Ending a book on dissent with the year 1980 is far different from ending it with the year 1989 or 2009. Changing the endpoint reminds us that dissent deserves attention as a cultural phenomenon in its own right, and not just as a political strategy aiming at the fall of Communism, a philosophy of authenticity, or a problematic chapter in the historical memory of post-Communism. It also reminds us of the horizons of dissent itself, especially in its early years, when the collapse of the regime was unimaginable. Works like *The Czech Dream Book* or even "The Power of the Powerless" look entirely different if we keep in mind the coordinates of hope and despair, uncertainty and conviction, that oriented so much dissident thought before 1989.

The 1980s in Czechoslovakia, as elsewhere in the Communist bloc, saw a branching out of civic activities, especially after Mikhail Gorbachev rose to power in the Soviet Union in 1985 and began instituting a program of top-down liberalization there, similar in many respects to the Prague Spring seventeen years before. Czechoslovakia's rulers responded coolly to Gorbachev's perestroika and glasnost, but could not wholly ignore the warmer wind blowing from the East. An environmental movement gained strength, and a new generation of youth culture took shape, one that still listened to the Velvets and the Plastics, but also exchanged bootleg cassette tapes of punk and New

Wave music. The underground continued to evolve, developing its own samizdat press (in particular the lively magazine *Vokno*) and existing in a sometimes
uneasy alliance with the Charter. The Jazz Section, a semi-tolerated department of the official Musicians' Union, began to print banned literature "for
internal use only" and created a significant new outlet for samizdat publishing until it was shut down in the mid-1980s. Near the end of the decade,
signs of change were clear to many. A number of new political movements
were appearing, such as the Independent Peace Initiative, Emanuel Mandler's
Democratic Initiative, or Petr Placák's Czech Children, with its deadpan
call for a return of the monarchy. The Charter itself increasingly faced the
need to define its own position with respect to a younger, more confronta-
tional generation that took hard-fought victories like *INFOCH* for granted
and tended to see its predecessors as a bit tame and square. Meanwhile, the
ill-defined sphere known as the "gray zone"—the world of professionals and
academics who worked in official structures but maintained their sympathy
for dissent and cooperated with dissidents, usually anonymously, when possible—became a more and more identifiable phenomenon and opened up possibilities for well-placed people who saw no need to sign the Charter but also
wanted to participate, for example, in drawing up its documents about the
state of Czech society.[1]

This growth of independent activities has cast a shadow back over the first
years of dissent and Charter 77, creating a retrospective illusion that a small,
isolated community of dissidents was gradually supplemented by more and
more civic activities, some of which had little to do with the Charter at all.
There is some truth to this account, although it is difficult to answer the coun-
terfactual question as to how quickly and successfully these later initiatives
would have developed if the Charter hadn't broken the ground for them, and
if it hadn't continued to soak up a great deal of the attention of the police and
the foreign press, creating a sheltered space in which other initiatives could
grow without forcing the regime's hand against them.

But this branching out of activities also created a deceptive distinction
between a more activist world of the 1980s, as the ice was beginning to thaw,
and a supposedly philosophical or theoretical world of dissent based around
the Charter. New forms of activism gave the false impression that the earlier
dissidents were somehow too passive, too intellectual, too legalistic. These
reproaches reflect the ideology of a younger generation that wanted to distinguish itself from its predecessors (and often its parents), as well as a tendency

to equate all of dissent with the figure of Václav Havel, whose own halting emergence onto the terrain of high politics was closely monitored at home and abroad in 1988 and 1989.[2] But such reproaches also reflect a stereotyped view of the "older" dissent, seeing it as more idealistic and philosophical than active and practical. VONS, for example, is difficult to fold into this narrative of increasing activism in the 1980s, and it is often difficult to gauge whether the younger generation's samizdat appeals reached more people simply by virtue of being more militant. Above all, however, the activities leading up to the fall of Communism in 1989 raise the question of whether "activism," or dissent in general, *could* have looked different under the far harsher conditions of the late 1970s and the early 1980s.

This is one sense in which the flatter view of dissent created by the Helsinki and parallel-polis narratives has distorted historical narratives of normalization. By painting dissent as a relatively well-organized and homogenous phenomenon with clear boundaries, they have, paradoxically, underestimated its significance. One of my goals in this book has been to show that these two narratives function best "at a distance," in broad brushstrokes. They are like an impressionist painting that only makes sense when you are standing far away. The Helsinki Effect explains some of the larger global connections of dissent, but it says little about the psychology of the Charter signatories, the choices they made, the varied reasons for their activism, or the actual institutions of dissent. The parallel-polis narrative, too, disguises many different motivations and levels of commitment under a single sign. Its ideal of an independent political community captures the yearnings of many dissidents, but it also obscures the forms of *intersection* between dissent and the rest of society—and, indeed, the ways in which dissent simply *was* part of the rest of society. The parallel polis represents one strain of dissident thinking, rather than dissent as a whole, and it neglects the many writers like Pithart and Vaculík who devoted so much time and creativity toward breaking down the idea of a separate community.

As we move in for a closer focus, we realize just how many gaps in the history of dissent remain to be filled. In fact, the historiography of Czech dissent is still in an early stage, and there are any number of pressing questions to answer. A largely Prague-based account of dissent needs to be supplemented by greater attention to different regions of the country. A largely secular view of dissident politics needs to take into account religious dissent, a story that overlaps with Charter 77 in many ways but also encompasses a great variety of other activities. The overwhelming attention paid to a few male dissidents needs to be expanded in order to include more women, and to consider gender roles inside dissident thinking. And more generally, an account centered around a few names like Havel and Patočka needs to open up to include a wider range of personalities and viewpoints. Contacts with exile journals, publishing houses, and foundations have yet to be fully mapped and assessed as an integral part of dissent at home. And finally, accounts of dissent that treat it as a timeless phenomenon need to pay more attention to chronology and evolution—a year-by-year account of the life of Charter 77 would open up a sense of its turning points, the ongoing debates inside dissent, and the ever-changing landscape of police persecution.

But the gaps do not result simply from a lack of knowledge or sources—they cannot be filled simply by conducting more interviews, gathering more information, or recovering and translating more dissident texts. Rather, the blank spaces on the map of dissent have followed logically from the questions that have been asked (and, indeed, have produced many excellent studies)—above all questions about its philosophical background and political effectiveness. If we hew to those questions, many elements of dissent will never come into focus. In a 1990 interview, Anna Šabatová was asked why women played such an important role in the Charter but had not been prominent in politics in the months following November 1989. She replied:

> The social life and work of the Charter was basically carried out in apartments, in homes. A person didn't have to go outside in order to participate. At most, you might go to another apartment headquarters. From the practical point-of-view, this gave women with children the possibility to take part in any kind of activity—this was my case. Now political life has moved from the home into the public, and some of us have no possibilities, or limited ones, to follow it there. In that dramatic development [after 1989], when suddenly it was necessary to be somewhere from morning to evening, some women were naturally excluded. To a certain extent, that's my personal situation as well. I just can't sit at meetings from morning until ten P.M. And I have no desire to fulfill myself in this way, at the expense of my children.[3]

In a real sense, Šabatová's apartment has been invisible to historical knowledge. Her reply suggests that the emphasis on public and philosophical positions has obscured all those facets of dissent whose political effects are speculative or difficult to grasp. As I argued in Chapter 1, these invisibilities are not simply questions of gender roles; they pertain to many different aspects of the varied worlds of dissent. If we want to know why the Communist regime fell, then it will probably never make sense to study, say, the handful of dissidents who braved the regime in Ostrava but did not make a dent in the regime's control over its heavily industrial and mining power base there. A similar caveat applies to interpretations of dissent focused on persecution and heroism. If we read *INFOCH* simply as a series of reports on interrogation and imprisonment, than we will never understand the important differences in tone, language, and genre that characterize these reports—and that made *INFOCH* so important for the imagination of a diverse dissident community.

In this book I have tried to reawaken a sense of that diversity, and to introduce some shifts in perspective that might make the gaps in historical knowledge more visible. I have tried to show that dissent emerged, not from a lofty realm of moral convictions, but from specific forms of persecution in the mid-1970s, as well as from a particular way of imagining cultural life. I have also tried to rethink some of the fundamental questions facing intellectuals who were considering taking the step into open opposition—the choices involved in signing the Charter, for example—and to explore how far-reaching decisions emerged from specific encounters, such as Havel's meeting with Jirous, or the conversations that led Patočka to become a Charter spokesman. This approach has also meant paying more attention to the individual biographies that entered into dissent—the quirks of fate and personality that placed someone in an outsider's position to begin with. Without neglecting Havel's importance, I have tried to open the philosophical and political stage to figures such as Ludvík Vaculík, Karel Pecka, František Janouch, Petr Uhl, Anna Šabatová, Eva Kantůrková, Jan Vladislav, Pavel Landovský, and Petr Pithart. There are, of course, many others who deserve equal treatment, and I hope some of the perspectives I have suggested may continue to provide a way to bring more characters into our stories of dissent.

I have also tried to turn attention away from the political program of dissent, and toward the types of stories and legends that helped constitute a dissident community. One of the main effects of Charter 77, indeed, was to provide a nucleus around which such stories could accumulate. In Tom Stoppard's play *Rock 'n' Roll*, a friend of the Plastic People in Prague tells a visiting British reporter: "Actually, the Plastic People is not about dissidents." The reporter replies: "It's about dissidents. Trust me."[14] Of course, the reporter is right, because he is wrong; the reason we have to trust him is that Western journalists created the character of the "dissident" far more than the dissidents themselves. Historians, however, should play a different role. Some of the myths of the Charter *are* mere journalistic fictions, such as the story of Patočka dying under police interrogation; others are more subtle, as in the whole story of "the trial of the Plastics." Seeing dissent as a world of legends and stories does not mean ratifying or rejecting these different versions of events, but rather recognizing them for what they are, asking why they caught hold, and thinking about the purposes and interests they served. If we say that Charter 77 emerged from the trial of the Plastic People, we should realize that we are endorsing Havel's "metaphysical" version of the Charter's origin as an appeal to morality and conscience. An understanding of the stories of dissent also helps reveal why dissent is born and thrives in a regime of censorship and imperfect information, in which certain people and events naturally acquire a larger-than-life aura, while others recede into the background no matter how much attention they deserve. History should not only recover such marginalized voices, but also help us understand our own shifts in attention.

An awareness of how information circulates is thus another essential precondition for the study of dissent. In Chapter 5, I suggested that the dominant account of Charter 77 still works on the "download" model—as if every decision to sign or not to sign were made under the same conditions. In fact, such decisions were shaped by information channels—they were a response to how the Charter reached you as much as to what it said. Patočka's conception of the Charter as a moral epiphany with direct access to everyone's conscience—"the message is the medium"—has obscured the fears, preconceptions, logistical questions, and sound reasoning that different people brought to their decision to sign or not. In fact, at every step, the history of dissent needs to pay more attention to how different ideas were presented, and who knew what when. As the rise of the Internet makes it easier and easier to find information, it is more and more difficult to think back to the samizdat era. Czech dissent in the 1970s and 1980s was shaped, as much as anything else, by typewriters and carbon paper. The clandestine handoffs of samizdat texts should interest us, not because they were clandestine, but because they inculcated an entire culture with far different habits of reading, writing, note-taking, and criticism than we might imagine today.

The question of information leads to the larger question of the dissident public that I raised in Chapter 6. If, today, the dissidents are sometimes reproached for being elitist or out of touch, it is important to realize that there is nothing new about these reproaches. They uncomfortably mirror the regime's own language of *ztroskotanci a samozvanci* (failures and usurpers), but more important, they were part of the dissidents' own self-conception from the very beginning. In fact, it was the dissidents who were reliably doing the most interesting thinking about this question (and had far more to say about it than many of their critics today). One of the main reasons Havel rallied to the defense of the music underground was because he feared that he and his friends had achieved a special status rendering them immune to persecution—and thus irrelevant to the rest of society. These questions intensified with Charter 77, and led to the heated debates about the railway workers' ball, VONS, and the provocative essays by Pithart and Vaculík—as well as to Havel's meditations on the greengrocer and the brewer. "The Power of the Powerless" is nothing if not a discussion of the relationship between dissent and the rest of the world.

There were dozens of opinions *inside* dissent as to how widely known it was *outside*, and if so many political scientists, sociologists, psychologists, literary critics, journalists, novelists, and other intellectual lights were unable to resolve this question at the time, it would seem unlikely that historians will be able to answer it today. The more interesting question, it seems to me, is to map out the different ways in which people, both inside and outside of dissent, conceived of the dissident community. Was it open or closed? Was it built around old friendships or new ones? Philosophical ideals or personal connections? Did signing the Charter mean crossing the border into dissent, or was it just the first step in a long process of rearranging one's own community of friends and acquaintances? I have framed some of these questions by borrowing Michael Warner's account of publics, because it nicely poses a fundamental paradox: for many people, dissent was *both* closed and open, both a bounded polis and a potentially infinite community founded around a common ideal, both a "scene of practical activity" and "a hope for transformation." History can map its movement back and forth between these two poles, rather than trying to assign it a definitive location.

Finally, I have hoped to show why writing, and in particular self-writing, was so fundamental to dissent. (By a happy corollary, this in turn may suggest just how much work is yet to be done on the wide range of texts that have not appeared on the radar of studies of dissent.) When Havel said that dissidents were "writing people," he was lamenting the fact that only writers seemed able to reach a Western audience and garner the attention necessary to be labeled as dissidents. But in fact, writing was a crucial *practice* of dissent, not just an outward sign of its existence. Petr Pithart has coined a distinction between what he calls "dissent of activity" and "dissent of reflection."[5] This was part of his larger project, carried out in essays such as "Dissi-risk," to shift attention away from the "active minority" of VONS and public protest, aiming it instead at the wide range of intellectual activity carried out by dissident historians, writers, philosophers, and critics. Pithart is absolutely correct to draw our attention to this distinction, although he is mistaken when he suggests that Havel was the main figure who combined both forms of dissent. In fact, there were many others. Pithart himself, like Jiřina Šiklová, made important contributions to dissident thought while also organizing the information channels that brought exile journals and other clandestine literature to Czechoslovakia.[6] Ludvík Vaculík organized samizdat publishing as well as writing feuilletons; he not only wrote *The Czech Dream Book*, but also staged the extensive discussion that helped make the book such an event. Petr Uhl, the archetypal "activist" in Charter circles, also edited *INFOCH* and wrote countless articles, reports, and announcements for it; these must be read with some rhetorical sophistication, not just as transparent channels of information but as the creation of an alternate "voice" of the Charter and an essential mechanism of its self-understanding. Our knowledge of dissent today derives to a great extent from these figures who crossed the line between reflection and activity.

At the same time, Pithart's category of "dissent of reflection" needs to be expanded and made more subtle. Dissident writing—like all writing, but perhaps in a special way—was as much about the writer as it was about his or her immediate topic. But this aspect of dissident writing was particularly clear in a whole world of first-person texts, from letters and interviews through feuilletons (nearly always written from a first-person perspective) all the way up to sophisticated projects like *The Czech Dream Book*. It was Vaculík, above all, who saw that self-writing, far more than just a form of exhibitionism, was *necessary* if the opposition in Czechoslovakia was going to create room for its many unusual and brilliant personalities. Dissent would only become a "public sphere" when it created maximum freedom for the "private spheres" of its diverse thinkers. Through its first-person writing, dissent evolved from a moral appeal and political tactic into a form of performance and experimentation with different genres, tones, and styles. Self-writing helped keep alive a sense of the many different personalities in dissent—a task that was just as important as defending political prisoners or commenting on the state of Czechoslovak society at large. An account of dissent must make room, not just for its constructive debates and harmony of ideals, but also for its individuals and eccentricities.

What We Argue about When We Argue about Dissent

Unhappy is the land that needs heroes—but so is the land that has no use for them. In writing this book, I have tried to steer a middle course between glorification and demystification. I am skeptical of heroic narratives, with their one-dimensional psychology and their suspicious tendency to replicate the dreams of the teller; what's more, like many scholars who have looked deeply into a particular culture, I am also struck at how often they are just plain wrong, if only because the texts that get translated are often those that reinforce existing models. On the other hand, as the history of Communism disentangles itself from earlier obsessions with fear and the police, I think it does need to come to terms with the dissidents, rather than embarrassedly shoving them off to the side and invoking a fictitious "ordinary person" or "everyday life" as a measure of what was possible. The history of Communism should not ignore this group of creative and resourceful people who devoted so much energy to imagining an alternative that was tolerant, open, and committed to nonviolent change and spirited debate. My argument in Chapter 1 might be distilled as follows: in order to understand the courage of the dissidents, we need an account of their behavior that is not built around courage.

I have tried to supply such an account, and above all to suggest new questions and perspectives that may spark the interest of other researchers. This account has drawn me into a detailed and textured narrative that, I hope, is not devoid of interest on its own terms. Nevertheless, the reader may well ask for a briefer statement of why all this matters.

In a 2003 interview, Jan Urban emphasized the political failures of dissent after 1989, and the fact that dissidents had disappeared from political life in the first phases of the transformation: "That doesn't mean that dissidents are better or worse. They are simply different. [. . .] That element of dissent—I once compared it to a part of the landscape. It's a ruin somewhere on the horizon, in which no one will ever live again, but it simply belongs to the landscape, and it helps shape that landscape."[7] In one sense, this perspective is useful. I am convinced that, in the main, the signatories of Charter 77 were not more or less courageous than other people—they simply cultivated a different kind of courage. Reading the interviews in the oral-history project *Ordinary*

People. . . ?!, in which many speakers sidestep the historian's questions about May Day parades, Charter 77, or the shortage of consumer goods in order to talk about their families and careers, I was struck by the rich texture and the *plausibility* of these "ordinary" life narratives—their complicated mixture of outside circumstances and personal plans, even when they avoid politics. It is important to remember how challenging an ordinary life can be. Disease, disability, unemployment, separation from loved ones, failures at school or work, and the slow dissipation of dreams—these require their own kind of courage, which need not always be a political virtue. No history of Communist society can safely assume that all these individual lives were missing something—that because they were not politically engaged, they were somehow limited or incomplete.

But does that mean dissent is a ruin, something to be explored as a historical relic but not taken as a model? Here I cannot agree. For one thing, the 1989 question—did the dissidents bring down Communism?—has woefully restricted understandings of what their political effectiveness might consist of, and underestimates the political significance of moral authority. It is true that, among the many causes of the fall of Communism—Gorbachev's reforms, his support for constructive change, exhausted and discredited elites inside the Communist Party, economic problems, new forms of protest in the late 1980s—dissent probably does not rank near the top of the list. Even during the first few days of the Velvet Revolution, veteran dissidents lagged behind more radical students in organizing and demanding change. But dissidents ultimately played an important, indeed crucial role in 1989, supplying leaders with the moral authority to guide the energies of massive crowds of demonstrators, and to shape the revolutions as nonviolent debates about the structure of a tolerant, liberal democracy.[8]

One way of understanding the authority of dissent is to remember Havel's "multiplier metaphors" for high culture. Novels, plays, concerts, and political essays are not weights on a scale; they are sources of light and shadow. Dissent is a reminder that we cannot always judge art, culture, and scholarship by their supposed political or real-world effects; at some level, dissent is always a call to explore the complexities of a world that others have tried to simplify. Dissent is what should happen whenever a society's rulers try to lower its horizons, corrupt its aspirations, and turn its population inward. This is why a mere head count of dissidents will never be very enlightening. Arguments about the political influence of the Czech dissidents sometimes mention a seemingly eloquent statistic, according to which the Czechoslovak state security in 1989 had only some five hundred people on a list of active dissidents, with an active core of sixty or so people.[9] I would not want to make the secret police an arbiter of who is and isn't politically important, but in any case this seductively quantitative fact simply postpones the question of why these particular people wielded so much influence over the police. I imagine that just about everyone can agree that the dissidents had more influence than a random population sample of equal size; they may have had more or less influence than an equal-size grouping of Party leaders or, say, economists or sociologists working at an official academic institute. But none of this solves the question of just what influence they did have. Neither an appeal to numbers nor a narrative of political failure during or after 1989 will resolve this question.

Nevertheless, in asking why dissent is worth studying today, it would be a mistake to limit oneself to models of political influence. Dissent deserves study in its own right, as a cultural phenomenon, and even as a phenomenon linked intimately to artistic endeavor. And so it is useful to ask: why does the culture of dissent remain so vital and fascinating today? I hope a fine-grained account of the problems and writings of Czech dissidents has helped the reader imagine his or her own answers to this question. I can suggest a few reasons of my own.

First, dissent was a community of remarkable tolerance and heterogeneity. One of the things it was good at was cultivating diversity, and its taste for loose organization and cooperation—not to mention the ethic of legal and nonviolent resistance—left room for many different personalities. Its flair for myth-building lent many of its figures a larger-than-life character—this, for once, is not just an artifact of Western attention—and they, in turn, helped foster an appreciation for individuality, even eccentricity. Once again, we should be careful about ascribing individualism to the dissidents alone; "ordinary life" was full of interesting people, including many artists and eccentrics who had nothing to do with dissent. But the preservation of individualism in the face of police repression was a notable achievement. For many people, dissent was not just a political movement but an invitation to imagine oneself differently, against a world that placed a great many restrictions on what could be said publicly. These projects of self-imagination, so widespread in the first-person writing of dissent, remain one of its most vital legacies.

A second strength of dissent, worthy of emulation, was its refusal to dissolve its own internal tensions and paradoxes. Charter 77 was notable, in part, because of its many fault lines. In a 2007 interview, Petr Uhl was asked to briefly summarize the basic ideological divisions within the Charter; he replied that there were too many to summarize briefly. (In a response to a 1999 questionnaire of Charter signatories, he had identified twenty-six.)[10] The Charter should be seen as helping to orchestrate these debates, rather than as unifying them under a common cause. Debate *was* the common cause. The Charter wasn't always successful in this effort, and from the outside it could sometimes look like a closed club, or even a clique, rather than an open discussion. But on the whole it has few analogues in Czech culture of the 1970s and 1980s. This is one of the most difficult things to remember today, when the effort to fit dissent into larger narratives of protest, Communism, or human rights often reduces it to a few prominent figures armed with theses about living in truth and the parallel polis. Dissent is better understood as an exploration of what was necessary to keep public debate alive in the face of censorship, police surveillance, and the threat of arrest and imprisonment. And its lessons are useful even to those living under less daunting political circumstances.

Finally, it is worth remembering that much of the debate within dissent was about what dissent means. That is, one of the tasks of being a dissident was figuring out what it meant to be a dissident. And one of the things that made dissent different was an ongoing commitment to articulating its own relationship to society at large. This commitment sets dissent apart from many other forms of local opposition, and should also undermine efforts today to frame popular apathy or irony as a form of resistance. The question of the dissidents' public created a lively debate, analyzed in Chapters 6 and 7, in the first few years of the Charter. When politicians and historians today argue about the meaning of dissent—its philosophical positions, its strategies of resistance, its relationship to "ordinary people," the nature of heroism—they are continuing that debate, whether they mean to or not. If there had been no dissidents, the "ordinary-people" narrative would have quickly become the default setting for a social history of Communism that did not encompass the imagination of alternatives. The dissidents thus continue to pose the same challenge to historians as they did to the people around them—to cultivate one's own imagination and think about how it fits into greater projects of imagining society. The dissident horizon was not the only one on offer, and it should be (to borrow a phrase from literary theory) interrogated as strictly as any other political project. But it should not be ignored. In this respect, one of the most intriguing legacies of dissent is the ongoing historical and political discussion about what it was, what it meant, and whether it mattered.

Communication and Cultural Life: A Coda

In 1979 and 1980, František Kautman and Jan Vladislav began to discuss an idea that had occurred to both of them independently: building on the publishing activities of Edice Kvart to set up a samizdat journal that would draw together criticism in many different fields—from literature and theater to history and even psychology. From the beginning, the editors of *Kritický sborník* (Critical Almanac) aimed for it to be a substantial undertaking, one that would establish a reputation and last for more than a few issues. A third founder, Jindřich Pokorný, gives credit to the French poet Pierre Emmanuel for arranging financial support; funding later came from František Janouch's Charter 77 Foundation in Sweden. The thorough preparation and fund-raising, however, took some time, and by the time the first issue was ready, Vladislav, under severe police pressure because of Edice Kvart, had emigrated to France. The editor who replaced him, and helped guide samizdat criticism to a new plane, was Josef Vohryzek.[11]

Vohryzek—whom we met earlier with Václav Havel, signing the Charter at a gas station outside Prague—was an ideal choice for editor: sharp, patient, selfless, and hardworking. He had learned to be independent from an early age. Born in 1926, he grew up in an assimilated Jewish family in Prague; in 1940, during the first year of the Nazi occupation, his parents entrusted him to the family of a Quaker schoolteacher from Sweden, who had offered to take him out of the country and care for him. (Vohryzek's parents died in Auschwitz, although his sister escaped to Palestine in 1939.) He was thirteen when he went to Sweden and, since the teacher's family had few resources of its own, he ended up leaving school at the age of fifteen; he spent the next ten years fending for himself in Sweden, spending two years on a farm and then working at various factories in Stockholm. He joined the Social Democrats and then the Communist Party. He spent the war as a stateless person, since his Czechoslovak passport was from a country that, after the Nazi occupation, no longer existed. He finally returned home to Prague in 1950, at the age of twenty-three. He didn't have a high-school diploma, but he managed to enter college and finished his college degree in Czech literature and literary theory in 1956, when he was thirty. In 1956 he also broke with the Communist Party when news arrived of Soviet premier Nikita Khrushchev's "secret speech" revealing Stalin's crimes. "It was like an earthquake, it was like a bomb," he said in a 1995 interview. "It was as if you told an Ursuline nun that there was no God and Voltaire was better than the Pope." His critical essays departed further and further from the official line, until he was expelled from the Party in 1959 and was only able to find work translating Scandinavian literature. After signing Charter 77, he worked as a night watchman as well as "in a trailer" for the water company, although he did not suffer the extremes of harassment that some other signatories did.[12]

Vohryzek suffered from a serious eye condition that eventually forced him to give up editing in 1985, but he saw *Kritický sborník* through its important first years and helped set it on the high level it would maintain until 1989 and beyond. In a 1990 interview, Vohryzek said: "I had expected that critics who had long been silenced would be glad to have a place to publish, but it turned out that the lack of publication opportunities had led to a paralysis of critical work. Criticism seems to be, far more than literature, dependent on the communicativeness of cultural life."[13] As was always the case with samizdat, creating the virtual space of communication—the journal itself—required the establishment of personal networks and personal contacts. This took a lot of walking. Vohryzek had to arrange all the contributions in person, with minimal use of telephone or mail. He would live for several days at a stretch in the trailer in the countryside, testing the water level at drilling sites, and then return to Prague, again for a few days at a time, where he would spend hours picking up manuscripts, cajoling late authors, talking with writers about possible essays—everything a magazine editor normally does, except without a telephone. He later described his editorial years as consisting of little more than "making the rounds," crisscrossing Prague from the medieval downtown to the vast apartment blocks in the suburbs, often at dusk or in the dark—no easy task, as Jindřich Pokorný pointed out, given his eye problems. He was helped by a number of other editors, including Jan Lopatka, Luboš Dobrovský, Miloš Rejchrt, and Karel Palek (who also wrote numerous articles under his pen name, Petr Fidelius).

The journal that emerged from all this hard work was impressive, and feels as lively and vital to today's reader as it did in the 1980s. *Kritický sborník* was not the only samizdat journal, but it was one of the broadest-based, ranging over all the humanities and specializing in critical essays, reviews, and polemics. It was also an early effort to cultivate criticism as a form of communication.

By his own account, Vohryzek played an important role in reshaping the journal's mission, altering the original plan for a literary-journalistic review and establishing it as a more exclusive, demanding journal. For this reason, he had trouble finding contributors at first, but the journal took off after Olga Havlová gave Vohryzek some of Václav Havel's prison letters, which sparked widespread interest. Eventually he had so many submissions that he needed to publish one or two extra issues during the year.

Thanks to the funding secured from abroad, *Kritický sborník* was able to pay honoraria to its contributors, as well as to pay for copying and copyediting. Palek, who joined the editorial board at the end of 1981, remembers that he was paid four hundred crowns for editing and laying out an entire issue of about a hundred pages; the copyists received five crowns a page. Jiřina Čílová would type up two to three "master copies" in the usual run of ten or twelve carbon copies, which Palek would then proofread and correct by hand. During the first years, Vohryzek remembers distributing about a hundred copies to various subscribers. Starting in 1985, Dagmar Tesařová joined the copying team and began to use an electric typewriter; after 1985, some issues were photocopied as well. Some of the "originals" went to subscribers; the rest were passed on to members of the editorial board, who would arrange for further typed copies of the masters. (Issues were also sent abroad, where they could be photocopied and distributed to libraries or among émigrés.) By the late 1980s, Palek estimated, the editorial team could produce 150 to 200 copies with relatively accuracy; Lopatka thought there were about three hundred. (The exact numbers are hard to reconstruct, since the editors avoided telling each other too much about their own activities; the less each one knew about the mechanics of the operation, the better.) Kautman thought that "the actual number of readers was doubtless much higher than those three hundred. Samizdat had one advantage. With the exception of those fastidious collectors who stored their copies away in their bookcases, it was constantly in circulation and generally spent one to two weeks with each subscriber."[14]

Samizdat created the usual difficulties for the reviewer. As Jiřina Šiklová wrote in a 1983 book review: "I had borrowed the book for only two evenings and two nights, and then it circulated further; what I cite here is only according to the notes and excerpts I wrote down." It was no easy matter to review a book that one no longer had access to. And did it even make sense to review a book when only a few copies existed? "In this absurd situation of ours," wrote Šiklová, "a review isn't actually a review; it's an attempt to familiarize readers as precisely as possible with the content of the book." Petr Pithart hoped that such summaries would generate interest and result in a "new edition"—another ten copies, that is—of a work; only after it had spread more widely would it be fair to criticize it.[15]

Perhaps even more problematic was the way in which samizdat publishing, by its very nature, tended to discourage criticism. The phenomenon of bad samizdat literature was familiar to all—being banned was the only thing that some writers had going for them. As Zdena Tominová suggested, the samizdat writer "is isolated even from his limited readership; he gets a response only from a few of his closest friends, and this response can often be too tolerant to be healthy."[16] František Kautman had pointed out that, without consistent feedback, "the author lives in thrall to his own self-reflections, and this can be tricky: sometimes it lulls him on the waves of his own conviction that he is a genius (and that he is unrecognized, it is so nice to add—an unrecognized genius!), at other times he succumbs to nihilistic moods and fortifies his own conviction that his work is worth nothing."[17]

Nevertheless, *Kritický sborník* would become one of the first journals to establish a samizdat forum for structured debate—both heated polemics and constructive criticism—and to create the framework for a consistent and long-running cultural, historical, and literary criticism within the opposition. It helped pave the way for later journals such as *Střední Evropa* (Central Europe) or Václav Benda's *PARAF*—but at the same time, it printed reviews (sometimes critical) of new issues of these samizdat journals. *Kritický sborník* participated in a wide range of debates, including discussions about samizdat itself: what it should be called, how it should be edited, whether it was different from "official" literature in any meaningful way. In the spirit of Edice Kvart, *Kritický sborník* also paid attention to questions of editing and philology, holding samizdat (and official) publishers to higher standards in their efforts to establish accurate or definitive texts. In general, it sought to break the taboo whereby everything in the "second culture" had to be praised and nurtured. It featured cultivated debates—on Milan Šimečka's guarded defense of utopian thinking, on Ladislav Hejdánek's understanding of socialism, on Václav Černý's memoirs. Some of its harshest and sharpest attacks came from Palek, writing under the pseudonym Petr Fidelius, and the philosopher Petr Rezek. Rezek, not himself a Charter signatory, was a sympathetic but tough critic who subjected dissident thought, in particular Havel, to a range of withering criticisms in *Kritický sborník* and *Střední Evropa*. One of the most notable achievements of dissent was to create a space whereby someone who didn't sign the Charter could analyze Havel's use of Patočka as a kitschy glorification of suffering.[18]

Another important step that *Kritický sborník* took was to begin breaking down the barriers between dissident and nondissident authors and literature. If it was, in some ways, a classic example of samizdat's "second culture," it also tried to erase the implicit lines between the parallel polis and official culture. Although it focused on samizdat, it also printed articles about officially published literature (and occasionally caused trouble for an official author whose work it praised). It also printed anonymous articles. This was sometimes seen as a step back from the hard-won principles of publicity, dialogue, and openness that stood at the heart of the Charter. After all, Petr Uhl and Anna Šabatová printed their names and address on the first page of every issue of *INFOCH*; when VONS declared its existence, the founding members signed the proclamation with their names and addresses. But anonymity created a more forgiving standard, allowing people to participate in the "second culture" without making an open proclamation of their disagreement with the regime. To some extent, this was a result of the conditions of samizdat publishing: Palek later wrote that "texts often arrived by quite tortuous paths, so that the editors themselves didn't always know whose contribution they were publishing."[19] But it was also the result of a conscious decision to create a more open space for critical discussion. Šiklová, still preserving her anonymity so that she could organize the import and export of clandestine literature, could take part in *Kritický sborník*—even writing an article on "The Ethics of the Anonymous Author" (by A. Nonymová). "Even someone who does not want to be harassed, who wants to remain in the structures and work in them, has every right to contribute to the 'second culture,' to the unofficial one, and we [. . .] should be grateful to him or her for enriching us; we should respect and defend his or her right to anonymity."[20] *Kritický sborník* thus created a less personalistic space in which criticism had more of a chance to flourish.

Vohryzek and his fellow editors were a different brand of dissident; they were neither human-rights activists nor philosophers of authenticity. They were editors, critics, and publishers; while some of them were active in the Charter—Vohryzek was even a spokesman in 1987, several years after he had passed the journal on to the new editorial team—others did not sign it. But their contribution to critical thinking in and around the dissident community was important. They did not see themselves as striking a blow against the regime, but rather as trying to resurrect and preserve cultural traditions and what Vohryzek called "the communicativeness of cultural life." It would be wrong to idealize *Kritický sborník*, but it did represent the kind of unbounded and critical community that I have tried to highlight as one of the achievements of dissent—not perfect, but able to talk about its imperfections in a framework that was both familiar and impersonal; engaged in a common project but open to new voices; emerging from the Charter but moving beyond it and, in the spirit of Ladislav Hejdánek's closing letter to his student friend, conducting a discussion that no longer distinguished between who had signed and who hadn't.

Vohryzek's critical essays had a slightly peculiar way of phrasing things, oddly direct, with shifts of emphasis that were logical but sudden. In a 1992 interview, he mused about his own unusual relationship to language. He had undergone a classically unsentimental twentieth-century education: raised in two different cultures, buffeted by the winds of both Nazism and Communism, he was an orphan and perennial outsider who entered college in his twenties and spent much of his working career as a translator, moving among several different languages. When he returned from Sweden in 1950, he remembered, "I was missing certain unspoken, subconscious information," making him vulnerable to misperceptions. It took him a while to see the show trials for what they really were, and as an orphan, he did not immediately recognize how Communist rule was breaking up and destroying families. Ultimately, though, his unusual perspective would give him critical leverage:

> I wasn't so sensitive to signals that, even then, others understood differently (during the show trials, for example). Maybe it was because I was uprooted, but not in a negative or pejorative sense. I accepted words in their original meanings and I didn't consider their connotations; I didn't have a feel for the euphemisms and hyperbole that were so abundant in the language of the totalitarian state. After all, I came from a free country and I didn't have any team here—I didn't have the background of relatives, the only place where genuine communication functioned, in the intimacy of families and communities of relatives. All of that had a lot of disadvantages for me, but then I reacted all the more vigorously.[21]

This is a striking meditation on the movement back and forth from an open to a closed society, from a free environment to a dangerous one, from a familiar to a foreign world. It suggests that genuine communication relies on communities that both nurture our ideas and resist them. Our family and friends give meaning to our words; yet any society does well to listen to its own outsiders, who can restore to words their original meanings and then put them back into circulation. Opposition doesn't mean stepping completely outside a society, but rather finding new ways to participate in it, even as one imagines better worlds. A culture that fosters such unions of generosity and creativity has gone a long way toward defeating conformity and repression.

Notes

Introduction

Note on Translations. Where possible, I have cited existing English-language translations of Czech sources. In these cases, I have specified the English title and translator in the appropriate footnote. Other translations are my own.

1. Václav Havel, "The Power of the Powerless," in *Open Letters: Selected Writings, 1965–1990*, ed. and trans. Paul Wilson (New York: Vintage, 1992), 127. Wilson's elegant English translation has taken on a life of its own; the original Czech is even more direct: *Východní Evropou obchází strašidlo, kterému na Západě říkají "disidentství"* ("A specter, which in the West they call 'dissidence,' is haunting [or: making the rounds of] Eastern Europe").

2. Karl Marx and Friedrich Engels, *The Communist Manifesto*, ed. Gareth Stedman-Jones (London: Penguin, 2002), 128. Stedman-Jones discusses the "specter" imagery on 11–12 and 27–39.

3. Havel, "Power of the Powerless," 132–148.

4. Ibid., 167–168.

5. Zdeněk Mlynář, "Místo 'disidentů' na politické mapě dneška," in Václav Havel et al., *O svobodě a moci* (Cologne and Rome: Index and Listy, 1980), 227.

6. I draw from the clips of Procházka's speech in *V žáru moci*, directed by Jordi Niubó (Televizní studio Ostrava—Česká televize, 2001).

7. On the end of censorship and new forms of civic organization in 1968, see Jiří Hoppe, *Opozice '68: Sociální demokracie, KAN a K 231 v období pražského jara* (Prague: Prostor, 2009).

8. Heda Margolius Kovály, *Under a Cruel Star: A Life in Prague 1941–1968*, trans. Franci Epstein and Helen Epstein with the author (New York: Holmes and Meier, 1997), 180–181.

9. Milan Šimečka, *The Restoration of Order: The Normalization of Czechoslovakia 1969–1976*, trans. A. G. Brain (London: Verso, 1984), 17.

10. The full text of "Two Thousand Words" is in Jaromír Navrátil, ed., *The Prague Spring 1968: A National Security Archive Documents Reader*, trans. Mark Kramer, Joy Moss, and Ruth Tosek (Budapest: Central European University Press, 1998), 177–181. See also Jakub Končelík, "Dva tisíce slov: Zrod a důsledky nečekaně vlivného provolání," *Soudobé dějiny* 15, no. 3–4 (2008): 485–544.

11. The full text of Kohout's appeal is in Navrátil, *Prague Spring*, 279–280.

12. "Final Report on the Activities of the American Poet Allen Ginsberg and His Deportation from Czechoslovakia," ed. and trans. Karel Vodrážka and Andrew Lass, in *The Massachusetts Review* 39, no. 2 (Summer 1998): 187–196; see also "The King of May: A Conversation between Allen Ginsberg and Andrew Lass" in the same issue, 169–184.

13. Jan Zábrana, *Celý život* (Prague: Torst, 1992), 1:208.

14. Miloš Forman and Jan Novák, *Turnaround: A Memoir* (New York: Villard, 1994), 172. Forman's account of the evening is closely echoed by Jean-Claude Carrière in his own memoir, *Les années d'utopie: 1968–1969, New York-Paris-Prague-New York* (Paris: Plon, 2003), 114–117.

15. Zdeněk Mlynář, *Nightfrost in Prague: The End of Humane Socialism*, trans. Paul Wilson (New York: Karz, 1980), 176–177. The journalist Jiří Lederer would later write: "The days following August 21, 1968 were the most fantastic film I've ever seen" in his memoir *Touhy a iluze II* (Toronto: Sixty-Eight Publishers, 1988), 7.

16. Josef Koudelka, *Invasion 68: Prague* (New York: Aperture, 2008).

17. Pavel Kosatík, *Ústně více: Šestatřicátníci* (Brno: Host, 2006); the photograph is between 160 and 161.

18. On Hrádeček and the Havels in the summer of 1968, see Pavel Kosatík, *"Člověk má dělat to, nač má sílu": Život Olgy Havlové*, 2nd ed. (Prague: Mladá Fronta, 2008), 99–108. Jan Tříska's reminiscence of the summer is in *Milý Václave: Přemýšlení o Václavu Havlovi*, ed. Anna Freimanová (Prague: Nakladatelství Lidové noviny, 1997), 62–73.

19. Václav Havel, *Disturbing the Peace: A Conversation with Karel Hvížďala*, trans. Paul Wilson (New York: Vintage, 1990), 107–108. The removal of street signs was widespread and much remarked upon; for a less enthusiastic view of this common motif, see Milan Kundera, *The Unbearable Lightness of Being*, trans. Michael Henry Heim (New York: Harper Perennial, 1999), 165–166 (part 4, section 25).

20. Jirous describes his experiences during the summer of 1968 in "Za čtyři roky se dá zapomenout na všechno," his 1994 book-length interview with Jan Pelc, in Ivan Jirous, *Magorův zápisník*, ed. Michael Špirit (Prague: Torst, 1997), 536–539.

21. Milan Kundera's comment comes from his 1968 essay "Český úděl," which is reprinted in Václav Havel, *O lidskou identitu: Úvahy, fejetony, protesty, polemiky, prohlášení a rozhovory z let 1969–1979*, ed. Vilém Prečan and Alexander Tomský (Prague: Rozmluvy, 1990), 187–193; Pavel Landovský, *Soukromá vzpoura: Rozhovor s Karlem Hvížďalou* (Prague: Mladá fronta, 1990), 55.

22. Ludvík Vaculík, *Český snář* (Brno: Atlantis, 1992), 399. Vaculík's rendering, in Czech, of his own uncertain English makes this scene all the more amusing and

indicative of the imperfect communication between the dissident and his Western admirer.

1. The Impasse of Dissent

1. Václav Havel, "Stories and Totalitarianism," in *Open Letters: Selected Writings, 1965–1990,* ed. and trans. Paul Wilson (New York: Vintage, 1992), 332.

2. Havel, "Dear Dr. Husák," in *Open Letters,* 60.

3. Michal Kopeček and Matěj Spurný, "Dějiny a paměť komunismu v Česku," *Lidové noviny,* January 9, 2010, www.lidovky.cz (accessed 2/7/10). See also Michal Kopeček, "Paměť národa new style," *Lidové noviny,* November 18, 2006, www. aktualne.usd.cas.cz (accessed 8/18/10). The sociologist Ivo Možný characterized dissent as a "counter-elite" as early as 1991 in an insightful account that explained the dissidents' lack of popular support without merely dismissing them: *Proč tak snadno . . . Některé rodinné důvody sametové revoluce,* 3rd ed. (Prague: Knižnice Sociologické aktuality, 2009).

4. See, for example, Paulina Bren, *The Greengrocer and His TV: The Culture of Communism after the 1968 Prague Spring* (Ithaca, NY: Cornell University Press, 2010), or Charles Maier, *Dissolution: The Crisis of Communism and the End of East Germany* (Princeton, NJ: Princeton University Press, 1997).

5. Petra Soukupová, *K moři* (Brno: Host, 2007), 76–77.

6. Michal Viewegh, *Vybíjená* (Brno: Petrov, 2004), 207–208.

7. Sergei Alex Oushakine, "The Terrifying Mimicry of Samizdat," *Public Culture* 13, no. 2 (2001): 191–214.

8. Alexei Yurchak, *Everything Was Forever, Until It Was No More: The Last Soviet Generation* (Princeton, NJ: Princeton University Press, 2005), 103–104 and 130. On popular ambivalence toward dissent, see Ladislav Holy, *The Little Czech and the Great Czech Nation* (Cambridge: Cambridge University Press, 1996). For a historical account by a former Charter signatory that nevertheless sees the dissidents as a small and isolated group, see Milan Otáhal, *Opozice, moc, společnost 1969–1989* (Prague: Ústav pro soudobé dějiny, 1994); Vilém Prečan offers a spirited reply in *Novoroční filipika 1995: Disent a Charta 77 v pojetí Milana Otáhala* (Prague: Ústav pro soudobé dějiny, 1995). See also Gil Eyal, *The Origins of Postcommunist Elites: From Prague Spring to the Breakup of Czechoslovakia* (Minneapolis: University of Minnesota Press, 2003), for an insightful sociological account that sees the dissidents as engaged in a struggle with other elites to redefine political and moral authority after the defeat of the Prague Spring.

9. Tony Judt, *Postwar: A History of Europe since 1945* (New York: Penguin, 2005), 569.

10. William Hitchcock, *The Struggle for Europe: The Turbulent History of a Divided Continent 1945–2002* (New York: Doubleday, 2002), 303.

11. Jeffrey Isaac, "The Meanings of 1989," *Social Research* 63, no. 2 (Summer 1996): 310 and 312.

12. Melvyn Leffler, *For the Soul of Mankind: The United States, the Soviet Union, and the Cold War* (New York: Hill and Wang, 2007), 234; see also Vladislav Zubok, *A Failed Empire: The Soviet Union in the Cold War from Stalin to Gorbachev* (Chapel Hill: University of North Carolina Press, 2007), 192 and 237–238.

13. Daniel Thomas, *The Helsinki Effect: International Norms, Human Rights, and the Demise of Communism* (Princeton, NJ: Princeton University Press, 2001), 95.

14. From the poems "21. 8. 1975" and "Pan Lopatka předpokládal" in Egon Bondy, *Básnické dílo,* ed. Martin Machovec (Prague: Pražská imaginace, 1992), 8:122 and 123.

15. John Lewis Gaddis, *The Cold War: A New History* (New York: Penguin, 2005), 190.

16. Tony Judt, "The Dilemmas of Dissidence: The Politics of Opposition in East-Central Europe," *East European Politics and Societies* 2, no. 2 (March 1988): 193. Judt also discusses this question in *Postwar*, 564–567.

17. Thomas, *Helsinki Effect*, 21.

18. On the international context of human rights in the 1970s, see Samuel Moyn, *The Last Utopia: Human Rights in History* (Cambridge, MA: Harvard University Press, 2010). Moyn is persuasive in explaining why human rights inspired so many in the West in the 1970s, but his framework is less useful for explaining the motivations of dissent. For a discussion of Charter 77's use of the "Helsinki Effect," see Jacques Rupnik, "Charta 77 a zrození evropského veřejného prostoru," in *Charta 77: Dokumenty 1977–1989,* ed. Blanka Císařovská and Vilém Prečan (Prague: Ústav pro soudobé dějiny, 2007), 1:xxvi–xxx.

19. See, for example, Odd Arne Westad, "Beginnings of the End: How the Cold War Crumbled," in *Reinterpreting the End of the Cold War*, ed. Silvio Pons and Federico Romero (London and New York: Frank Cass, 2005), 68–81; Silvio Pons, "The Rise and Fall of Eurocommunism," in *The Cambridge History of the Cold War,* ed. Melvyn Leffler and Odd Arne Westad (Cambridge: Cambridge University Press, 2010), 3:45–65; or the September 1975 interview that Zdeněk Mlynář and Jiří Hájek recorded for Swedish television and radio, "Záznam rozhovoru," in *Hlasy z domova 1975,* ed. Adolf Müller (Cologne: Index, 1975), 87–98.

20. Miroslav Kusý, "Chartism and 'real' socialism," trans. Paul Wilson, in *The Power of the Powerless: Citizens against the state in central-eastern Europe*, ed. John Keane (Armonk, NY: M. E. Sharpe, 1985), 153.

21. Jan Patočka, *Kacířské eseje o filozofii dějin* (Prague: Academia, 1990). For an excellent treatment of the philosophical background of Czech dissent, see Aviezer Tucker, *The Philosophy and Politics of Czech Dissidence from Patočka to Havel* (Pittsburgh: University of Pittsburgh Press, 2000). For an interpretation of dissent as a negotiation between an existentialist language of authenticity and a discourse of legal legitimacy, see Jiří Přibáň, *Dissidents of Law* (Burlington, VT: Ashgate/Dartmouth, 2002).

22. Gaddis, *Cold War*, 190.

23. Thomas, *Helsinki Effect*, 286. In general, Thomas overestimates the level of popular support for Charter 77, and the seriousness of the threat it posed to the

regime. He suggests that the regime was forced to move quickly from "harassment and intimidation" to "reasoned arguments" in opposing the Charter (183), but harsh repressions continued throughout the 1980s, and the state never entered into any serious dialogue with the Chartists.

24. See the interview with Hejda in Petr Placák, *Kádrový dotazník* (Prague: Babylon, 2001), 113–114.

25. Václav Havel, *Disturbing the Peace: A Conversation with Karel Hvížďala*, trans. Paul Wilson (New York: Vintage, 1990), 122. The phrase "victories written by history" comes from Václav Bělohradský, another philosopher whose thinking at the time drew heavily on Heidegger and existentialist themes. It is not surprising to hear the poet and novelist Jiří Gruša in a 2004 interview speaking of human rights, the American founding fathers, and Heideggerian *Dasein* all in the same breath— the dissidents' language of rights was often quite personal and eccentric. Jiří Gruša, *Umění stárnout: Rozhovor s Daliborem Dobiášem* (Prague: Litomyšl, 2004), 171.

26. The full text of the Final Act is available at www.osce.org (accessed 11/5/11).

27. See Havel, "The Power of the Powerless," in *Open Letters*, esp. 192–196.

28. H. Gordon Skilling, "Introductory Essay," in *Civic Freedom in Central Europe: Voices from Czechoslovakia*, ed. H. Gordon Skilling and Paul Wilson (New York: St. Martin's Press, 1991), 3–32. For a useful contemporary discussion, see Timothy Garton Ash, "Reform or Revolution?", *in The Uses of Adversity: Essays on the Fate of Central Europe* (New York: Vintage, 1990), esp. 270–279.

29. Isaac, "Meanings of 1989," 316–318. See also his "The Strange Silence of Political Theory," *Political Theory* 23, no. 4 (1995): 636–652, as well as "Rethinking the Legacy of Central European Dissidence," *Common Knowledge* 10, no. 1 (2004): 119–129.

30. See Barbara Falk's comprehensive and invaluable *The Dilemmas of Dissidence in East-Central Europe* (Budapest: Central European University Press, 2003), 339 and 344.

31. Václav Benda, "The Parallel 'Polis,'" in Skilling and Wilson, *Civic Freedom*, 41.

32. Falk, *Dilemmas of Dissidence*, 248.

33. Skilling and Wilson, *Civic Freedom*, x. Skilling has also discussed these questions in his *Charter 77 and Human Rights in Czechoslovakia* (London: Allen and Unwin, 1981) and *Samizdat and an Independent Society in Central and Eastern Europe* (Columbus: Ohio State University Press, 1989).

34. Ladislav Hejdánek, *Dopisy příteli* (Prague: Institut pro středoevropskou kulturu a politiku/Oikumene, 1993); Petr Šámal, "Literární kritika za časů normalizace," *Literární archiv* 37 (2006): 170–171.

35. Benda, "Parallel 'Polis,'" 37.

36. It is interesting, for example, to note that Adam Michnik's 1976 essay "A New Evolutionism," which would become a touchstone of civil-society narratives, argues closely from the situation in Poland (and suggests several comparisons with a "Spanish model") even as it gestures somewhat vaguely toward an East European strategy for dissent. See Adam Michnik, *Letters from Prison and Other Essays*, trans.

Maya Latynski (Berkeley: University of California Press, 1985), 135–148. Despite many parallels (and transnational connections) with the rest of the Communist bloc, the Polish case rests uneasily in comparative East or Central European models of Communist society and opposition. The strength of the Catholic church in Poland and a tradition of revolts against Russian authority, among other things, led to more extensive independent publishing and distribution networks and a more widespread oppositional culture in general. On this point, see also Stephen Kotkin and Jan Gross, *Uncivil Society: 1989 and the Implosion of the Communist Establishment* (New York: Modern Library, 2009), 99–104.

37. An exception to this rule is Barbara Day's fascinating book *The Velvet Philosophers* (London: Claridge Press, 1999), a detailed discussion of underground university lectures in Czechoslovakia during the 1970s and 1980s, including those sponsored by the Jan Hus Educational Foundation, a sophisticated, multinational collaboration that brought historians and philosophers such as Paul Ricoeur, André Glucksmann, Charles Taylor, Roger Scruton, Jacques Derrida, Tony Judt, and many others to give unofficial lectures in private apartments. Day's focus on the underground university makes her book seemingly more narrow than more comprehensive accounts of dissent, but in fact it is an essential complement that changes the overall picture dramatically. Notably, the longest-running and arguably most successful of the underground lecture series, organized in Brno by Jiří Müller, programmatically rejected the idea of its own "parallel" existence and sought to increase contacts between open dissidents and people in the "gray zone" who disliked the regime but did not oppose it openly.

38. Ludvík Vaculík, *Český snář* (Brno: Atlantis, 1992), 25.

39. Day, *Velvet Philosophers*, 89–96.

40. See, for example, the discussion among former VONS members in Petr Blažek and Jaroslav Pažout, eds., *Nejcitlivější místo režimu: Výbor na obranu nespravedlivě stíhaných (VONS) pohledem svých členů* (Prague: Pulchra, 2008), 65–83.

41. Gruša, *Umění stárnout*, 173. For another former dissident's forceful statement against the parallel-polis narrative, see Petr Pithart, *Devětaosmdesátý* (Prague: Academia, 2009), esp. 20–34.

42. On the presidential vote, see Jiří Suk, *Labyrintem revoluce: Aktéři, zápletky a křižovatky jedné politické krize (od listopadu 1989 do června 1990)*, 2nd ed. (Prague: Prostor, 2009), 212–229. For a former dissident's account of this episode, see Pithart, *Devětaosmdesátý*, 146–159.

43. From a vast and varied scholarship we could mention Stephen Kotkin's *Magnetic Mountain: Stalinism as a Civilization* (Berkeley and Los Angeles: University of California Press, 1995); Sheila Fitzpatrick's *Everyday Stalinism: Ordinary Life in Extraordinary Times: Soviet Russia in the 1930s* (New York: Oxford University Press, 1999); or Jochen Hellbeck's *Revolution on My Mind: Writing a Diary under Stalin* (Cambridge, MA: Harvard University Press, 2006).

44. See Yurchak, *Everything Was Forever*, especially his theory of the "performative shift" in Chapter 1.

45. Corey Ross, *The East German Dictatorship: Problems and Perspectives in the Interpretation of the GDR* (London: Arnold, 2002).

46. Mary Fulbrook, *The People's State: East German Society from Hitler to Honecker* (New Haven, CT: Yale University Press, 2005), 1–2.

47. Charles Maier, "What Have We Learned from 1989?," *Contemporary European History* 18, no. 3 (2009): 266.

48. Miroslav Vaněk, "Úvod," in *Obyčejní lidé. . . ?! Pohled do života tzv. mlčící většiny,* ed. Miroslav Vaněk (Prague: Academia, 2009), 1:10.

49. Cited in ibid., 13. The full article, "17. listopad v českých dějinách," is available on Klaus's website at www.klaus.cz (accessed 10/19/11). Even Klaus puts the term "ordinary citizens" in quotes the second time he uses it—this term, like the word "dissident" itself, is fraught with its own inadequacy.

50. See, for example, Havel's short reply, "Byli jsme zbyteční?" ("Were we unnecessary?"), available on Havel's website at www.vaclavhavel.cz (accessed 10/19/11).

51. Vaněk, "Úvod," 12.

52. Bren, *The Greengrocer and His TV,* esp. 89–103.

53. Miroslav Vaněk and Pavel Urbášek, eds., *Vítězové? Poražení? Životopisná interview,* 2 vols. (Prague: Prostor and Ústav pro soudobé dějiny, 2005). These volumes contain over two thousand pages of interviews with former dissidents and Communist Party functionaries. They build on several earlier oral history projects, including Květa Jechová, *Lidé Charty 77: Zpráva o biografickém výzkumu* (Prague: Ústav pro soudobé dějiny, 2003); Milan Otáhal and Miroslav Vaněk, eds., *Sto studentských revolucí* (Prague: Lidové noviny, 1999); and Petr Blažek, Jaroslav Cuhra, Libuše Cuhrová, Miroslav Vaněk, and Pavel Žáček, *Ostrůvky svobody: Kulturní a občanské aktivity mladé generace v 80. letech v Československu* (Prague: Ústav pro soudobé dějiny and Votobia, 2002).

54. Two notable exceptions to this rule are Day's *The Velvet Philosophers* and Padraic Kenney's *A Carnival of Revolution: Central Europe 1989* (Princeton, NJ: Princeton University Press, 2002). With both verve and acuity, Kenney examines oppositional movements of the 1980s in terms of street happenings, theater, performance, and other practices. Even Kenney, however, sometimes assumes that this world of practices only came into its own in the second half of the 1980s, when the "older generation of dissident intellectuals" (191) gave way to a more dynamic, younger generation interested in practical problems. In fact, the dissident intellectuals were also highly attuned to questions of self-presentation and performance, although in somewhat less public terms.

55. Eva Kantůrková, *My Companions in the Bleak House* (Woodstock, NY: Overlook Press, 1987). Kantůrková's sharp-edged portraits are more insightful than, for example, Havel's romanticized view of his fellow prisoners: "Almost every prisoner had a life story that was unique and shocking, or moving. As I listened to those different stories, I suddenly found myself in something like a pre-totalitarian world, or in the world of literature" ("Stories and Totalitarianism," 338).

56. Jiří Müller, who helped organize the enormously successful underground lecture series in Brno (over sixty lectures from 1985 to 1989, without a single police intervention), emphasized the importance of couples for dissent: "There was more than one case where I turned for help, if I can put it this way, to a marriage, not to one person or the other. Because difficult moments come, and if they are going to manage them, then both of them will have to do so." The Brno seminar was co-organized by Petr Oslzlý and Eva Oslzlá. See Müller's 2004 interview with Pavel Urbášek in Vaněk and Urbášek, *Vítězové? Poražení?*, 1:599, as well as Day, *Velvet Philosophers*, 141–172.

57. See, for example, Marta Marková, *Olga Havlová a ty druhé: Ženy ve vnitřní emigraci* (Brno: Barrister & Principal, 1996); Pavel Kosatík, *"Člověk má dělat to, nač má sílu": Život Olgy Havlové*, 2nd ed. (Prague: Mladá Fronta, 2008); Jan Bárta and Dana Němcová, *Lidé mého života* (Prague: Portál, 2003); and Eva Kantůrková, *Sešly jsme se v této knize* (Prague: Toužímský a Moravec, 1991).

58. Mary Hrabik Samal, "Ženy a neoficiální kultura a literatura v Československu v letech 1969–1989," in *Prítomnosť minulosti, Minulosť prítomnosti*, ed. Jolaná Kusá and Peter Zajac (Bratislava: Nadácia Milana Šimečku, 1996), 84.

59. Shana Penn, *Solidarity's Secret* (Ann Arbor: University of Michigan Press, 2005), 181; see also Padraic Kenney, "The Gender of Resistance in Communist Poland," *American Historical Review* 104, no. 2 (April 1999): 399–425, as well as Kenney's review of *Solidarity's Secret:* "A Solidarity Still Unexamined," HABSBURG H-Net reviews, October 2007, www.h-net.org (accessed 8/18/10), which points out the affinity between research on women and research on "the *praxis* of opposition." In the Czech case, this question has received less systematic attention. See, for example, Samal, "Ženy a neoficiální kultura"; Kamila Bendová, "Ženy v Chartě 77," in *Opozice a odpor proti komunistickému režimu v Československu 1968–1989*, ed. Petr Blažek (Prague: Dokořán and Ústav českých dějin FF UK, 2005), 54–66; Jiřina Šiklová, "Podíl českých žen na samizdatu a v disentu v Československu v období tzv. normalizace v letech 1969–1989," *Gender, rovné příležitosti, výzkum* 9, no. 1 (September 2008): 39–44; or Jechová, *Lidé Charty 77*, esp. 69–72.

60. See, for example, Timothy Garton Ash's still indispensable *The Magic Lantern: The Revolution of '89 Witnessed in Warsaw, Budapest, Berlin, and Prague* (New York: Random House, 1990), or more recently Jiří Suk's superb *Labyrintem revoluce*.

61. Možný, *Proč tak snadno . . .* , made this case brilliantly in 1991. The most forceful statement in English is Kotkin and Gross, *Uncivil Society*. For a reply, see Timothy Garton Ash's review, "1989!", *New York Review of Books* 56, no. 17 (November 5, 2009), www.nyrb.com (accessed 9/18/2011).

62. An early statement of this view came from Juan J. Linz and Alfred Stepan, *Problems of Democratic Transition and Consolidation* (Baltimore, MD: The Johns Hopkins University Press, 1996): "Unfortunately, the atmosphere of dissident life in frozen post-totalitarian Czechoslovakia did not generate much attention to formal institutional matters. Indeed, the style of Havel and many of his closest advisors [. . .] was actively anti-political and anti-institutional" (331). For a more nuanced

view, but one still shaped by the perspective of 1989, see Alan Renwick, "Anti-Political or Just Anti-Communist? Varieties of Dissidence in East-Central Europe and Their Implications for the Development of Political Society," *East European Politics and Societies* 20, no. 2 (2006): 286–318. Jiří Suk's account in *Labyrintem revoluce* gives a detailed and sophisticated account of how dissident philosophy flowed into revolutionary politics.

63. Falk, *Dilemmas of Dissidence*, 354–364.

64. As Falk points out, in the late 1980s many dissidents as well as Western theorists would have associated dissent with socialist aspirations (ibid., 337). It is instructive to read, for example, Tony Judt's "The Dilemmas of Dissidence," written just before the fall of Communism, or Timothy Garton Ash's classic essays from the 1980s, collected in *The Uses of Adversity*, for a refreshing open-endedness about the many possibilities contained in dissent.

65. Jacques Rupnik, "In Search of a New Model," *Journal of Democracy* 21, no. 1 (January 2010): 105–112.

66. On backshadowing, see Michael André Bernstein, *Foregone Conclusions: Against Apocalyptic History* (Berkeley: University of California Press, 1994), and Gary Saul Morson, *Narrative and Freedom: The Shadows of Time* (New Haven, CT: Yale University Press, 1994).

2. The Stages of Demobilization

1. František Janouch tells his story in *Ne, nestěžuji si: Malá normalizační mozaika* (Prague: Acropolis, 2008), first published in 1978; the 2008 edition contains reproductions of documents relating to Janouch's various protests and legal cases. His statement to the Party expulsion commission is on 61–63; the letter dismissing him from his job is reproduced on 73; the appeals court decision is cited on page 126; on Sakharov, see 183–188.

2. Ibid., 208.

3. The minutes to Clifford's staff meeting are in Günter Bischof, Stefan Karner, and Peter Ruggenthaler, eds., *The Prague Spring and the Warsaw Pact Invasion of Czechoslovakia in 1968* (Lanham, MD: Rowman and Littlefield, 2010), 471. On the invasion, see also Mark Kramer, "The Czechoslovak Crisis and the Brezhnev Doctrine," in *1968: The World Transformed*, ed. Carole Fink, Philipp Gassert, and Detlef Junker (Washington, DC: German Historical Institute and Cambridge University Press, 1998), 111–172. On the "technically magnificent" peaceful resistance of invasion week, see Kieran Williams, "Civil Resistance in Czechoslovakia: From Soviet Invasion to 'Velvet Revolution,' 1968–1989," in *Civil Resistance and Power Politics: The Experience of Non-violent Action from Gandhi to the Present*, ed. Adam Roberts and Timothy Garton Ash (New York: Oxford University Press, 2009), 110–126.

4. Milan Šimečka, *The Restoration of Order*, trans. A. G. Brain (London: Verso, 1984), 30. For discussion and a translated text of the Moscow Protocol, see Jaromír

Navrátil, ed., *The Prague Spring 1968: A National Security Archive Documents Reader*, trans. Mark Kramer, Joy Moss, and Ruth Tosek (Budapest: Central European University Press, 1998), 477–480; see also Kieran Williams, *The Prague Spring and its Aftermath* (Cambridge: Cambridge University Press, 1997), 137–143.

5. Šimečka is quoted in Vilém Prečan, "Velké a male dějiny Milana Šimečka," in *V kradeném čase: Výběr ze studií, článků a úvah z let 1973–1993*, ed. Milan Drápala (Prague: Ústav pro soudobé dějiny, 1994), 456; on the name of the Moscow agreements, see Prečan's analysis in "Zpráva o Černé knize" in ibid., 252–256.

6. Williams, *Prague Spring*, 148–150. In addition to Williams's excellent account, which provides a harsh and disillusioned perspective on the whole Prague Spring leadership, the best recent analyses of the post-1968 crackdown are Zdeněk Doskočil, *Duben 1969: Anatomie mocenského převratu* (Brno: Doplněk and Ústav pro soudobé dějiny, 2006), a blow-by-blow account that is somewhat more sympathetic to the reform leaders, and Paulina Bren, *The Greengrocer and His TV: The Culture of Communism after the 1968 Prague Spring* (Ithaca: Cornell University Press, 2010), focusing particularly on the mass media. Older, but still valuable, accounts are Milan Otáhal, *Opozice, moc, společnost 1969–1989* (Prague: Ústav pro soudobé dějiny, 1994), which downplays the influence of dissent; Galia Golan, *Reform Rule in Czechoslovakia: The Dubček Era 1968–1969* (Cambridge: Cambridge University Press, 1973); and Vladimir V. Kusin, *From Dubček to Charter 77: A study of 'normalisation' in Czechoslovakia 1968–1978* (New York: St. Martin's Press, 1978).

7. See Doskočil, *Duben 1969*, 29–31, and Williams, *Prague Spring*, 147–149.

8. The four who voted against were František Kriegel, Gertruda Sekaninová-Čakrtová, František Vodsloň, and Božena Fuková. All of them would come under fire in the following months; the first three would eventually sign Charter 77.

9. Doskočil, *Duben 1969*, 35–36. Williams characterizes the Warsaw meeting more unequivocally as "essentially his [Brezhnev's] monologue of demanded corrections" (*Prague Spring*, 177). Mlynář's resignation speech is in his memoir *Nightfrost in Prague: The End of Humane Socialism*, trans. Paul Wilson (New York: Karz, 1980), 261–266.

10. Jiří Lederer, *Touhy a iluze II* (Toronto: Sixty-Eight Publishers, 1988), esp. 30–42; Květa Jechová, "K historii Koordinačního výboru tvůrčích svazů," in *Proměny Pražského jara*, ed. Jindřich Pecka and Vilém Prečan (Brno: Doplněk, 1993), 91–122. Jechová also reprints Lederer's speech; the quotation about culture is on 119.

11. Williams, *Prague Spring*, 178. In Williams's apt phrase, Husák "defined his own agenda as a messianic yet pragmatic man of power" (158).

12. Ibid., 186.

13. Jaroslav Putík, *Odchod od zámku* (Prague: Hynek, 1998), 51–52. Suppressing his usual clear-eyed cynicism, Putík continues: "Who was it that said sometimes only tragedy prevents us from seeing how laughable events are? But never mind. The moral pathos of this deed overlays everything. I can't help myself; tears come into my eyes. Something irrevocable has happened; this nation has heroes again." See also Eva Kantůrková's meditation "On the Ethics of Palach's Deed," trans. Milan Pomichalek and Anna Mozga, in *Good-Bye, Samizdat: Twenty Years of Czech*

Underground Writing, ed. Marketa Goetz-Stankiewicz (Evanston, IL: Northwestern University Press, 1992), 175–180.

14. On Palach, see especially the extensive materials in Michala Benešová, Petr Blažek, Patrik Eichler, Veronika Jáchimová, Jakub Jareš, and Viktor Portel, eds., *Jan Palach '69* (Prague: Togga, 2009), as well as Williams's brief but enlightening discussion in *Prague Spring*, 188–191.

15. On the hockey riots, see Doskočil, *Duben 1969*, 96–113; on the question of StB provocation, see especially 100–103. The exact role of the secret police in these events is difficult to determine, but evidence now seems overwhelming that much of the violence was provoked, including in the most visible case of the ransacked Aeroflot offices.

16. Ibid., 106.

17. Ibid., 129–131.

18. Williams, *Prague Spring*, 202.

19. Doskočil, *Duben 1969*, 147.

20. Williams, *Prague Spring*, 204.

21. Putík, *Odchod*, 50; Šimečka is quoted in Prečan, "Velké a male dějiny," 456–457. After April, Václav Havel, in whose apartment the secret police had installed listening devices, was recorded as saying that "Dubček is a dreamer and lyric poet" while Husák "has a genuinely firm conception and can lead the nation out of the crisis situation" (Williams, *Prague Spring*, 208–209; Doskočil, *Duben 1969*, 267). Such opinions were widespread.

22. Petr Pithart, *Devětaosmdesátý* (Prague: Academia, 2009), 11–12.

23. On the Ten Points manifesto, see Kusin, *From Dubček*, 148–150; Martin Lakatoš, Luděk Pachman, and Ludvík Vaculík, "Osudy a smysl petice 'Deset bodů' ze srpna 1969," in Pecka and Prečan, *Proměny Pražského jara*, 281–310; and Luděk Pachman's memoirs, *Jak to bylo: Zpráva o činnosti šachového velmistra za období 1924–1972* (Toronto: Sixty-Eight Publishers, 1974); a shortened version of this memoir is available in English as *Checkmate in Prague*, trans. Rosemary Brown (New York: Macmillan, 1975). One of the best sources on Ten Points is Ludvík Vaculík's diary entries from the end of 1969, where he details how he came to draft the petition despite his skepticism toward it; see Ludvík Vaculík, *Nepaměti 1969–1972* (Prague: Mladá fronta, 1998).

24. On Uhl's life and political opinions, see especially his memoir, *Právo a nespravedlnost očima Petra Uhla* (Prague: C. H. Beck, 1998), as well as his 2003 interview with David Weber in Miroslav Vaněk and Pavel Urbášek, eds., *Vítězové? Poražení? Životopisná interview* (Prague: Prostor, 2005), 1:985–1027. On the Movement of Revolutionary Youth, see also Jaroslav Suk, "Československá radikální levice," *Svědectví* 17, no. 67 (1982): 613–629, which reprints sections of the 1969 "Proclamation."

25. On the 1971 elections and 1972 trials see, for example, Kusin, *From Dubček*, especially 116–118 and 145–170; for interviews with Anna Šabatová, see Marta Marková, *Olga Havlová a ty druhé* (Brno: Barrister and Principal, 1996), and Eva Kantůrková, *Sešly jsme se v této knize* (Prague: Toužímský a Moravec, 1991).

26. Williams, *Prague Spring*, 240–241.

27. On the Party purge, see Jiří Maňák, *Čistky v komunistické straně Československa v letech 1969–1970* (Prague: Ústav pro soudobé dějiny, 1997); Kieran Williams, "The Prague Spring: From Elite Liberalisation to Mass Movement," in *Revolution and Resistance in Eastern Europe: Challenges to Communist Rule,* ed. Kevin McDermott and Matthew Stibbe (New York: Berg, 2006), 101–118; Williams, *Prague Spring*, 226–244; Bren, *The Greengrocer and His TV*, 35–60; and Josef Belda, "Konečná fáze likvidace obrodného procesu," in Miloš Bárta, Ondřej Felcman, Josef Belda, and Vojtěch Mencl, *Československo roku 1968* (Prague: Parta and Ústav mezinárodních vztahů, 1993), 2:83–121.

28. Maňák, *Čistky*, 36.

29. Williams, *Prague Spring*, 228.

30. Ibid., 228–229. See also Maňák, *Čistky*, 37n62.

31. Pachman, *Jak to bylo*, 181 (on the Soviet press) and 196–197 (on his expulsion).

32. Šimečka, *Restoration of Order*, 42.

33. Bren, *The Greengrocer and His TV*, 44.

34. These figures come from Maňák, *Čistky*, 58. The actual numbers vary slightly depending on when we take the endpoint of the purges to be. For a summary, see Bren, *The Greengrocer and His TV*, 215n33.

35. Williams, "Prague Spring," 108.

36. Prečan, "Společenské vědy ve svěráku 'konsolidace,'" in *V kradeném čase,* 294. On "disciplinary mechanisms," see Michel Foucault, *Discipline and Punish*, trans. Alan Sheridan (New York: Vintage, 1995), especially his section on "the examination," 184–194.

37. Bren, *The Greengrocer and His TV*, 45. For an interpretation of the meaning of "intellectual" in the context of Czech history, see Bradley Abrams, *The Struggle for the Soul of the Nation* (Lanham, MD: Rowman and Littlefield, 2004), esp. Chapters 2 and 3. There is no good English translation for the term *inteligence*; the Russian-flavored *intelligentsia* encodes a set of assumptions about intellectuals' aspirations, often for society-wide or revolutionary change, that were losing their force in Czechoslovakia in the 1970s. "University-educated people" might give a better approximation, although we would have to include many artists, actors, poets, novelists, and so on, who might not have a university degree. There is also the important cohort of non-Communist intellectuals whose educational opportunities were severely limited in the 1950s, and yet who went on to write, teach, or research starting in the 1960s—a well-known case being Václav Havel himself.

38. Williams, *Prague Spring*, 235. Despite the massive loss of white-collar members, the Party still "permeated these professions more deeply than it did the working class" (ibid.).

39. Maňák, *Čistky*, 63, including notes 106 and 107. Maňák reprints the Central Committee's own reports and calculations over the course of 1970, 87–125. The figure of 56 percent comes from the Central Committee report of December 1970 (ibid., 109).

40. This evaluation also comes from the December 1970 Central Committee report (ibid., 110). See also Bren, 44–45.

41. Maňák, *Čistky*, 77.

42. See the Central Committee report from April 1970, reprinted in ibid., 88–95.

43. Kateřina Blahová, "Svaz českých spisovatelů (1)," in *Slovník české literatury po roce 1945*, www.slovnikceskeliteratury.cz (accessed 7/27/10).

44. Vaculík, *Nepaměti*, 83–84.

45. Růžena Hamanová, "Václav Černý," in *Slovník české literatury po roce 1945*, www.slovnikceskeliteratury.cz (accessed 7/27/10); John Connelly, *Captive University: The Sovietization of East German, Czech, and Polish Higher Education, 1945–1956* (Chapel Hill: University of North Carolina Press, 2000), 129–130. For the Ministry of Education decree on retirement, see Prečan, "Společenské vědy," 287; for the moral striptease, "Oni o sobě," *Rudé právo*, April 23, 1970, 1–2. The best source on Černý's life and opinions is his own memoirs: Václav Černý, *Paměti*, 3 vols., 2nd ed. (Brno: Atlantis, 1992). He describes his dismissal in 2:380–381; the discovery of the manuscript in 2:443–447; and the media smear campaign against him and Procházka in 2:618–628. Some fifteen years later, Milan Kundera's characters would discuss the campaign in the novel *The Unbearable Lightness of Being*, trans. Michael Henry Heim (New York: Harper Perennial, 1999), 132–134 (part 4, section 2) and 228–230 (part 5, section 19).

46. On Patočka's life, see, for example, Skilling, *Charter 77*, 20–23; Přemysl Blažíček, "Jan Patočka," in *Slovník české literatury po roce 1945*, www. slovnikceskeliteratury.cz (accessed 7/27/10); and the tribute published after his death by Charter 77, reprinted in Blanka Císařovská and Vilém Prečan, eds., *Charta 77: Dokumenty 1977–1989* (Prague: Ústav pro soudobé dějiny, 2007), 2:34–36. For Patočka's return to lecturing, see Michal Jůza's poem "Filozof" in *Haňta Press* 8 (December 1990): 1.

47. See Urban's interview with David Weber in Vaněk and Urbášek, *Vítězové? Poražení?*, 1041.

48. Prečan, "Společenské vědy," 298n26.

49. Putík, *Odchod*, 183; Vaculík, *Nepaměti*, 101–102 and 110–112; Pavel Kohout, *Kde je zakopán pes* (Brno: Atlantis, 1990), 26–28. On Procházka, I have also drawn on the documentary *V žáru moci*, director Jordi Niubó (Televizní studio Ostrava—Česká televize, 2001). Funerals of reformers and regime opponents were symbolically fraught for both the state and the mourners; another notable case is dramatized in Slovak journalist Ján Rožner's remarkable account of the funeral of his wife, the well-known translator Zora Jesenská, in December 1972: *Sedem dní do pohrebu* (Bratislava: Albert Marenčin, 2009).

3. The Shadow World

1. Jaroslav Putík, *Odchod od zámku* (Prague: Hynek, 1998), 110.

2. As Kieran Williams points out, the term "entered Soviet parlance as a euphemism for the restoration of communist control" after the Polish and Hungarian

uprisings of 1956. *The Prague Spring and its Aftermath* (Cambridge: Cambridge University Press, 1997), 40.

3. Robert Alison Remington, ed., *Winter in Prague: Documents on Czechoslovak Communism in Crisis*, trans. Michael Berman (Cambridge, MA: MIT Press, 1969), 377–378.

4. Ibid., 390.

5. Milan Šimečka, *The Restoration of Order*, trans. A. G. Brain (London: Verso, 1984), especially 137–145; Antonín Liehm, "The New Social Contract and the Parallel Polity," in *Dissent in Eastern Europe*, ed. Jane Leftwich Curry (New York: Praeger, 1983), 173–181.

6. Quoted and translated in Williams, *Prague Spring*, 40. Williams himself argues against the "social contract" as an explanation of popular acquiescence with normalization, 40–46.

7. Paulina Bren, "Weekend Getaways: The Chata, the Tramp and the Politics of Private Life in Post-1968 Czechoslovakia," in *Socialist Spaces: Sites of Everyday Life in the Eastern Bloc*, ed. David Crowley and Susan Reid (New York: Berg, 2002), 123–140; Kieran Williams, "The Prague Spring: From Elite Liberalisation to Mass Movement," in *Revolution and Resistance in Eastern Europe: Challenges to Communist Rule*, ed. Kevin McDermott and Matthew Stibbe (New York: Berg, 2006), 111.

8. Zdeněk Doskočil, *Duben 1969: Anatomie mocenského převratu* (Brno: Doplněk and Ústav pro soudobé dějiny, 2006), 39.

9. Pecka tells his own story in Jan Lukeš, *Hry doopravdy: Rozhovor se spisovatelem Karlem Peckou* (Prague and Litomyšl: Paseka, 1998). See also Petr Blažek, "'Podkopávej ze všech sil dnešní režim!' Ilegální tiskoviny odbojové skupiny *Za pravdu* (1949)," *Paměť a dějiny* 1, no. 1 (2007): 134–161.

10. Šimečka, *Restoration of Order*, 85.

11. Remington, *Winter in Prague*, 394.

12. Quoted in Doskočil, *Duben 1969*, 214 and 217. The Ten Points petition had, by contrast, declared: "We don't believe assurances that legality will be upheld in the future and that repetitions of the institutionalized violence of the 1950s will not occur, unless security is placed under the visible and effective control of civilian organs, above all the legislative bodies." Jindřich Pecka and Vilem Prečan, eds., *Proměny Pražského jara* (Brno: Doplněk, 1993), 285.

13. Pavel Juráček, *Deník (1959–1974)*, ed. Jan Lukeš (Prague: Národní filmový archiv, 2003), 671.

14. On the function of show trials, see István Rév, "In Mendacio Veritas (In Lies There Lies the Truth)," *Representations* 35 (Summer 1991): 1–20.

15. On the postponement and eventual burial of the Piller report, see Doskočil, *Duben 1969*, 305–306 and 351–352. The report was eventually published in the West, first in German and then in English: *The Czechoslovak Political Trials, 1950–1954*, ed. Jiří Pelikán (Stanford, CA: Stanford University Press, 1971).

16. See Doskočil, *Duben 1969*, 176–199, for a good account of Husák's character and background.

17. Ludvík Vaculík, *Nepaměti 1969–1972* (Prague: Mladá fronta, 1998), 30.

18. Janouch, *Ne, nestěžuji si*, 198–199.

19. Vaculík, *Nepaměti*, 79.

20. Šimečka, *Restoration of Order*, 78–79. On Husák's approach to legality, see also Peter Bugge, "Normalization and the Limits of the Law: The Case of the Czech Jazz Section," *East European Politics and Societies* 22, no. 2 (May 2008): 282–318.

21. Putík, *Odchod*, 86.

22. Zdeněk Mlynář, *Nightfrost in Prague: The End of Humane Socialism*, trans. Paul Wilson (New York: Karz, 1980), 242–244.

23. Putík, *Odchod*, 30; Jiří Lederer, *Touhy a iluze II* (Toronto: Sixty-Eight Publishers, 1988), 10.

24. Lederer, *Touhy a iluze II*, 110–112; Luděk Pachman, introduction to the anonymous volume *Motáky z Ruzyně* (Cologne: Index, 1973), 18.

25. Ludvík Vaculík, *A Cup of Coffee with My Interrogator*, trans. George Theiner (London: Readers International, 1987); Václav Havel, "Zpráva o mé účasti na plesu železničářů," in *O lidskou identitu: Úvahy, fejetony, protesty, polemiky, prohlášení a rozhovory z let 1969–1979*, ed. Vilém Prečan and Alexander Tomský (Prague: Rozmluvy, 1990), 280–290. See also Havel's entertaining "Reports on My House Arrest," in *Open Letters*, ed. and trans. Paul Wilson (New York: Alfred A. Knopf, 1991), 215–229.

26. Janouch, *Ne, nestěžuji si*, 87; Lederer, *Touhy a iluze II*, 146–150. Ledererová does not mention this anecdote in her 1979 interview in Eva Kantůrková, *Sešly jsme se v této knize* (Prague: Toužimský a Moravec, 1991), 30–42, although she does discuss losing her job as an interpreter in 1973.

27. Janouch, *Ne, nestěžuji si*, 183–184.

28. This at least happened to Jan Šimsa when he improvidently paid a year in advance for *Tvář*. Jan Šimsa and Ludvík Vaculík, *Vážený pane Mikule: Dopisy 1967/1968* (Olomouc: Nakladatelství Olomouc, 2003), 32.

29. Ivo Možný, *Proc tak snadno . . . Některé rodinné důvody sametové revoluce,* 3rd ed. (Prague: Knižnice Sociologické aktuality, 2009), 55; on Pecka's apartment, see Lukeš, *Hry doopravdy*, 221–225.

30. Pachman, *Jak to bylo*, 263–274; Ivan Klíma, *Moje šílené století* (Prague: Academia, 2010), 2:189 and 204; Lukeš, *Hry doopravdy*, 220–221.

31. Zdeněk Mlynář, "Místo 'disidentů' na politické mapě dneška," in Václav Havel et al., *O svobodě a moci* (Cologne and Rome: Index and Listy, 1980), 229–230.

32. On parasitism, see also Havel's essay "Article 203" in *Open Letters*, 117–124. Havel suggests that parasitism charges were rarely brought against out-of-work intellectuals, but were quite common against ordinary workers.

33. Vaculík, *Nepaměti*, 98 and 106.

34. On Dilia and foreign royalties, see Pavel Kosatík, *Fenomén Kohout* (Prague and Litomyšl: Paseka, 2001), 254–258, as well as the documents in Radek Schovánek, ed., *Svazek Dialog: StB versus Pavel Kohout* (Prague: Paseka, 2006), especially Part 1. In later years, an important source of stipends for Czech writers was the Charter 77 Foundation, first set up by František Janouch in Sweden

in December 1978. See Václav Havel and František Janouch, *Korespondence 1978–2001*, ed. Květa Jechová (Prague: Akropolis, 2007), including Jiří Suk's introduction, "Podrobná zpráva o paralelní polis," 9–29, as well as František Janouch's article "Stockholmská Nadace Charty 77 a podpora nezávislé literatury a jejích tvůrců," in *Česká nezávislá literatura po pěti letech v referátech*, ed. František Kautman (Prague: Primus, 1995), 98–122.

35. As might be expected, this could be a complicated relationship. There are stories of both great selflessness and of exploitation, in which the "covered" person might have to pay for the service. In 1973, historian Vilém Prečan recorded a more negative term, "Aryanizer"—after the "Aryans" who took over Jewish property, whether nominally or for real, during the Nazi occupation: "Some 'Aryanizers' collect up to fifty percent of the honorarium from their 'Jews.'" "Společenské vědy ve svěráku 'konsolidace'," in *V kradeném čase: Výběr ze studií, článků a úvah z let 1973–1993*, ed. Milan Drápala (Prague: Ústav pro soudobé dějiny, 1994), 300. There seems to be relatively little historical work on this phenomenon of "covering" others' publications and the different forms it took.

36. Janouch, *Ne, nestěžuji si*, 83.

37. Putík, *Odchod*, 204; Jan Zábrana, *Celý život* (Prague: Torst, 1992), 1:478 and 2:996.

38. Prečan, "Společenské vědy," 282–283.

39. Milan Jankovič, "Osobní vzpomínka," in *Záznamník*, by Miroslav Červenka (Brno: Atlantis, 2008), 285–289.

40. Jiří Lederer, *České rozhovory* (Prague: Československý spisovatel, 1991), 33. Compare Václav Havel, *Disturbing the Peace: A Conversation with Karel Hvížďala*, trans. Paul Wilson (New York: Vintage, 1990), 122.

41. Luboš Dobrovský, "O čepičce s kšiltem," in *Československý fejeton/fejtón, 1975–1976*, ed. Ludvík Vaculík (Prague: Novinář, 1990), 93–95.

42. Quoted in Jiří Suk, *Labyrintem revoluce: Aktéři, zápletky a křižovatky jedné politické krize (od listopadu 1989 do června 1990)*, 2nd ed. (Prague: Prostor, 2009), 123.

43. I am grateful to Dr. Jiří Holba of the Oriental Institute of the Czech Academy of Sciences for information about his experiences as a stoker.

44. "Vzpomínám. . . Rozhovor s Karlem Kaplanem," in *Gottwaldovi muži*, by Karel Kaplan and Pavel Kosatík (Prague and Litomyšl: Paseka, 2004), 322. On Kaplan's life, see also the biographical sketch by Milena Janišová and Karel Jech in *Stránkami soudobých dějin: Sborník statí k pětašedesátinám historika Karla Kaplana*, ed. Karel Jech (Prague: Ústav pro soudobé dějiny, 1993), 7–16.

45. On work "in a trailer," see Karel Pecka's account in Lukeš, *Hry doopravdy*, 211–219, as well as Pecka's July 1983 essay "Čtvrtá lokalita," a tribute to Petr Kopta—poet, translator, fellow pump operator, and Charter signatory—in *Obsah* 3, no. 9 (1983): 24-30. Here Pecka also wrote that over half of pump operators signed the Charter (26).

46. Putík, *Odchod*, 183; Vaculík, "On Heroism," in *A Cup of Coffee*, 50.

47. Lederer, *Touhy a iluze II*, 156; Putík, *Odchod*, 181.

48. Lederer, *Touhy a iluze II*, 142. My account of Klement Lukeš is based on Lederer, 142–144, as well as the obituary by Josef Smýkal and Eliška Hluší, "Kdo byl Klement Lukeš?," *Brněnský občasník* 9, no. 1 (January 2001), bo.webz.cz/obcasnik (accessed 7/15/10). On Lukeš's expulsion, see Jiří Pelikán, *Czechoslovak Political Trials*, 28–29 and 217–218.

49. Lederer, *Touhy a iluze II*, 143–144.

50. Vaculík, *Nepaměti*, 107. This was written in February 1971, but Lukeš's apartment continued to be a meeting place throughout the 1970s and 1980s. For example, Vaculík paints a similar portrait of Lukeš in his 1976 feuilleton "Jaro je tady" in *Sólo pro psací stroj*, ed. Ludvík Vaculík (Cologne: Index, 1984), 10. See also František Vaněček, *Všivá doba: Z deníku chartisty* (Středokluky: Zdeněk Susa, 2002), 120–121, for another appreciation of Lukeš from the late 1970s.

51. For accounts of the "Kolář table," see, for example, Jiří Pechar, *Život na hraně* (Prague: Torst, 2009), 106–131; Eva Kantůrková, *Památník* (Prague: Československý spisovatel, 1994), 244–247; or Karel and Ivan Kyncl, *After the Spring Came Winter*, trans. George Theiner (Stockholm: Charta 77 Foundation and Askelin and Hägglund, 1985), 43–46.

52. See the interview with Němcová in Kantůrková, *Sešly jsme se*, 147–162, or Jan Bárta and Dana Němcová, *Lidé mého života* (Prague: Portál, 2003).

53. Lederer, *Touhy a iluze II*, 131–132.

54. Putík, *Odchod*, 271; this entry is from 1978, even after the Charter and the delineation of a dissident movement. Putík first mentions the "Orphans" in November 1970 (164).

55. For a detailed history of the underground universities in their different manifestations, see Barbara Day, *The Velvet Philosophers* (London: Claridge Press, 1999).

56. See Klíma, *Moje šílené století*, 2:126–129; for a somewhat different view, compare Vaculík, *Nepaměti*, 102–104.

57. Lederer, *Touhy a iluze II*, 131; Petr Pithart, *Osmašedesátý* (Prague: Rozmluvy, 1990), 303–308. Pithart's text originally circulated anonymously (under the pseudonym of Sládeček) in the late 1970s, before being published abroad in 1980.

58. Havel, *Disturbing the Peace*, 120–121.

59. From the extensive literature on samizdat, see in particular Ann Komaromi, "The Material Existence of Soviet Samizdat," *Slavic Review* 63, no. 3 (Autumn 2004): 597–618; Tomáš Vrba, "Nezávislé písemnictví a svobodné myšlení," in *Alternativní kultura: Příběh české společnosti 1945–1989*, ed. Josef Alan (Prague: Lidové noviny, 2001), 265–305; Jiří Gruntorád, "Samizdatová literatura," in ibid., 493–508; Martin Machovec, "The Types and Functions of Samizdat Publications in Czechoslovakia, 1948–1989," *Poetics Today* 30, no. 1 (Spring 2009): 1–26; Gordon Skilling, *Samizdat and an Independent Society in Central and Eastern Europe* (Columbus: Ohio State University Press, 1989); Day, *Velvet Philosophers*; Zdena Tomin, "Typewriters Hold the Fort," *Index on Censorship* 12, no. 2 (April 1983): 28–30; Jan Vladislav, "All You Need Is a Typewriter," *Index on Censorship* 12, no. 2

(April 1983): 33–35; and Ludvík Vaculík, "A Padlock for Castle Schwarzenberg," trans. A. G. Brain, in Goetz-Stankiewicz, *Good-Bye, Samizdat*, 118–126. For an overview of debates about the various Czech terms used to designate samizdat, see the articles in Karel Palek, ed., *Kritický sborník 1981–1989* (Prague: Triáda, 2009), 2–29, as well as Vrba, "Nezávislé písemnictví," 265–271.

60. See Gertraude Zandová, *Totální realismus a trapná poezie* (Brno: Host, 2002); Martin Machovec, "Od avantgardy přes podzemí do undergroundu," in Alan, *Alternativní kultura*, 155–199; and Egon Bondy, *Prvních deset let* (Prague: Maťa, 2003).

61. Zábrana, *Celý život*, 2:886. The entry comes from the summer of 1981.

62. Vladislav, "All You Need Is a Typewriter," 34.

63. So-called "Catholic" or "religious" samizdat was an important subset of the overall samizdat publishing world; not all of its texts were religious in nature, but the publishing operations and networks tended to be run by devout Catholics, and there were a number that were much better equipped than the typewriter culture of Prague. See Marta Edith Holečková, *Cesty katolického samizdatu 80. let* (Prague: Vyšehrad, 2009).

64. Gruntorád, "Samizdatová literatura," 496.

65. On the history of Petlice, see, for example, Vaculík, "Padlock," as well as Vaculík's website www.ludvikvaculik.cz, where a number of texts about Edice Petlice are reprinted along with a list of all its publications. Klíma also discusses the early days of samizdat in *Moje šílené století*, 2:170–172; see also Pavel Kohout, *Kde je zakopán pes* (Brno: Atlantis, 1990), 179–183.

66. Vrba, "Nezávislé písemnictví," 286–287 and 304n12; Vaculík, "Padlock," 121. On Zdena Erteltová, see in particular Vaculík's 2007 obituary, "Umřela," at www.ludvikvaculik.cz (accessed 5/27/11). On women copyists, see Mary Hrabik Samal, "Ženy a neoficiální kultura a literatura v Československu v letech 1969–1989," in *Prítomnosť minulosti, Minulosť prítomnosti*, ed. Jolaná Kusá and Peter Zajac (Bratislava: Nadácia Milana Šimečku, 1996), 81–95.

67. Vaculík, "Padlock," 121. Samizdat publishing could be classified as "incitement," "damaging the interests of the republic abroad," "disturbing the peace," or other crimes based on what was published; see Gruntorád, "Samizdatová literatura," 500–501.

68. See Vrba, "Nezávislé písemnictví," 297–298, and Gruntorád, "Samizdatová literatura," 496–497.

69. Jan Vladislav, "O Edici Kvart po letech," in *Umíněnost jako osud*, ed. František Kautman, Vilém Prečan, and Milan Drápala (Prague: Nadace ČSDS, 1998), 89–92 (where there is also a list of all the titles published by Kvart), and "All You Need Is a Typewriter."

70. On Vladislav's life, see Vilém Prečan, "Tajný čtenář, tajný kritik, tajný vydavatel Jan Vladislav," in Vladislav, *Umíněnost*, 100–115.

71. Vladislav, "O Edici Kvart," 89.

72. Vladislav, "All You Need Is a Typewriter," 34.

73. Vladislav, "O Edici Kvart," 91.

74. Vrba, "Nezávislá literatura," 290–291.

75. Gruntorád, "Samizdatová literatura," 497–498.

76. Vaculík, "Padlock," 124.

77. Vladislav, "All You Need Is a Typewriter," 35.

78. Vaculík, "Padlock," 123–124.

79. Vrba, "Nezávislá literatura," 298.

80. Komaromi, "Material Existence," perceptively traces an older "heroic" view of samizdat as a fragile cultural entity preserving sacred truths from the depredations of the state. She shows how Soviet samizdat fed into a "baroque" duality between physical and spiritual reality: "the more wretched the material manifestation, the more sublime the impulse behind it" (615). "Russian readers," she suggests, "found a satisfying badge of their difference from the west in the wretched physical aspect of the samizdat text" (616). In the Czech context, heroic and sacral aspects of the samizdat text had much less traction; the faint typed copy may have been seen more as the trace of a *connection* to the West, as well as to the country's own democratic traditions, rather than as a sign of difference. Machovec, "Types and Functions," carefully avoids the sacralizing view, noting how much samizdat writing was bad, and emphasizing that the "editions" like Petlice were only a subset of a much larger and unmonitored activity of self-publishing.

81. Miroslav Červenka, "Dvě poznámky k samizdatu," in Palek, *Kritický sborník*, 25.

82. Červenka, "Dvě poznámky," 26–28.

83. Vaculík, "Padlock," 122.

84. Svatopluk Karásek, *Poezie* (Prague: samizdat, 1989), 51.

85. Today one can download scans of many samizdat periodicals from the Internet. The full runs of a number of samizdat journals, for example, are available at the excellent website www.vons.cz, run by Czech historian Petr Blažek. It is useful to keep in mind what is gained and lost in the shift of samizdat from a physical to a digital text. While making the "content" of these texts widely accessible, the scans supersede the communication networks that were an almost physical part of the reading experience.

86. Anna Kovaříková, "Z okna Vokna (Rozhovor se šéfredaktorem časopisu Františkem Stárkem)," *Iniciály* 1, nos. 8–9 (1990): 19–22.

87. -n [pseudonym for František Kautman], "Otazníky kolem ineditní literatury," in Palek, *Kritický sborník*, 9.

88. Kohout, *Kde je zakopán pes*, 386.

89. Jiří Trávníček, "Twenty-Two Years Later: A Second Reading of Milan Kundera's *The Unbearable Lightness of Being*," trans. Jonathan Bolton, *Eurozine*, June 15, 2007, www.eurozine.com (accessed 7/9/10). This was not samizdat in the strict sense, but the circulation of Czech books published by émigré publishing houses abroad—a significant part of illicit reading culture under normalization—bore similarities to that of samizdat, even if the material artifact was bound and printed.

90. Eva Kantůrková, *Záznamy paměti* (Prague: Hynek, 1997), 278. The quotation comes from Kantůrková's 1988 feuilleton "Jak se nám zachtělo svobody."

91. Lederer, *České rozhovory*, 351–352 (for Kliment) and 10–11 (for Vaculík).

92. Published translations, especially by such a skilled translator as Paul Wilson, should not be tampered with lightly; for clarity and accuracy, however, I have changed the translation slightly. Where Wilson has "especially in the sciences," I have written "in scholarship even more than in art," since Havel's phrase ("ve vědě ještě spíš než v umění") suggests he is most likely distinguishing academic work from the creative arts. Where Wilson has "politics, including the nuclear threat," I have written "a politics that takes into account the nuclear threat." See Václav Havel, "Dear Dr. Husák," in *Open Letters*, 68–69.

93. Havel, *Disturbing the Peace*, 123–124.

94. Lederer's speech is in Květa Jechová, "K historii Koordinačního výboru tvůrčích svazů," in Pecka and Prečan, *Proměny Pražského jara*, 116–120.

95. Havel, "Power of the Powerless," 155–156.

4. Legends of the Underground

1. Václav Havel, *Disturbing the Peace: A Conversation with Karel Hvížďala,* trans. Paul Wilson (New York: Vintage, 1990), 128.

2. For an account of the trials, see Petr Blažek and Vladimír Bosák, "Akce 'Bojanovice'—11. listopad 1976," *Paměť a dějiny* 1, no. 1 (2007): 120–133, as well as H. Gordon Skilling, *Charter 77 and Human Rights in Czechoslovakia* (London: Allen and Unwin, 1981), 7–16.

3. "Smysl tažení proti českému ,underground'," *Listy* 6, no. 4 (August 1976): 41–42.

4. "Dopis V. Jirousové," *Listy* 6, no. 4 (August 1976): 45.

5. Cited in Skilling, *Charter 77,* 16n4.

6. Václav Havel, "The Trial," in *Open Letters: Selected Writings 1965–1990,* ed. and trans. Paul Wilson (New York: Alfred A. Knopf, 1991), 108.

7. Sváťa Karásek, Štěpán Hájek, and Michal Plzák, *Víno Tvé výborné: Rozhovory* (Prague: Kalich, 1998), 143.

8. Jan Patočka, "On the Matter of The Plastic People of the Universe and DG 307," translated and reprinted in Skilling, *Charter 77,* 205–7.

9. Václav Havel, "Moc bezmocných," in *O lidskou identitu: Úvahy, fejetony, protesty, polemiky, prohlášení a rozhovory z let 1969–1979*, ed. Vilém Prečan and Alexander Tomský (Prague: Rozmluvy, 1990), 79.

10. Havel, *Disturbing the Peace*, 128 and 131.

11. Skilling, *Charter 77,* 7–16.

12. Gale Stokes, *The Walls Came Tumbling Down: The Collapse of Communism in Eastern Europe* (New York: Oxford University Press, 1993), 24. Similarly, Barbara Falk speaks of "the trial of Jirous and three of the PPU band members" in *The Dilemmas of Dissidence in East-Central Europe* (Budapest and New York: Central European University Press, 2003), 86.

13. A typical account comes in John Lewis Gaddis's *The Cold War: A New History* (New York: Penguin, 2005): "It is unlikely [. . .] that the aging leaders in Moscow followed the fortunes of a scruffy, anti-establishment Czechoslovak rock band, the 'Plastic People of the Universe,' formed in the aftermath of the invasion of that country in 1968. Given to performing in secret while dodging the police, the band ran out of luck in 1976, when its members were arrested. Their trial provoked several hundred intellectuals into signing, on January 1, 1977, a manifesto called Charter 77 [. . .]" (191).

14. My account of the Plastic People draws on Jaroslav Riedel, "The Plastic People of the Universe v datech," in *The Plastic People of the Universe: Texty,* 2nd ed., ed. Jaroslav Riedel (Prague: Maťa, 2001): 15–29; Ivan Jirous, "Pravdivý příběh Plastic People," in *Magorův zápisník,* ed. Michael Špirit (Prague: Torst, 1997): 237–387; and Mejla Hlavsa and Jan Pelc, *Bez ohňů je underground,* 2nd ed. (Prague: Maťa, 2001). The latter book includes excerpts from the *Kronika* (Chronicle) kept by fans of the band in the 1970s and 1980s. See also the essays in Josef Alan, ed., *Alternativní kultura: Příběh české kultury 1945–1989* (Prague: Lidové noviny, 2001), especially Martin Machovec, "Od avantgardy přes podzemí do undergroundu," 155–199, and Josef Vlček, "Hudební alternativní scény sedmdesátých až osmdesátých let," 201–264.

15. Hlavsa and Pelc, *Bez ohňů je underground,* 32.

16. Jirous, "Pravdivý příběh," 243. They later played for a while as the Lumberjacks—another close call. A better early candidate was Hlavsa's Fairy Factory (according to Hlavsa) or Hlavsa's Fire Factory (according to Jirous). In early photos, the band has "The Plastic People of Universe" (without the second "the") written on their drum (see Hlavsa and Pelc, *Bez ohňů je underground,* 33). The band's English remained shaky until Paul Wilson joined it in 1970.

17. For the UFO, see Hlavsa and Pelc, *Bez ohňů je underground,* 32; for Agrippa, see Jirous, "Pravdivý příběh," 245 and 249.

18. An anecdote explains the meaning of the term "psychedelic." When Jirous was giving an art history lecture to the band (as he was wont to do), he described "psychedelic" as a type of performance and "underground" as a spiritual stance. Guitarist Jiří Števich raised his hand and clarified: "So psychedelic is the one with fire, and the one without fires is the underground." Jirous, "Pravdivý příběh," 255–256; Hlavsa relates the same story. On the underground's "Platonic relationship" with drugs, see Vlček, 209.

19. Jirous, "Pravdivý příběh," 247.

20. Ibid., 263. See also Timothy Ryback, *Rock around the Bloc: A History of Rock Music in Eastern Europe and the Soviet Union* (New York: Oxford University Press, 1990), 129–130, and Hlavsa and Pelc, *Bez ohňů je underground,* 65.

21. Richard Witts, *The Velvet Underground* (Bloomington, IN: Indiana University Press, 2006), 42. Witts's account of the Velvet Underground in the context of American cultural politics of the 1960s will resonate with anyone following the Czech scene in the 1970s.

22. Ibid., 123–124 and 129.

23. Paul Wilson, "What's It Like Making Rock 'n' Roll in a Police State?" in *Views from the Inside: Czech Underground Literature and Culture (1948–1989)*, ed. Martin Machovec (Prague: Katedra české literatury a literární vědy, Univerzita Karlova v Praze, Filozofická fakulta, 2006), 33–48.

24. On this "underground" of the late 1940s and early 1950s, see Gertraude Zandová, *Totální realismus a trapná poezie: Česká neoficiální literatura 1948–1953* (Brno: Host, 2002), and Machovec, "Od avantgardy," 155–166, as well as Martin Pilař's *Underground: Kapitoly o českém literárním undergroundu* (Brno: Host, 1999). For Bondy's own account, see Egon Bondy, *Prvních deset let* (Prague: Maťa, 2002). On Bondy's life, see also Martin Machovec's tribute "Za Egonem Bondym," *A2*, April 18, 2007, www.advojka.cz (accessed 7/25/10). On Bondy as poet and mythmaker, see Oskar Mainx, *Poezie jako mýtus, svědectví a hra: Kapitoly z básnické poetiky Egona Bondyho* (Ostrava: Protimluv, 2007), and Jaromír Typlt, "Bondy nejen Bondyho," *Host* 3, no. 3 (1997): 21–35, both of which deal with Bondy's efforts to cultivate his own legend.

25. Zandová, *Totální realismus a trapná poezie*, 74–79, and Martin Machovec, "Židovská jména rediviva," *A2*, December 19, 2007, www.advojka.cz (accessed 7/25/10).

26. Jirous, "Pravdivý příběh," 304.

27. According to the the Plastic People's *Kronika* (*Chronicle*), average attendance at the band's concerts in the fall of 1969 (still in its "official" phase) was 250–300 people. Four hundred sixty-five people were invited to the June 26, 1973, concert on the steamboat *Vyšehrad*; 250 were invited to a DG 307 concert on June 21, 1975. See also Hlavsa and Pelc, *Bez ohňů je underground*, 216, 220, 222.

28. On the state campaign against long hair in the 1960s, see Filip Pospíšil and Petr Blažek, *"Vraťte nám vlasy!" První máničky, vlasatci a hippies v komunistickém Československu* (Prague: Academia, 2010). On the police use of the term in the context of the underground, see Pavel Ptáčník, "První festival druhé kultury," *Sborník archivu bezpečnostních složek* 5 (1997): 343–351; for the Hlavsa quote, see Hlavsa and Pelc, *Bez ohňů je underground*, 16. Underground novels and memoirs are full of references to the symbolism and conflicts surrounding long hair. See, for example, the young narrator's travails in Josef Vondruška's memoir *Vyšehradští jezdci* in his *Chlastej a modli se* (Prague: Torst, 2006), or Jirous, "Pravdivý příběh," 337–338, on police harassment. On style and dress as semiotic markers of underground culture, see Dick Hebdige, *Subculture: The Meaning of Style* (London and New York: Routledge, 2002).

29. See Jirous, "Pravdivý příběh," 332–344, for a contemporary account of the whole incident. Jirous was in jail during the actual "massacre" but came to the subsequent trial.

30. Ptáčník, "První festival," 343–348, and Jirous, "Pravdivý příběh," 342.

31. Jirous, "Pravdivý příběh," 337. Even in its "semi-unofficial" phase, the band had auditioned before a panel of state officials and state-approved musicians in May 1973, in an attempt to get professional qualification and hence permission

to record an album in a studio. As late as November 1975, they auditioned (again unsuccessfully) for amateur status (Riedel, "The Plastic People of the Universe v datech," 19). These attempts reflect a more flexible conception of the underground than would emerge from Jirous's writings.

32. Karásek, Hájek, and Plzák, *Víno Tvé výborné*, 88.

33. Pavel Zajíček, *Zápisky z podzemí [1973–1980]*, ed. Martin Machovec (Prague: Torst, 2002), 32. This text comes from Zajíček's *Mařenická kniha,* a book of his notes from 1973 to 1976; see also Machovec's useful annotations on 523–531. "Mejla" was Milan Hlavsa. Just as Bondy's reading of his novel became an underground legend, so did the fact that the two members of DG 307 "kept going outside to throw up" during the event.

34. Egon Bondy, *Invalidní sourozenci* (Brno: Nakladatelství "Zvláštní vydání," 2002), 16.

35. As Machovec notes in "Za Egonem Bondym," this was perhaps Bondy's "happiest creative period"; before and afterward his texts are often desperate and bitter.

36. Hlavsa and Pelc, *Bez ohňů je underground*, 128.

37. Jirous writes of the Plastics' turn to Czech lyrics: "contemporary music ought to speak to [*oslovovat*] people in the language they understand." Ivan Jirous, "Zpráva o třetím českém hudebním obrození," in *Magorův zápisník,* ed. Michael Špirit (Prague: Torst, 1997), 182. I have provided my own translations of the Czech text; an English version appears in Machovec, *Views from the Inside*, 7–32.

38. Jirous, "Zpráva," 196–197.

39. Ibid., 197.

40. Ibid., 192–193.

41. I draw here on Martin Machovec's remarks on "naïve," "indigenous," and "pseudo-primitivist" literature in his insightful overview of underground writers, "Šestnáct autorů ceského literárního podzemí (1948–1989)," *Literární archiv* 25 (1991): 41–75; see also Pilař, *Underground*, esp. 28–29. Where Czech distinguishes between *pseudoprimitivismus* and (genuine) *primitivismus*, I am simply using "primitivism" to refer to the aesthetic valuation of primitive behavior, whether it is "real" or feigned. The very point of primitivism is often the inability to distinguish between the two, so it seems desirable simply to speak of "primitivism," remembering that the term has different connotations from the pejorative word "primitive."

42. One of the greatest writers of Czech primitivism, Bohumil Hrabal—a key member of the early underground in the 1950s—worked with all these forms of "authenticity." For example, he often described Romani "authenticity" in explicitly primitivist terms, as in his novel *Too Loud a Solitude*.

43. Jirous, "Zpráva," 193.

44. Jirous, "Pravdivý příběh," 322.

45. Ivan Jirous, *Magorovy labutí písně* (Munich: Poezie mimo domov, 1986), 81-82.

46. Jonathan Bolton, "The Skeptical Imagination of Ivan Wernisch," in Ivan Wernisch, *In the Puppet Gardens*, ed. and trans. Jonathan Bolton (Ann Arbor: Michigan Slavic Publications, 2007).

47. Jirous, "Zpráva," 180.

48. Martin Putna, "Mnoho zemí v podzemí," *Souvislosti* 1 (1993), www. souvislosti.cz/archiv/ (accessed 11/5/2009).

49. Ibid. In his perceptive sociological study of the underground, Josef Alan makes a similar point, showing how the small, mobile, and intense groupings of the underground were founded on a "face-to-face" principle; works of art—whether songs, visual art, or literature—were presented and performed in an almost "ceremonious" way, and being at a performance was just as important as perceiving the work of art being presented. Josef Alan, "Alternativní kultura jako sociologické téma," in Alan, *Alternativní kultura,* 9–60; see especially 28–37. On underground mythmaking, see also Vlček, 216–217.

50. "Zbytečná starost," *Rudé právo,* April 8, 1976, 2; Blažek and Bosák, "Akce 'Bojanovice,'" 121.

51. See Ptáčník, "První festival," 344 (on the incorrect names) and 349 (on hostile activity).

52. Blažek and Bosák, "Akce 'Bojanovice,'" 121–122. This article contains a facsimile of the June protest, as well as secret-police photos from the appeals trial in November 1976. For the August open letter to Böll, I have used the English translation in Skilling, *Charter 77,* 199–200.

53. Initially, one of the few contacts between these two worlds were two psychologists, Jiří Němec and Dana Němcová, whose apartment on Ječná Street in downtown Prague became a gathering place for members of the underground, including the Plastic People. Němec, who had attended Jan Patočka's unofficial philosophy lectures, was also the first real link between Patočka and the underground. See, for example, Blažek and Bosák, "Akce 'Bojanovice,'" 128 (on Němec), or the interview with Dana Němcová in Eva Kantůrková, *Sešly jsem se v této knize* (Prague: Toužimský a Moravec, 1991), 147–162.

54. On Olga Havlová and the underground, see, for example, her interview in Kantůrková, *Sešly jsem se v této knize,* 14–15. Later, the Havels' cottage Hrádeček would become the venue for many Plastic People concerts.

55. Havel, *Disturbing the Peace,* 126.

56. Jirous, "Pravdivý příběh," 345.

57. According to Jirous (ibid., 345), one of the things they talked about was the amateur performance of Havel's play *The Beggar's Opera* in 1975. As Havel details in *Disturbing the Peace,* this performance had an enormous effect on him. He must have realized that it was just the kind of intense, onetime, *Gesamtkunstwerk* experience the underground specialized in. Jirous notes that "None of us [i.e., from the underground] was there," a clear indicator of how little contact the two worlds had at the time.

58. See Skilling, *Charter 77,* 199–200.

59. Havel, *Disturbing the Peace,* 126–127. Havel also discusses the Plastic People in texts like "On the Beginnings of Charter 77," "The Trial," and "The Power of the Powerless"; the account in *Disturbing the Peace* has probably been the most influential in the West.

60. Havel, "The Trial," 104.

61. Havel, *Disturbing the Peace*, 128.

62. Charlie Soukup, *Radio* (Prague: Torst, 1998).

63. Blažek and Bosák, "Akce 'Bojanovice,'" 123.

64. Machovec, "Od avantgardy," 186.

65. Havel, "The Trial," 107–108.

66. Karásek, Hájek, and Plzák, *Víno Tvé výborné*, 153.

67. From Stárek's 2003 interview with Milan Otáhal in *Vítězové? Poražení? Životopisná interview*, ed. Miroslav Vaněk and Pavel Urbášek (Prague: Prostor, 2005), 1:881–882.

68. A classic account of the drafting of Charter 77 is given by Václav Havel in *Disturbing the Peace*. Havel's account has been the basis for many English discussions of the Charter, even though, as he insists, "I'm not giving a history lecture here, I'm merely recalling how I experienced and observed these events at the time. My view may be one-sided; in fact, it probably has to be one-sided" (131). In general, there are many discrepancies among the remembered accounts of different participants; the best attempt to reconstruct the original events is in Blanka Císařovská and Vilém Prečan, eds., *Charta 77: Dokumenty 1977–1989* (Prague: Ústav pro soudobé dějiny, 2007), 3:1–24, where there is also a list of the first signatories. Zdeněk Mlynář described the background and drafting of the document in *Ideologische und politische Richtungen innerhalb der Bürgerrechtsbewegung in der heutigen Tschechoslowakei* (Cologne: Bundesinstitut für Ostwissenschaftliche und Internationale Studien, 1978); H. Gordon Skilling provides much valuable information and perspective in *Charter 77*. Pavel Kohout, who was also at the founding meetings, describes the beginnings of the Charter at length in *Kde je zakopán pes* (Brno: Atlantis, 1990), esp. 383–533; this work, written in 1984–1987, and drawing on Kohout's own notes and datebook entries, is relatively reliable, although highly dramatized. Petr Uhl gives many details in his memoir *Právo a nespravedlnost očima Petra Uhla* (Prague: C. H. Beck, 1998). For a further discussion of uncertainties around the original meetings, see also Petr Uhl, "Rozpaky pamětníka nad edicí dokumentů Charty 77," *Soudobé dějiny* 15, no. 1 (2008): 177–192 (among other things Uhl insists the initial meeting was December 10, International Human Rights Day, rather than December 11, the date recorded in Kohout's notes), and Vilém Prečan's response, "Rozpaky historika nad pamětníkem v roli arbitra," in ibid., 193–203. With the recent opening up of secret-police archives, it has been possible to cross-check the memories of the participants with secret-police reports; see Petr Blažek and Radek Schovánek, "Vznik Charty 77 očima StB," *Respekt* 17, no. 2 (September 1, 2006): 18, as well as Radek Schovánek, ed., *Svazek Dialog: StB versus Pavel Kohout* (Praha and Litomyšl: Pasek, 2006). Vaculík has occasionally revealed a few of his own memories; see, for example, his interview with Robert Malecký: "Písařky, obálky a jeden omyl" (printed in *Lidové noviny*, January 8, 2007; available at www.ludvikvaculik.cz, accessed 6/16/10). There are also a host of memories in the oral-history interviews in Vaněk and Urbášek, *Vítězové? Poražení?*, as well as in Blanka Císařovská, Milan

Drápala, Vilém Prečan, and Jiří Vančura, eds., *Charta 77 očima současníků: Po dvaceti letech* (Brno: Doplněk and Ústav pro soudobé dějiny, 1997). I have drawn on all these sources for my account in this chapter and the next.

69. Havel, *Disturbing the Peace*, 133; Mlynář, *Ideologische und politische Richtungen*, 38–39.

70. Kohout, *Kde je zakopán pes*, 393.

71. The StB's own categorization of the first signatories is not without interest. It divided them into overlapping categories such as "expelled from the Communist Party" (117), "pro-Zionists" (35), "punished after 1968" (35), "trotskyist" (12), "representatives of the church" (15), "former workers in science and culture" (81). See Císařovská and Prečan, *Charta 77*, 3:18.

72. On the choice of spokesman, see especially Havel, *Disturbing the Peace*, 134–136, and Uhl's interview in Vaněk and Urbášek, *Vítězové? Poražení?*, 1003–1004. On the spokesmen more generally, see Skilling, *Charter 77*, 19–38.

73. Havel, *Disturbing the Peace*, 136. According to Uhl's memories in a 2003 interview, the possibility of Černý came up immediately at the third meeting; Havel was designated to "pacify" him, while Němec was sent to persuade Patočka (Vaněk and Urbášek, *Vítězové? Poražení?*, 1004).

74. Patočka, "On the Matter of The Plastic People of the Universe and DG 307," translated in Skilling, *Charter 77*, 205–207.

75. Václav Černý, "Nad verši Věry Jirousové a o kulturním stanovisku našeho undergroundu" and "O všem možném, dokonce i o 'hippies' a o 'novém románu'," in *Tvorba a Osobnost*, ed. Jan Šulc (Prague: Odeon, 1992 and 1993), 1:900–908 and 2:553–562; Ivan Jirous, "Nebyla nikdy v troskách," in *Magorův zápisník*, 402–418.

76. Eva Kantůrková, *Památník* (Prague: Český spisovatel, 1992), 264–268.

77. Radek Schovánek, "Devět agentů mezi námi," *Lidové noviny*, January 9, 2007, www.lidovky.cz (accessed 9/18/11).

78. Kohout, *Kde je zakopán pes*, 395.

79. On the foreign publication of the Charter, see Císařovská and Prečan, *Charta 77*, 3:25–31. In the event, everyone forgot that *Le Monde* was an evening paper, so it was first to publish the news on the evening of January 6, whence it immediately passed to Western radio stations. In Kohout's estimation, this was a blessing in disguise; since the first arrests had already been made, the "early" Western interest in the Charter may have helped blunt the police's initial response.

80. Blažek and Schovánek, "Vznik Charty 77," and Schovánek, *Svazek Dialog*, 58–61. Police may have also been confused by one subterfuge of the Charter organizers, who dated the original drafts of the Charter with dates ten days later; surveillance of Kohout's apartment heard him mention that something would happen on January 17, 1977 (Císařovská and Prečan, *Charta 77*, 3:1–2).

81. The following account draws on Pavel Landovský's 1987 interview with Karel Hvížďala, *Soukromá vzpoura* (Prague: Mladá fronta, 1990), 64–67. On Landovský's fate under normalization, see also his 1976 interview in Jiří Lederer, *České rozhovory* (Prague: Československý spisovatel, 1991), 127–146.

82. The police report otherwise confirms the basic outlines of the chase. It is reprinted and analyzed in Blažek and Schovánek, "Vznik Charty 77," 18.

83. Jan Vladislav, "Otevřený deník," in Císařovská and Prečan, *Charta 77*, 3:82.

84. An early, spirited retelling of the tale made it to the West thanks to Tom Stoppard, who went to Prague that summer to report on the Charter. He visited Landovský, "a heavy, buccaneering figure with a Zapata mustache." In his "historical car," Landovský drove Stoppard along the route of the chase, telling him it "was just like the movies." See Tom Stoppard, "Prague: The Story of the Chartists," *New York Review of Books*, August 4, 1977, www.nyrb.com (accessed 5/19/2011).

5. Everything Changed with the Charter

1. Ludvík Vaculík, *Nepaměti 1969–1972* (Prague: Mladá fronta, 1998), 19. Vaculík's speech at the Writer's Congress is reprinted in Dušan Hamšík, *Writers against Rulers*, trans. D. Orpington (New York: Random House, 1971), 181–198. The text of "Two Thousand Words that Belong to Workers, Farmers, Officials, Scientists, Artists and Everybody," is in *The Prague Spring 1968*, ed. Jaromír Navrátil, trans. Mark Kramer, Joy Moss, and Ruth Tosek (Budapest: Central European University Press, 1998), 177–181. "Deset bodů" is reprinted in Vaculík, *Nepaměti*, 129–134.

2. This English translation is available at the website of Prague's samizdat library Libri Prohibiti, libpro.cts.cuni.cz/charta/ (accessed 7/22/10). According to the police documents reproduced there, it was translated by signatory Jan Petránek and confiscated by police from his apartment on January 7, 1977. An alternate translation (which brushes up the original Czech text to make it a bit more elegant) is in H. Gordon Skilling, *Charter 77 and Human Rights in Czechoslovakia* (London: George Allen & Unwin, 1981), 209–212.

3. This last sentence is mistranslated both in the Libri Prohibiti version and in Skilling's translation; it should read "to act as intermediary in any conflict situations caused by injustice." Injustice leads to conflict, says the Charter, and not the other way around.

4. See the interview with Kubišová in Eva Kantůrková, *Sešly jsme se v této knize* (Prague: Toužimský a Moravec, 1991), 171.

5. Blanka Císařovská and Vilém Prečan, eds., *Charta 77: Dokumenty 1977–1989* (Prague: Ústav pro soudobé dějiny, 2007), 3:40. Patočka's interrogation protocols, which he read over carefully before signing, are a model of courage and restraint, revealing Patočka as self-confident, steadfast, and intelligently careful—refusing to let himself be drawn out, or drawn into contradictions or traps of phrasing. He simply refused to answer most questions, although, since police could not read his handwriting on the manuscript of "What Charter 77 Is and What It Is Not," he did oblige them by reading the text aloud to the stenographer. By his own account, Patočka's first interrogations were civil in tone—"genuinely polite," as he told the German newspaper *Die Zeit* in responses written for a March interview—although

this would not have made them any less grueling or tense. See Císařovská and Prečan, *Charta 77*, 3:39–52, for the texts of Patočka's interrogations, and 63–65 for the *Die Zeit* interview.

6. Jan Patočka, "Čím je a čim není Charta 77," in Císařovská and Prečan, *Charta 77*, 3:37. I have used my own translations here; a full English translation of the text is available in Skilling, *Charter 77*, 217–219.

7. The handwritten comment is on the typescript of Patočka's essay contained in his interrogation protocol from January 11 (Císařovská and Prečan, *Charta 77*, 3:43). Patočka did not tell police who wrote this comment; Císařovská and Prečan have confirmed that it was Hájek by looking at the protocol of Hájek's own interrogation from January 11. See their explanation on 3:36n6.

8. Jan Patočka, "Co můžeme očekávat od Charty 77?," in Císařovská and Prečan, *Charta 77*, 3:60–63.

9. Václav Havel, "Anatomy of a Reticence," in *Open Letters*, ed. and trans. Paul Wilson (New York: Alfred A. Knopf, 1991), 309.

10. Petr Rezek, "Obec otřesených, nebo postižených?," in *Filozofie a politika kýče*, 2nd ed. (Prague: Jan Placák—Ztichlá klika, 2007), 106–120.

11. Patočka, "Co můžeme očekávat," 63.

12. Skilling, *Charter 77*, 22–23. On Patočka's final days, see especially the editors' commentary in Karel Palek and Ivan Chvatík, eds., *Sebrané spisy Jana Patočky* (Prague: OIKOYMENH, 2006), 13:438–441. The relevant documents are also collected in Císařovská and Prečan, *Charta 77*, 3:55–65.

13. Ludvík Vaculík, "Fatal Illness," in *A Cup of Coffee with My Interrogator*, trans. George Theiner (London: Readers International, 1987), 38.

14. Tom Stoppard, "Prague: The Story of the Chartists," *New York Review of Books*, August 4, 1977, www.nybooks.com (accessed 5/18/2011); Roman Jakobson, "Jan Patočka: From the Curriculum Vitae of a Czech Philosopher," *New Republic*, May 7, 1977, 28; Richard Rorty, "The Seer of Prague," *New Republic*, July 1, 1991, 36.

15. Císařovská and Prečan, *Charta 77*, 3:59–60 (for the police report) and 64 (for the *Die Zeit* interview). According to Skilling (*Charter 77*, 22), Patočka collapsed during questioning, and in Vaculík's account, he "became very ill" and his interrogators were forced to let him go; if this is true, Patočka did not see fit to mention it in the *Die Zeit* interview a week later.

16. Vaculík, "Fatal Illness," 39.

17. Jan Zábrana, *Celý život* (Prague: Torst, 1992), 2:570; Ladislav Hejdánek, *Dopisy příteli* (Prague: OIKOYMENH, 1992), 49.

18. The actual number of initial signatories turns out to be somewhat difficult to determine, in part because the list of signatories varied slightly in different versions of the proclamation. The version that Havel, Landovský, and Vaculík were carrying to the Federal Assembly, for example, had 236 names. At the time, most signatories thought the initial total was 242, the number that has generally been accepted by historians. Císařovská and Prečan conclude that the actual number of initial signatories was 241 (one of whom revoked his signature during January); they also

give a final total of 1,889 signatures. See Císařovská and Prečan, *Charta 77*, 3:17 and 3:337–378.

19. "Josef Vohryzek" (interview with Ilona Christlová), in Květa Jechová, *Lidé Charty 77: Zpráva o biografickém výzkumu* (Prague: Ústav pro soudobé dějiny, 2003), 146–167. Vohryzek describes his signature on 160–161.

20. Jaroslav Mezník, *Můj život za vlády komunistů (1948–1989)* (Brno: Matice Moravská, 2005), 224–225; see also Jaroslav Mezník, "Můj podpis Charty a jeho bezprostřední důsledky," in *Charta 77 očima současníků: Po dvaceti letech*, ed. Blanka Císařovská, Milan Drápala, Vilém Prečan, and Jiří Vančura (Brno: Ústav pro soudobé dějiny and Doplněk, 1997), 105–107.

21. See Kantůrková's response to the poll of Charter signatories in Císařovská et al., *Charta 77 očima současníků*, 229.

22. Robert Malecký, "Pisařky, obálky a jeden omyl" (interview with Ludvík Vaculík), *Lidové noviny,* January 8, 2007, www.ludvikvaculik.cz (accessed 7/1/2010).

23. "Václav Benda" (interview with Ilona Christlová), in Jechová, *Lidé charty 77*, 125–145. On Benda's signature, see 129–130.

24. See the interview with Šiklová in Michael Long, *Making History: Czech Voices of Dissent and the Revolution of 1989* (Lanham, MD: Rowman and Littlefield, 2005), 104. Šiklová was arrested in 1981, along with a number of other people (including Šimečka, Kantůrková, and others), after a secret-police informer infiltrated the operation and alerted the police that a French truck full of samizdat would be crossing the border. On this "camion" affair, see, for example, Lawrence Weschler, *Calamities of Exile* (Chicago: University of Chicago Press, 1998).

25. See also the interesting poll of "nonsignatories" in Císařovská et al., *Charta 77 očima současníků*, 273–291.

26. Jaroslav Putík, *Odchod od zámku* (Prague: Hynek, 1998), 248.

27. Ibid., 251 and 250. It is in an entry from January 1977 that Putík, so sensitive to language, first uses the word "dissidence," although in a slightly different form from Havel and other dissidents (*disidentstvo* rather than *disidentství*, 253) that suggests a group of people rather than a concept. Putík employs it with some skepticism and often uses the vaguely pejorative prefix "disi" (as in *disi-příběh*, "dissi-story" or "dissident story," 359).

28. Ibid., 249.

29. Ibid., 321, in an entry from 1981.

30. Ibid., 306, in an entry from 1980.

31. Jiří Pechar, *Život na hraně* (Prague: Torst, 2009), 108.

32. See his discussion of this stance in ibid., 108–109.

33. Putík, *Odchod*, 132.

34. Císařovská and Prečan, *Charta 77*, 3:15–16 and frontispiece. Klíma's wife Helena, who did sign the Charter, was also on the list; see her own account in Císařovská, Drápala, Prečan and Vančura, *Charta 77 očima současníků*, 83–85 and 231–233.

35. Ivan Klíma, *Moje šílené století* (Prague: Academia, 2010), 2:220.

36. Klíma, *Moje šílené století*, 2:224–225.

37. Ibid., 2:225.

38. Ibid., 2:224–225.

39. See the interview with Elžbieta Ledererová in Kantůrková, *Sešly jsme se*, 31–42, as well as Jiří Lederer, *Touhy a iluze* (Toronto: Sixty-Eight Publishers, 1984) and *Touhy a iluze II* (Toronto: Sixty-Eight Publishers, 1988).

40. Lederer, *Touhy a iluze II*, 247.

41. Kantůrková, *Sešly jsme se*, 37–38.

42. Pavel Kohout, *Kde je zakopán pes* (Brno: Atlantis, 1990), 396.

43. Müller in turn spent several years as a house-husband while his wife worked. See his 2004 interview with Pavel Urbášek in *Vítězové? Poražení? Životopisná interview*, ed. Miroslav Vaněk and Pavel Urbášek (Prague: Prostor, 2005), 1:609.

44. Marie Vaculíková, "Charta 77 u Vaculíků," in Císařovská, Drápala, Prečan, and Vančura, *Charta 77 očima současníků*, 191–192. See also Pavel Kosatík, *"Člověk má dělat to, nač má sílu": Život Olgy Havlové*, 2nd ed. (Prague: Mladá Fronta, 2008), 178–179, for an enlightening discussion of Olga Havlová's decision to sign the Charter in February 1982.

45. "Anna Marvanová" (1992 interview with Zuzana Sloupová), in Jechová, *Lidé charty 77*, 104.

46. See, for example, František Vaněček, *Všivá doba: Z deníku chartisty* (Středokluky: Zdeněk Susa, 2002), 7–8.

47. Václav Havel, *Disturbing the Peace: A Conversation with Karel Hvížďala*, trans. Paul Wilson (New York: Vintage, 1990), 137.

48. Lederer, *Touhy a iluze II*, 248.

49. Jan Vladislav, "Otevřený deník," in Císařovská and Prečan, *Charta 77*, 3:81. Vladislav quotes Patočka in an entry from January 3, 1977.

50. On the regime response to the Charter, see especially Skilling, *Charter 77*, 127–150.

51. The document is reprinted in Petr Blažek, ed., *"Tentokrát to bouchne": Edice dokumentů k organizaci a ohlasům kampaně proti signatářům Charty 77 (leden–únor 1977)* (Prague: Univerzita Karlova v Praze—Filozofická fakulta and Odbor archiv bezpečnostních složek MV ČR, 2007), 27.

52. Ibid., 85–86.

53. Ibid., 87–89.

54. On February 1, *Rudé právo* wrote: "The so-called Charter 77 may be formally addressed to organs of the Czechoslovak state, but before that it was sent to Western agencies and published in the bourgeois press. Only after publication in the West was it also sent to some organs of the Czechoslovak state." Quoted in Císařovská and Prečan, *Charta 77*, 1:20–21.

55. Peter Bugge, "Normalization and the Limits of the Law: The Case of the Czech Jazz Section," *East European Politics and Societies* 22, no. 2 (May 2008): 282–318.

56. Václav Havel, "The Power of the Powerless," in *Open Letters*, ed. and trans. Paul Wilson (New York: Alfred A. Knopf, 1991), 185–190. Peter Bugge also emphasizes

the idea of the law as "a system of canonized explanations of the state of society"; he points out another aspect of the legal alibi, which was "to offer future protection to those in power. The brutal experiences of the 1950s—or perhaps rather the unpleasant consequences of their being revealed in the 1960s—dissuaded the leadership from using the most extreme measures" (Bugge, "Normalization," 300 and 305). On the relationship of dissident legalism to peaceful resistance, see Kieran Williams's suggestive "Civil Resistance in Czechoslovakia: From Soviet Invasion to 'Velvet Revolution,' 1968–1989," in *Civil Resistance and Power Politics*, ed. Adam Roberts and Timothy Garton Ash (New York: Oxford University Press, 2009), 110–126.

57. See Müller's interview in Vaněk and Urbášek, *Vítězové? Poražení?*, 1:595.

58. Bugge, "Normalization," 297–298 and 314nn84–85.

59. "Ztroskotanci a samozvanci," *Rudé právo*, January 12, 1977, 2.

60. *Rudé právo*, January 18, 1977, 1.

61. On the "Anti-Charter Rally," see Paulina Bren, *The Greengrocer and His TV: The Culture of Communism after the 1968 Prague Spring* (Ithaca: Cornell University Press, 2010), 104–107. Vladislav recorded the event in his diary and wrote about it at length over the following days: Jan Vladislav, *Otevřený deník*, in Císařovská and Prečan, *Charta 77*, 3:85–87.

62. *Rudé právo*, January 29, 1977, 1–2. The list of signatories was printed on page 1 and continued in subsequent issues of *Rudé právo*.

63. Havel, "Power of the Powerless," 169. The point is a bit more clear in the original Czech: "For 'dissident' means, as is well known, *odpadlík*—but the 'dissidents' do not feel themselves to be *odpadlíky*, because they haven't fallen away from anything" (my translation). See Havel, "Moc bezmocných," in *O lidskou identitu: Úvahy, fejetony, protesty, polemiky, prohlášení a rozhovory z let 1969–1979*, ed. Vilém Prečan and Alexander Tomský (Prague: Rozmluvy, 1990), 92.

64. Vaněček, *Všivá doba*, 21. Vaněček went through quite a few different jobs before he and his wife emigrated in 1980; his diary offers one of the most interesting portraits of an intellectual doing blue-collar work, and analyzing the morale and customs of the socialist workplace.

65. Ibid., 85.

66. Kamila Bendová, "Ženy v Chartě 77," in *Opozice a odpor proti komunistickému režimu v Československu 1968–1989*, ed. Petr Blažek (Prague: Dokořán and Ústav českých dějin FF UK, 2005), 54–66; Vaněček, *Všivá doba*, 25, 44, 79–80.

67. A few of the first signatories were put on a "Do Not Interrogate" list by the secret police, at least for the time being. These included several people who had recently returned from prison, like Jaroslav Šabata and Jiří Müller, as well as, for example, the widow and son of Rudolf Slánský; presumably the regime thought it would be too unpopular to harass these icons of the show trials. The writers Jaroslav Seifert and Dominik Tatarka were also spared, presumably because of their wide popularity (Císařovská and Prečan, *Charta 77*, 3:18).

68. Petr Blažek, "Akce 'Přednáška'–sledování Ivana Dejmala," *Paměť a dějiny* 2, no. 2 (2008): 55–61.

69. *Informace o Chartě 77* 1, no. 7 (1978): 12–13.

70. *Informace o Chartě 77* 1, no. 7 (1978): 4–5 (Medek); *Informace o Chartě 77* 1, no. 7 (1978): 14–15 (Doležal).

71. Forty-nine women signed a protest letter to President Husák, describing the case and asking him to intervene. *Informace o Chartě 77* 1, no. 11 (1978): 21–22.

72. Tominová describes this incident in a letter written from the hospital and published in *Informace o Chartě 77* 2, no. 9 (1979): 6–7.

73. *Informace o Chartě 77* 4, no. 1 (1981): 9–10 (Malý); *Informace o Chartě 77* 4, no. 9 (1981): 9–10 (Soukup); *Informace o Chartě 77* 4, no. 7 (1981): 6–7 (Třešňák); on Třešňák, see also Kosatík, *"Člověk má dělat to, nač má sílu,"* 216–223.

74. Alexandr Kliment, *Tři žině* (Prague: Torst, 2009), 76.

75. *Informace o Chartě 77* 1, no. 5 (1978): 24.

76. Kohout described this whole affair, interlocking it with vignettes from his life in the 1970s, in his *memoáromán* ("memoir-novel") *Kde je zakopán pes.* See also Radek Schovánek, ed., *Svazek Dialog: StB versus Pavel Kohout* (Prague: Paseka, 2006), which gathers togethers the StB files on the harassment and surveillance of Kohout, and Pavel Kosatík, *Fenomén Kohout* (Prague and Litomyšl: Paseka, 2001). After examining the StB files, Kosatík concluded that it was not entirely clear who was responsible for the bomb, the poisoning, and the rest of this harassment. The police certainly took advantage of the affair, however, to increase the strain on Kohout and Mašinová in hopes of forcing them to emigrate.

77. Vaněček, *Všivá doba,* 79.

78. On Mašinová, see Kohout, *Kde je zakopán pes,* 404–406. On Šimsa, see his wife Milena Šimsová's account in *Informace o Chartě 77* 1, no. 8 (1978), 17–20. On Šabata, see *Informace o Chartě 77* 1, no. 11 (1978), 17–18, as well as the reports on his trial in *Informace o Chartě 77* 2, no. 1 (1979), 15–19.

79. See Jan Šimsa, "Předmluva," in *Dopisy příteli,* by Ladislav Hejdánek (Prague: OIKOYMENH, 1992), 8.

80. From Václav Malý's 2004 interview with David Weber in Vaněk and Urbášek, *Vítězové? Poražení?,* 1:434.

81. From Jan Urban's 2003 interview with David Weber in Vaněk and Urbášek, *Vítězové? Poražení?,* 1:1034.

82. Jiří Fiedor, "Bílé vrány v černém kraji: Chartisté a nezávislé iniciativy na Ostravsku," *Dějiny a současnost* 29, no. 2 (2007), www.dejiny.nln.cz (accessed 6/19/10). The publication of Prečan and Císařovská's documentation suggests that Fiedor's memories about who signed the Charter, and when, are not entirely accurate, but his larger point about the intensity of police harassment and surveillance is.

83. Anonymous [Petr Uhl], "Zpráva o Chartě 77 k 6. březnu 1977," in Císařovská and Prečan, *Charta 77,* 3:104.

84. On the number of Slovak signatories, see Císařovská and Prečan, *Charta 77,* 3:393.

85. On the Charter and Slovakia, see Miroslav Kusý, "Slovensko a Charta '77," *Sme*, February 1, 2007, komentare.sme.sk (accessed 7/23/10); Miroslav Kusý, "Slovenský fenomén," a May 1985 lecture reprinted in *Eseje* (Bratislava: Archa, 1991), 155–174; Norbert Kmeť, "Opozicia a hnutie odporu na Slovensku 1968– 1989," in *Opozice a odpor proti komunistickému režimu v Československu 1968–1989*, ed. Petr Blažek (Prague: Ústav českých dějin FF UK and Dokořán, 2005), 41–53; and Michal Piško, "Charta 77 znela Slovákom cudzo," *SME*, October 22, 2009, www.sme.sk (accessed 7/25/10). For an English analysis of some of the issues, see Carol Skalnik Leff, *National Conflict in Czechoslovakia* (Princeton, NJ: Princeton University Press, 1988), esp. 263–268.

86. Kusý, "Slovensko a Charta '77."

87. Alexander Dubček, *Hope Dies Last*, ed. and trans. Jiří Hochman (New York: Kodansha International, 1993), 264. Dubček's own lack of contact with the Charter may be indicated in his misconception that "[o]ut of some 2,000 signatories of the charter, there were only three Slovaks, two of whom lived in Prague" (264). In 1981, Skilling reported: "I was informed that Dubček was deliberately *not* asked to sign Charter 77, so as to avoid too direct a link between the Charter and 1968, and to maintain its character as an initiative 'from below,' as well as to leave his hands free for future political action" (*Charter 77*, 57). Whoever may have told Skilling this, it is hard not to perceive it as a rationalization, mainly because there was so little effort among the Prague signatories to bring a cross section of Slovak intellectual life on board.

88. On Hejdánek's apartment university, see Barbara Day, *The Velvet Philosophers* (London: Claridge, 1999), and Skilling, *Charter 77*, 29–31. Hejdánek would successfully combine the various seminars into a single weekly meeting that, despite police harassment, ran consistently from 1980 to 1989.

89. Hejdánek, *Dopisy příteli*, 13. This 1993 edition contains only the first "cycle" of letters, from February 10 to September 1, 1977; Hejdánek would write several more cycles throughout 1978 and 1979, using the letters as a way of weighing in on the major debates within the Charter community.

90. Ibid.

91. Ibid., 17 and 41. At the end of May 1977, Hejdánek uses the term "dissident" for the first and last time in this first cycle of letters, but his usage makes it clear that it is a derivative, pejorative term—he is angry that some Chartists are said to be "playing their role as 'dissidents' in return for foreign money" (88).

92. For these openings, see ibid., 24, 44, 50, 62, and 105.

93. Patočka, "Čím je a čím není Charta 77?," 37.

94. Hejdánek, *Dopisy příteli*, 124–126.

95. Ibid., 127.

96. Ibid., 134.

97. Ibid.

98. Císařovská and Prečan, *Charta 77*, 3:17.

99. Ibid., 1:23.

100. In her account of Czech dissent, Barbara Falk speaks of a collective "voice" of the Charter, but she has something different in mind from what I mean by the Charter "spokesvoice." Falk suggests a unity of philosophical thought underlying all the Charter documents; to my mind, this not only underestimates the real diversity of thinking among Charter signatories (as well as underestimating the extent to which many documents were cowritten by nonsignatories), but also reduces dissent to a philosophical position rather than a practice. In speaking of a "spokesvoice," I mean to suggest that the Charter documents tended to be written in a somewhat objective and clinical tone of voice, no matter how myriad the topics they were talking about. For the collective "voice of the Charter," see Barbara Falk, *The Dilemmas of Dissidence in East-Central Europe* (Budapest: Central European University Press, 2003), 251–256.

101. On the beginnings of *INFOCH*, see Petr Uhl, "Slovo úvodem," in *Informace o Chartě 77: Článková bibliografie*, ed. Jiří Gruntorad (Brno: Doplněk and Libri Prohibiti, 1998), 9–16. Research on INFOCH would hardly be possible if Gruntorád had not assembled this indispensable volume, containing an abstract of every article published in INFOCH along with an index of authors and names.

102. A few days later, spokesmen Patočka and Hájek would issue an "Overall Report [Přehledná zpráva] on State-Organized Campaigns and Slanders against Charter 77 and Individual Signatories." A full "balance sheet of activities" would not appear among the Charter's official documents until April 25. See Císařovská and Prečan, *Charta 77*, 1:21–25 and 1:39–43.

103. All eight reports are reprinted in Císařovská and Prečan, *Charta 77*, 3:97–127. Although Císařovská and Prečan present these reports as anonymous, Uhl's authorship is undisputed.

104. Ibid., 3:102.

105. Information about the poll is sketchy. See Císařovská's brief remembrance in ibid., 3:236, as well as Uhl, "Slovo úvodem," 10; Uhl suggests that "about 90 percent" of the 750 signatories at the time were questioned. A third poll question asked about Šabata's suggestion of forming some kind of regional representation for the Charter; about half approved, but few steps seem to have been taken in this direction.

106. Uhl, "Slovo úvodem," 9.

107. Kantůrková, *Sešly jsme se*, 77.

108. A great many other people were involved in publishing, copying, and distributing *INFOCH* at home and abroad; see Uhl, "Slovo úvodem," for an accounting of the dozens of people who made contributions.

109. *Informace o Chartě 77* 2, no. 1 (1978–1979): 13–18.

110. Padraic Kenney, *A Carnival of Revolution: Central Europe 1989* (Princeton: Princeton University Press, 2002), 150.

6. The Public of the Powerless

1. Blanka Císařovská and Vilém Prečan, eds., *Charta 77: Dokumenty 1977–1989* (Prague: Ústav pro soudobé dějiny, 2007), 3:247–248.

2. *Rudé právo*, January 21, 1977, 1.

3. František Janouch, *Ne, nestěžuji si: Malá normalizační mozaika* (Prague: Acropolis, 2008), 82. A collection of open letters from 1975 is in Adolf Müller, ed., *Hlasy z domova 1975* (Cologne: Index, 1975). On open letters, see also Vladimir Kusin, *From Dubček to Charter 77* (New York: St. Martin's Press, 1978), 280–286.

4. See Václav Havel, "Letter to Alexander Dubček," trans. A. G. Brain, in *Open Letters: Selected Writings, 1965–1990*, ed. Paul Wilson (New York: Alfred A. Knopf, 1991), 36–49.

5. The letter and reply are reprinted in Ludvík Vaculík, *Nepaměti 1969–1972* (Prague: Mladá fronta, 1998), 112–113.

6. Janouch, *Ne, nestěžuji si*, 126–134, reprints Janouch's open letter, Wichterle's reply, and Janouch's 1973 letter to *Der Spiegel*. Wichterle's own memoirs reveal that he was more experienced at the personal appeal; when a newspaper printed lies about him and his father, he went to the editor directly, rather than making the dispute public. See Otto Wichterle, *Vzpomínky* (Prague: Nakladatelství Evropského kulturního klubu, 1992), 193–203.

7. Václav Havel, "Dear Dr. Husák," in *Open Letters*, 50–51.

8. Ibid., 60.

9. Ibid., 76.

10. Ibid., 77.

11. Pavel Landovský, *Soukromá vzpoura: Rozhovor s Karlem Hvížďalou* (Prague: Mladá fronta, 1990), 64.

12. Jiří Lederer, *České rozhovory* (Prague: Československý spisovatel, 1991), 31. This passage is left out of the abridged English translation of the interview in *Open Letters*.

13. Jürgen Habermas, *The Structural Transformation of the Public Sphere*, trans. Thomas Burger and Frederick Lawrence (Cambridge, MA: MIT Press, 1989). See also the essays in Craig Calhoun, ed., *Habermas and the Public Sphere* (Cambridge, MA: MIT Press, 1992), as well as James Van Horn Melton, *The Rise of the Public in Enlightenment Europe* (Cambridge: Cambridge University Press, 2001).

14. Michael Warner, "Publics and Counterpublics," *Public Culture* 14, no. 1 (2002): 49–90.

15. Ibid., 50.

16. Ibid., 50 and 59.

17. Ibid., 62.

18. Ibid., 56.

19. Ibid., 77.

20. Ibid., 64.

21. "None of my essays has been so frequently quoted, both approvingly and polemically [. . .]. At the same time, none of my essays was more improvised," wrote Benda in reply to Gordon Skilling's questionnaire; see H. Gordon Skilling and Paul Wilson, eds., *Civic Freedom in Central Europe: Voices from Czechoslovakia* (New York: St. Martin's Press, 1991), 48. In 1995, Benda said that he drew up the argument at "a period of deep doubts about the possibilities of continuing further in civic dissent."

See his interview with Ilona Christlová in Květa Jechová, *Lidé Charty 77: Zpráva o biografickém výzkumu* (Prague: Ústav pro soudobé dějiny, 2003), 143.

22. Václav Benda, "The Parallel 'Polis,'" in Skilling and Wilson, *Civic Freedom*, 35–41.

23. Ibid., 40.

24. Pavel Kohout, *Kde je zakopán pes* (Brno: Atlantis, 1990), 491. In addition to Kohout's account of the ball, written a few years after the fact, see Ivan Klíma, *Moje šílené století* (Prague: Academia, 2010), 254–257, as well as the reports on the ball and subsequent arrests in the first issues of *INFOCH* in 1978. A detailed account was written up by Havel shortly after he returned from jail: "Zpráva o mé účasti na plesu železničářů," in *O lidskou identitu: Úvahy, fejetony, protesty, polemiky, prohlášení a rozhovory z let 1969–1979*, ed. Vilém Prečan and Alexander Tomský (Prague: Rozmluvy, 1990), 280–290.

25. Petr Pithart, "Disi-rizika," in Václav Havel et al., *O svobodě a moci* (Cologne and Rome: Index and Listy, 1980), 270–271.

26. The opening statement appeared in *INFOCH*; an image of an early copy is available at www.vons.cz. On VONS, see Jaroslav Pažout, "Výbor na obranu nespravedlivě stíhaných," in *Opozice a odpor proti komunistickému režimu v Československu 1968–1989*, ed. Petr Blažek (Prague: Ústav českých dějin FF UK and Dokořán, 2005), 96–110; Petr Uhl, *Právo a nespravedlnost očima Petra Uhla* (Prague: C. H. Beck, 1998), 46–59; and Petr Blažek and Jaroslav Pažout, eds., *Nejcitlivější místo režimu: Výbor na obranu nespravedlivě stíhaných (VONS) pohledem svých členů* (Prague: Pulchra, 2008), the transcript of a 2007 discussion among former VONS members.

27. See the discussion in Blažek and Pažout, *Nejcitlivější místo*, 18.

28. According to Petr Uhl, a founding member, an *ediční komise* (editorial or publishing commission) was a feature of the earliest conceptions of VONS (ibid., 21). Although it worked out channels for transmitting information abroad (ibid., 26), VONS did not overcome the communication gap between Czechs and Slovaks. Carol Skalnik Leff calculated that the time lag between rights violations and their report in VONS was three times longer for Slovak cases than for Czech. See her *National Conflict in Czechoslovakia* (Princeton, NJ: Princeton University Press, 1988), 267.

29. Luboš Dobrovský, "Několik vět o jedné možnosti," in Havel et al., *O svobodě a moci*, 151.

30. *Informace o Chartě 77* 1, no. 9 (1978): 10–11.

31. *Informace o Chartě 77* 1, no. 10 (1978): 5–6.

32. *Informace o Chartě 77* 1, no. 12 (1978): 11–16.

33. On the case, see *Informace o Chartě 77* 1, no. 13 (1978): 7; on the hunger strike, see *Informace o Chartě 77* 1, no. 15 (1978): 23, as well as 2, no. 4 (1979): 15.

34. Julius Tomin, "Jsem jenom vrátná . . . ," in the samizdat collection *Československý fejeton/fejtón 1977-1978*, ed. Ludvík Vaculík (Prague: Petlice, 1978), 69–74. I would like to thank Daniel Green for drawing this essay to my attention.

35. Jakub Trojan, "Disi-šance," in the samizdat anthology *Diskuse*, 192. This anthology lists no editor or publication information except for the year of publication, 1979.

36. Václav Havel, "The Power of the Powerless," in *Open Letters*, 127.

37. Kohout, *Kde je zakopán pes*, 122–123. Kohout suggests that "super-progressive intellectuals of the West" were avoiding the word because of its antisocialist tinge; a German visitor told him that the dissidents shouldn't throw out the baby of socialism along with the bathwater of the regime's "errors."

38. Císařovská and Prečan, *Charta 77*, 3:30.

39. Ibid., 3:46.

40. Ibid., 1:10.

41. Václav Havel, "Nedělíme se na disidenty a ty ostatní, bezpráví bude kritizováno bez ohledu na to, na kom je pácháno," in *O lidskou identitu*, 260.

42. Havel, "Dear Dr. Husák," 54–55.

43. Havel, "Power of the Powerless," 132–133.

44. Ibid., 141.

45. Ibid., 141–142.

46. Ibid., 143–144.

47. Ibid., 148.

48. Ibid., 148–149.

49. Ibid., 149.

50. Ibid., 176–178.

51. Ibid., 177.

52. Ibid., 167.

53. Ibid., 167–168.

54. Ibid., 169.

55. Ibid., 173–174.

56. Ibid., 158, 170–171, and 212–214.

57. Ibid., 179–180.

58. Ibid., 180.

59. Ibid., 171.

60. Václav Havel, "Reports on My House Arrest," in *Open Letters*, 221.

61. Ludvík Vaculík, "On Heroism," in *A Cup of Coffee with My Interrogator: The Prague Chronicles of Ludvík Vaculík*, trans. George Theiner (London: Readers International, 1976), 47–51. I have used Theiner's translation, although I have altered "man" to "person" and have retained Vaculík's original title. His "Poznámky o statečnosti" or "Notes on Courage" is (intentionally) modest and unimposing.

62. Vaculík offers fascinating background to this feuilleton in the opening pages of his diary *The Czech Dream Book*, which will be discussed in the next chapter. The feuilleton originally got a good response from his wife and some of his friends, including Alexandr Kliment and Helena Klímová. Vaculík heard that Pithart was working on "his own formulation of some similar considerations," but also that "deep in the Charter, there were arguments" about the questions they were raising.

The forcefulness and anger of some of the replies, particularly from Jiří Gruša and Havel, took him by surprise and shook his confidence. See Ludvík Vaculík, *Český snář* (Brno: Atlantis, 1992), 12–13 and more generally 7–47.

63. Petr Pithart, "Bedra některých," reprinted in Havel, *O lidskou identitu,* 207–211.

64. See, for example, Zdeněk Pinc's comment about the "Uhlian tendencies" from which VONS had developed, in Ludvík Vaculík, ed., *Hlasy nad rukopisem Vaculíkova Českého snáře* (Prague: Torst, 1991), 105, or Eva Kantůrková's questions about Uhl's activism in her interview with Anna Šabatová, in *Sešly jsme se v této knize* (Prague: Toužimský a Moravec, 1991), 76–77.

65. Václav Havel, "Milý pane Ludvíku" and "Milý pane Pitharte," in *O lidskou identitu*, 204–206 and 211–217.

66. In her 1979 interview with Eva Kantůrková, Olga Havlová said of Havel's letter to Vaculík: "Vašek's answer seemed unnecessarily emotional to me. Maybe he shouldn't have written it right away, when he was so angry." Kantůrková, *Sešly jsme se*, 10.

67. Anna Marvanová, "Poznámky proti lhostejnosti," in *Diskuse*, 39. This 1979 samizdat anthology, which lists no editor or place of publication, gathers together most of the responses to Vaculík and Pithart.

68. A.R., "Vážený příteli," in *Diskuse*, 65.

69. Jan Příbram, "Mea res agitur" (My Affairs Are at Stake), in *Diskuse*, 137–142. We can assume this is a pseudonym, both because there is no Jan Příbram listed among the Charter's signatories or in Jiří Gruntorád's index of all the issues of *INFOCH*, and because Jan of Příbram was the name of a fifteenth-century Hussite preacher who spoke out vehemently against the radical wing of the Hussite forces.

70. Jaroslav Suk, "Etika aktivní menšiny," in *Diskuse*, 128.

71. A.R., "Vázený příteli," 62.

72. Pithart, "Disi-rizika," 279–280.

73. Pithart's views on dissent were worked out in a number of essays; most recently, he has summarized them in *Devětaosmdesátý* (Eighty-Nine), the sequel to his earlier work *Osmašedesátý* (Sixty-Eight). See Petr Pithart, *Devětaosmdesátý* (Prague: Academia, 2009), esp. Chapter 2.

7. Dreams of a Dissident

1. Madla Vaculíková, *Já jsem oves: Rozhovor s Pavlem Kosatíkem* (Praha: Dokořán, Jaroslava Jiskrová—Máj, 2002), 78–81.

2. Ibid., 82–87.

3. See Jiří Pechar, *Nad knihami a rukopisy* (Prague: Torst, 1996), 90–91, for a contemporary discussion of confusion about Vaculík's writing.

4. In 1987, Vaculík wrote: "One autumn—it was either in '75 or '76, I can't be sure—the police gave me three options: I could leave the country, give up Petlice, or . . . The third, very uncouth option was to become a reality in January 1977. It is something I have yet to write about." Ludvík Vaculík, "A Padlock for Castle

Schwarzenberg," trans. A. G. Brain, in *Good-Bye, Samizdat*, ed. Marketa Goetz-Stankiewicz (Evanston: Northwestern University Press, 1992), 123.

5. After many years of alluding to this affair obliquely in his feuilletons, Vaculík discussed it explicitly in "Poučení z krizového vývoje," in *Charta 77 očima současníků: Po dvaceti letech*, ed. Blanka Císařovská, Milan Drápala, Vilém Prečan, and Jiří Vančura (Brno: Ústav pro soudobé dějiny and Doplněk, 1997), 189–190. Marie Vaculíková describes her side in *Já jsem oves*, especially 102–105. Most recently, Vaculík reprinted the photos themselves in his *Tisíce slov* (Brno: Atlantis, 2009). For contemporary reactions, see Jan Vladislav's *Otevřený deník*, in Blanka Císařovská and Vilém Prečan, *Charta 77: Dokumenty 1977–1989* (Prague: Ústav pro soudobé dějiny, 2007), 3:81–96; or Jaroslav Putík, *Odchod od zámku* (Prague: Hynek, 1998), 253.

6. Vaculík encoded a description of Sidon's favor in his feuilleton "Moc práce" (Císařovská and Prečan, *Charta 77*, 3:71–72). This is the same arrest that the Charter spokesvoice, with its talent for wan objectivity, merely glossed by saying: "it is necessary to conclude that his [Sidon's] personal freedom was illegally restricted [. . .]" (Císařovská and Prečan, *Charta 77*, 1:23).

7. Vaculíková, *Já jsem oves*, 105.

8. Císařovská and Prečan, *Charta 77*, 3:52.

9. Vaculík, "Poučení z krizového vývoje," 190.

10. Ludvík Vaculík, *Český snář* (Brno: Atlantis, 1992), 448.

11. Ibid., 17–19.

12. Pavel Kosatík, *Fenomén Kohout* (Prague-Litomyšl: Paseka, 2001), 352–355; Radek Schovánek, ed., *Svazek Dialog: StB versus Pavel Kohout* (Prague-Litomyšl: Paseka, 2006), 300–304.

13. Vaculík, *Český snář*, 200.

14. Ibid., 265. Kantůrková had written a letter to Margaret Thatcher protesting the VONS arrests.

15. Ibid., 388 and 107. Vaculík also refers to "our dissident cyclotron" in his thoughts on Havel's letter (18).

16. Ludvík Vaculík, ed., *Hlasy nad rukopisem Vaculíkova Českého snáře* (Prague: Torst, 1991), 90.

17. Vaculík, *Český snář*, 398.

18. Pechar, *Nad knihami*, 75. Vaculík himself, discussing a story by Drahomira Pithartová, says that she has found a good position "from which to deglorify dissidence" (*Český snář*, 389).

19. Vaculík, *Český snář*, 214.

20. Ibid., 379.

21. Putík, *Odchod*, 308; Pechar, *Nad knihami*, 99. In a 1994 interview with Michael Špirit, Vaculík compared his writing to a salon: "The idea is for it to be a sort of salon, where the reader walks in and is right there with the characters [. . .]" ("Postscript: A Discussion with the Author," trans. Alex Zucker, *Trafika* 3 [1994]: 73).

22. Jan Lukeš, *Hry doopravdy: Rozhovor se spisovatelem Karlem Peckou* (Prague-Litomyšl: Paseka, 1998), 261–262.

23. Vaculík, *Hlasy*, 122 (Lukeš) and 115 (Klánský); Václav Černý, *Eseje o české a slovenské próze* (Prague: Torst, 1994), 179.

24. Vaculík, *Hlasy*, 97 (Kantůrek) and 69 (Šimečka); Lukeš, *Hry doopravdy*, 261 (Pecka).

25. Vaculík, *Hlasy*, 90.

26. Ibid., 91. Whether or not Fišer assimilated the whole book, of course, it was surely processed thoroughly by the StB, a fact of which Vaculík was well aware. On the question of giving information away to the police, see also Vaculík's 1994 interview with Špirit: "Postscript: A Discussion with the Author," 72.

27. Vaculík, *Hlasy*, 93.

28. Černý, *Eseje*, 186–187; emphasis in the original.

29. Vaculík, *Hlasy*, 130.

30. Vaculík, *Český snář*, 153. Barbara Day describes the "real" version of this event, a lecture by Oxford philosopher Kathy Wilkes, in *The Velvet Philosophers* (London: Claridge Press, 1999), 36–38.

31. Vaculík, *Český snář*, 93.

32. Ibid., 128–131.

33. Ibid., 31. "Thinking" (*mysl*) might also be translated here as "thought" or "mind."

34. Ibid., 314 and 421.

35. Ibid., 60–61.

36. Ibid., 361.

37. Ibid., 115.

38. Ibid., 152 and 251. Vaculík referred to Fišer as "Major (?)" until he was sure of his rank.

39. Ibid., 230.

40. Ibid., 332.

41. Vaculík, *Hlasy*, 124–127.

42. Václav Havel, *Disturbing the Peace: A Conversation with Karel Hvížďala*, trans. Paul Wilson (New York: Vintage, 1990), 161–162.

43. Václav Havel, "Odpovědnost jako osud," in Vaculík, *Hlasy*, 136.

44. Ibid., 134.

45. Ibid., 134–135.

46. Vaculík, *Český snář*, 71.

47. Ibid., 402.

48. Ibid., 181.

49. Ludvík Vaculík, *A Cup of Coffee with My Interrogator*, trans. George Theiner (London: Readers International, 1987), 49.

50. Vaculík, *Český snář*, 415.

51. Ibid., 157–158.

52. Ibid., 332. *Prosazovat*, the verb I have translated as "advocate," means to push (an idea or proposal) through or try to get it realized; *předvádět*, which I have translated as "display," could also mean "perform" or "demonstrate."

53. Jürgen Habermas, *The Structural Transformation of the Public Sphere,* trans. Thomas Burger and Frederick Lawrence (Cambridge, MA: MIT Press, 1989), 49 and 55.

54. Vaculík, *Český snář,* 420.

55. Vaculík, *Hlasy,* 10 (Jungmann) and 68 (Šimečka).

56. Eva Kantůrková, *Památník* (Prague: Český spisovatel, 1994), 66.

57. Ibid., 229.

58. Ludvík Vaculík, *Milí spolužáci!* (Prague: Mladá fronta, 1995), 14.

Conclusion

1. On the 1980s, see Padraic Kenney, *A Carnival of Revolution: Central Europe 1989* (Princeton: Princeton University Press, 2002); Miroslav Vaněk, et al., *Ostrůvky svobody: Kulturní a občanské aktivity mladé generace v 80. letech v Československu* (Prague: Ústav pro soudobé dějiny and Votobia, 2002); and Paulina Bren, *The Greengrocer and His TV: The Culture of Communism after the 1968 Prague Spring* (Ithaca: Cornell University Press, 2010). For the evolution of dissent into a political force, see especially Jiří Suk, *Labyrintem revoluce: Aktéři, zápletky a křižovatky jedné politické krize (od listopadu 1989 do června 1990),* 2nd ed. (Prague: Prostor, 2009), and Aviezer Tucker, *The Philosophy and Politics of Czech Dissidence from Patočka to Havel* (Pittsburgh: University of Pittsburgh Press, 2000). A classic discussion of the "grey zone" is Jiřina Šiklová, "The 'Grey Zone' and the Future of Dissent in Czechoslovakia," *Social Research* 37, no. 2 (Summer 1990): 347–355. On Mandler, see Růžena Hlušičková and Milan Otáhal, eds., *Čas demokratické iniciativy 1987–1990* (Prague and České Budějovice: Nadace Demokratické iniciativy pro kulturu a politiku, 1993), as well as Tucker, *Philosophy and Politics,* 194–195, and Bren, *The Greengrocer and His TV,* 96–100; on Czech Children, see Petr Placák, *Fízl* (Prague: Torst, 2007), as well as Kenney, *Carnival,* 184–190. On relations between the Charter and the underground, see Luboš Veselý, "Underground (Charty 77)", in *Opozice a odpor proti komunistickému režimu v Československu 1968–1989,* ed. Petr Blažek (Prague: Dokořán and Ústav českých dějin FF UK, 2005), 111–118; on relations between the Charter and the younger generation, see Milan Otáhal and Miroslav Vaněk, eds., *Sto studentských revolucí* (Prague: Lidové noviny, 1999).

2. Suk, *Labyrintem revoluce,* 80–91.

3. Marta Marková, *Olga Havlová a ty druhé* (Brno: Barrister and Principal, 1996), 145.

4. Tom Stoppard, *Rock 'n' Roll* (New York: Grove, 2006), 74.

5. Petr Pithart, *Devětaosmdesátý* (Prague: Academia, 2009), 20–34.

6. See Pithart's interview with Milan Otáhal, from 2003 and 2004, in *Vítězové? Poražení? Životopisná interview,* ed. Miroslav Vaněk and Pavel Urbášek (Prague: Prostor, 2005), 1:757–761.

7. Vaněk and Urbášek, *Vítězové? Poražení?,* 1:1044.

8. See, for example, Kieran Williams, "Civil Resistance in Czechoslovakia: From Soviet Invasion to 'Velvet Revolution,' 1968–1989," in *Civil Resistance and*

Power Politics, ed. Adam Roberts and Timothy Garton Ash (New York: Oxford University Press, 2009), 110–126.

9. This number comes from an unpublished paper by the skeptical Jan Urban called "The Powerlessness of the Powerful." See, for example, Stephen Kotkin and Jan Gross, *Uncivil Society: 1989 and the Implosion of the Communist Establishment* (New York: Modern Library, 2009), 10 and 149n12. Urban's paper has cast a long shadow; it is also quoted, for example, in Juan J. Linz and Alfred Stepan, *Problems of Democratic Transition and Consolidation* (Baltimore, MD: The Johns Hopkins University Press, 1996), 321 and 321n85, and Mark R. Thompson, "Why and How East Germans Rebelled," *Theory and Society* 25, no. 2 (April 1996): 276 and 295n52.

10. Lukáš Rychetský, "Odpověď na nesvobodu" (an interview with Petr Uhl), *A2*, January 3, 2007, www.advojka.cz (accessed 5/22/11); Petr Uhl's response to the questionnaire is in Blanka Císařovská, Milan Drápala, Vilém Prečan, and Jiří Vančura, eds., *Charta 77 očima současníků: Po dvaceti letech* (Brno: Ústav pro soudobé dějiny and Doplněk, 1997), 264–267. See also Martin Palouš, "Poznámky ke generačním sporům v Chartě 77 v druhé polovině osmdesátých let," in Emanuel Mandler, ed., *Dvě desetiletí před listopadem 89: Sborník* (Prague: Ústav pro soudobě dějiny/Maxdorf, 1993), 35–44.

11. My account of *Kritický sborník* in this and the following paragraphs draws on Karel Palek, ed., *Kritický sborník 1981–1989: Výbor ze samizdatových ročníků* (Prague: Triada, 2009), especially Palek's introduction, "Předmluva vydavatele," vii–xix. See also "Řeč kritiky: Rozhovor s redaktory Kritického sborníku," an interview with the journal's editors, in Jan Lopatka, *Šifra lidské existence,* ed. Michael Špirit (Prague: Torst, 1995), 467–470; "'Ideální je pro mě metodu vůbec nemít': Rozhovor s Josefem Vohryzkem," an interview with Vohryzek, in *Kritický sborník* 14, no. 2 (1994): 58–64; and Petr Šámal, "Literární kritika za časů normalizace," *Literární archiv* 37 (2006): 149–179.

12. On Vohryzek's life, see his interview with Ilona Christlová in Květa Jechová, *Lidé Charty 77: Zpráva o biografickém výzkumu* (Prague: Ústav pro soudobé dějiny, 2003), 146–167, and his 1992 interview with Ivo Fencl, "Rozhovor s Josefem Vohryzkem," in Ivo Fencl, *Vize a iluze skupiny Květen* (Prague: Pražská imaginace, 1993), 147–158. See also František Kautman, "Kritik Josef Vohryzek," in *O literatuře a jejich tvůrcích* (Prague: Torst, 1999), 205–210.

13. Quoted in Palek, *Kritický sborník 1981–1989*, xi.

14. Quoted in ibid., xiii.

15. Jiří Otava [Jiřina Šiklová], "Rozhovory s českými spisovateli v zahraničí," in Palek, *Kritický sborník 1981–1989*, 445, and Petr Pithart, "První léta T. G. Masaryka v Praze," in ibid., 176.

16. Zdena Tomin, "Typewriters Hold the Fort," *Index on Censorship* 12, no. 2 (April 1983): 29.

17. -n [František Kautman], "Otazníky kolem ineditní literatury," in Palek, *Kritický sborník 1981–1989*, 9.

18. See the essays collected in Petr Rezek, *Filozofie a politika kýče*, 2nd ed. (Prague: Jan Placák—Ztichlá klika, 2007). On Rezek, see also Tucker, *Philosophy and Politics*, esp. 115–123, and Bren, *The Greengrocer and His TV*, 101–103 and 205–206.

19. Palek, *Kritický sborník 1981–1989*, xvii.

20. A. Nonymová [Jiřina Šiklová], "Etika anonyma 1983," in Palek, *Kritický sborník 1981–1989*, 15.

21. Fencl, "Rozhovor s Josefem Vohryzkem," 149, 157–158.

Acknowledgments

I have been working on this project for a long time, and I have relied on the criticism, encouragement, and goodwill of more people than I could name here. Nevertheless, some thanks are in order. Writing a book about dissent has often led me to think about why we imagine better worlds than the one we live in. But it has also reminded me, over and over, of my own good fortune.

I am grateful to the several institutional homes I have had at Harvard during my work: the Society of Fellows, which gave me the time and freedom to work on varied projects at my own pace; the Davis Center for Russian and Eurasian Studies, which welcomed me into an interdisciplinary group of scholars working on many different regions; and Harvard's Department of Slavic Languages and Literatures, where I have been blessed with colleagues who are unflagging in their support and thoughtful in their advice. I would like to thank them here: Svetlana Boym, Julie Buckler, Michael Flier, George Grabowicz, John Malmstad, Joanna Niżyńska, Stephanie Sandler, William Mills Todd III, and Justin Weir. Judy Klasson and Stuart Robbins-Butcher provided far more than administrative support with unfailing good humor. I received financial support for my research from Harvard University and the Society of Fellows, and I wrote much of this book during a sabbatical funded through a John F. Cogan Junior Faculty Leave Grant from the Davis Center. I have also been fortunate to draw on the holdings of the Czech collection at Harvard's Widener Library (including its remarkable collection of samizdat from the 1970s and 1980s) and the help of its exceptional librarians. Jiří Gruntorád of Libri Prohibiti in Prague graciously provided me with materials from their own samizdat holdings. Vladimír Štvrtňa at Czech Television's studio in Ostrava and director Jordi Niubó kindly arranged for me to see two of their documentaries, on Jan Procházka and Egon Bondy. I am grateful to Kathleen McDermott, my editor at Harvard University Press, who believed in the project from its beginnings and offered a great deal of helpful advice along the way.

Jindřich Toman has been giving me both encouragement and friendly criticism since I began my Ph.D. studies at the University of Michigan; he has taught me to go beyond received wisdom and test out new perspectives. The long-running series of Czech Cultural Studies workshops that Jindřich founded at Michigan in 2000 has helped create an intellectual community of scholars of Czech history and literature, and I have been fortunate to draw on their advice and criticism over the years. I continue to learn from the friends I made during my graduate studies in Ann Arbor, including Charles Sabatos, Anne Fisher, John Hope, and Joe Peschio. I have also benefitted from the comments, insights, and often challenging questions of under-graduate and graduate students in my Harvard courses on Central European literature and history, and I have learned a great deal from the graduate teaching fellows for my course on postwar Czechoslovakia, Ana Olenina, Maryana Pinchuk, and Philipp Penka. I am also grateful to Maryana Pinchuk for her invaluable research assistance, and to Jan Straka for help with research in Prague.

Charles Sweetman, Thor Polson, and Alex Star have been patient interlocutors and friends. I owe a special debt of thanks to Elizabeth Papazian for her stubborn encouragement and guidance. In addition to their own comments, David Danaher, Urs Heftrich, Bettina Kaibach, Terry Martin, Chad Bryant, and Hana Píchová gave me helpful opportunities to present this work to fellow scholars in Madison, Hei-delberg, Cambridge, and Chapel Hill. For their comments on earlier drafts, I am especially grateful to Julie Buckler, Peter Bugge, Rajendra Chitnis, Marek Nekula, Joanna Niżyńska, John Plotz, Andrew Roberts, Jacques Rupnik, and Peter Zusi. Her-bert Eagle, Jiří Holba, Marek Nekula, Jacques Rupnik, Jiří Trávníček, Jiří Voráč, and Ivan Wernisch generously shared their knowledge, experiences, and insights into the world of samizdat and Czechoslovakia in the 1970s. The two anonymous readers for Harvard University Press offered invaluable suggestions, not to mention corrections, and I learned a great deal from their advice.

Bonnie and Douglas Wagner and Kija Bolton have been models of good spir-its. Christopher Bolton, artfully combining the roles of brother, advisor, and friend, has shaped this work in more ways than he can realize. My parents, Roger and Julia Bolton, have always known how to balance guidance and freedom. This book is dedi-cated to them.

And as I keep imagining my own better worlds, I am thankful to find Raquel in all of them.

Index

Eastern Bloc, 6

Eastern Europe, 1, 20, 25, 208, 289n36

East Germany, 5–6, 34

economy, 19, 57, 65; barter, 109; command, 4; consumer, 21

Edice Expedice (Dispatch Editions), 101–103

Edice Kvart (Quarto Editions), 101–103, 106, 278, 281, 302n69

Edice Petlice (Padlock Editions), 98–103, 106, 109, 114, 167, 240–249 passim, 302n65

Edice Půlnoc (Midnight Editions), 98

emigration, 20, 48–49, 93, 103, 181, 182, 241, 247, 254, 257, 278, 315n64, 316n76; attempt at, 74, 75; émigré journals, 163

Emmanuel, Pierre, 278

employment, 42, 47, 64, 85, 86, 90–94 passim, 113, 125, 145, 169, 171, 179, 186, 222, 226, 227, 230; as a requirement, 88, 100, 171; employer's stamp, 88, 100; loss of, 13, 14, 20, 38, 62, 70, 86, 87, 88, 89, 98, 119, 139, 179, 183, 293n1, 299n26, 315n64; types of, 60, 64, 65; the un- and under-employed, 104, 185, 275; *v maringotce* ("in a trailer"), 92, 279, 300n45. *See also* parasitism

Engels: *Communist Manifesto,* 1

Enlightenment, the, 45, 147

environmental movement, 266

Erteltová, Zdena, 99–100, 180, 240, 244, 247, 248; as scribe of Charter, 148; obituary "Umřela," 302n66

"Ethics of the Anonymous Author" (A. Nonymová). *See* Jiřina Šiklová

existentialism, 26, 67, 131, 142, 264, 289n25; themes of, 81; vocabulary of, 27, 288n21

"Failures and Usurpers" editorial *(Rudé právo). See* "Ztroskotanci a samozvanci"

Falk, Barbara, 289n30, 318n100

feuilletons, 39, 99, 187, 194, 197, 217, 231, 232, 234, 235, 236, 237, 241, 243, 244,

251, 273, 301n50, 304n90, 321n62, 323nn5–6

Fidelius, Petr. *See* Karel Palek

Final Act (Conference on Security and Cooperation in Europe). *See* Helsinki Accords

Firemen's Ball (Forman, director), 8

"First Festival of the Second Culture," 123, 133

Fišer, Zbyněk. *See* Bondy, Egon

Forman, Miloš, 8, 82, 286n14; *Firemen's Ball* (film), 8, 82; *Loves of a Blonde* (film), 8, 82

For the Truth, 74, 75

Foucault, Michel, 21; *Discipline and Punish,* 63

freedom of the press, 13, 25, 52. *See also* censorship; human rights; publishing

French Communist Party, 58

Fuková, Božena: vote against treaty on foreign troops, 294n8

Garton Ash, Timothy, 289n28, 292n60, 293n64

Gesamtkunstwerk, 131, 308n57

Ginsberg, Allen: as "The King of May," 7; "Howl," 7

glasnost, 266

Glucksmann, André, 290n37

Gorbachev, Mikhail, 266; reforms of, 275

"gray zone," 193, 267, 290n37, 325n1

Grechko, Andrei, 56

greengrocer's tale (Havel), 2, 142, 220–226 passim, 237, 238, 260, 272. *See also* "The Power of the Powerless"

Gruntorád, Jiří, 130, 318n101, 322n69

Gruša, Jiří, 33, 163, 236, 247, 289n25, 322n62

Guinea Pigs, The (Vaculík), 99, 241

Habermas, Jürgen, 208, 259

Hájek, Jiří, 26, 51, 143, 144, 164, 177, 196, 201, 312n7; comments on Patočka's essay, 156; open letter to the National Assembly, 205; "Overall